MW01295606

The Bucko Mate: Twenty Years in the Merchant Marine

By

Kevin Zahn

Published by CreateSpace Independent Publishing Platform

Cover design by: **www.ebooklaunch.com**
Back Cover photo: K. Zahn

Table of Contents

Dedication

To those who have gone down
with their ships, and those
who will.

Foreword

"Any fool can carry on in a storm; it is the wise man who knows when to shorten sail in time."-- Joseph Conrad

There is a way of life that is almost gone. This book is an attempt by one who lived a small part of it to get some of it down in writing before it disappears. The sea has been man's greatest challenge. It holds our fascination even now, in this era of space exploration. Men have gone up against the sea, now women as well. Why? What drives a person to set out across thousands of miles of ocean? Adventure? Excitement? The challenge? Escapism from the rest of the world? Probably all of these things and more, but elements that have driven people to sail have been changing over the last twenty years, and will never be the same again.

This is a personal look at going to sea, through the eyes of a merchant marine officer, or a "mate." One question is, "What the hell is the merchant marine?" Everyone knows that if you join the navy, you are a sailor, and you are a member of the Armed Forces. However, many other sailors are in the merchant marine. They are not usually part of the Armed Forces, although they can be in wartime, and many members of the merchant marine are members of the Naval Reserve. Simply put, if you are in the merchant marine, you are a civilian sailor.

The proper term for a merchant sailor is "seaman," although on the ships, seafaring men use the term "sailor," usually for members of the crew. You don't have a rank like in the navy; your job determines that. You are a mate, an engineer, a bosun, AB, oiler, or a cook. No one salutes. You wear work clothes, and only the mates wear required khakis. In the old days, the deck officers, or mates, wore shoulder boards with stripes, and frequently wore ties to dinner. You wore one stripe as a third mate, two for second mate, three for chief mate, and four for the captain. There is no dress code for the crew, and no one can tell you to get a haircut; you are a civilian.

The major concern in merchant marine operations is that you sail a ship for a private steamship company (although some are government owned) and the goal, like any other business, is to make money for the owners. You sail here and there at their orders. You are in business -- the business of transporting cargo, whether break bulk (general), liquid, bulk, natural gas, military, or whatever needs to be taken somewhere in the world, for a price.

Owners register merchant ships in a home country, and its name is painted on the stern, and governed by their rules; in foreign ports, you abide by other, local rules, and woe to those who forget this. You need a document -- papers for the crew, or a license for the officers, to do this. There are different ways to get a license to be an officer on a merchant ship. In the United States, you can become an officer by attending an academy for that purpose, a four year program. You can also sail in the crew for several years, and then take the same license exam that the students do. In the U.S., the Coast Guard issues the license, if you are qualified to take the test, and you pass it. License exams take a full week. Then, like anybody else in the world of work, you go look for a job. You can go union or non-union. Some countries will recognize the license of another country, and you can work for shipping outfits there, if you can live on the wages.

The crew of a merchant ship consists of three departments: deck, engine, and steward. The captain, who is the boss of all, heads the deck department. Below him are the mates -- chief mate, second mate, and one or two third mates. The chief mate is in charge of ship maintenance, cargo loading and unloading, stability, and personnel matters with the crew. The 2nd mate and 3rd mates stand watches, navigate the ship, prevent collisions and groundings, plus help with the cargo, crew, and paperwork. One of the mates is the medical officer. The captain does what the hell he wants to do.

The rest of the deck department is in the crew, and their boss in the bosun. He is like a foreman for all the work done on deck. There are ABs, or Able-Bodied Seamen, and OSs, or Ordinary Seaman. An AB steers the ship in addition to his deck work, an Ordinary doesn't. They all clean, paint, haul lines, run the windlasses, drop the anchor, and whatever else superiors tell them to do on deck.

The chief engineer leads the engine department. Like the chief mate, he usually doesn't stand a watch, and is the head of his department, in control of keeping the "lights burning and the screw turning," as well as maintenance, repairs, and fuel oil. His right-hand man is the 1st Assistant Engineer, called "The 1st." He is the foreman of the engine department, and is usually a whiz at makeshift or jury-rigged repairs. The 2nd and 3rd engineers stand watches down in the engine room, four hours on and eight off, 24 hours a day, every day, like the mates. In modern times, this has changed; a modern, automated ship has no watch-standing engineers. The engineers quit at 1700 hours (5:00 p.m.) and lock the engine room down for the night. Automatic alarms ring in the engineer's rooms if something is wrong.

There are also crewmen who work in the engine room. In past times, they were oilers or wipers, but now, with combined duties, they have titles like DeMac, for Deck/Engine Mechanic. Life is changing for them, too. They might have to know more about computers than how to light off a boiler.

The boss of the steward's department is the chief steward, known as "The Steward." He supervises the cooks and utility men who do all of the food preparation, take care of the linen, and attend to passengers, if they carry them. In the heyday of the merchant marine, this department included waiters who served all three meals to everybody on the ship. Today, on the automated ships, there are no waiters. Cooks serve meals cafeteria style, and even the captain goes down the line with his tray. It would have been unthinkable twenty years ago.

If you consider that the merchant marine includes any commercial, non-military vessel, then you might add things like fishing boats, research vessels, cable-laying ships, salvage boats, treasure hunters, and tugboats, to the types of merchant marine craft. Besides the merchant marine and the navy, you can also go to sea, for a ways at least, in the Coast Guard. Navy subs are full of sailors, of course, but their experience is so different from the surface vessel guys, it seems a separate category. There are also thousands of people who go out in pleasure craft, power and sail, but merchant sailors consider this a vastly different type of sailing. They have respect for the serious sailboat guys who cross the ocean in small boats, even though many of them are crazy. If you go back in time, you might add crews of lightships (almost gone now) and lifeboat rescue crews, guys who rowed out to wrecks in storms, to the list. Passenger ships are certainly part of a nation's merchant marine (not much for the U.S.), but that type of work is foreign to the rest of the seamen who work the freighters and tankers. A guy working his butt off on an old freighter would consider a passenger ship a vacation.

Who goes to sea? Where do these seamen come from? Anywhere is the answer. Sean Connery sailed in the British Merchant Service, and Carol O'Connor, Peter Falk, Mike Douglas and Jimmy Dean sailed in the American Merchant Marine. Cliff Robertson did, too, and Japanese aircraft hit his ship. Sometimes there is a family history of seafaring; often there is not. It is amazing how many sailors come from farming backgrounds, or lumber jacking and other outdoor work. At least in the crew, there is usually a pattern of doing hard, physical work. The only bond one might see with such diverse backgrounds is a love of the sea, and a desire to sail across the damn ocean and see what's over the horizon. In this, even a modern sailor has a link to the past, to those who sailed out for similar reasons, but had no idea what they would find, or if they would be lucky enough to return.

To be a mate on a merchant ship in the heydays of the freighters was to be a man in the middle -- in the middle of maritime chaos, living a lonely but colorful life that few can imagine. Yet changes in the business part of a seaman's life have taken away much of the color and adventure of it. The ships have gotten much bigger, the crews smaller, and they don't stay in port long. The U. S. Merchant Marine, ships that sail with an American crew and the stars and stripes aloft, is rapidly disappearing. U.S. flagged ships carry less than 5% of the nation's foreign commerce. If things continue, someday they will carry nothing. The way of life will be gone. This effort is my way of getting some of that colorful way of life on paper before it all fades away.

"Being in a ship is being in a jail,
with the chance of being drowned." – Samuel Johnson

* * * * *

Part One

Youngblood

Chapter 1: Memory Lane

The bar was long and narrow, and the door opened out onto the main street near Journal Square, in New Jersey. Winter was over, but it was still cold. A guy about 40 years old came in, hauling a canvas sea bag and a small wooden case with him. He walked the length of the bar slowly, glancing all around. It was nearly deserted. He went to the back of the bar, where it took a right angle. He sat in the corner, with his back to the wall, and faced the front door. From there, he could see the whole place. He propped the sea bag up next to him, with the canvas handle on top, where he could grab it. He put the small case underneath him, and placed his left work boot on top of it. The case contained his nautical sextant, now twenty years old.

He was dressed in khaki pants, a long-sleeved plaid shirt with a dark blue jacket over it, heavy socks, and work boots. The wind, rain, snow and sun had weathered his face beyond his years, but he was still fairly trim and muscular. He had a hard look on his face. He ordered a vodka straight, no ice. He did not speak to anyone but the bartender. It was the middle of the day and there were only a few others in there. It was a blue-collar kind of bar, the kind that might present problems late at night if you were a stranger. It would do for a quick drink or two during the day. A large, ugly dog lay on the floor behind the bar. It eyed him carefully and snarled a little. The mate could imagine this dog would be trouble if you tried to mess with the barkeep. *Christ -- four months at sea, and this is the first place I go after my last North Atlantic crossing. I need to get out of this dump,* he thought. An old, beaten guy came in and sat near him. The old-timer started talking nonsense to him; he was angling for the seaman to buy him a drink. That did it. With all that was happening in his life, he didn't need a conversation with some old drunk. He tossed a bill on the bar, grabbed his bags and went out to the street. Watching everyone on the sidewalk carefully, he whistled down a cab. The driver offered to put his bags in the trunk, but he put them in the back seat with him.

"Where to, pal?"

"Newark Airport."

The cabbie drove off, happy to have a long fare. He checked his fare out a couple of times in the rear-view mirror. "Hey, you one of those guys from the union hall back there, ain't 'cha?"

"Yeah, that's right."

"You're one of those mates that sails all over, right? Am I right?"

"Yeah, you're right."

"You guys got it made, pal. Hell, you been everywhere, right? Make lots of money, chase girls all over, right?"

"Yeah, that's right." *I've been all over in the last twenty years, he's right about that.* But the mate wasn't going to ruin the cabbie's fantasy by telling him about the hard times. People like him had a vision of it right from the television. They even thought it was fun to go through a typhoon. You couldn't tell them anything different. It would do no good to tell him how he couldn't find work, or that his ex-wife's lawyers were taking all his money, or what little he had to go home to, and how little he had to show for the last twenty years. Still, there had been some good times, at least before the business changed. It seemed so long ago. He leaned back in the dirty cab and wondered how it had all started. *I could have done so many things, how the hell did I end up at sea?*

~ ~ ~ ~ ~

The young boy stood poised on the top of the only hill around. The main campus of Jacksonville University, in northern Florida, was behind him; the tennis courts and baseball field were below him, and to the right. He looked at the crude device again. He and his brother had cut a roller skate in half with a hacksaw. They had nailed each half to one end of a piece of wood. The idea was to balance on the 2x4 and go like hell down the hill. It was hard to turn the damn thing, but if he made it to the bottom, it would be all right if he couldn't turn, 'cause he would be in the parking lot, and after that there was a large grassy area before you got to the river. The St. Johns River was not a threat; it was too far away. He had done this before and survived falling off. The trick was to time it right.

As he watched for traffic below, he looked over the wide river. A ship was coming into port. Soon, it would go underneath the Mathews Bridge and dock. There were a couple of other ships on the far side of the river already alongside. Cargo was going off and on, and tugboats were working in the harbor; there was a great deal of activity. He wondered where that ship came from, where it was going, and who was on it. It seemed like great adventure to him.

The traffic cleared, and he got on the wood beam and pushed off. He made it down to the bottom but couldn't turn it, flew across the parking lot and into the grass. The crude skateboard stopped when it hit the grass, and he flew off headfirst, but onto the field. It felt great. As he picked himself up, he again looked across the river. The cargo ship was now almost under the bridge. A couple of tugboats were going alongside of it, to help it to the dock. He wondered again where it had come from, and what cargo it had. He picked up the board and headed up the hill.

Five years later, the young boy, now a senior in high school, was home one day watching the news when Congressman Bennett came on the television and read off his nominations to the U.S. Merchant Marine Academy. His name was one of them. Years later, he would remember that the hardest part, in all the celebration that followed, was convincing people that he did not have an appointment, only a nomination. It was not a direct political appointment, as you might get to Annapolis. There was a pool of over 3,000 young men nominated from all over the country. The school would then choose a freshman class of 334. His odds were still ten to one, but no one wanted to hear that. Everyone had acted as if it was a done deal. He worried incessantly, but a few months later, it was a done deal. The academy had chosen him, among others, to attend from Florida. He would be no burden to his family for college. It was a four-year scholarship, and he would go to sea. It had been his dream for years.

By August that year, he was on Long Island, New York, at the school that would change his life. He was still seventeen years old. A year after that, he went to sea, as a cadet, or midshipman. He was an apprentice officer learning his trade on regular merchant ships, as part of his academy education. The young boy had gone to college, and now had gone to sea. He was eighteen, but felt older.

Chapter 2: Easy Money

His very first day at sea, aboard the freighter *S. S. Thompson Lykes*, the chief mate sent him out on deck to work with the deck gang. The bosun, a guy the crew called Nervous after his habit of mixing drugs and alcohol and then running around like a maniac all day, shaking but working his butt off, asked him if he knew how to coil wire.

"Yessir." He had done it once in school.

After getting chewed out for calling the bosun "sir," ("Save that shit for the officers," Nervous said), the kid, Nervous and a dayman they called Deck went up to #4 hatch.

"We're going to renew the wire on the winch up there," Nervous said. "Get down there forward of the hatch coaming, and when we feed you this wire, you coil it right there."

"No problem." He got the end of it, and the bosun began running it off the winch, from a platform about ten feet above the kid's head. Wire can be difficult to deal with, especially if it is 3/4-inch thick wire. You had to man-handle it, and coil it alternately clockwise and counter-clockwise, depending on the lay of it, and how it wanted to go, from years of being wound around the winch. At first, he did fine, thinking he could keep up with physical work as well as any of the old salts in the crew. Lykes Brothers Steamship Company would be glad they had an apprentice like him aboard on the run to Viet Nam. Then Nervous decided to have some fun.

The maniac ran the winch faster and faster, the wire running straight down on the kid desperately trying to coil it on deck. It flopped all over the place; it hit him on the head, it hit him on the back, the shoulders, ran up against his legs, and left marks all over him. Nervous loved every second of it, and laughed out loud. Deck just stood at the railing looking down at the kid. When the wire reached the bitter end, it lay all over the place. The kid had to re-coil the whole thing. He said nothing.

When he went into the officer's lounge for morning coffee time, the chief mate told him that he couldn't come in there "like that." He had heavy grease, the kind used on the wire to keep it supple and prevent rust, all over his tattered clothes and tired body. The mate wanted to know how his student had gotten that way.

"I just coiled up some wire, that's all," was the kid's answer. He made no complaint. Lesson One was over. His first set of work clothes went over the side the first night. He would not have enough. He would get some more from the ship's small store, the slop chest, when the captain opened it, usually once a week at sea. It had tax-free cigarettes, candy, gum, work clothes, shaving cream and things like that. You signed for what you took and the captain deducted the amount from your pay.

The S.S. Thompson Lykes was 495 feet long, cruised at 18 knots, and held 11,042 tons of cargo in its five hatches; she displaced 16,870 tons of seawater. She had 568,000 cubic feet of cargo space, including 16,000 feet for reefer, or refrigerated cargo, and cargo oil tanks in hatch #3. She was launched in 1960, one of a class of merchant ships they called "Gulf Pride." She had a "split house," that is, part of the living quarters were separated from the bridge and passenger deck by a working cargo hatch. There were two crewmen to a room, and two of their rooms shared a head, or bathroom. Officers had their own rooms, as was by then traditional. She had rooms for twelve passengers as well, but on this trip, two U.S. Army lieutenants and ten enlisted men occupied them, going off to war. It was the kid's first voyage and the ship's 27th.

The chief mate set the cadet's work schedule. He would begin work with the bosun and the deck gang during the day, from 0800 to 1700, a normal eight hours of physical work with the guys from below decks. In order to complete his sea project, his homework from the school meant to teach him more about ships and the business of sailing, he would have to find time on his own. At sea he asked to be called, or awakened by the AB, the Able-Bodied Seaman, on the 4-8 watch, a half hour before star time, if the 2nd mate thought that some stars would be visible to shoot with a sextant and determine the ship's position. The weather going across the Pacific was mostly good. The seaman on watch usually called him at 0430. The AB was a dark, ugly, creepy guy. In order not to awaken the kid's engine cadet roommate, the guy would open the unlocked door, tiptoe in the dark next to the upper bunk where the kid was sleeping, and tap him on the shoulder. Sitting up with a start, the young man would see the guy standing there, just pointing up towards the sky with his crooked finger. He would say nothing, and slink back out without a sound, quietly closing the door behind him. It wasn't like Mom calling you for breakfast.

After a couple of hours on the bridge taking and working out his sights and talking things over with the 2nd mate, the kid would go below to his room. He'd get dressed for day work and go to breakfast about 0720. By 0750, he was down in the passageway outside the crew's quarters, waiting for the bosun to appear and give out the work assignments for the morning. The cargo ship carried two daymen, sailors who worked on deck maintenance, repair, and so forth, and did not stand a watch on the bridge. They liked having this kid working with them, as the kid was young, and eager to prove he could work as hard as they did. As the trip went on, the kid sometimes went down to their quarters to drink with them. The officers didn't like it, so the kid learned to keep quiet about it. Hell, if he was going to work with these guys all day, he felt he could have a beer or two with them. Besides, they seemed to know more about seamanship than anybody else on the ship. They could rig booms, splice rope or wire, and fix just about anything. On many other nights he played cards for small stakes with the army troopers, who had little to do, but did not seem to mind boredom.

A lot of the time they chipped and painted. This was the main task of the deck gang at sea. During these days of working "on deck," the kid squeezed time for his sea project. At morning coffee time, he would run up to the bridge to get a sun line observation and figure out local apparent noon, the time the sun crossed the meridian. During lunch he shot local noon with the mate on watch, later went back up during afternoon coffee to do a compass observation and maybe another sunline. He had to keep records of all this in his navigation notebook. When the deck gang knocked off near 1700, he cleaned up, went to supper, then back on the bridge. Now he figured out the optimum time for evening stars -- that small window of time when the stars are visible through a sextant, but there is enough daylight to see the horizon clearly. Then he took stars again with the 2nd mate and worked them out with pencil and trig tables, in those days before hand-held calculators or computers, and plotted them on the ship's chart. The 2nd mate was a helpful old-timer. His eyesight seemed to be failing, however, and sometimes he used the kid's sights and erased his own. A U-boat had torpedoed his ship in The War, and he frequently saw conning towers when everybody else only saw fishing boats, or the tops of merchant ships hull down near the horizon.

After some time with the 2nd, he went down to his room and worked on his other homework, all kinds of projects about seamanship, ship construction, cargo loading and securing, docking, radar, and the rest. Usually he took a tour of the ship about 2200. Some of the Cajun crew played bouree for heavy stakes, in their messroom. Sometimes an officer invited him in for drinks, or he went down to the crew's quarters to see if the daymen were up. If they were, the door would be open, and they would have beer cans stuck in a washtub of ice. With luck and some sense, he would get to bed about 2300. Sleep quickly, and wait for the creepy guy to come wake him the next morning to start all over. *All this fun and a salary of $111 a month, with no overtime,* he thought. The pay for cadets was the same as it had been in World War II. It came to about $90 a month after taxes -- three bucks a day. The two daymen nicknamed him "Easy Money," or "Easy," for short.

Most of the times that Easy was on rust removal he chipped paint off the ship with a small chipping hammer, and covered the exposed metal with a goop called red lead, as a rust preventative. Then, he applied two coats of whatever color that part of the ship was, on top of the red lead. One of the first things he painted was a watertight door. He started to paint over the gasket, without thinking, but one of the old-timers stopped him. He got the rubber piece cleaned before the bosun saw it, which was fortunate, since Nervous would have been convinced that he had an idiot on deck. The old salt also told him not to whistle. "Only a queer bosun whistles on a ship," he told the kid.

After several days of this, the ABs working on deck gave him some turns with the hurdy-gurdy. This was a heavy, air-driven device that had rotating metal spools, which spun, faster and faster, around and around, and took the paint off anything they hit. This made one hell of a racket, produced tons of vibrations, and if you used it a lot, you were either beat to hell, or developed strong arms. They used it to chip paint off larger areas, like the decks and hatch covers. It was a man's job, and the kid was glad he would become an officer and not have to make a living with things like the hurdy-gurdy.

This first trip of his was in 1965. Weather reports weren't great. Most weather maps sent by radio on fax transmissions were the result of weather observations that ships and planes made and sent in to the weather bureau. Meteorologists mapped out the readings taken for pressure, temperature, wind speed and direction, and made educated guesses made for areas without reports. The effect of this was that sometimes you would come up on a storm that no one knew was there, or knew how strong it was, until some ship sailed through it and radioed in a report.

They had sailed from New Orleans through Panama, and then fueled up in San Pedro, California for the crossing to Viet Nam. About half way across the Pacific, the weather reports started showing a low-pressure area ahead of them. The reports listed the maximum winds at about 30 knots. Captain Hamilton kept up with the reports, but didn't alter course for it. That was too damn bad, for when they got to the area a couple of days later, it was a full-blown typhoon.

Typhoons and hurricanes are the same thing; different names for different oceans. It's a bitch wherever you are. People who think it is exciting to be in one have watched too many movies. No good sailor wants to go through one; he always wants to go around. It isn't just the danger of sinking, but bad storms cause delays, since you can't make much headway, and the heavy pounding can damage ships. Men can get hurt just trying to get around a ship in a storm, and cargo, particularly deck cargo, can be ruined or washed overboard. All this costs money to the shipping company, and merchant ships need to make a profit to keep sailing. Besides, even if you are an old salt and don't get sick, it is unpleasant.

The first notice that you are in for it would be that the glass, or barometer, starts falling rapidly. Ships have a barograph too, which constantly tracks the barometric pressure with a pen that moves along graph paper. The closer you get to the center of a storm, the more it drops. In this case, the line went down sharply. That meant that the isobars, or lines of equal pressure, were close together. The closer they are together, the stronger the wind gets -- the stronger the winds, the higher the seas. It was simple, but brutal. A large, modern ship, thousands of tons of steel welded together, seems like the proverbial cork on the water. You learn quickly how insignificant the ship is.

Soon, the line traced on the barograph began to look like it fell off a cliff. Everyone who came up to the bridge would look at it, hoping that it would level off, indicating that they would have reached the lowest pressure on their course, and would start out the other side of the storm. But, the damn line kept going down, the winds and seas got higher, and the cargo ship began to pitch into higher seas, and roll heavily. The weather reports were now calling it a gale, but the guys on the ship knew better. The anemometer, the wind speed indicator high up on the mast, broke off at 110 knots. They were in for it. The captain ordered the watertight doors that led out on deck secured, and signs placed forbidding anyone out on deck. The sailors lashed down everything that was loose. The cooks secured most of the stoves. They would fix mostly sandwiches and cold food, with one hot pot a meal, soup maybe. For his part, Easy got sicker than hell, and could not hold down anything.

He had not been sick before this, and did not realize that they had been lucky with the weather. The seas had been nearly calm. He thought he had it knocked, that sailing wasn't so tough after all. He thought going to sea was easy, now he couldn't hold down soup. He would get up to the bridge and try to help do some work there, but up high in the ship, you felt the rolls and pitches even more. Eventually, he would run into the head, lose his lunch, and the officers would order him to go down to his room.

There, all he could do was lie in his bunk, and even that was difficult. He propped himself into a kind of a wedge with a mattress and pillows, but even then, when the ship took a violent lurch from side to side, he had to hold onto the side rail to keep from being pitched out of the bunk and onto the deck. A padeye in the deck secured his desk chair with a small turnbuckle. If you dared sit in the chair, the motion of the ship would lift your butt right up off the seat of the chair when the ship dropped into the trough of a wave. He thought he had everything in his room safely put away in lockers, or lashed down, but during one hard roll to port, the trash can lifted right up out of its lasso, off the deck, flew across the room and crashed into the bulkhead, spilling crap all over the place. He crawled over to it on hands and knees, and stuffed it into the clothes locker, which was now a jumbled mess anyway. Then he felt sick again and crawled right over to the toilet. He was in the absolute misery of a sailor's first storm. He could not understand how he could retch again, when he had emptied his stomach so many times. He would not ask for any medication; real sailors don't, and there wasn't much you could do anyway. It was okay to be sick, but it was not okay to whine about it. Everybody on the ship had been through this before. You were supposed to lose it your first time; if you kept getting sick in future storms, however, it meant that you were not cut out for the sea, and would have to quit the school and change your career plans. The first bad night of all this was made worse for him when the old, crusty, chief engineer, whose room was next to his, came into his room with a bottle of whiskey, and tried to get Easy to drink with him. The thought of it made him sick again. The old bastard left, laughing.

Sailors told him it would help to get fresh air, and look at the steady horizon. He ventured out on the deck by his room, in the morning, in spite of orders not to go on deck. It did help, too, until he looked up at the radar mast, the highest point of the ship. The crosstree on top of the mast reminded him of a cross in church, only this one was swinging violently to starboard and port, across a huge, ugly sky. It looked like a giant, upside-down pendulum, totally out of control. *Is this a sign?* He wondered. *Are we in for it? Is God that mad?* He mumbled what he could remember from a church prayer and went back inside.

On the second bad day, the kid went back up on the bridge. The helmsman was having a hell of a time trying to steer. The ship was now rolling as much as 40 degrees. The kid did not yet know enough about the real stability of a ship to realize how dangerous this was getting. He would learn that every ship, depending on its design, how it is loaded, the amount of fuel in the tanks, the amount of free surface liquid, whether the cargo is secure or loose, and so forth, has an angle of no return. At that point the forces that give a ship its righting moment to return from a roll begin to work in the opposite way, and theoretically, if you roll past this angle, you will keep on going and capsize. He would learn that for most cargo ships, properly loaded, this angle is about 55 degrees. If things got much worse on his first trip, they could reach this angle, and prove or disprove the theory.

Years later, he thought it was better that he did not know so much his first time out. Even without this detailed knowledge, Easy knew they were in danger. He felt it from the captain himself. The captain liked him, treated him fairly, and taught him things. The Old Man was competent, and he told the kid that he wanted to turn the ship around and sail away from the center of the typhoon, which was now clearly dead ahead. He wanted to put the seas on the stern and ride the storm out that way. He told Easy that he was afraid to turn the ship that much. If she broached to, or turned sideways in the trough of a large enough wave, she might roll over before he could complete the turn. Easy didn't need to know the details of the stability calculations to realize that this was more dangerous a storm than he had thought. Being sick now was secondary. *If an intelligent, sober captain were worried, hell, who wouldn't be?* You could not show it. Everybody had his macho face on.

Easy also began to give more importance to the engineers and "black gang," or engine room crew who kept the plant operating and the steering engine working. If you lost the boilers, and propulsion, all hell would break loose. You could not make headway or steer at all. You would broach to the seas, and only fate, luck, or God, whichever you wanted to believe in, would decide if you kept the stack up or not. He also heard the mates talking about the cargo, in the holds and on deck. If the deck cargo washed over the side, the ship would have more relative weight below decks, and the ship would become stiffer. A stiff ship rolls more violently, that he knew. He began to understand how a ship that seems so large at the dock could be lost with all hands in a storm, sometimes without a trace. The ships he saw in the Saint Johns River as a kid, the ones that seemed so huge, were tiny out here, compared to the vastness and power of the ocean in turmoil.

By the end of his second day in deepest hell, the barograph leveled off, and began to go up. The news spread around the ship quickly. They had gone right through the center of the damn storm, exactly what you don't want to do. The kid thought about all the ships that had sailed over the centuries with no weather reports at all. All those guys had was a sailor sense of when a storm was near, but they were mostly helpless to get away from it. No wonder so many ships had wrecked or been sunk. It took another day of steaming at reduced speed to get out the other side of the typhoon. On the fourth day, Easy held down food, and had a drink of whiskey with the chief engineer.

Work on board the westbound ship got back to normal. The bosun asked Easy one day if he knew how to go aloft.

"Yeah, I do." *No more "sir" for that son-of-a-bitch.* He also knew that cadets on most ships, when working with the deck gang, did not go aloft, up the masts. There was too much explaining to do if the kid got hurt. It was a sign that he was proving himself with the deck gang, as he was also doing with his navigation work with the officers.

His job was chipping and painting, up on a ladder where a vang guy, a wire used to brace the block at the head of the boom, secured it to the side of the ship. This was only about fifteen feet above the deck, but on a rolling ship, a fall, even from that height, to the solid steel deck below, could mess you up good. They made him take a safety belt, and asked him if he knew how to secure it.

"Yeah, yeah, I've used 'em before," Easy lied. It seemed simple enough. It was a wide belt, like weight lifters used, with about four feet of line, or rope, spliced onto the buckle. You used the line to tie yourself wherever you were working. A sudden movement of the ship, or a shift in your weight would not throw you backwards onto the deck.

He climbed up the ladder, chipping hammer tucked into the belt, paint bucket with the goddam red lead dangling from the same belt with a small line, and a brush hanging from another small line. He got up to the top, to start there and work his way down, as he had seen the old salts do. He got there, one hand for the ship and one hand for himself, in true sailor fashion -- one hand for the work, and one to take care of you. He took the end of the safety line and tied it around the top rung of the ladder by the vang guy. It was just after 0800, the ship was rolling, but the weather was decent. It was hot, but that was better than being cold. He felt good, but still, he wished he had not been drinking with the daymen down in their room the night before. He wondered how they could do it -- work so hard all day long, eat mountains of food, then drink tubs full of beer, or shots of whiskey, 'til everyone got fucked up, go to sleep for five or six hours, and do it all over again the next day, every day, weekends and holidays included, for months at a time. You simply had to push yourself and punish yourself.

He had two hours of physical labor until coffee time at 1000. He chipped for a time, and then had to lean out and back to reach the side of the stanchion. He let go with his hand, and stretched out -- at that time, the ship rolled to starboard, away from his side. His weight, then, strained against the safety rope. The knot slipped, and then gave way. He started to fall straight backwards. Dropping the hammer, he reached as far as he could and managed to grab a rung of the ladder with one hand. Using all his strength, he pulled himself up and got the other hand on it. The hammer clattered to the deck below. Sweating and cursing, he looked around. No one had seen this. He had not secured the line correctly. He climbed down, got the hammer, and went right back up again. He wondered later what his priorities in life were since he was more worried about someone seeing him and thinking there was a dummy aloft, than whether or not he would get hurt. He made it to morning coffee time a wiser young man.

As the trip progressed, Easy leaned more safety lessons one at a time. One of the most important happened in port. After unloading most of the cargo from one of the tween decks in a hatch, the hydraulic hatch cover would not rise up all the way. It was stuck partly open. Easy went down into the hatch with Deck, and they quickly determined that a piece of shoring, used to brace the crates in the space, had fallen down on the track that the wheels of the hatch pontoons rolled on. If they forced the wheels up against it too much, the wheels could jump the track, and the heavy hatch cover could drop down into the open space below this deck, causing huge delays and expensive repairs. The solution was simple--get rid of the damn lumber that was wedged on the track.

"I've got it," Easy hollered. "You get the controls." Deck went over to the hydraulic control box. When the pump was running, you pushed a handle one way to raise the hatch cover, the other way to lower it. Easy lay flat on his stomach and leaned over the edge of the hatch opening. Deck could not see him, and it was noisy. Easy reached out, fully extended and grabbed the wood. It took some grunting, but he finally pushed it over the edge. It fell harmlessly to the hold below. Easy was shouting to Deck, but he couldn't hear him, and suddenly it hit him. One instantaneous, wrong move during this, and the steel hatch cover would come down, snapping his arm off like a twig. Blood would spurt all over the place. Maybe Deck knew enough to save him, or maybe he would bleed to death right there. By the time Deck could get help, it would be too late. He would die right there, in that smelly tween deck, alone. The captain would fill out a report and notify the company and his next of kin. What a stupid way to go -- all because he had done a dumb thing. He knew instantly that he should have found another piece of shoring, or a turnbuckle, or some damn thing, and shoved that under the cover, not his arm

He yanked his arm back, rolled over on his back, and took a deep breath. He yelled to Deck to try it. The dayman pushed the control handle, and the hatch cover came up quickly. It fetched up and the locking latches dropped down, to secure the sections, one to another, like an accordion. Deck returned the handle to the stop position and walked over to Easy.

"What are ya' doin' fuckin' around? Let's go."

The kid knew he had gotten away with one yet again. Deck would have known better. Learning lessons this way wasn't going to work. Eventually, he would get himself killed, or maimed for life. He cursed himself and swore to do better, to think all the time, even with simple tasks. He also feared that when he became an officer he might get someone else hurt. Maybe handling mooring lines, a lot of guys got hurt that way. Maybe rigging booms . . .maybe . . . hell, he couldn't let that happen; he would do better. The worst thing would be to have a collision, or crack a ship up on a rock somewhere, or cause a fire on a tanker, hell, a thousand things could go wrong, and how could he live with that? He would pay more attention. He would watch the older sailors carefully, since they had been doing this kind of work for years and most still had their fingers and limbs, when others didn't. The trick was not to avoid work that was necessary for the ship, but not get yourself or anyone else hurt in the process. They climbed up the ladder to the main deck, Easy checking each rung of the ladder before he put his weight on it.

Easy learned more how to keep one hand for himself, and one for the ship, which meant he had to think more about safety. Sometimes, though, he got too comfortable with the deck work. When the ship arrived in port, he and Deck would go from hatch to hatch, and unsecure the cargo booms from their cradles, getting them ready for the stevedores to work as soon as they came aboard. Easy learned to handle the winches, guy wires, and booms. One of them worked the winches while the other loosened the cargo hook from its padeye on deck, and other chores. They were both young, physically fit, and, in spite of the near accidents he had, Easy felt that he had it now, and could not fuck up again.

As they went from hatch to hatch, they sometimes did stupid things. Deck would be on the winches, slackening the cargo runners until Easy could let go the cargo hook from the padeye. Easy would sometimes hang on to the hook, and Deck would hoist him up in the air with the winches, setting him back down on the winch platform, ten feet off the main deck. It was this bit of horseplay that got them in trouble. The chief mate, who was in charge of the deck gang as well as the cadet's work schedule and training, witnessed it. The ass chewing was a little different for each, with Deck getting the worst of it, since he was the more experienced sailor. Still, Easy thought it was obvious that the chief mate secretly enjoyed having two young bucks on deck who showed no fear, and would do any job at any time, one for three dollars a day, the other for union scale.

After discharging their cargo in Qui Nhon, Vietnam, the U. S. government, which had chartered the ship for the trip, ordered them to return to the states empty. They had not refueled, and had just enough bunker C for the return across the Pacific, through the Panama Canal, and back to New Orleans.

Therefore, the ship only had fuel for weight, and they were burning that all the time. The ship burned about a barrel of Bunker C fuel oil for every mile it traveled. The weather reports on the way back began to show another typhoon in their path. The reports were better this time, and the captain changed course to avoid it. Still, you never knew for sure which way a storm would track, and if another typhoon hit them now, empty of cargo, the ship would be in more danger than before. As all the mates discussed these things on the bridge, the kid listened to it all. Then the captain called the bridge and told the mate on watch to send the cadet down to his room.

The kid figured that the Old Man had some errand for him, a normal thing for an eighteen-year old cadet. The skipper, however, invited him in his room, told him to sit down, and offered him a cold beer. Not wanting to be rude, and a cold beer being difficult to obtain, Easy accepted. This was highly unusual. The only other time he had sat down in the captain's cabin was when he was guarding a stowaway earlier in the trip. He also knew that captains usually had no social contact with kids like him.

The captain told him that he thought the kid was one of the best cadets he had ever sailed with, and he wanted to talk to him about the storm ahead and how he was going to handle it. It was a high compliment for the kid. The Ol' Man began talking about the strength of the storm ahead, its uncertain course, and his efforts to avoid it, and to prepare the ship if they hit it. It seemed he was trying to teach him things for the future. He told Easy that he had just ordered all four cargo oil tanks, in #3 lower tween deck, a thousand tons total capacity, to be filled with sea water ballast. This, he said, was strictly against company policy. If they were to go through another typhoon like the other one, however, with no cargo in the holds, and low on fuel, he doubted whether the ship could take it. You couldn't wait until you were in trouble to start ballasting, he explained. While the tanks were filling up, you actually had less stability than before. Only when they are full and pressed up did the weight in there help you, at that point the water being just as good as solid cargo, or in the old days, rock ballast.

Out at sea, his word was law. The company could not stop his orders. What would happen when they reached port was another matter. If he thought it necessary for the safety of the ship he could do it, but the company could reprimand him by reassigning him to another ship, or just fail to find work for him. He could lose his job, in effect. Salt water in the cargo tanks could contaminate future cargo oil. Even after a thorough cleaning, residual salt could remain, start rusting the tanks and damage cargo, causing a loss of revenue or expensive repairs to the tanks. He was taking the time to explain his decision, which was unnecessary, and to teach him. It felt great to have this veteran do this, and drink a beer or two with him in the process. The kid could tell when the lesson was over, and thanked the Captain as he left.

The cargo oil tanks were soon full of seawater, and the thousand tons of weight in them gave the ship needed stability as well as a more comfortable ride in the seas. This time, the captain's course change to the southeast worked, as this storm tracked more predictably to the northwest. They only sailed through the southern edge of the storm, and the ride wasn't too bad. Easy didn't even get sick this time. When they arrived in New Orleans, the company took the skipper off the ship for vacation, and a new captain came aboard. Easy would not find out if the company was sanctioning the Ol' Man or not. Easy would never meet a captain he respected more.

Back from the trip to Viet Nam, the ship loaded cargo in several ports along the Gulf of Mexico for the next trip, a commercial run to the Mediterranean. Easy was looking forward to this, his first commercial trip, some good ports in Spain, Italy, and elsewhere, some good times in addition to his work. The Viet Nam trip had many days at sea, but it had been good for learning ship work, and he had gotten months ahead on his sea project homework for the school. He figured he could afford to party some this trip. On future ships, he would not associate with the crew much, but on his first he had to work with them every day, and do his officer training on his own time, so it fell into place. On the coastwise run, Easy and Deck went ashore together in Houston, up at the Turning Basin. This was a place where a ship could turn around and head back out to the Gulf, there not being enough width to the Houston Ship Channel for a large ship to turn around in most of it. A freeway went right by the Basin, but it was a long way into town. The main attractions of the Basin were the cowboy and Mexican bars that littered the area. It was a night they would both regret the next day, but what the hell, when you're young and putting out to sea again the next day after a long trip that just ended, you don't care much.

The next day he tried to remember all that had happened in the Basin bars the night before. He recalled getting separated from Deck and wandering into a cowboy bar. He ran into the engine cadet and they had Lone Star beer together and shot some pool. At one point, a couple of girls had come into the place. The two kids, after a long trip at sea, noticed them right away. The girls had a quick drink at the bar, some conversation with the woman bartender, and left. A minute later, the barkeep had come over to them and told them that the two girls who just left were looking for a couple of guys to go to a party with, and they would wait outside in their car for a few minutes. If the guys were interested, she said, they should go out right then.

Hell yeah, they were interested! They went outside. The one driving rolled down the window. There was a short conversation, wherein the Texas girls invited the boys to get in the back seat. The girls seemed a couple of years older than the sailors were, but they were both attractive; after a little more time at sea, they would both seem gorgeous. The driver asked them if they wanted to party. Their response was quick and positive. She then wanted to get it straight who was going with who. Easy liked the looks of the driver and said so. The engine cadet said that pairing was fine. Easy could not believe his luck. *These cowgirls sure are friendly; hell, they seemed hot to trot,* Easy thought.

He remembered being surprised when they pulled into a motel parking lot a few minutes later. He had expected a drive to someone's house for the party. Easy now thought that maybe they were married, and this was how they got away and fooled around. They were shipping out again the next day, so what did he care? If that was the case, it would be their problem, not his, he thought. As soon as they all got out of the car, his girl took him by the hand and led him to a room. His pal went down the hall in the other direction. Damn, they were quick. His date had her room key out, and they were inside in seconds. She put her purse down in the corner, came back over to him and started rubbing her body all over him. He was extremely interested. Then she took off her clothes. Everything he had been dreaming of during the voyage was right there in front of him. She was slender and pretty. He could not contain himself. He was yanking off his clothes when she came over to him again. She took his hands and placed them on her body.

"Slow down, hon'. We're going to have a good time, but business first. That'll be twenty bucks."

It hit him hard. *Stupid!* You might be still eighteen, but you should have known. *Damn!* She was a real pro. *What kind of girls did you expect to meet in the Turning Basin bars, socialites?* His shock must have shown on his face, but she knew how to handle the rookie. He couldn't recall everything she said after that, but it was about how she didn't do this all the time, she just needed to make some money for some reason or other. She had promised to perform all kinds of tricks for him, told him how good she was in bed, and again taken his hands and passed them all over her body. His brain said no, you don't pay for it, but his body didn't care. It was a struggle between brain and body, but his body won out in about ten seconds. He fumbled for the twenty. She ran over to the dresser, stuffed in it her purse, and came back to bed.

"Now let's get you undressed, hon'. You'll have a good time, don't worry." And, he did. He would remember that once he got past the ugly business part of it all, it was a good time. Maybe she went out of her way for the naive rookie, but she did perform tricks in the sack, said nice things the whole time, and he forgot about the sea for a while. He had especially liked the way she could put her bare feet on his back and push his body down to hers, in rhythm.

They soon got back out to the car, and within a few minutes, his buddy came out of another room with his girl. The two girls had great timing. They got a ride back to the Basin, and the girls dropped them off at the gate to the dock. The kids walked back quietly, had a last drink up in their room, and went to bed. They didn't discuss what had happened, but it was clear that the experience was about the same for both, and they both felt funny about it.

The next morning, the ship undocked early. Easy went up on the bow and handled mooring lines with Deck and the other sailors. They drank coffee on deck after that, before breakfast, and Deck asked him what happened after they had separated the night before. Easy felt embarrassed, but he told him about the party. Deck provided counseling.

"Ah, fuck it. You had a good time, right? That's what girls like that are for. What did you expect to find around the docks at night, a fuckin' museum to go to? Don't worry about nothin'. Every sailor pays for it once in a while. Any sailor who says he hasn't is either a liar or a goddam fag, and you can't trust neither one. The married guys pay for it too, every month when they pay their bills. Lots of single guys send money to girlfriends in Korea or home. You ain't no different, you just paid up front. Now go to breakfast, then meet me back aft. Nervous wants me to splice a mooring line this morning, and I told him I needed your help. I'll show you how to do it right; those fucking eight-inch mooring lines are a bitch to splice."

They went different ways to eat, Deck over to the crew's mess, and Easy to the officer's saloon. Deck seemed to have a little smile on his face. His young, officer-candidate, college-student pal was becoming more of a sailor all the time.

They got the line spliced and did other work around the ship. Easy spent some time on the bridge with his navigation in the afternoon and even got permission to do some steering in and out of port during the rest of the coastwise trip. He needed to know this for his own skills, and because when he became a mate, he would be supervising the sailors who steered. The ship made a few other ports in the Gulf; Galveston, Beaumont, Gulfport, then topped off cargo back in New Orleans before going across the Atlantic to the Med. During the brief stay in New Orleans, the kid went to the academy office, which the rules for student sailors at the time demanded.

In the cadet year of sailing, part of the four-year course of study at the academy, kids shipped out on regular, in service, merchant ships. They left out of New York, San Francisco, or New Orleans. The kid was from Florida, so he was sent to New Orleans, the nearest of the three to his home. The school maintained a small office there. The secretary had the run of the place, and it paid to be nice to her. She was the one who arranged with a shipping company to put you on board for a trip. The company got cheap labor; the kids got real life experience. It was a good system. Easy was there to request a second trip on the same ship. This was unusual, but he got it. It was a different run, and the secretary knew that they had screwed the kid with his first assignment. He had given up his 30-day annual leave to ship out early. He had requested Far East, meaning commercial Far East, to Japan, Korea, and Hong Kong, and all that. Instead, the jerk in charge had put him on a military charter to Viet Nam and back -- no fun. The other good news for him was that he was months ahead on his sea project. He went down to the French Quarter for a visit to the Attic Bar, as tradition at the time demanded.

Guys from the school who had already been to sea passed down practical knowledge to the younger guys. If you shipped out of New Orleans, they said, go down to the Attic Bar at night. You could meet other guys from your school there and trade stories. The bar even kept a logbook where you made entries telling what ship you were on, or left comments on the captain, advice on places to go in different ports, or hints on where to meet girls, or cheap places to stay, eat, or drink. Graduates of the school would write in it for a year or so after graduating, but gradually give that up as a juvenile thing to do. They would, however, uphold the tradition of buying beer for cadets who were in the bar. The older guys with good paying jobs, in other words, would front for the kids who were in the same situation they had been in only a few years before. Easy had been in there before, and true to tradition, had beer slid down the bar from grads, sometimes never knowing who in the place had paid for it. The tradition ended many years later when the owner sold the place. The new owner changed everything. It was the way things went, but it was a shame.

The bar was across the street from the old Courthouse. The downstairs had a long bar and some tables. There were French doors all around which opened to the street. There was another room upstairs, hardly used except when the place was packed, like during Mardi Gras. The guy who owned the place was an ex-seaman himself. In between the two floors, there was a secret room. Legend had it that Jean Lafitte, the pirate, who helped Jackson defend the city against the British, used this room as a meeting place in the War of 1812. It made a good story, and many a sailor had used it to impress a date.

The location of the Attic was good. If you met a tourist girl down at Pat O'Brien's you could get her away from the hustle and expense of Bourbon Street and take her there for a more intimate setting. If things were going right, you could then go right across the street to the Napoleon House. The legend of that old restaurant and bar was that it was the house prepared for Napoleon to come and live in when he decided to abdicate the throne. In this place, they played classical music on an old record player, and there were old pictures on the walls. The whole place was old, damn old, and a nice place to have a glass of brandy.

Easy hung out in the Attic for a while, trading stories with a few guys in the same business. It was a drinking bar in those days, and, as usual, there weren't any girls unless you brought your own. He had a few bucks in his pocket, but did not feel like going over to Bourbon Street and buying over-priced drinks for tourist girls. His ship was leaving the next day. He'd be in the Strait of Gibraltar in about a week, and he would save what he had for the Med. ports. To save money, he rode the trolley uptown, then caught a bus, then walked down to the Nashville Avenue Wharf, where the ship was docked, loading the last of her cargo.

He paused for a minute on the wharf and watched the work. It was noisy. Longshoremen were shouting and sweating all the time, working the cargo. He thought about his learning experiences so far with watching out for himself, and wondered, in those days when a lot of the cargo was handled by hand and fork lift truck, why more of these guys didn't get hurt. In his short time around the ports, Easy had already witnessed several near misses with cargo handling. He remembered a pallet with drums stacked on it, flat end down, with some netting around it that had seemed safe enough to load. The winch driver, however, had swung the load too much, and he saw the drums come tumbling off, falling 30 feet or more, where the longshoremen in the hatch were standing. He had watched them scramble to get out of the way, all "assholes and elbows," as the expression goes, and seen the 55-gallon drums hit the steel deck below and split open. No one had been hurt, but there was a lot of cussing, mostly directed at the winchman. The guys in the hatch had then refused to do any more work unless the boss replaced the asshole running the winches, and they used chime hooks to load the drums. With chime hooks, you laid the drums on their side on the dock, and stretched these hooks, which were on chains, until one was one each end of each drum. When the winch driver picked up the cargo runner, the cargo hook pulled up all the chains, the chime hooks tightened on the drums, and they all came off the dock together. When landed in the hatch opening, the only problem was that they were now not on a pallet where a forklift could pick up the load and put it in place. The damn drums were on their sides, and they had to roll them into place and then set upright again. The hatch boss went for the chime hooks, and replaced the winchman. Still, Easy thought there was always a tradeoff. Something like this seemed so simple at first, but it wasn't. You had to balance ways of handling cargo that were the fastest with ways that were the safest. He thought it did no good to save the company a thousand dollars in labor costs with a method of work that got a guy hurt or killed, and his lawyers tore into you. He was only beginning his second trip to sea, but he was acting more like a seaman, and thinking more like an officer, all the time. He never thought about it at that age, but that is exactly why students went to sea.

Chapter 3: A Night in Beirut

The trip to the Mediterranean was a lot different than the military charter to Viet Nam the kid had just completed. The captain and chief mate were new guys. The engine cadet had gotten off to join another ship, and Easy had a room to himself. At sea, on the way over, the new chief mate started coming up to his room on weekends, bringing the ship's paperwork with him. The officers normally left cadets alone at sea on weekends, to do their homework. This guy was using him more than normal, but the kid was catching on with this game. Finally, the mate brought him the crew's overtime and payroll to figure out. Easy knew, even on his second trip to sea, that he should not be doing this. There were union rules to follow, and the mate made overtime pay doing the paperwork. If the crew knew that the cadet was doing their payroll, there would be hell to pay. He did it for a few days, and then made his move.

He went to the mate's office one night at sea when no one else was around, and laid it out to him. He, the kid, would work weekends at sea, doing whatever paperwork or other work the mate wanted, but when the ship was in port in the Med the mate shouldn't look for him around the deck, cause he'd be ashore. He would go sightseeing during the days, and partying at night. That was the deal; otherwise, he would have to go to someone else to see if all this was acceptable. It was clear that the "someone else" would be the captain. The kid knew the mate could work his ass off every day, in port as well as at sea, and there would be nothing he could do about it, and he would not get overtime pay. Yet, the captain was a fair man, and he liked the kid, so Easy had the upper hand. The mate hated paperwork. The kid was good with the numbers and typed fast for a sailor. The mate turned red, but he agreed. Easy didn't feel badly; it was a fair deal, and he was learning that you had to stand up for yourself in this business, or guys would run over you. He would work his ass off at sea, but have some free time to see the sights in Spain, Italy, North Africa, and wherever else they went. His dreams of seeing some of the world were beginning to come true. The vision he had years before, standing on the hill, watching the big ships sail up the St. Johns River was no longer just a vision. He could make it a reality, and he did not care if he had to work fourteen-hour days to make it so.

The mate, for his part, worked the kid more than ever. Easy did not mind. He thought the background in physical work on deck and the paperwork he did on weekends would come in handy in three years when he was an officer. Even though he would be one of "them college graduate mates," he would know a thing or two about deck work, and would relate to the crews better than if he only did office work, which happened on some ships. On many ships, the rules forbid cadets to work with the crew, except for docking and undocking, when all deckhands took part.

On this ship, the crew was an unusual bunch. It is difficult to imagine, perhaps, but most of the crewmembers would put on a coat and tie to go ashore. The kid fell in with the new bosun, his pal Deck, and four or five of the ABs, who went ashore in a group. They attacked each port with a vengeance. One of their best efforts was in Genoa, Italy. The ship lay at anchor, but there was a launch service. Every couple of hours, a small boat pulled alongside the gangway and brought guys back or took those off duty ashore. The group left shortly after supper and started hitting bars. Eventually, the new bosun and Easy separated from the rest of the group. The bosun knew a couple of good places to go, and the kid tagged along. The drinking got serious. When the drinking gets serious, there is no more chasing women, no more reason to anything, except to see how much you can drink. In this state, the two of them missed the last launch back for the night. When they realized this, they had two choices. Find a place to sleep a little, or take the bosun's choice -- go to some after-hours clubs he knew, and keep drinking until the first boat out at 0530 in the morning. Their sense and judgment, added together, did not amount to spit. They started walking to the first club. It was a true sailor's solution; keep going all night long, and to hell with tomorrow.

Before the sun came up, they somehow stumbled their way to the docks and amazingly found the right boat that the company had hired for launch service. They got back to the ship about 0600, and the kid got to his room by crawling the last part on his hands and knees. He lay down, fully clothed, but had not been in the sack five minutes when the chief mate came into the room, physically shook him, and told him that the ship was shifting to a dock right away, and he had to turn to for docking.

"I can't, mate, I'm all fucked up." It was the first time in his life he ever said he couldn't work.

"Well, that's too bad, you have to. The bosun's drunk; I can't get him up. You have to come up to the bow and run the anchor windlass." The mate shook him again, and left.

"The bosun's drunk? The goddam bosun's drunk? Of course he's drunk! We're both drunk; we were together! He's the smart ass who knew all those after-hours clubs! He's supposed to be the toughest guy on the goddam ship, for chrissakes, I'm supposed to take his place?" The mate heard none of this. Then, the concept of being a good shipmate took over his befuddled mind. You never left a shipmate in a bad spot ashore or in trouble with work on the ship. If a guy screwed you, then you could abandon the son-of-a-bitch -- no more good shipmate then. But the bosun was a good guy. He had treated the kid well, even though he worked him hard, and now it was up to the kid to cover for him. If he didn't, maybe they would fire the bos' at the end of the trip. He had to do it. The kid somehow stumbled into some work clothes and made it to the bow. He ran the windlass that lifted the anchor off the bottom. Deck and the ABs hosed down the anchor chain. The chief mate was up there, calling out on his radio how much chain was still down. "Three on deck," then "two in the pipe," finally, "one in the water," indicated how many shots of anchor chain were out, a shot being fifteen fathoms. He called out "anchor's aweigh" when the hook was off the bottom, and the ship moved ahead towards Genoa. The kid had to steady himself the whole time, but within an hour or so, they had docked the ship, and the usual swarm of workers scrambled up the gangway to rig booms and guy wires, take cargo off, and load cargo on. Easy went aft, into the house, and towards his room. Unfortunately, the passageway to his room went right by the mate's office.

"You going ashore today?" the chief mate shouted as he went by.

"Hell no, I'm going to bed."

"Well, if you stay aboard, I'm going to work you on deck." The mate had him. He must have worked on that angle for days. The deal was that Easy would go ashore in port. He never anticipated wanting to sleep during the day in port.

"Well, in that case, I am going ashore; all day." Easy showered and changed, then went down to breakfast in his shore clothes. The mate eyed him pretty good, but the kid held up, held down his food, and went down the gangway.

After much asking and wandering around, he found the train station and bought a third class ticket to Pisa. He spent the day there, seeing the Tower, taking pictures, sending postcards home, and even had enough for lunch at a sidewalk cafe. He felt better after eight or nine cups of coffee, the espresso kind that could knock your socks off. He got back to the docks early in the evening, with every intention of going quietly up to his room, on the outside ladder this time, not by the mate's office, and getting some sleep. Walking along the dock, however, he met up with the bosun and the gang. They made serious arguments for him to turn around and go out with them. He figured he had them when he said that he had spent most of his money, and couldn't afford to go drinking. The bosun, now completely sober and ready to go again, insisted he would cover Easy. Hell, he had covered him for docking, maybe saving his job, and he would not listen to a negative answer. Easy gave in, although he knew what would happen. Sure enough, it was long after midnight when he finally got back to the ship. At least the damn thing was at a dock now, and he could get to it. He was young, and he didn't care. The ship was leaving early in the morning for Beirut. He had now been over 43 hours without sleep, gone ashore, seen some sights, and had gotten drunk twice and sobered up twice in this time. He loved it. He had also gotten the best of the arrangement with the mate. The other mates liked his work on the bridge and on deck, and the crew treated him as one of them, especially after the bosun incident. *I can sleep at sea,* he thought. Perhaps he was getting the hang of it. They headed for the anchorage off Beirut.

In the 1960's, Beirut was the playground of the Middle East. It had fine hotels, good beaches, and was a safe place. American money was welcome. Rich Arabs went there to play; it was like the Miami Beach of the Middle East. Sailors rated it a good shore port. The deck gang dressed for the occasion, dragging along their daytime helper, Easy Money, with them. They left the ship on the launch right after supper, in a pack, as was their custom. Even the Ordinary Seaman, the lowest rank in the deck department, had on a coat and tie. As usual, there was a lot of discussion and bullshit trying to decide where to go first. The guys who had been to the port before usually got their way, although you could easily walk by a place, like the looks of it, and go in. This particular time, someone had heard of a place called the American Bar, and they all agreed to start the night's fun there. Any bar would probably do, since their routine was to go drinking for a while first. They would look for places with women later. Places that had good food were unimportant.

Inside, they saw that there was a bar to the right, and some tables to the left. They pushed a couple of tables together, and the group of eight guys ordered drinks. Everything seemed normal, but Easy, perhaps because he was the newest at all this, looked around and watched more than the veterans. After a while, he spoke to the group.

"Hey guys, I don't know about this place."

"What are you talkin' about, Easy?"

"Well, there are no women in here, for one thing. The guys are real friendly, and they keep disappearing in the back room in pairs. There are booths back there, and some of these guys are sitting on the same side of the booth, with no one across from them."

"Goddam it!" the bosun, rested and full of realization, exclaimed. "The American Bar is a fag joint!"

"Let's get the fuck out of here!" many seemed to say at once.

For his part, Easy did not know why they were so upset. They seemed to be insulted, somehow, even though it was common knowledge that a degree of homosexuality was common in most countries. He decided they were pissed off that the owner called his place the American Bar. They got out to the street quickly, and the kid had made his reputation with them. He had gotten this group of tough guys out of a fag bar before they were there long enough to be embarrassed, or drunk enough to start a fight. They all insisted on buying his drinks.

They went from place to place, and lit for a while at the New York Bar. Every port in the world seemed to have a New York Bar, and it was always a sailor's bar. This was no exception. They felt at home. There were Danish sailors from a merchant ship who were joking around, and everyone seemed to be having a good time. There were a few women in the place, the most notable of whom was a 300-pound prostitute. She was wearing a dress the size of a circus tent, and sitting at the bar, drinking. She laughed and drank constantly, and if hers was a sad lot in life, it didn't show on this night.

Easy was clearly the youngest sailor in the place, not being quite nineteen yet. Some of the other sailors, from different countries, seemed to make note of that. He eventually went into the men's room, and stood in front of an old, beat-up urinal. The next thing he knew, the fat broad was in there with him, catching him in a compromising position. She was laughing her ass off, if that was possible, and blocking the door. She made it clear, in the English she knew, that the group of guys he was with, along with the Danes, had paid her to have sex with him, right there in the men's room, and right then. He was horrified. He finished his business, embarrassed, and wanted to leave.

She locked the door. By now, he could hear the guys in the bar laughing, and yelling to him things about having a good time, and all that. *What the hell now? There is no way,* the kid thought, *that I am going to do this.* If he wanted a girl from this bar, it certainly wouldn't be her. The men's room was no place for this anyway. He made a move to push her out of the way and open the door. He was strong, but weighed only 160 pounds. She was immovable. Her response was to repeat the arrangement and lift up her circus tent-like dress. *My god, no, I've got to get out of here,* he thought. *A window? Not big enough.* He couldn't hit her. What then? She was drunk, immovable, and insistent on removing her clothes. She was still laughing, and thought the whole thing was a riot. The noise from the bar got louder.

He decided to appeal to her sense of humor. He took out some money, forced her to take it, and explained that they would both go out into the bar and pretend that they had consummated the act. That way, all her patrons would enjoy their joke, she could keep the money they had given her, and his tip as well, and everyone would have fun with it. Easy would keep his mouth shut about the solution, building his reputation with the gang as a real sailor, and one who could take a joke. She stuffed his money into her bra, rearranged herself, laughed some more, and let him out. As he came out of the bar, he got a standing ovation from the jerks in the bar. Everyone was in on it, locals as well as seamen. *Christ.* He just smiled sheepishly, and let them think what they wanted to. The girl also got a round of applause when she emerged, rearranging her clothing, proof enough to all the drunks in the place that yes, indeed, it had happened. The kid put up with all the jokes. People he didn't know bought him drinks, he had some new Danish friends, and all was right in the New York Bar in Beirut, Lebanon. At one point, just before the pack left to go somewhere else, the kid had gone up to the bar to fetch drinks, and stood next to the fat broad. He said, "Thanks." She looked at him and started laughing again. That was how they left it, although Easy now had the habit of looking over his shoulder when entering men's rooms.

From there, the gang went to a huge, fancy nightclub called the Kit Kat Club. They sat at a bar and ordered drinks. There were European businessmen, Arabs in traditional garb, and some gorgeous women in the place. One of the girls came up behind Easy, "accidentally" rubbed her chest across his back, then docked alongside of him and asked for a light for her cigarette. Easy didn't smoke, but carried a lighter just for these occasions. As he turned, he could see that she was one of the most beautiful women he had ever seen, including in pictures. He lit her smoke as calmly as he could. She steadied his hand, blew a puff of smoke over his head, gently stroked his hair, and called him "sexy Blondie." She was the type of girl you would dream about. She acted like Lauren Bacall, but Easy thought this girl was better looking. She sauntered away, turned left, and sat in a booth.

Easy was in love. He would have done anything, paid anything, and mortgaged his soul to spend an hour with her; hell, a few minutes even. The older sailors could see all this in his eyes. They asked the bartender about her. They had to hold him back from chasing her around the club. She was, they found out, one of those European call girls who worked the expensive clubs in Beirut, for the pleasure of the super wealthy. If they put all their money together, it would still not be enough. *She could have been a model or a Playboy bunny,* Easy thought, but it didn't matter. He wasn't going to get her out of there, even for an hour, not even for ten minutes. The Kit Kat was the most elaborate place they went to that night. It had a floorshow with Flamenco dancers, and a stripper that was even better looking than the blonde he was crazy about. When the deck gang left the Kit Kat, he didn't think he would ever find any place in the world as wonderful.

Easy and Deck wandered away from the group. They drifted into a small bar in the center of the city. There was a four-piece jazz band playing. Although it didn't seem like much of a place, the musicians wore tuxedos. There were no girls and very few patrons in the place. Deck didn't like it much, but Easy wanted to listen to the music, so they settled in for a drink. The kid liked the band. He had played drums in high school, and was familiar with some of their pieces. Eventually he went over and talked to the guys in the band. With some sign language to supplement his English, he made it clear that if the drummer wanted to take a break, Easy would buy him a drink, and sit in. They went for it. He never did know if the guys in the band enjoyed having a little fun with a customer, or just put up with the tourist, but he didn't care. They played some big band pieces he knew, and some jazz he could improvise. It was great. He forgot all about the bathroom incident, the Kit Kat girl, and the sea. Deck was unsettled, but kept quiet. It was a good break from their work, and the barhopping they did ashore. When Easy turned the sticks back over to the band's drummer, they both smiled. Maybe, just for a brief moment, they bridged the culture gap between them. Maybe just as sailors from all over the world could meet and usually get along, musicians could also. *And,* he thought, *if sailors and musicians could find common ground, hell, why couldn't everybody?* It was an ethereal thought for a sailor who was getting drunker all the time, but it was a thought that would haunt him for the next twenty years. It would seem that the more you traveled, the more you realized that people the world over are pretty much the same. All the fuss over different languages, religions and customs that drove some to hate each other, others to kill each other, was all bullshit.

Deck still seemed uncomfortable, so they left. The bad part of the jazz bar experience was that they now realized that they had missed the last launch back out to the anchorage. It was, as Yogi Berra said, "Deja vu all over again." Easy was beginning to hate anchoring out, and wished the damn ship would just go straight to a dock. He was determined, however, not to repeat the mistake he made with the bosun. He would not drink all night; they could find a cheap place to get some sleep, and take the first boat out of the harbor early in the morning. Deck agreed. The hotel they found was beat-up looking, but good enough for two sailors who had been drinking all night. At least the price was right. They got separate rooms next to each other. Easy had trouble locking the door to his room. Examining it through his alcohol-fueled haze, he saw that the goddam thing did not have a lock. He propped a chair up against the door handle, took off his shoes, and lay down. He was too tired to argue or go look for another place. He then hoped that one of the two of them would wake up in time, since there was no phone, and they didn't know if the guy at the desk understood them when they had told him that they wanted to be awakened at five.

It wasn't an hour later, however, when the kid awoke with the sound of Deck pounding on his door. He stumbled to the door, recognized the voice, and removed the chair to open it. Easy struggled to clear his head. The fat broad, the Kit Kat girl, the drummer, and many drinks were pounding in his head. Deck looked terrible.

"What the hell's the matter?" the kid asked.

"That asshole from the front desk just sneaked into my goddam room and crawled into bed with me. When I woke up, he was rubbing my leg. This is a fag hotel!"

"What'd you do?" Easy asked, as he ran over to find his shoes. He sensed there was a slight problem.

"I beat the hell out of him! Come on, we got to get the fuck out of here!"

Easy needed no more encouragement. Visions of Middle Eastern jails, and the stories he had heard of what they were like, spurred him on. They went down some back stairs and out into the street. They walked quickly through alleys and narrow streets, always working their way down towards the waterfront. When they got to the docks where all the small boats were, they checked for police before venturing along the docks. It was clear. They woke up a guy who had a small boat, and bribed him with a few dollars and some cigarettes to take them out to the anchored ship right then. It was still several hours before daylight, and the first scheduled company launch. There was a heavy swell running outside the breakwater, but they did not care, the boatman did not care, and the little boat got them out there. Easy felt ahead of the game this time. He was not as drunk as he was in Genoa, and would get a few hours' sleep before work. Another night of learning was over. As he might have predicted, the mate called him out at 0530 for weighing anchor, shifting into port, and docking. At least the damn bosun showed up this time.

They made a quick stop in Turkey, at a place called Iskenderun. The only things memorable were the army tanks they discharged with the heavy-lift boom, and the "cages." The tanks were so heavy the wire creaked and groaned with each lift, and it sounded like the wire would break. Even at the dock, the ship took a list when the heavy weight hung over the dock and it took a lot of effort from the guys handling the ropes to keep the load from swinging.

The cages were at the local jail, and on the ground floor. Dozens of girls yelled at him as he walked by on the sidewalk, and reached out their arms through the bars. The ones who spoke English promised all kinds of sexual delights, and the price was incredibly cheap. A jail guard stood watch at the door to the prison and eyed him. You could go up to the guard, make a financial deal, and then he would take you inside, to view the girls in the cages, or cells. You could have your pick, and have your way in a separate cell. Supposedly, the girl you would choose would get something out of it, but who knew what -- better treatment, cigarettes, or a dollar? He walked by, not being that desperate and wondered what these women had done to be in there.

With the exception of some time in Barcelona, Spain, the rest of the Med part of the trip was uninspiring, and the ship headed westbound, past Gibraltar, and for home. His shipmate, the dayman, resumed something he had started the trip before, on the long ride back across the Pacific. He had asked Easy how difficult it was to learn to navigate. Deck was 27-years old, and a good sailor, but it seemed that he could see how hard his job was going to be when he got older, and thought maybe he could become an officer. Many guys had become mates this way, rather than go to an academy. "Coming up the hawsepipe," they called it. On the older ships, the crew had lived forward, on the bow, or in the forecastle. Since the hawsepipe was also on the bow, he figured that the expression meant that a guy had worked his way "up the pipe" to the officer's quarters. You had to study at night from many books, have at least three years of experience as an AB, and then you could take an exam that lasted a full week.

It was a good time to try it. The mates' union had opened their books to new members, since some ships sailed short-handed. Crewmen all knew that if they were ever going to make a try to be an officer, the Vietnam War had handed them the opportunity. The mates' union would take hundreds of new members in during the war. A third mate's license issued by the U. S. Coast Guard and a thousand dollars was all you needed to join. It was very difficult to get a license on your own, though. Even if you had the three years of sea time as an Able-bodied seaman there was that test, the one that took a full week. A passing grade was 90% on some sections of it, too.

Easy had the college to go back to, and even though some of the courses were strictly for the degree, there were plenty of others in navigation, cargo handling, and so on, to get you ready for the exam. Easy thought he owed Deck some help, with all that Deck had done to teach him the practical aspects of shipboard work. It might be a fair trade, but Easy didn't know if Deck liked to read and study.

Deck had started coming up to the kid's room on weekends and sometimes at night during the week. Deck had looked a little pale when he saw all the books in Easy's room. Easy started with the basics of piloting -- courses and bearings, compasses and chart symbols, those kinds of things. He wrote down the titles of some of the books Deck would need to buy and study. Easy decided to stick to the practical aspects, and got permission from the mates who stood the watches on the bridge to bring Deck up there with him to work with actual charts. One of the three watch-standing mates had come up the hawsepipe himself, and seemed to encourage them, but it didn't go so well.

By the time they were halfway back across the Atlantic from the Med, it had become apparent that years of physical work and no book learning had made Deck a terrific sailor, and a poor student. With his rough, beaten hands he had a difficult time even holding the dividers to measure mileage off the latitude scales and transferring it to a place on a chart. By the time they had rounded Dry Tortugas, in the Florida Keys, and headed for New Orleans, Deck had given up. He stopped asking about coming to the bridge, and didn't want to borrow any more books.

The kid was due to get off the ship in New Orleans, and sail on a different one. The bond between the two sailors was being broken. Even at his age, Easy could tell that from the looks he got, and how Deck avoided him. One was destined to be a college graduate and a mate, and the other would likely pound his way around the decks of many ships, doing whatever hard work was required. *If only Deck had done better in school, if only he had spent more time reading and less time hanging out when he was in high school,* Easy thought. *Hell, he would make a better officer than I will.* One would wear a khaki collar, the other a blue collar, for life, and there was nothing the kid could do about it. In New Orleans, on payoff day, an academy representative came down to visit the ship, and get reports from the officers on the kid. Easy, therefore, wore his academy uniform, with the bright buttons and stripes. The rep got good reports, and told Easy that he would have a day or two off, and then ship out again. He should find a place to stay, and come up to the office the next morning. Then he offered the kid a ride uptown. Easy said he would get his gear. He went out on the deck of the ship for the last time, to find the guys he had worked with, and gone ashore with, and say goodbye. The bosun asked him how much money the chief mate had given him.

"Nothin', bosun." He didn't understand the question.

"That son-of-a-bitch! I know he's been having you do his work -- he should piece you off. He ought to give you at least a hundred or two!" Bosun was pissed. He had taken a drink or two, normal for payoff day, and mumbled something about going up to the mate's office and telling him off.

"No, bos' don't do it. He and I had a fair deal. He worked my butt off at sea, and gave me paperwork of his on weekends, but I had off in port. Don't get into a hassle; it's okay."

The bos' backed off. The chief mate would have been claiming overtime pay for the work the kid did on weekends. It would have been fitting to pay the kid a little of it, but screw it, it was a fair deal. Easy had already seen the captain and mates, and now he went around the deck; the guys made crude jokes about the bathroom girl and so on, and Easy just smiled. The academy guy was waiting on the dock. Easy had to find his pal, Deck. He found him by the gangway. They shook hands. Deck smiled and cracked a joke or two. The grease and paint on his clothes were in sharp contrast to the kid's clean, crisp uniform. They had reached a parting of the ways, each going in a different direction. The kid said he would run into him again, and all those things. He told Deck to keep up the studies, that he would become a good mate someday, but they both knew that would not happen. Still, it made the dayman happy to hear it. Easy threw his sea bag over his shoulder, and headed down the gangway. He was Uneasy that day.

Chapter 4: Under the Marks

His next assignment was on an old, Delta Lines, C-1 diesel freighter, running from the U.S. Gulf Coast to Brazil. The *Thompson Lykes* had steam propulsion, with boilers and turbines, and was an "S. S." for "steamship." This ship had a diesel engine, giant pistons, and was the *M. V. Del Campo*, the "M. V." for "motor vessel." It was a small, dirty, busy ship, about 550 feet long, and the kid thought it was full of odd characters and hard cargo work. It had some refrigerated cargo holds, all kinds of booms and guy wires on deck, and needed chipping and painting badly. It was just the kind of thing he had dreamed of when he was in high school. Winter in the Northern Hemisphere was approaching, so it was good to be going south. He would turn nineteen on the trade route seamen called the "romance run."

They were in Galveston, topping off the cargo spaces, and would sail foreign from there, at night. The kid had been looking over the remaining parts of his sea project. A lot of it seemed like bullshit, but he noticed there was a naval architecture assignment that he hadn't done yet that seemed reasonable. He would need to take a bunch of measurements around the ship, loading conditions, freeboard, the draft of the ship at several places, and so on. He decided to take the measurements that night, and work on the project on the way to Brazil.

While the longshoremen were loading the last of the cargo, the kid went onto the dock. He had paper and pen, a long tape measure, and a plumb bob. He took draft readings on the bow, the stern, and amidships. He measured the freeboard, the distance from the water to the uppermost continuous watertight deck, at several points. He had already checked the clinometer, to see if the ship was listing to either side, to account for that. The official ship's measurements were posted in the passageway, as required, and he could get the official distances off that.

Over the next couple of days at sea, he worked on the figures. Things didn't add up right. He rechecked the official blueprints of the ship. The location of the plimsol mark on the side of the ship was clear. This circle, with some lines around it, showed how deep the ship could be in the water, by regulation. There were marks for fresh water and salt water, and for different climates. The distance from the water to the main deck was your freeboard. A ship was required to have a certain amount of freeboard, as one of the measures of the ship's safety for going to sea. There was only one answer and it troubled him. He easily could have faked his measurements, done the damn project, and no one at the school would have known the difference. Yet the plausible answer, the true answer, was something he really wanted to find. He had started standing the 4 to 8 watch with the 2nd mate, a guy they called Red, and one morning, when they were alone out on the wing of the bridge, he decided to ask him about it.

The kid told Red about all his measurements. He seemed very interested.

"Second, the figures don't add up except one way. We sailed under the marks the night we left Galveston, didn't we?"

"Have you mentioned this to anybody else?"

"No, sir."

"Well, keep this to yourself. Come to my room after breakfast, and we'll talk about it."

After eating, the kid went to the 2nd's room. Red invited him in and shut the door behind him. He took a cold beer out of a little fridge he had, handed it to him, and leaned back against his desk. He stared right at him, and he wasn't smiling.

"You seem like a savvy cadet, so I'm going to tell you a little story. You pay attention." Red told him that at first he thought he would just tell him that he was wrong; he should go redo his figures. He hadn't done that, he said, because the kid seemed too smart for that. He told him that he was right. The ship sailed foreign under the marks. It was late at night, and the Coast Guard wasn't around to check. The mark on one side of the ship was pressed up against the dock. The only way you would see the other mark, on the outboard side of the ship, would be to nose around in a small boat, with a light, in the middle of the night. You had to know what you were looking for. Of course, you could take measurements, as the kid had, and figure it out. That part seemed to impress ol' Red. He added that one of the more traditional methods of overloading a ship was to load right down to the legal marks, but be low on fuel. Then you sailed over to Freeport, in the Bahamas, a foreign country, and filled up on fuel. Then, you would be below the marks, but out of the reach of the Coast Guard. You could sail across the ocean, and burn out enough fuel to come back up to the legal load line before you reached your next port.

He went on to explain that only the captain, chief mate and himself knew about it. They sometimes loaded a few hundred tons of extra cargo when the company had it to load. If the trip was good, meaning no serious problems with the cargo handling, the company made a little extra money with the freight rate on the additional cargo. At the end of the trip, they would piece off the captain, chief mate and the 2nd -- no one else.

The kid now figured he could get in on the action -- a little supplement to his $111 a month salary. This was a safety violation; it was dangerous. *People could get in trouble for this;* even he knew that. He made a suggestion to the 2nd in this regard.

"There's no way. Look, it doesn't amount to much. Besides, you don't know Captain One Lung yet. He really does have one lung, and he's near the end, you understand? He's a tough old son-of-a-bitch who can be your best friend or your worst enemy. He likes you so far; don't fuck it up with this. An old timer like him thinks everyone has their place, especially kids. You got to earn your stripes, get it?" The kid got it, all right. Red was telling him to shut up. His negotiating position was getting weaker.

"I get it, 2nd, but don't you think if the crew's union knew about this there would be trouble? You and I might know that the ship is okay, but they might not care, since none of them are in on it." He had upped the ante a bit.

"Well, yeah, that could be a problem, but you could have problems too. Your school gets a report on you at the end of every trip. The chief mate and I write them up, and One Lung signs them. We would deny everything, and you could be in trouble with the school, maybe serious enough that you don't finish or get your license, and then where are you?" The stakes were now higher.

"Well, I don't know how I could get into trouble just for doing the report I'm required to do. It's not my fault how it turned out. And what if I mailed in that part of my project from Brazil, and someone at the academy turned a copy over to the Coast Guard? That would be unfortunate, but it would be out of my control." *Fuck you -- I can learn how to play this game,* he thought.

"I'll tell you what would be unfortunate," the 2nd shot back. "If some customs agent in South America were to find contraband or drugs in your room, that would be a mother-fucker for you, and I'm telling you that the Ol' Man has been running down there for twenty years and knows them all, on a first name basis. Instead of going to the beach in Rio, you might be in a hellhole jail somewhere. Now that's unfortunate." Red had put his last card down. He and the captain clearly had the better hand, but the kid did not want to give in.

"That would be a bitch, but I'll tell you, if anything like that happened to me, I wouldn't go quietly, I'd be pissed." Then he remembered a saying he learned on his last ship. "I don't like getting fucked without taking my clothes off first."

"Hey 'Gadget,' don't get excited, we can work this out." Red smiled for the first time. The negotiation was over; it was time to settle it. "Look, you want time off in port, right? That's what all you young guys want. I'll fix that up for you. And, if you're a good worker, the mates can pass the hat before each port and give you some spending money. How's that?"

"I won't have to look over my shoulder on this ship, will I?"

"No, no, come on, it's not like that. You'll have a good trip. You're sharp, you can learn a lot on this old tub. Look, the Ol' Man is burning the candle at both ends, and the chief mate doesn't know his ass. You listen to me, stand watches with me, and I'll teach you a few things."

They shook on it. The kid had come out of it with some advantages for himself. *One hand for yourself,* he thought. He now knew he would have a good time in Brazil, and would not be abused for cheap deck labor as he had been on his first ship. He would work mostly with the 2nd mate, and sharpen his navigation and radar skills. He already knew how to work a goddam hurdy-gurdy; if he was going to make it as a ship's officer he needed to spend more time with the mates.

For his part, the kid went back to his room and falsified his readings. The 2nd mate kept up his part of the bargain as well. He passed the hat when they reached port. He would come around the deck in the early afternoon in port, when the kid worked the day watch, from 0800 to 1700, put twenty dollars in his hand, and suggest that he take the rest of the day off and go ashore. The youngster was happy to follow these orders. He got time to see some sights. He planned to go up to Corcovado in Rio, and see the famous statue of Christ. He might be able to walk along the beaches of Ipanema and

Cococabana, and still have a few bucks left over for nightlife. He was learning the business, and getting around the world a bit --just what the now nineteen-year old had wanted.

As the trip wore on, Red gained more confidence in the young apprentice, and taught him a few things. The student's radar plotting got better, and he could lay down some good lines on the charts. Red also advised him on other aspects of seafaring. One of the best of these was when he showed the kid a bunch of gems and stones he had in his room. He showed the kid how he bought blue diamonds in Brazil, for far less than you could in the states. When the ship returned each trip, he would declare them on his customs forms as aqua marine stones, similar in color, but worth far less. That way, the worst thing that could happen was that a customs agent could argue about the value of the stones, but could not accuse him of smuggling. Red said that there was not one customs agent in a hundred who could tell the difference. He took them off in Houston on each coastwise leg of the voyage, and took them to a jeweler he knew. The jeweler would mount the diamonds and sell them, and split the profits with Ol' Red. The crafty 2nd even showed him his magnifying tools and test kits that he had learned to use. No seller in Brazil would stick it to him. He had studied it all for years. He had a steady source on one end, and a reliable seller on the other. He was the middleman, and would retire early because of it.

Red, as a part of the bargain, had help on the 4 to 8 watch. The kid would do the routine weather reports and other mundane chores, was a good lookout, and made coffee. In port, he climbed up and down the ladders into the cargo holds, checking stowage and lashing. It saved Red and the third mates a lot of legwork. He did embarrass the 2nd on watch one day, however. They had been sailing along on a clear day, and another ship had appeared on the horizon, dead ahead. It was "stem on" or nearly so, meaning the two ships were on nearly opposite courses. The uninitiated might view this situation as dangerous, but it is the easiest collision to avoid. Each ship changes course slightly to starboard, just like cars, and they pass "port-to-port," following the international rules of the road for this situation. Red did not want to change course. He did not have the radar on. This was normal for ships at the time in good weather. You learned not to burn out the tube on the damn thing by using it when you didn't need it. He stood in the exact middle of the wheelhouse and eyeballed the other ship. It would pass close to port without him changing course. There was no need to be so close. If either ship lost steering or the use of its engine, the plant, at a crucial time, there could be a stupid disaster.

It seemed to be a little macho game between the two mates. No one wanted to give in to the other, or let the other mate think that he was afraid to pass so closely. It seemed stupid to the kid, but it wasn't his watch. The two ships sailed past each other so close the kid could clearly see the men on the deck of the other ship, even without binoculars. The kid was out on the wing of the bridge, looking her over as they passed. It was just astern of their ship when he hollered into the wheelhouse.

"Hey, 2nd, how far did we pass that ship, a couple of hundred yards?"

"Jesus Christ, no, it was at least a mile and a half!" Red was yelling. Unbeknownst to the kid, Captain One Lung had come up on the bridge while he was outside. Now the Ol' Man came out on the port bridgewing, closely followed by Red.

"Your distance judgment needs some goddam work!" he shouted.

The kid knew that he had spoken out of turn. One Lung looked at the other ship, now astern of them, stared at the 2nd, grunted, and went below to his room. He was shitfaced, as usual.

"Sorry, 2nd," he said.

That was all that needed to be said. Watch-standing mates liked to be alone to run the ship. Red was embarrassed because he was wrong. The future mate knew that they had passed that ship much closer than they should have, and nowhere near even a mile. He said nothing else the whole watch, but filed this little lesson away in his head.

Another day at sea they were sailing along near the hump of Brazil, where the depth of the water was relatively shallow. It was a fishing ground, but the kid did not know that. He had seen many shrimp boats in the Gulf and some other deep-sea trawlers, but he was unprepared for these guys. He began to see little black dots on the water ahead. They seemed to be buoys, although it was clear from the chart that there were no buoys that far out. The kid thought that maybe they were oil drums that someone had thrown overboard. If you didn't puncture the drums, they would float for a long time. That wouldn't be much of a hazard. The bow wake would wash an empty oil drum to the side. The closer they got, the more he saw. There were now dozens of little black dots, spread out ahead, to the port and starboard sides of the bow.

The second mate played along a little with the kid. He toyed with his pupil, asking him whether he would recommend going into hand steering. He quizzed the cadet on whether if he were in charge he would change course or not, and if so, when, and to what course. All this was great practice. Red had done this with other traffic situations, involving large ships, sometimes on collision courses. He was living up to his promise to teach the kid some things that would make him a better mate. Everything wasn't in the damn books, you had to get out there and see the practical side of it all. As they got close enough, the kid could see that the objects on the water were little boats. They were fishing dories, about ten feet long. In each one, a guy was fishing with a line, standing up in his boat. Nearby was the mother ship, a vessel much smaller than the Delta Lines ship, but large enough to hoist the dories up with a winch at the end of the day. The fishermen would start out at first light, fish all day standing up, then row back to mother, hook up the boats to be hauled up to the deck. Then, they would unload their catch for the day, and help to store and process the fish. After a late meal, they would get some sleep aboard the smelly ship, and do it all over again the next day. They typically stayed out at sea until the storage holds were full of fish. This could take weeks. There was no time off. The kid felt lucky that he was sailing the way he was.

As they got close to this fishing fleet, their ship was a danger to the fishermen. The dory guys had the right-of-way, and the second would have to change course for them. It wasn't enough just to avoid hitting them; you had to give them enough leeway that the wake of the larger ship did not swamp the little boats. The kid thought that they should have changed a long time ago, and avoided the whole fleet. Red explained that doing it that way would take them miles out of their way. There were fishing fleets in various parts of the world that numbered in the hundreds.

You couldn't sail around all the damn fleets, it would cause too much of a delay. The way he did it was to sail right ahead until he was almost in the middle of the pack, then make a sharp turn or two and be out the other side of the fleet without going more than a half mile or so off their own course. The kid noticed how this was done, and remembered it. He also noticed that the second stood out on the wing of the bridge, taking quick bearings with the compass repeater. He was simply taking sights on open water between the boats, and would holler in the course changes to the quartermaster. He could also see what the helmsman did with the rudder by watching the rudder angle indicator on the wing, and tell what course he steadied up on with the compass repeater. The visibility all around was better out there, away from the masts, booms, and guy wires that impeded your view if you stayed inside the wheelhouse. It was rude to run somebody over and kill him, and it could have a negative effect on your career.

The cargo work in the various ports had gone well enough. The kid now had the habit of walking the deck on the offshore side. It seemed easier and safer than watching the loads of pallets and crates swing by your head all the time. He knew which hatches had broken or rusty rungs on their ladders, so when he climbed in and out of them, he was aware of the hazards. He knew how to start up the pumps for the hydraulic winches, and how to work the refrigeration machinery to cool down the spaces where they carried reefer cargo.

The mates also taught him some more tips for dealing with foreign longshoremen. He had to guard some cargo in the special cargo locker up in #1 hold a few times. What they kept in there was more valuable than other things, carried a higher freight rate because of that, but was highly pilferable. The guys who unloaded these things were all poor. The kid already knew, from his early trips, about some of the corruption on the waterfront. How much cargo longshoremen stole or damaged was important to the ship, the mates, and the company.

One of the games he learned to play was simple but effective. He used it while watching the unloading of some valuable goods that included cases of whiskey. The kid went down the ladder into the hold first. He unlocked the sliding door to the space, and went inside and waited. The hatch boss came down and looked things over. Soon, about a dozen of the grubbiest workers you could ever see joined him, and they all eyed the cases over real good. He just stood there, watching everything. Soon, the first pallet from the winchman landed in the square of the hatch. The longshoremen muscled the crates and cases from the locker onto the pallet. The pallet had rope netting around it to prevent things from falling off while the winchman, with the guidance of the signalman, hoisted it up and over the side of the ship, and landed it on the dock. There, other workers would lift the cases off the pallet and onto a truck. There was a guard on the dock, and a tallyman who counted everything. Once cargo was on the dock, the ship was not responsible.

As soon as the work began, the kid took one case of whiskey, put it aside, and put his work boot on top of it. He then called the hatch boss over, and explained that he thought this case had been damaged. He could see the interest in his eyes. The kid then told him that when the rest of the cargo was safely off the ship, with nothing damaged or stolen, he would determine what to do with the damaged case. The hatch boss understood immediately, and smiled. As the workers carried the special cargo out of the locker, they eyed the cadet and the case under his foot real good. The kid kept a harsh look on his face. In thirty minutes, everything was gone except the damaged case. He eyeballed the hatch boss, and then smiled. He told him that he and his men did very good work. He took out his pad of cargo exception reports, and wrote up the case under his boot. "Insufficient packaging" was the entry. He then took out his jackknife and ripped the case open. He stood aside and the hatch boss started passing out bottles, taking one for himself first. He left a few bottles in the case, secured it with some tape, put it on the pallet, and signaled to the winch driver to land it ashore. There were smiles all around. The bottles quickly disappeared into coats and bags. The kid motioned the workers to leave the hatch first. He locked up the specials locker and climbed out last. This was far better than trying to be a hard ass with these guys, and seeing them purposely steal and damage your cargo. It was no problem for the winchman to swing a load into the side of the ship, for example, and smash far more cases than the one he had given them. As long as everyone understood the rules of the game, it worked. He had learned that it did you no good to piss off the longshoremen. You were in their country, and they were the ones who had friends on the docks.

The chief mate, however, in spite of his years of sailing, did not seem to understand all this. Red had warned the kid that the mate was incompetent, and the kid learned that he was right. As long as he let the 2nd mate and the two 3rd mates handle the deck work, things went well. On the southbound leg, however, the chief mate had lost it while they were in Bahia. He had run around the deck, ranting and raving at all the longshoremen. He had embarrassed the hatch bosses in front of their men. They got out of port seemingly without incident, and didn't think about it until they docked in Rio de Janeiro.

In a lower tween deck, the middle level of the three spaces in the hatch, the cargo had been floored off with dunnage, or scrap lumber; there was a layer fore and aft, then athwartships. On top of this flooring, they had loaded a brand new limousine for the American ambassador in Brazil. It was for discharge in Rio. The ship had not quite finished docking, but the ambassador's representative was already standing there, waiting impatiently for the crew to put the gangway down. He came up first, even before the workers, and went right to the captain's cabin. One Lung was recovering from his hangover, however, and did not know, and could care less, about the auto. The Ol' Man sent the ambassador's boy down to see the chief mate. The mate fell all over himself assuring the diplomatic errand boy about the car. The kid went out on deck with the mate on watch, an old 3rd mate who was a very good sailor, but who said little. The chief mate rushed around to find the walking boss, the dockworker in general charge of cargo unloading ashore, and got him to open the hatch with the car first. With all the commotion, a crowd gathered around the hatch. The upper tween deck was now empty, and the workers went down the ladder and opened the cover to the lower tween deck, just below, where stevedores had stowed Mr. Ambassador's car. When they opened the cover however, everybody deck got a surprise.

The ambassador's car was there, all right, but all smashed up. It looked like someone had "turned to" on it with 2x4 pieces of lumber. Every window and light was broken, and there were dents and scrapes all over the sides, front and back.

"How can this be?" the ambassador's boy kept saying. The cadet and the 3rd mate knew how it could be. In the last port, after the mate had pissed off all the longshoremen, some of them had gotten down into the manhole and into the cargo space and worked the car over in retaliation. It would be difficult to blame them now, since the ship had left that port, and all the cargo reports were on file. The damage could have happened anywhere during the voyage, they would say, how could you prove somebody in Bahia had done it? You didn't claim any damage when you were there. The third mate on watch had the best response.

"It seems the ambassador's car is in need of a little repair," was all he said, and he left to write up some kind of report.

The chief mate got apoplectic, and went to his room, where he retreated into his bathroom and drank whiskey he kept hidden there in his mouthwash bottle. The state department guy left, mumbling to himself. Eventually, they lifted the car up with wheel chocks, and put it on the dock. There was cargo underneath it. No one would accept delivery in that condition, of course, so it sat on the dock until the ship left Rio, when it was loaded back on for return to the states. God only knew who would argue over repair or replacement costs. Probably a different car would come back, on a different ship. They stayed in Rio for two days, and the kid noticed that during their stay, the limo on the dock was a source of great amusement for local dockworkers. Perhaps it had retained some value after all.

The kid had a good time in Rio, his main sightseeing port. The 2nd got him off the day watch early both days they were there. He didn't intend to chase girls, but he saw a few he would jump ship for. He and the engine cadet, a tall kid the engineers called the Crane, had gone to Ipanema Beach. They had walked along, barefoot, and seen many beautiful girls. There was one the kid could not just walk past. She had on a tiny bikini, in those days before the girls in the states would dare wear one. She was perfect. He tried to talk to her and her friends, but the American knew only a word or two in Portuguese, and none of the girls spoke any English. He would have done anything just to take her out for an innocent date, but it was impossible to arrange. Finally, in desperation, he took out his camera, and with some sign language, got his girl from Ipanema to pose for a picture. He would look at that picture for years afterwards, thinking correctly that this girl could have made any magazine. No wonder everyone in Rio talked about the beaches. It wasn't the damn water.

Having given up on meeting local girls, they had taken the tram up to the top of Mount Corcovado, where the statue of Christ looked down on the whole city. It was a fantastic view. They went back down just before dark. By the time they found a place to eat that they could afford, it was dark. As they made their way back to the waterfront, they found a bar called the Florida. There were tables out on the sidewalk, and some of the officers and crew from the ship were there. They had a few beers, and some of the guys dragged them over to a place called the Subway Bar.

It was "The Subway" because you entered from street level, and then went downstairs to a large room. It featured a small dance floor with lights all around it, and neatly groomed waiters in white dinner jackets. It also featured girls for hire who cruised around the place and asked you if you had a cigarette, or would buy a "drink para mi?" Some of them were very attractive, and made it clear that there was a hotel right across the street that had rooms for rent at hourly and half-hourly rates, to which they would be happy to accompany you for a price. The girls were different from the ones in Belem and Santos. They did not pester you. They did not dance on tables, or act rudely. The kid politely refused their offers, however. Maybe he was dreaming of the girl on the beach, and did not want to take a lesser path to the same end. He was also nearly broke. Some of the guys from the ship sent drinks over to his table, and after several of these, he fumbled his way out and back to the ship.

Their next port was Santos, the port city for Sao Paulo, and a large city in its own right. It was also a notorious place for sailors. Near the docks was an area seamen called Monkey Wrench Corner, after the twists and turns the trolley made there on the main street. There were sailor bars, working girls, and souvenir shops everywhere. A short ride away was the beach area, which had more regular restaurants, beaches, and shops. There were bars down near Monkey Wrench that had Scandinavian names to appeal to those sailors, American names for those guys, Oriental names, and so on. They were all pretty much the same. In the ones that were more like nightclubs, you could meet girls who came down from Sao Paulo on weekends. Many of these working girls had day jobs in the mountain city, and secretly came down to the port on weekends to earn extra money. These girls worked the better clubs, and sailors held them in high regard. The street girls were different. A lot of them were drug addicts, or just plain crazy. On this, his first visit to Santos, the kid had gone down to the corner with his buddy, the 2nd mate, and one of the engineers. The old cargo ship had docked within spitting distance of the first bar, the ABC. It was the first stop on the way out, and the last stop on the way back. Some guys became so enamored of the girls on the street that they never made it past the ABC. Red got them past this den of evil, but they settled in the Scandinavian Bar not far away.

The engineer had a camera with him, and was looking for an attractive girl to pose for pictures. For some reason, the girls turned him down. They would do anything you wanted in private, but did not like having their picture taken. Finally, a girl they called Bird Legs came over and sat down at their table, between Red and the engineer, and across from the kid. Other girls tried to sit with the young American, but he kept them away. He had thoughts of getting out to the beach area, and away from all this corruption. The more they drank, however, the farther away the beach seemed, and the better Monkey Wrench seemed.

Red explained some things to him, while he sat closer and closer to Bird Legs. If you were a young, pretty girl in a poor country, or poor area of a city, like in Santos, Brazil, you had two choices for your future, he said. You could stay a virgin, and hold out for marriage to a rich man, or you might end up on the streets, like the girl at their table. There wasn't much of a middle class. Just trying to get a job didn't get you anywhere in places like this, according to Red. That's why, in countries away from America, you saw some of the prettiest girls in bars like they were in. They made more in a month in Santos than they could in a year in their own towns. All during this discourse, the kid swore he could see the expression on the girl's face change. She stared at him in a peculiar fashion. With the engineer on one side, and the mate on the other, she sat in between them and fidgeted, and smiled at the kid. She seemed to be trying to tell him something. She motioned with her eyes beneath the table. He pretended to drop something, and looked under the tablecloth. He sat up and smiled back. The joke was that Bird Legs, so named for her skinny but shapely appendages, had on a very short skirt. While they were all talking, dirty ol' Red had been running his hand up her port leg, and the engineer with the camera and a lecherous eye, had been rubbing his hand up her starboard leg. There wasn't much of a skirt there, and she did not care when their hands met in the middle. She thought the whole thing was funny, and wanted the young, sandy-haired cadet in on the joke. It wasn't long before the engineer was propositioning every girl in the bar to have some photos taken. Red seemed to like Bird Legs, but the kid had kept all the girls at bay. He didn't want to spend his first night in Santos on Monkey Wrench Corner. He left the others to their pleasures, and found a cab. After a little negotiation, the driver and he agreed on a price to go out to the beach.

When he got to the beach area, he was happy. There were restaurants and clubs, and "regular" people around. He went in and out of some shops, just looking. At some point in his meanderings, he met a blonde Brazilian girl, about his age. Her English was good, and they ended up at a sidewalk cafe, and had some seafood and beer. The seafood in Brazil was excellent. The shrimps were large and fresh. His ship would load some frozen shrimp to bring back to the states, he would find out. Eventually he asked the blonde about clubs they could go to for dancing. The English Club sounded the best. This private club was only open to the public one night a week, and tonight was that night. The American said they should go there, but the blonde, hippy-looking girl seemed astonished at this suggestion. With some difficulty, he began to understand that she had never been there because it was for upper-class people. She lived in a poor section of town, and didn't feel she was dressed right for the club. She was slim and pretty, and he liked her a lot. Hell, if they had a dance open to the public and young people went there, paying an admission to get in, they would fit right in. He convinced her to go. She looked fine.

She was happy that her date thought she was acceptable to go to a place full of upper class Brazilians, and a few foreigners. The club seemed just like those back home to the young American, but it impressed his date. Yeah, maybe some of the other young people there were dressed a little nicer, but they fit in just fine, no one hassled them, and he was now determined to show her a good time. He was from another country, and did not care what part of town the other young people called home.

The English Club was large, and had a live band with a dance floor, two bars, and a patio area where you could just sit out and drink and talk. They drank Cuba Libras, or rum and coke, and after a couple of these, the blonde warmed up nicely. She got more physical while dancing, and even kissed him. What he thought would be just a cultural experience with a Brazilian girl now escalated into a different experience. He noticed more and more how slim and pretty she was. This little Brazilian girl would put many of the girls he had met in the states to shame. They left before the dance was over. They got a cab and she gave the driver directions to her apartment. She seemed to be trying to tell him that it wasn't much of a place, but he did not care.

When they got to her place, he understood why she had tried to apologize. By American standards, it was a dump, and a tiny one. They went in, and he pretended not to notice. She only had a room, not really an apartment. A few pieces of furniture and some clothes in the closet was all she had in the world. She did say that she had something special, however, and he found out that she had a joint of dope rolled up, hidden in a drawer. It seemed to be a big deal to her that they smoke it. Hell, he didn't even smoke cigarettes, let alone dope. She lit it, and he gave it a few puffs. He "got off" a little, but not like she did. She lost what inhibitions she had left. He spent the night there, and she was wonderful.

The next day was Sunday. He left her early in the morning, to go back to the ship, change clothes, and see if he had to work that day. He tentatively arranged with the girl to meet about noon. Things went smoothly on the ship, and the mates let him go. He met up with the girl, and they went out to the beach, and after that, the movies. Again, she seemed surprised that he would take her to so many nice places. The kid could not understand it. She was very attractive, what the hell did the guys she dated do? Why was it a big deal? It didn't matter. Neither did the money. He had borrowed a little from Red. He had understood perfectly, and knew the cadet was good for it, probably because he knew how many cartons of cigarettes the kid was smuggling in the smaller ports, and how much profit he could make from it. Yeah, ol'

Red was proud of him. He spent a second night with the Brazilian girl, and the ship sailed the next day. They did not exchange addresses, or make stupid promises to see each other again. They both knew it had been a fun weekend between two young people from different worlds. It would be more than two years until he finished school anyway, and could return. A lot could happen in all that time. Besides, no one had used the word "love." Still, when the ship undocked and slowly moved downriver towards the sea, the kid felt strangely. The sailors on the ship would be proud of him because he had scored, but he did not feel that way about the weekend.

Chapter 5: Small Port Paradise

After Rio and Santos, the kid was flat broke. He resumed his cigarette business in the smaller ports. Even though he did not smoke, he had arranged for a steady supply of cartons of cigarettes to end up in his room on the ship. The guys on the ship could buy them tax-free at sea, but were limited to only three cartons a week. You could sell them for triple their worth ashore, but it was illegal. He took the full allotment each week, even though he never smoked them. Then he arranged with some of the officers and crew who did not smoke to go down to the weekly slop chest opening, and take their full amount. The kid paid these guys for the cartons they took. After Santos, he went around the ship and collected his accounts. It was routine. He had done it in Belem, Sao Luis, and Niteroi, and would do it the rest of the trip.

When ships docked in a new port, among all the people who streamed up the gangway there were always a few moneychangers, smugglers, and assorted other criminals. They would go around and offer to exchange money, or sell or buy different things, especially smokes. The trick was not to get too anxious with the smoke sale, or the exchange rate. You could usually do better ashore, but sometimes, the trick was to get ashore with your contraband. The local guys would imply that only they had the contacts to get things off the ship without a hassle with the local authorities. Unless you had dope, however, you could usually buy your way out of a hassle. It was easier, though, to let them come up on the ship, make your best deal out on deck, then sneak the guy up to your room and conduct business there.

The kid checked his stash of cartons. The captain would let him draw, or take part of his salary in advance, anytime. The rules let a sailor take only up to half of what he had earned, but, because the cadet's pay was so low, Ol' One Lung would let him draw it all. That, with some pass-the-hat money from the mates, and his cigarette business, would get him through. His roommate, The Crane, did not participate in this business. He went ashore mostly with the engineers, and maybe they were paying his way, or maybe he felt he was above it, but the deck cadet did not care. He only knew that he did not sail thousands of miles around the world only to sit on the damn ship because he did not have a few dollars to go anywhere. He would have spending money somehow. A carton of Marlboros cost a sailor $1.25 at sea. He had gotten anywhere from $3 to $5 for them in Brazil. The funniest customer was a customs officer himself who ended up in the cadet's room, bought his cartons, and then taped them to his legs and waist to get ashore with them undetected.

Not only were the smaller ports better for the cigarette business, but other things as well. Drinks in bars were cheaper. There wasn't so much of a hustle from the locals as you walked around; in fact, many people seemed to regard the ship as a source of amusement. On Sunday mornings, whole families would walk down to the waterfront after church, and the parents would explain about the ship to the kids. Prices for souvenirs seemed to be better than in the big cities, provided you learned to negotiate a little. Some vendors even came down to the ship, and if they had a friend in the security detail, came right up on deck to show you their butterfly trays, or hand-made bird cages.

In one of these little ports, the ship had docked port side to a wharf along the river. After the ship was secure, the kid noticed that a few canoes were paddling around on the offshore side of the ship. They seemed rather crudely built. A bulky guy would be in the stern, paddling and fighting the current. He noticed that the others in the canoes were mostly young girls. As the sailors worked on deck after breakfast, the canoes had come closer and closer to the side of the ship. The girls in the boats seemed to be yelling at the American sailors, but no one could understand them. One of the ABs, a deckhand who was a big, strong, rough guy, was particularly interested. He kept shouting at the girls. Soon, one of the boats came right alongside the ship, and the girl in the bow took off her shirt and exposed her young chest for all to see. Her intentions were now clear, but the canoe was still about twenty feet below the level of the main deck of the ship. The big AB could not stand it anymore.

He dragged the ship's pilot ladder down the deck. You hung this rope device over the side for a harbor pilot to climb up to the ship from a small boat. It would certainly do for a topless girl as well as a harbor pilot. The nearly naked girl was laughing as she realized she could get up to the ship, and the game was on. Other canoes quickly paddled over, and soon there were several of them alongside. A small crowd gathered on deck where the AB, with help, was rigging the ladder. There were now several sailors, the kid, and a few longshoremen all waiting. As the ladder went over, and the first giggling girl came up, the kid expected to see the police appear. They were just across the deck, guarding the gangway. He wondered who they would arrest, or how much the pay-off would be to either avoid jail, or let the game continue. The half-naked one climbed over the bulwark and put her bare feet down on the deck.

"What in the hell is goin' on here?" A loud, gruff voice had shouted. It was Captain One Lung himself, standing right there. He had obviously witnessed the whole affair from his deck, above, and come down at just the right time. He had been drinking, as usual, even in the morning.

"You see what's going on, Cap'. We just want to have a little fun," big AB answered for all.

"All right, then, goddam it!" the old bastard shouted, and he grabbed the first girl by the hand, and led her up the outside ladder. A couple of decks more and he'd be into his cabin with her. The game now had the sanction of the Old

Man himself. Several more girls from different boats scrambled up, and sailors and officers alike led them away. The kid didn't take one; he just watched the whole episode with amusement. If not for Santos, he might have been first in line. He did notice that these were certainly not city girls. They did not wear city clothes or jewelry, and were either barefoot or wore just hand-made sandals on their feet. They spoke no English, but communicated quite effectively. One of the waterfront workers told him later that the girls came from a little village upriver. They would stay on the ship until they got ready to sail. Then their friends in the canoes would come back and take them home. He said he had even seen them jump into the water and swim to the boats.

The youngster thought this was all pretty wild, but many of the guys on the ship told him that things used to be even more open. It used to be fairly common, they said, for ships to pick up women on the southbound leg in Brazil, and keep them on board from port to port, until they hit the same port on the way north. Anyone who wanted one could have a girlfriend right on the ship for a week or two. Of course, they bribed customs officials, but that used to be no problem. Some ships even tried to make it look legal by signing the girls on as crew, listing them on the crew manifest as "librarians," or "hairdressers," or some such nonsense. In recent times, however, if you had a girlfriend in one port in Brazil, and wanted to see her again as the ship unloaded and loaded cargo up and down the coast, you gave her train or bus fare, and she would meet the ship in the next port, and the next.

Most of the girls were in it just for the money. Americans seemed to have more than anybody else and tipped better. Others, however, hoped to find an American to marry and take them back to the states. This was not a new idea, the old timers told him. American soldiers and sailors had been bringing back war brides from other countries since the revolution. They weren't all virgins that the guys met in church. Most were so grateful to escape their lives of poverty in South America, or the Far East, or any poor country that they usually made extremely loyal partners. The kid understood better why sailors called this the romance run. The people back home who did not understand this didn't see the shapely young bodies that came up the ladder. They did not hear about how incredibly sexy an oriental girl could be, either. The guys he sailed with weren't trying to become accountants, for chrissakes, they were goddam sailors, and occasionally, they acted like it.

Their ship stayed in that port for two days. No one saw the captain until just before sailing. The sailors put the ladder down again, and went around to the rooms, rounding up the canoe girls to get them off the ship. One Lung came down with his, and wasn't the least bit embarrassed about it. Most of the girls went down the ladder with plastic bags full of laundry powder, soap, and things like that. One of them did jump off the deck into the river instead of backing down the ladder.

One of the small ports they stopped in that trip was Paranagua. It would become memorable to the kid for one reason. He ventured out after dark with his roommate, the engine cadet, or Crane, and big AB, known as Curly for his lack of hair and three stooges' antics. They found a bar in the jungle and drank all night. Just after dawn, Crane remembered that they all had to be at work on the ship at 0800. Curly stumbled up the stairs in the bar with two young girls. As drunk as they were, the kids thought the only thing he would "get" was robbed. They profanely bid him goodbye and made their way outside.

The morning sun hit them hard. As they wound their way, crookedly, they tried to focus on the time, and were not sure they could get to work by 0800. It would be close. Another obstacle was actually finding the ship at all, but this was not impossible since the road only led to the dock area. In spite of the odds, they found their way back to the gate to the dock. Unfortunately, the future mate noticed a bicycle leaning against the fence just inside the gate. There was a young, uniformed guard, with a rifle, in a little shack by the gate. The guard watched in amazement as the kid hopped on his bicycle and pedaled off, totally unstable, down the dock.

The scene that resulted was a confused one, and probably comical to those lucky souls who, having gotten up in time for work on the ship or the docks, witnessed it. The drunken cadet wheeled crookedly towards the ship, his mind fixated on getting there in time. The guard, who was about the same age, ran after him, shouting and cursing in Portuguese and waving his rifle in the air. Following him was the Crane, shouting in English to both of them, and, also being drunk, making no sense. The spectators on the sidelines divided into two groups, as if they were in a sports stadium. The local dockworkers lined up along the warehouse on the right side, yelling encouragement to the guard, and curses at the thief. On the left side was the ship, and along the railing of the main deck, the sailors who had gotten up for work lined up with their coffee, laughing and cheering for their favorite cadet.

The future navigator made it to the ship first, parked the bike, and stumbled up the gangway on all fours, to the delight of the sailors on deck. They seemed happy that it was their cadet, the deck one, who was causing all this commotion, and had been up all night drinking. It must have brought back fond memories of youthful indiscretions to all of them. As the young idiot reached the top of the gangway, he looked straight up and saw Captain One Lung staring right down at him from his deck. He must have seen the whole thing. It was the first time the kid had seen a smile on the captain's face; he usually sported an ugly scowl. He was clearly proud of his trainee.

It wouldn't be until the next day that the young fool would realize that the guard could have shot him for being a thief, and no local court in Brazil would have blamed him. The young thief was lucky that the guard just either did not want to shoot him, or didn't have any bullets for his rifle. Either way, the guard did not come up on the ship to arrest him, but seemed satisfied to get his bike back in one piece, and ride off to the guard shack, to the cheers of his fans, the locals. When sober and reflective, the trainee would make a vow to himself not to repeat this behavior elsewhere.

There was no time to eat breakfast, but they could still make it to work on time. It was one of those unwritten rules about going to sea. No matter how fucked up you were, you made it to work on time, and worked without whining. The kid got a quick shower and put on his work khakis. The Crane dropped his lanky body on his bed, fully clothed, and did not move. The roommate could not persuade him to get his ass down in the engine room, where he belonged, or even to move at all; after ascertaining that he was not dead, he left him there. The bike thief went out into the dining room, grabbed a mug of black coffee, and wandered out on deck for his eight hours of cargo watch duty. It was one minute before 0800. He got out on deck where the 2nd mate was organizing the cargo operations, and there were longshoremen and hatch bosses all over the place. Booms were being swung out, guys were opening the hatches to be worked, and the usual shouting about where to land the pallets, and who was going to run the winches, was going on. The kid went over to the open number four hatch, took another sip of coffee, leaned over the hatch coaming to look down at the cargo, and threw up. It was another day in Paradise.

By the time supper was over, however, the kid began to change his mind about never going ashore again. He felt better, held down food, and still had some ill-gotten spending money. He would not go to the same bar again, but ride into town with a couple of the other guys, and take it easy in a sidewalk cafe. He didn't stay out all night, either, and felt he was beginning to learn about moderation. The Crane would not hear of it, though, and stayed aboard the ship to get some extra sleep. The kid thought that maybe a life at sea was not for the Crane.

The kid held true to his plan, and stayed relatively sober, returning to the ship about midnight. The only excitements of the evening were the cab rides, at night, down the road to and from the dock. The cab driver had kept his headlights off, and only turned them on if he saw an approaching car. Then he would flash his lights to show the other driver that he was there. Other cars along the lonely road did the same thing. The older sailors told the kid that this was common in the rural areas. The drivers wanted to save their headlights for when they really needed them. Why burn out your lights if you don't need to?

Curly had not made it back to work at all that day in Paradise. The captain logged him a day's pay, and now had a legal excuse to fire him when the ship returned to the states. Curly expected no less, and it did not seem to bother him. The deck cadet did not see much of this guy until the ship stopped in Recife on the way north. Recife was on the hump of Brazil, and the last stop before the return to the states on the trip. One of its most notable features was a bar called the Moulin Rouge. All the merchant sailors went there, at least for a beer on the way uptown or as a last stop on the way back to the ship. You went up a flight of stairs to get to the bar. It was quite large, with a long bar, dozens of tables, and a dance floor. The only people who used the dance floor, however, were the bar girls who didn't have a date for the night yet. They would go out there alone, or in pairs, and shake it for all to see. If you liked what you saw, you simply called the girl over to sit at your table. They would also make the rounds of the tables and ask the guys for a cigarette. If you gave a girl one, she would then ask for a drink. You buy her a drink, she sits down with you. Everyone understood the arrangement and it was similar to those in many other places. The sailors also knew that in Brazil, if you picked out a girl like that, you were hers for the night. She would claim you for a prize, and the other girls would not mess with you. If you tried to pick up another girl instead, they were offended and called you "butterfly boy," or "queer," in Portuguese, English, or Spanish. You would have to leave and go somewhere else. The Moulin Rouge also had another floor, above the bar. It had small rooms where the girls lived, and if you wanted more than casual conversation, that was where they took you. "Going upstairs" was a phrase with a special meaning to sailors round the world.

As the kid had never been there, the guys he went ashore with insisted that he see it. Older sailors had explained the rules of the game in other ports, so he knew what the deal was. He did think that this den of evil was much larger than most, and had numerous girls to choose from. He didn't really want a girl right then, so he only gave away cigarettes. He still did not smoke, but kept a pack of Marlboro's in his pocket. It was considered polite to give a bar girl one, you just had to be clear that you didn't want her to sit down with you. He had learned to say "maybe later," which they accepted without a hassle. In Brazil, the bar girls liked cadets, and gave them special treatment. The kid did not know if it was because of their age, or relative innocence, but he had learned this to be true. The girls would joke about being the first to get a cadet, or him being a "cherry boy," and so on. It seemed to be a mark of honor for them to actually find a virgin sailor, as rare as they were. If a girl thought she was the first, she would buy you drinks, and even take you upstairs for free.

The student sat in the midst of all this, trying to be only an observer. There were a couple of officers from his ship at the table, and some of the deckhands, including Curly, across the room at another table. Other merchant seamen, from a variety of other ships from around the world, sat at their own tables. Everybody seemed to be having a good time until Curly got into an argument with a table full of Greek sailors. He probably already had too much to drink, and apparently had made some unwise remarks to the Greeks, things about their sexual preferences, to which they took exception.

It didn't take long for Curly and a Greek to square off and start throwing punches. If this was all there was of it, there wouldn't be much of a problem. The bouncer and bartender would stop it, throw the two guys out, and the party would go on. Some of the Greek guys, however, stood up to back the play of their guy, maybe because Curly was a large, beefy type, and the Greek was smaller. That's when it changed. There is an unwritten rule that you can't let a shipmate get the hell beaten out of him, especially by more than one guy at a time, so the Americans ran over to save Curly's butt, even though it was known that he was a trouble-maker and had probably started it. The kid went too, but thought that they could all just break it up. You can't reason with a drunk, however, and the fight escalated into a goddam brawl. A dozen or more guys were beating each other with fists, bottles and chairs. The kid would recall years later that it was the only time he had ever been in a fight like the brawls he had seen in the movies. The fight got even more confused when the girls in the bar started screaming, some even running into the middle of it all to try to pull their boyfriends away. The reason for this behavior became instantly apparent when the local cops came up the stairs. They came running with their clubs already out, and started beating anyone who was in the way, even the girls. The fight stopped, but the arguments about who did what continued. The kid felt lucky that he had not been hurt, and the police only hauled away Curly and a couple of other guys, including one of the Greeks.

The music started up again, and soon the Moulin Rouge was back to normal. The kid knew that in the middle of the brawl one of the girls had tried to save him from the cops. She had pulled at his arm just as they had run through the bar, swinging clubs. Maybe she had saved him from a beating or an arrest. She now wanted to take him upstairs. He gave her some money for helping him, but decided to seek a calmer environment, and left the bar with a couple of the officers.

The ship sailed the next day. The kid did not see Curly until the ship undocked. He was handling lines back aft, and Curly, who normally worked with that bunch, showed up with his arm in a cast. He did not work, of course, but sat on the bitts, and told the story of how the cops broke his arm with a club, and took him to jail. One Lung had bailed him out in the morning, and the ship's agent had taken him to the doctor to set his arm. He now knew he would be getting off the ship at the end of the voyage. Delta Lines would either fire him, or declare him medically unfit. He didn't care, in fact, he seemed proud of being such an Ugly American.

The real shame of the brawl was that the ship's electrician, a guy they called Dirty John, had not been there. All up and down the coast of Brazil, Dirty John had gone ashore with his camera, bounced around from sailor bar to sailor bar, and taken pictures of the sailors and the girls, in spite of the reluctance of his subjects. He developed the pictures, as slides, right in his room on the ship, and on alternate nights at sea, would have slide shows -- one night for the officers, another night for the crew. At first, it was mostly pictures taken in the bars, and the guys would comment or laugh about how they looked, or the girls who would show some leg or other things. This was tame enough, but some of the girls showed no embarrassment at all, and the slide show became more pornographic as the trip progressed. One of the most amusing results was when two guys recognized the same girl in the show as being one they had gone upstairs with, sometimes even on the same night. According to an old sea-going tradition, the guys then became "brothers-in-law."

As the voyage had progressed, the slide shows got more explicit. If you appeared in one of his pictures, he would give you the slide afterwards, in case you did not want it to be in anybody else's possession, or be part of the show the next voyage. However, Dirty John had gone from taking pictures in the bars to paying girls to go to a room, and posing for pictures. By the time they were hitting the last few ports, he had gone even further. He took a tripod ashore with him, and started taking pictures with himself as one of the naked stars. He would get drunk on slide show nights, slip some of these personal favorites in with the others, and laugh and giggle uncontrollably when they appeared on the screen. The kid thought this was going too far, even for a typically shameless sailor. The rest of the guys on the ship had a mixed reaction, but all seemed thankful when they left Brazil for the run up the Caribbean for home, and there were no more slide shows.

Their arrival in the Mississippi River was no big deal, with one exception. The chief mate, walking back from the bow, at night, tripped over a chain that secured a huge block of granite to the deck. He broke his hip, although no one on board knew at the time that was his injury. By the time they approached New Orleans, he was bed-ridden and spitting up black bile. The ship was going farther upriver, to Baton Rouge, for cargo work, then down to New Orleans. It would be another 24 hours before they docked in their home port. Captain One Lung was drunk; in fact, he was sipping mixed drinks right on the bridge, while the river pilot took the ship up. The kid and the chief engineer looked in on the poorly chief mate just before they were going to pass New Orleans. They could see that he had internal injuries. The bastard couldn't get out of bed, was spitting up ugly stuff, and could hardly talk.

The chief took the kid with him up to the bridge. The engineer asked the captain if he was going to slow down and anchor off New Orleans, so a rescue boat could come out and get the mate. "No, fuck him," was the answer. "He can wait until we come back downriver." With that, the chief told One Lung that if he did not stop off the downtown area, the chief would go down to the engine room and stop the ship himself. No engineer would answer bells from the bridge. He meant it. One Lung gave in, had the radio operator call ashore for emergency help, and they anchored. The Old Man bitched about the chief not following his orders, but he knew he was wrong, and didn't fight it. They lost a couple of hours on the schedule, no big deal. The cadet helped get the mate into a stretcher and down to the boat. The captain was a fun guy to make a trip with, but he had his ugly side, and it showed. He was dying, and didn't care who else suffered.

Chapter 6: Tankeritis

When the old Delta diesel got back to New Orleans, the academy representative came down to visit the ship and get the reports on the kid. Red had fixed them up with One Lung and the chief mate, and they glowingly told of his efforts and progress; they left out a lot that didn't seem suitable for academy review. The academy rep had good news and bad news for the kid. The good news was that he would get a trip on the *Nuclear Ship Savannah,* which the kid had written to request. It was still fairly new, and the wonder of the American Merchant Marine. It was apparent that the reports on him from the first captain he had sailed with, and the parts of his sea project that he had already mailed in had gotten him this assignment. He would go to New York to get on it in about a month, and sail back to the Mediterranean. The cadet immediately figured that he could go home for a couple of weeks, then spend some time up north with his older brother, at his private college. That's when the rep gave him the other news.

He told the kid that he would have just enough time to make a few coastwise runs on a tanker, and he was taking him upriver that same day to join the *S. S. Key Trader,* a tanker operated by the Keystone Tankship Company. The kid tried to bring up the fact that he had volunteered to ship out early, and would have more than enough sea time for the school, so it would be fair to give him a break. The rep guy countered with the theory, unfortunately valid, that the more ships of different kinds he sailed on, the better an officer he would make. The other fact, that the kid had no plans to sail coastwise when he graduated, but rather wanted only to go foreign, meant nothing to the rep. The rep seemed to think he was doing the kid a big favor by taking him up to the tanker dock right then in his car. The youngster had entertained ideas about a night in New Orleans, or at least a quick trip to the French Quarter, to check in at the Attic Bar. He couldn't fight it. He would make the best of it. He would learn about a different kind of ship, and what the hell, he was here to go to sea, even if it was only coastwise on a tanker. He said his goodbyes to Red and the gang, and grabbed his bags and sextant case. He was on his way to the exciting port of Norco, Louisiana.

An hour or so later they drove through a security gate and on down near the Keystone Tanker Company's dock. Tanker docks were very different from the cargo docks in New Orleans. First, they were far away from cities, mostly in case of an explosion. There were no smells of bags of coffee beans piled up on the docks on pallets, or crates and barrels of all kinds of goods from all over the world. There were just pipes and storage tanks all over the place, and the smell of fuel oil, gasoline, jet fuel, and a dozen other chemicals that these ships routinely carried. High vent pipes were all around, giving off noxious odors of their own.

The tanker was an older T-2, about the same size as a cargo ship. Neither the kid nor his shipmates in those days would dream of the size tankers would get to after the oil embargo, and shipping companies realized how much more money they could make with supertankers. This ship was one of what some called the Jones Act fleet. The Jones Act, he knew, was a law that said if you carried cargo only from and to United States ports, you had to register the ship in the states, and have a U. S. crew. Most people did not know that the law was the only reason companies like Texaco and Exxon had any U.S. ships, or that most of their tonnage, the Persian Gulf ships, were built overseas, registered in countries like Liberia, where the regulations were lax, and crewed by the cheapest labor they could find. So-called red-blooded Americans owned most of these ships. Most of the coastwise tankers were non-union ships, or had company unions, a real oxymoron. So far, the student had sailed only on union ships. Most tanker guys felt more loyalty to the company than to any union.

The rep left him off by the dock, and he went aboard with his gear. The ship was sitting high in the water, as it was still mostly empty. It would take on liquid cargo all night long, and sail in the morning for Fall River, Mass. There were pipes and valves all over the deck, and no booms or masts, except a small boom for loading supplies. They would load it with bulk oil, heating oil, jet fuel, chemicals of different kinds and float the time bomb to New England, and pipe all that stuff into storage tanks there. Then they would turn around to the south, cleaning and gas-freeing the tanks on the way, arrive in Louisiana to do it all over again. Over and over, the same route, the same places, week in and week out. He was bored already. No adventure here and worse yet, there were additional homework projects to do, since he was on a different type of ship. He would have to do written reports and make many drawings of piping systems, and so on, with only a month to complete it.

The amazing thing to the kid was that some guys liked tankers, and became homesteaders. That meant that the tanker company permanently assigned them to the same ship. They sailed for years and years, back and forth, hardly ever leaving the ship in port. They did whatever the company said, took whatever money they offered, and never wanted anything else. This kind of life wasn't what the kid had imagined years ago standing atop the hill, watching the ships come into port from all over the world. He had no choice for now. He would make the best of it. *Save what little money you earn for your next foreign trip*, he thought.

Stow your gear in your room, introduce yourself to the captain and chief mate, and then get your work clothes on. Go out on deck, find the mate on watch and do whatever he tells you. Learn. Observe everything. Work hard and impress them all. All these things he did in the first hour aboard. The mate on watch asked him the obvious question.

"You ever been on a tanker before?"

"No, sir."

"Okay, Youngblood, well, first thing, you see that large valve wheel over there, the red one? Shut it down, we're ready to top off this tank."

"No problem." Youngblood went over to the wheel. It was horizontal to the deck, a couple of feet off it, and about 30 inches in diameter. He had no idea which tank it went to, or what kind of liquid they were pumping aboard. It looked like it would be a bitch to close, a valve wheel that big. *I'll close the son-of-a-bitch, all right,* he thought. He was no longer the skinny little kid who had graduated from high school weighing 122 pounds. A year of starchy food and weekend beer at school, lifting weights, running cross-country, and rowing, together with many months at sea eating heavily and doing lots of physical work had added 40 pounds of muscle to his frame. *I'll close it, better than any other bastard who ever tackled it,* he thought. *You'll be glad you've got a workhorse like me aboard this trip, you'll see, and maybe somewhere I'll earn some time off somewhere. Get up to Boston, maybe.* He started turning the wheel clockwise, which spun the reach rod attached to it in the same direction and somewhere far below, deep in the tank that was rapidly filling up with some kind of oily goo or another, a valve was closing.

After many spins of the wheel, it fetched up, or seemed to reach the end. It wouldn't turn any more. *I'd better close this real tight,* Youngblood thought. *That's probably real important; you can't have the goddam oil spilling out anywhere.* He opened up the valve counterclockwise to get a start on it, squatted down with his knees bent, and heaved it clockwise again with all his might and 40 new pounds. When it fetched up again, he got a better grip with both hands together, leaned left with all his weight and pulled some more. Suddenly, the wheel started spinning freely. He spun it around and around, with one finger even, still clockwise, but it would not fetch up at all. The 3rd mate on watch saw this and came running over. He grabbed the wheel and tested it. He had an ugly look on his face.

"You dumb bastard, what the fuck did you do? You broke the reach rod!"

"I just closed it real tight!"

"Shit. The rod attached to this valve is only about an inch thick. The goddam wheel is large to help close it fast. You must have really yanked on the damn thing."

Commotion reigned on deck. Guys he did not know were running around doing things he would find out about only later. They were quickly re-routing the oil flow through the manifold so the tank would not overflow. They all ignored him. He had fucked up in his first hour on the tanker. No one would speak to him. *It's not my fault,* he thought. *Nobody said how hard to close the damn thing.* He later got a lecture about the delay this would cause in discharging the oil up north, and how someone would have to repair the rod on the return, when the tank was empty, gas free, and safe to enter. The repairs would cost more than he made. Only one of the crew had any sympathy at all. An old AB had mumbled to him that the ship was getting old, and the rod was probably rusty.

He got off the deck at suppertime, and ate alone, in silence. He unpacked in his room but couldn't stand it. He hated tankers. He wasn't near any place anyone had ever heard of. He walked up the dock and went ashore. He found only one bar around, and went in. It was a local, Cajun kind of a place, and the only people in there seemed to be guys from his ship or local refinery workers. No one knew him. There were no young guys in there, and no women. He had a beer at the bar and wished he were at sea with Deck, Red, One Lung, or even Curly. He became aware of three or four guys who were officers on the tanker. They were playing pinball, in the corner of the little dock bar, for $50 a game. *Thank God, they don't know I'm the fool who broke the valve,* he thought. He went back to the ship.

One of the sailors called him out to help undock the ship at 0500. He got through that okay; at least handling lines was about the same from ship to ship. He finished the 4-8 watch on the bridge. He felt at home up there. Navigation was the same, tanker or cargo ship, and his skills on watch were good. He went down for breakfast. No one paid him much attention, but no one cussed him out, either. He went to his room, having some time off before turning to again. He unpacked the rest of his stuff, and looked over his tanker project.

He also found a meerschaum pipe that he had bought in Turkey. He still did not smoke, but seamen told him that you had to smoke this pipe, with its carved sultan's head, for it to turn the right color, and look really cool. He found some old pipe tobacco, stuffed the sultan's head with it, lit it up, after some trouble, and walked out of his room and down the passageway. He almost reached the door to the outside. Coming in the door was one of the engineers. As Youngblood almost got past the guy, the engineer grabbed him by the shirt and pulled him back.

"Are you fuckin' nuts!? Are you going to go out on deck with that goddam thing?"

"No, I was just going to look out the door," he mumbled, instantly realizing his mistake.

"Bullshit. You want to blow up the ship, get us all killed?" The guy was rightly furious.

The kid slunk back to his room. He knew better. A single spark on the deck of a tanker that wound up in the wrong place could indeed blow them all to bits. He had been on the ship less than 24 hours, and committed two unpardonable sins. He just hadn't made the transition to tankers yet, but it didn't matter. He was a cursed young man. He had heard of guys getting "tankeritis." This condition affected guys who sailed only tankers for years. Maybe it was their exposure to a lot of chemicals, or the boring routine of the trade. Sailors who had this condition could not sail other ships. They went to work day after day in a tanker stupor. Youngblood knew he would never get it; he hated tankers more than ever, and it was only his second day.

On the third day, the chief mate, a grumpy guy who had to suffer the consequences of being in charge of the cargo loading and unloading, as well as the tank cleaning, deck work and safety, came into the cadet's room.

"You college boys are supposed to be smart. Figure out these cargo figures for arrival in Massachusetts."

In those days, there were no computers, or even hand-held calculators. The report he had to do was tedious; long calculations of how much of each liquid product they had on board. The depth of the tanks, capacity, ullage readings, temperature at loading and expected temperature on arrival, all had to be taken into consideration. He had never done it before. *No problem,* he thought. He took out some notes had gotten from a graduate of his school. There was a similar report included in the material.

He worked his pencil to the nub. Scratch paper and numbers representing millions of gallons of cargo flew about the room. He worked for hours, sure that all was perfect, and turned it into the mate on his way to the bridge for the evening 4 to 8 watch. At last, he would show these guys that he had value as an officer-trainee. He went down for supper at 1700. Youngblood had just begun eating when the chief mate came into the saloon, threw the entire stack of papers on the table in front of him, and shouted for all the officers in the room to hear.

"These are all wrong. You used the wrong coefficient of expansion. Do them all over."

It was another pleasant day at sea. *God, how I hate tankers,* he thought.

The next three weeks he spent on the ship were miserable to him, although there were no more major fuckups. He stood watch from 4 to 8, morning and night, with the old 2nd mate, did some deck work during the day, and worked on his reports at night. He sometimes played chess with the radio operator. He was about the only officer who would even talk to him. There was almost no time to go ashore in the oil ports. He did get around Fall River a bit. He went by the Borden's house; he had read about Lizzie and thought she was innocent. He found a bar in a bowling alley to have a couple of beers in. That was all there was to do there. It was typical for a tanker port.

The 2nd mate didn't seem to like him at all. Every watch was full of little tests of his that were designed to try to show that he, the high school graduate 2nd, was smarter than any college kid. It didn't matter how hard he worked, or how good his navigation was, the guy kept putting him down. His four weeks on the tanker were almost over when the 2nd came up with a new one.

"You college sailors take math up there in that school, right?"

"Yeah, 2nd, that's right."

"Well, I've got a problem here for ya. Solve this with your fancy math." He handed him a math riddle on a sheet of paper. It seemed insoluble. There were three unknowns, but you couldn't get three equations. It was the type of thing that you would get out of a magazine, and if you spent years trying out different numbers, you might eventually discover numbers that worked. Yet, the riddle seemed familiar to the kid. He decided to play.

"Let me take this down to my room after watch. I'll work on it then."

The second mate snickered in his usual, old bastard, smug way. What he didn't know was that on Youngblood's last ship, Ol' Captain One Lung, as crazy as he was, had a hobby with problems like this, and had shown some of them to the kid. Down in his room, Youngblood tore through his sea bag, and found some notebook paper with One Lung's solution to problems like these. By using the same principles, he could solve the 2nd's riddle. It involved quadratic equations and graphs, and he had it all! He worked it out carefully, and got the right answers.

He went up to the bridge early the next morning for the 0400-0800 watch, before the 2nd mate came up. Youngblood placed the two-page solution on the chart table. He went out into the darkened wheelhouse and waited with the 3rd mate on watch. The 2nd came up and relieved the watch, then went into the chart room, aft of the wheelhouse. The trainee poured himself a cup of coffee, sat down in the captain's chair, a privilege strictly forbidden to him, and put his feet up on the engine order telegraph. Twenty minutes went by before the 2nd appeared again in the wheelhouse. Youngblood did not move.

"Say, cadet, if you have time, could you explain to me how you got this? I mean, the answers are right, but, uh, you know, I'm not sure about all your figuring," he fumbled.

Finally, the cadet had gotten the best of him. He would listen to no more bullshit on the 4 to 8 watch. The tanker docked upriver from New Orleans in a few days, and his time was up. He would go up to New York to get on the *Savannah,* and away from this oily madness. No one seemed sad to see him go. He felt like some sort of survivor, and hoped he would never see a tanker again, except while passing one on the open sea.

Chapter 7: The White Elephant

He got down to the *N. S. Savannah* in Hoboken, New Jersey. The world's first nuclear merchant ship was still new looking, with its coat of white paint, and the symbol of the atom painted on both sides, amidships. American-Export Isbrandtsen Lines operated it. She wasn't any larger than the average cargo ship, about 600 feet long, but it was different in many respects, not just the lack of a boiler. There were rooms for 60 passengers, although they had none this trip. The ship had carried all kinds of dignitaries on voyages. Many people did not trust anyone in the merchant marine to operate a nuclear plant safely. They feared a radiation leak, a collision that would damage the core, or an explosion that could wipe out a whole city. There had been three years of stroking people since it had sailed out on its first commercial voyage in 1962. Although the U.S. and Russian navies had nuclear ships, this was different. Officials had to be convinced to allow the damn thing into their ports.

For a deck cadet, the power plant was a mystery. He was lucky, as there was an engineer called the nuclear advisor aboard, and he was helpful. Part of this shore-based nuclear expert's job was to train new hands. The ship even had a classroom for holding group lessons at sea. This trip, he and one new 3rd mate were the only rookies, and they both learned a lot about nuclear power from the advisor. The kid was relieved to discover this, since he again had a special sea project to do about this special ship. The *Savannah* could cruise about 300,000 miles without needing any refueling. Even after that, she would have used only about 100 pounds of uranium. In addition, the cargo gear on deck was all a new design. It also had stabilizer fins; the only commercial cargo ship he had ever heard of that had them. Only the big passenger ships had those things, which dampened the roll of the ship in the seas.

He already knew that the ship's name was in honor of the steamer *Savannah,* the first ship ever to sail the Atlantic with a steam engine, although she had sails, too. That ship had been a pioneer effort in 1818, and this version would break her own new ground. The old *Savannah* had made a lot of smoke on those rare occasions when she steamed instead of sailed. The new one gave off no smoke at all.

The inside of the ship was a lot fancier than any American ship he had ever seen. It had elevators, a hospital, and even a salt-water swimming pool. The promenade deck had tiled ceramics. It also had air conditioning, still new in those days, still considered unnecessary for sailors, and colored televisions. The engine was smooth and quiet compared to steam and diesel ships. The ship did not vibrate and shake like some.

The ship also carried people known as health physicists (HPs) as part of the crew. Their job was to constantly monitor radiation levels all over. Everyone wore radiation badges, and there were sample points all over the ship where they took readings. The cadet soon learned that they had the best jobs on the ship, since, if there were no problems, they had little to do. He felt lucky, though, that while in Hoboken, New Jersey, they shut down the plant. During this shutdown, one of the HPs offered to take all three cadets, two deckies and one engine, into the containment vessel, and the reactor area itself. They put on radiation suits, but everyone kept saying how safe it was. The containment vessel was a specially built layer of protection for the nuclear plant. There were layers of steel, polyethylene and lead. Outside of this was a collision mat made of steel and redwood two feet thick, and a thousand tons of concrete outside of that. The idea was that if the biggest ship in the world hit the *Savannah* bow on at full speed, the reactor would still be safe.

The bridge was the most luxurious he had ever seen. It had large work areas and the latest in equipment, including the new true motion radar. It would be a good experience to work on this bridge. Artwork adorned the public areas, like the dining room. The cargo ships he had seen would never have had such finery. No American shipping company wanted to spend a dime on any luxuries, it seemed. The fact that sailors spent months at a time living on a ship meant nothing to them. The cadet had visited some foreign ships that had paneling and things just to make the sea-going employees feel better. In some other cultures, going to sea was a respected way of life, but not in the good ol' dollar-conscious U.S.

By the time they had crossed the Atlantic and were beginning to hit ports in the Med, he had become aware that the officers and crew referred to it as the "White Elephant." It had cost over $46 million to build, most of that paid by the U. S. Government, an unheard of sum at the time. It would never turn a profit. The ship carried a huge crew for a commercial vessel. There were so many engineers on it you could not keep them all straight. Special training was required of all the officers. The labor cost was not the only problem. There were so many safety regulations written just for this one ship that the operating cost would always be high. Maintenance and inspections on the nuclear plant caused delays and more expense.

The mates tried like hell to make as much profit on the cargo as possible, but the balance sheet would always be negative. The cadet had never seen the mates and cadets spend so much time down in the hatches, trying to reduce breakage and theft of the cargo. In spite of the newness of the ship, it carried one holdover from the old cargo ships, in the person of the bosun. He had reputation as being the "leg breaker" from Export Lines. He was now in his mid-forties, but none of the deckhands messed with him. The legend included the routine of the company assigning him to any ship where a deckhand was a troublemaker. He would assign the guy work back aft or in a hold, and, when no one else was around, beat the hell out of the guy. On one ship, he saved time and trouble by simply smashing a heavy, ceramic coffee cup over a guy's head right in the crew's messroom, sending him to the hospital, and a clear message to the rest of the deck gang.

The *Savannah* was a pioneering effort, meant to pave the way for many others to follow. If they could just prove the safety of the damn thing, the unit cost of other nuclear ships, built later, would come down. The designers could find ways to reduce the construction costs. Without a large expense on fuel, and carrying fewer crew than the first one, eventually nuclear ships could turn a profit. The believers on board talked about a whole fleet of these ships sailing all over the high seas, helping save the American Merchant Marine from foreign competition. The cadet would sail long enough to see the *Savannah* high and dry, just laying around at a dock, with nowhere to go, and no one who wanted it, even for a museum piece.

His two months on the White Elephant went by very quickly. There always seemed to be work to do, and reports to write. The two deck cadets worked overtime, even in port. There wasn't much time to go ashore. The only positive was that the mates arranged to pay the cadets extra for excess work. A 3rd mate made $4.23 an hour for overtime work. They could not officially pay the cadets any overtime, so the 2nd mate kept track of their excess hours, and added it to the mates' payroll. Since they had to pay taxes on the extra money, he allowed the cadets to collect $3 an hour from the mates' pay at the end of the trip. As broke as all cadets were, at least it would be something at the end; on most ships they would work you all they wanted to, and didn't have to give you anything extra. The bad news was that they frequently spent twelve hours or more a day on deck, and in the hatches. There would be no days off, and no arranging for time off in port to see any sights. Cadets on this ship were cheap labor, and everyone called them "cadet." There were no nicknames or parties with the officers. Their rooms were not even amongst the officers' quarters, like on most ships. They lived down on C deck, the lowest deck for living spaces, just above the waterline. They had rooms designated for bellhops and extra messmen, necessary when the ship had carried passengers.

He also found out that whenever the ship entered or left port, the deck officers and cadets all wore complete blues uniforms, stripes and all. Even when he was on the bow, he had to wear his academy uniform, with high-pressure hat and all. This made for nice pictures, but cadets never expect to wear their academy uniforms on commercial ships. Neither deckie had brought an overcoat to go with the blues. Sailing into Boston in March with no overcoat was cold work.

The extra work and low-class treatment offset their educational experiences. Neither deck cadet felt like an officer-trainee. Even at night, at sea, if they walked by an officer's room where several officers were having a little drinking party, no one invited them to join it. The officers seemed to consider themselves part of some elite group, better than the guys out there on the cargo ships and tankers, and they acted like it; they were invited in by one of the 3rd mates for drinking only once or twice.

By the time the Elephant got back to New York, the cadet looked back on a trip that was almost all learning and work. Other cadets said he was crazy to ask for more work than normal, and an additional sea project to do. He didn't think so. It had been an unusual opportunity, one of a kind. Years later he would sail past the laid-up *Savannah* and think that he was lucky to have been on it. Twenty years later he still would be one of the relatively few who had experienced this part of sailing history. Still, it hadn't been a party trip like the Brazil run. There had been only a few memorable moments.

One of them happened in Genoa, Italy. The cadet went with a couple of guys up to Jenny's Bar. Jenny was an American who had married an Italian, and ran a little bar that was a favorite spot for merchant sailors. Everyone was pretty drunk when one of the ship's officers passed out on the floor. The laughing stopped when no one could bring him to. Jenny called for an ambulance. A long time passed, as the drunks all checked the poor guy out and argued whether to give CPR or not, or what to do or not do. Jenny said that ambulance service in Italy was terrible, and told the group to pick the guy up. The cadet got one end of the guy, somebody got the other end, and they carried him out of the bar. Jenny pulled up in her Maserati. They crammed the guy in the back, and the cadet stuffed himself in as well. He then got a ride to the local hospital he would never forget. It was just like the damn movies, he thought, as Jenny ignored streetlights, careened around corners, stomped on the gas, and cussed out the local emergency services. He was amazed when all three of them got to the hospital alive. The unconscious guy recovered. He had some kind of severe reaction to something or other, or maybe alcoholic poisoning.

A quick stop in Livorno, or Leghorn, Italy was a place where the cadet bought a marble chessboard and pieces. Sailors told him that the area was famous for marble work, and he wandered in, by accident, to a dirty shop where workers were making all kinds of things. It wasn't a retail store, but the workers liked his attitude, and he made a cash offer right there. They wrapped the set in newspaper for him. Some of the officers fell in with some English merchant officers, who, in typical fashion, took them around drinking. When the *Savannah* sailed, later that night, they came to the dock and sang songs until it was clear of the pier; drinking and singing were traditional for them, and the kid thought they had a great time with it.

The ship also stopped in Venice, which the cadet had never been to, and he did manage to get a few hours ashore.

It surprised him to discover that he could walk all over the city. There were narrow walkways along the canals, and hundreds of little bridges to cross. He went to St. Marks Square, just because he had seen so many pictures of it. The weather was cool, however, and it wasn't tourist season, so the canals were not full of gondoliers. He learned that there were water taxis that were more efficient, anyway. He took one to Harry's Bar. It was a famous place, and had been a hangout for many American writers, including Hemingway. He had a drink at the bar, just to say he had done it, but could not afford to go upstairs for a meal. Still, he was happy that he had gotten somewhere interesting on the trip. He walked back to the ship at night, and found another unusual thing about Venice. He noticed that more than once, a girl had walked ahead of him and dropped a handkerchief on the walkway. The first time he hesitated, and the girl came back, picked it up, and went away quickly with a girlfriend. A few minutes later, the same girl passed him, and dropped it again. He understood the game now, and picked it up for her. This was a local method of meeting a guy, if a girl liked his looks. The girl spoke no English, and since the cadet spoke no Italian, a real date was unlikely. He had to get back to the ship anyhow, and could not explain that either. Still, he had a good memory of the young girl, and hoped that she did not go away thinking he didn't like her.

Another port new to him was Rijeka, Yugoslavia. He had seen posted warnings to be careful in that communist country, but went ashore at night with his deck cadet partner anyway. The boys were told what places were open to them, and they stuck to the list. They were very surprised to visit a nightclub where foreigners could go, and see a floor show that included a strip tease. The difference with this stripper was that she wore regular street clothes, not a fancy costume. They were more surprised when she stripped all the way, and paused stark naked for the applause. They hadn't expected that in a restrictive, communist country. Maybe it happened only in certain places, to attract some tourist dollars. They ended the evening in a large bar where there seemed to be a lot of sailors and girls. They drank the local specialty, slivovitz, a plum brandy that would, and did, give you one hell of a headache the next morning. There was a dance floor, and they both danced with a few girls. Then his partner, the other deckie, got interested in a particular girl, who was sitting at a table near them. She did not want to dance, but invited the interested American to sit with her. After checking that his shipmate was okay for money and directions back to the ship, the kid left him there. He did not see him again until they both turned to on deck at 0800 the next morning. Things seemed a little strange. The other cadet did not want to talk about the night before, or the girl, and he wore a neckerchief wrapped around his throat. The kid did not want to ask, but the 3rd mate on deck was typically more direct, when he saw it.

It became obvious that the 3rd mate, and others on the ship who had been ashore in Rijeka, knew why the cadet had the kerchief on. He was hiding bite marks and scratch marks. The girls there liked to mark their men with blood-sucking hickeys and fingernail marks. A few other guys on deck that morning had them too. The kid was glad he went back to the ship when he did. His partner was embarrassed, and would not talk about it, even when the older mates joked around with him. Then the 3rd mate took the kid aside and told him the rest of it. Guys from the ship had seen him with the "girl who didn't dance." They knew her. They knew why she didn't dance, too. She had a wooden leg. She had a reputation as a maniac in the sack. The kid would have liked to hear his partner's side to this, but he left it alone. Their sea year was indeed a learning experience. Besides, he had to work with the guy every day as they sailed back. His room was next door to his. He was a good guy, and a good shipmate. They had several cases of beer to drink on the return trip, and the partner had the only music. He had brought a cassette player along. That was good, but the only tapes he had were all Bob Dylan. They would drink every night, down on C deck, and listen to the same songs repeatedly. The kid had liked Dylan at the beginning of the trip, but by the time they arrived in New York, he was sick of him. They parted in New York as friends, but the kid wished he had found out if the stories about the "girl who didn't dance" were true.

This time he had to report to the academy office in Manhattan. He now had more sea time than the school required. He had volunteered to do an extra project, and had it ready to turn in. Classes for his junior, or 2nd class year, would start in a month. He had a little spending money saved up, thanks in part to the $3 an hour overtime the mates had let him earn. He had a brother at a civilian college in New Jersey, and he was looking forward to going there and relaxing for a few weeks. His hair was a little longer now than the last time he had been to New Jersey, and he would do a little better with the girls from other schools around the area. The academy rep had other news.

He had just enough time to make a few trips on a coastwise tanker, he explained. He would leave right away for Fall River, Massachusetts, and join the *S. S. Key Tanker*, a Keystone tanker. It was a sister ship of the one he had already sailed. The kid again made the argument that he had volunteered to ship out a month early on his cadet year, but this was to no avail. There was the usual advice on sailing all you could. He had already done the tanker sea project, he offered. "Good, then you won't have to do that, you can just work on the ship," the rep said. There was no hope. He went right back to sea on a hated tanker. The only good news was that he had learned something about tankers, and didn't think he would repeat the mistakes he had made before. He prayed that no one on that ship had been on the other one; that he could start anew with these officers, and earn some respect.

All these things turned out to be true. The chief mate was glad to have a cadet who had a little experience with tankers. He was a good guy, liked the kid, and helped him learn some more without berating him. He even offered him cold beer in the evening. He had a roommate this time too, a cadet who had recently changed from deck to engineering, and was trying to find his way around an engine room. The run was boring, and he still hated tankers, but, with the sea project all done, and some guys to drink and play cards with, it wasn't too bad. When it was over, he had two days left to party in New Jersey on his way back to school. Some people wondered how you could finish a degree in four years if you spent a year at sea. The answer was that you went to class eleven months a year, and took eighteen credit hours or more at a time. Just two more years of that and he would graduate, and return to the sea as a licensed 3rd mate; a bona fide, hell-bent-for-leather, bucko, young mate. He would be ready for it.

The author's first ship, in the Panama Canal. Photo: Ron Heimburger

Working cargo on the Nashville Avenue wharf, New Orleans (circa 1965). Photo: Ron Heimburger

The N. S. Savannah

Looking aft along the catwalk, S. S. Key Trader. Photo: K. Zahn

Part Two

The Bucko Mate

Chapter 8: Going Oriental

When he graduated from the academy in 1968, he went home to Jacksonville, Florida and joined the deck officers' union, the Masters, Mates and Pilots, or MM&P. He was broke, but had a bachelor's degree, a third mate's license, an ensign's commission in the naval reserve, and felt he had it all. The decision to go union wasn't just because of the higher union wages, but also the opportunity to sail to different places in the world. If you became a company man, you could spend years on the same ship, sailing to the same places, over and over again. You could join a tanker outfit and never see any place but a tanker dock in Louisiana and an other in New England. This wasn't why he had joined the merchant marine.

Shipping was good that summer, because of the Vietnam War. Many inactive ships, many from the "mothball fleet," were activated, crewed up and sent with military goods to the war. This added hundreds of new mate jobs for all trade routes, not just Southeast Asia. The mates' union was actively taking in new members, a rarity. Some ships even sailed short-handed. He made up his mind to make a commercial run to the Far East. Even as a new union member, without first choice of jobs off the board, there were jobs he turned down. After a couple of days, he didn't even bother to go down to the hall for job calls. He told the dispatcher to call him at home when there was an open 3rd mate's job on a freighter to Japan. The guy called the next day and gave him a choice of two different ships, both headed for Japan. One was in Panama, the other in New Orleans. The steamship company would be happy to fly him free of charge to either place to join. He decided on New Orleans. It would feel good to go back there as an officer with a good job, not a poor cadet.

He figured he would make New Orleans his home, and ship out of there in the future. He was 21-years old, and had life by the throat.

The ship was an old, C-2 freighter, operated by Lykes Lines, named the *Almeria Lykes*. It was 460 feet long, had launched in 1945, had five cargo hatches, a steam turbine engine, and could hold about 9000 tons of cargo. She was a little rusty, but he wouldn't be chipping and painting this trip. He would take his place up on the bridge with the captain and the other mates. Many older ships had been running longer than normal, due to the increased need for cargo ships going to Viet Nam. His ship was sailing with three mates instead of four. It meant more work, and more overtime. The main difference from cadet year was that he would be the only officer on the bridge during the 8 to 12 watch, morning and night. He would be the only one to determine the ship's position, avoid collisions, make the course changes, and give orders to the helmsman. He officially signed ship's articles for his first trip as a licensed mate on August 8, 1968.

After a few days of checking on him, tall, lanky Captain Bloomquist left him alone. Once a captain determined that a new mate was competent, he would leave him to run things, with only spot checks on his navigation work, weather map construction, and collision avoidance. The bucko mate had learned well when he was an apprentice and felt proud that the captain trusted him so much on his first trip as a mate. The crew on his watch was one man short. He had only one AB instead of two. This guy was also a 21-year old, and making his first trip as an AB, which meant that he had never officially steered a ship before. The OS, or Ordinary Seaman, on his watch, was seventeen, and making his first trip to sea. The average age of his watch, then, was nineteen and a half. It would never be so young. These were the days to join up if you wanted to sail. All the unions were taking on new members. Many of the World War II guys were retiring. The other reason things were so good for shipping was the war.

The sailors all wondered why it took a war every damn time to make people realize they needed a merchant marine. Nobody seemed to care what nationality of ships actually carried the damn goods around in peacetime. As long as they got their cars and other products as cheaply as possible, it didn't matter. Hell, most of the people the mate knew did not have any idea what the merchant marine was. A guy in the steamship company office he met while taking his physical and filling out paperwork had given him a warning. "Things are great for you union officers now," he had said, "but it won't last." He advised him to get a permanent assignment to a ship, and keep it. "Someday," he said, "you'll be stuck in the union hall without work." Hell, he was the one who didn't get it. Job security meant nothing to him. He had managed to stay single and unattached. He was responsible only to himself. If something bad happened to him, he wasn't hurting anyone else, really. It was his damn life, and if he wanted to spend it bumming around the waterfronts of the world, so be it. *Steady job? Nah, you could do that anytime.*

They loaded cargo in the Gulf ports before steaming down to Panama. The new mate worked on deck in port, and looked the part. He had new khakis, clean, leather work gloves dangling out of his back pocket, steel-toed work boots, and a notebook and pen in his shirt pocket, to make notes about the cargo. He carried a folded cargo stowage plan; he had colored it in himself, with each port's cargo coded with a different color. He paced the deck constantly, on the offshore side, away from the swinging pallets that came out of the hatches and over to the wharf. He sought out the longshoreman boss for each hatch, and let him know that he, the mate, would be checking everything.

They got through the ditch without problems and headed north towards San Diego. From there, they would head across for Yokohama. The new mate was determined to handle things on his own. Some new guys would call the captain every time a ship or fishing boat got on a collision course -- not him. He had it in his mind never to call the captain. He would prove how well he could handle the ship. The Old Man had come up to the bridge enough times by now to see that the young 8 to 12 watch did not need help. It made his job easier if those kids could handle things.

All this went well until one night on his watch when he began to notice all kinds of lights on the ocean ahead. Soon they were all around him, most of them moving. Some of the lights were identifiable as large ships, and he could tell their direction of travel. Others had different lights he could not make out. Then there were red lights, flashing red lights, and lights that moved up and down, instead of across the water. He had the old, little, World War II era radar warmed up. He turned it on to help plot the targets, but there were so many of them on the little screen that many of the blips ran together on the tube. The young lookout was going nuts trying to report each new light he saw. The mate called him on the phone and told him just to report anything dead ahead. The rookie AB went into hand steering, and the mate left the radar to stand out on the starboard wing of the bridge. He would maneuver through this mess like he had learned from Red. He couldn't plot all the targets even if he tried. He would take visual bearings of the lights that were a problem, and change course for those in danger of collision. There was, as usual, no thought of slowing down the ship. Merchant ships don't do that at sea, and it would take too long even if he ordered it.

As he sailed into the middle of this confusion, he scanned the lights with binoculars, and determined that the navy fleet from San Diego was out on exercises. There were destroyers, carriers, escort and supply ships; you name it, it was out there. Some of the lights were helicopters taking off and landing. There were special navy lights, some for aircraft operations. He figured that at least some of these ships had the right-of-way. Others were moving in more or less straight lines, underway. He would treat these as meeting or crossing situations, even though the normal Rules of the Road were different when so many ships were involved. Common sense and quick decisions would be his goddam rule.

He got into the middle of the exercise and began to zig and zag, as Red had taught him. The AB answered the commands correctly, although his eyes got bigger all the time. They went right, they went left, and then they went right again. He thought they were just about clear of most of them when a large ship changed course off his starboard bow, and headed towards his port side on a steady bearing, or collision course. He went right again, and passed it port to port. Before he could get back to his original course, the navy guy turned around again, and headed across his bow from port to starboard. Now the mate figured he had the right-of-way, and held course. The navy guy got in front of him, closer than normal, and did not seem to be giving him any room. Cursing, the mate went to the left and passed the same guy again, starboard to starboard.

The captain appeared on the bridge, apparently having seen lights all over the ocean. He sat in his chair, but said nothing. Eventually, the young mate got free of the fleet, and resumed his course. The captain went below. The mate felt that his abilities were now evident to his commander.

After a quick stop for bunkers in San Pedro, California, they sailed west across the Pacific. The weather was mostly good, and everyone settled in to the routine. For a third mate, this meant standing a watch twice a day for four hours, with a little other work in between. The old ship was slow, and only made sixteen knots on a good day. It became boring. Standing a watch meant exactly that. You had to stand all the time, and you watched. You watched the horizon for other ships, you watched the compass for the course steered, and you watched the weather. In the sixties, the mates still navigated mostly with celestial observations. You took sights on the sun or moon during the day with a sextant, and stars on the 2nd mate's watch morning and night. You spent time working out your sights with tables and math formulas. You checked the accuracy of the ship's gyrocompass by comparing bearings of the setting sun, or low stars. You used the Nautical Almanac and other publications to determine what the bearings of these bodies, from 000 to 359, should be for your position on the surface of the earth. You adjusted course, filled out weather reports and made your own weather maps from information received by radio. You hardly ever used the old radar. You saved that for bad visibility, and going along a coast.

Off watch, you ate meals, played cards or chess if anyone was interested, read books, and had one or two movie nights a week. Guys would congregate in someone's room from time to time, and guys would share beer or whiskey, and stories. Even this became monotonous. As a full officer this time, he did not socialize with the crew. You couldn't be too friendly with guys you might have to get fired. It wasn't done. So, after a week or more of this, the young mate realized that there was more boredom than he had thought. As a student-seaman, he always had homework to do, things to investigate or learn, extra work on his off time, or guys from the deck gang to share a drink. It wasn't all exciting, fun times. You could get lonely at sea. Stories about guys going nuts after going to sea too long began to make more sense to him.

One of the engineers on a different watch than his showed up on the bridge one quiet night, and asked permission to come into the wheelhouse. The bucko mate said "sure," and was glad to have some company. The engineer was much older than he, and had been going to sea for about twenty years. They got coffee, and went out to the bridge wing. There were no other ships around, the radar was off, and the ship was being steered automatically by "Iron Mike," the name the sailors had for that device. A gentle breeze wafted astern, and the sky was full of stars. The old engineer was quiet for a while, and then spoke.

"You know, in all my years at sea, I have never been up on the bridge at sea."

"No kidding. What do you think?"

"You could plan your whole life up here, on a night like this. Engine rooms are hot and noisy, and all you see is the equipment." He seemed to have regrets about his choice of careers, but it made the mate feel better that he had chosen to be a mate, not an engineer. Still, he felt he had to make the guy feel better.

"Yeah, this is real peaceful, but when you're steaming through traffic, or rolling your ass off in bad weather, or when you're standing out here in the snow or rain, it's not so much fun. Many times I have wished I was down in the warm engine room on days like that." It seemed to make the engineer feel better, but still, he was quiet and stood there, looking at the horizon, and the stars. He went down below soon after, and the young mate invited him to come back anytime.

They crossed the Pacific with no major shipboard problems, and no typhoons. Their first port was Yokohama, the port city for Tokyo. They would make a couple of other ports in Japan, then cross the China Sea to Korea, and return to Yokohama through the inland sea. From there, they would head straight back through Panama to New Orleans. In the sixties, seamen still considered Japan to be a good country for American sailors. The dollar was welcome, and if you behaved yourself, you could have one hell of a time. There were beautiful young girls in nightclubs who would spend the night with you for about $25. You could get a room in a fancy hotel for about the same price, or go to a good restaurant or a bathhouse. The mate remembered what he had read about the Korean War, that the American soldiers in Japan who went there were totally unprepared for war. After a few days in Japan, he didn't wonder. Those guys had been having the time of their lives with the girls, the food, the great service, hiring housemaids and all that.

He also heard of guys "going Oriental." Unless you went to the Orient, it was impossible to understand how an American would suddenly change his whole way of life to embrace Oriental habits. The older guys were still fighting World War II, but the younger guys were more open-minded. He discovered, in Japan and Korea, and years later, in China, that Orientals were polite. Their homes and cities were clean. It was against their culture to cheat you or rob you. Violence was not the answer. They were service-oriented. They smiled and thanked you for every little thing. Guys who went nuts over all this would marry Oriental girls, buy Oriental furniture, wear robes and sandals, and even leave their shoes off at home. They learned to cook with rice and sometimes got very colorful tattoos. American guys who had never left the farm would never understand the attractiveness of a 90-pound Oriental girl. But if you had one hop into a hot tub with you, or give you a complete body massage, with the incense burning and the oils rubbed onto your tired body, she could make you forget your high school sweetheart in a second.

There were differences on the ship, too. The longshoremen did not come up the gangway yelling and cursing, and refuse to do what you wanted them to do. They said, "Good morning," smiled, and went about their work. They seemed happy to have work for that day, even if it was hard, dirty work. The ship stayed in Yokohama for three days on its first call, and the mates changed to eight-hour work shifts. The mate got the 1600-2400 shift. His first night in charge of cargo operations, he realized that he was alone. The captain, chief mate, and every other officer on the ship except the engineer on watch, were ashore. So was most of the crew. It was good experience for the bucko mate. He alone ran around the deck with the stowage plan, discussing with the bosses what hatches to work, and what cargo was theirs. He learned that he didn't need to worry much about workers stealing cargo, or breaking equipment on purpose, to delay the ship. It wasn't in their nature to do those things.

Everything was going smoothly on his first watch in port. Then one of the hatch bosses came up to him, excited, and told him, with limited English, that something was wrong with the cargo booms at #3 hatch. The mate went up there and found that the one of the cargo runners, a wire that ran from the cargo hook, up through a block at the head of the boom, and down to another at the heel of the boom, then to the winch, was broken. Normally, he would tell the chief mate, who would get the bosun and an AB or two, and they would re-rig the thing, but they were not aboard the ship. He tried to decide if he could send this gang to another hatch to work, and leave the problem for the morning. The hatch boss, however, seemed distraught. Maybe if they could not work that hatch, their boss would send them home, and they would earn less money for the night's work. Maybe it was some kind of honor thing, that his boss had told him to work this hatch tonight, and it didn't matter if there was a problem. At any rate, he made it clear that he wanted to know if there was a spare wire aboard the ship.

The mate took him back aft, to the bosun's locker. He had a key to it, but had no idea if there was a spare or not. Inside, the boss and several workers looked everything over, chatting rapidly. They pointed to a large, heavy, coiled-up wire. The mate said "Dai jobo," meaning, "okay," and they dragged the damn thing back up to the hatch. The mate was amazed. In the U.S., no longshoreman would help you do anything like this. Equipment problems were yours. They would spend the whole night lying around, getting paid for sleeping, or drinking, while you fixed something. The mate knew the basics, and went down the crew's quarters, where he found one AB alone, drinking coffee. He said he would help. The mate, the AB, the Japanese hatch boss, and several workers then spent the next hour or so re-rigging the boom and the broken wire.

When the new wire was in place, the winchman picked up a pallet load from the hatch, swung it over the side, and set it down perfectly on the dock. There were smiles all around. The mate was not used to seeing such a reaction. He told the hatch boss it was "Ichi bon," or "Number one." There were more smiles. He thought back to the trip he had made to Brazil, when the chief mate had treated some workers like dogs, and they had responded by smashing up the ambassador's car. He began to think that cargo work was hard work, and if guys were doing it well, you should treat them like people, no matter where you were in the world. He motioned the hatch boss to follow him, and he took him up to the ship's office, where all the cargo papers and plans were. He motioned him to wait there, and went to his own room and got two cold beers and brought them back. The Japanese hatch boss seemed astonished. They drank the beer together, but there must have been 40 bows and "thank you's" all around. A simple gesture had apparently earned him a friend for life. He did not completely understand their fierce loyalty to the job, but it sure was helping him, and the ship. No wonder the captain and chief mate had both gone ashore at the same time, something he had never seen. They had been here before, and knew how the work would go.

His relief showed up on time, and the mate showered and went ashore, after midnight. He felt safe walking the streets, unlike many other places. He had a difficult time finding anything open, however. He found a little bar, went in, and had a couple of beers. He was the only foreigner in there, but no one seemed to mind. He was watching his back, with his normal heightened instincts, but after a while, he relaxed. He went back to the ship and went to bed. During the next day, he mentioned his night to the radio operator, Sparks. Merchant sailors called radio operators names like "Sparks." Sparks told him that places closed early in Japan, but that there were some late night clubs and bars open, if you knew where to go. He was a vet at this run, and he offered to show the mate a place or two after midnight, if he wanted. Hell, yes, he wanted. Sparks was the only bastard on the ship who did not have to work in port. He could stay out all night and not have to get up for work in the morning. Because of his work schedule in port, the mate could party all night, as long as he got to sleep by morning, and took over the watch at four in the afternoon. They arranged that Sparky would come back to the ship just after midnight that night with a cab. The mate went on duty at 1600 with anticipation.

Things went better on his second eight-hour cargo watch. The hatch boss from the previous night smiled every time he passed him. His gang did exceptional work. Towards the end of the shift, however, the mate had an unusual decision to make. There had been some bags of graphite stored in the deep tanks in the bottom of a hatch. When the cargo was all out, a cleaning gang had gone down there to soogie the tanks with cleaning solution, and wash them down. Some of the bags had leaked, and some had broken. The tanks were a goddam mess. In typical Oriental fashion, however, the gang of cleaners worked until the old spaces were spotless. They, however, were not. They were covered in black, dirty graphite and dust. The head of the gang had come up to the mate and asked if they could take showers aboard the ship. The only available showers were the crew's stalls; they had a common shower, with about six showers in there. But if the crew got mad at the mate for letting longshoremen in there, there could be some union trouble about it. In addition, some of the cleaners were women. The mate was ready to just say no, when the AB who had helped him out the night before appeared. He heard the request, and told the mate that it would be okay. He said that he "knew these people," and there would be no trouble with it. Plus, he was a tough guy, and he said that he would handle any complaints from the crew. The mate told the boss it was dai jobo, and the AB went and got them some soap. He also got some cleaning solution, which the mate did not understand, at first.

After a while, the mate made a round through the crew's quarters. He heard a lot of noise from the crew's "head," or bathroom. He peeked into the space. What he saw was a dozen members of the cleaning crew, men and women, all naked, cleaning themselves and the showers. They were chattering and happy. He had heard that Orientals took baths together, and liked everything to be clean, but that sight on the old freighter was a first.

His watch was almost over, and, by tradition, he was standing by the gangway waiting for his relief. The cleaning crew filed past him, and down the gangway. They looked like different people, with their scrubbed faces. Every one gave him a slight bow and a smile as they passed him. *Christ, such a simple thing -- let 'em have a shower, and they thought it was a holiday.* The AB came out on deck and told the mate to have a look in the shower when he went topside. After his relief showed up, he did. The place was the cleanest he had ever seen it.

He then showered in his room quickly, as Sparks had said he would be along about a quarter after midnight. He went back down by the gangway, and sure enough, a few minutes later, a cab drove up next to the ship, and the crazy redhead got out. The mate went down the gangway, expecting to be ferried to some bar that stayed open late. When he got to the cab, however, he looked inside it, and there was a surprise. Sparks had not come alone. Two pretty, young girls were with him. Sparks pulled him aside.

"Look, Third, most places are closed. You can have either of these girls; I don't care, I like them both."

"You picked these girls up for us for the night?"

"I was just trying to save time; if you don't like them, we'll drop them off where I got them, and go drinking somewhere. This cabbie is all right, he knows lots of clubs."

The mate bent down and looked closely in the cab. The girls were smiling and he could see slim figures and a lot of leg. They were wearing what Americans called "Suzie Wong" dresses, with the slit up the side.

"They look fantastic, Sparky, what's the deal?"

"Well, they'll take us to a hotel. We can have a drink there, and if you want, you take one of them to a room for the night. In the morning give her some money and ask the Mama-san to call you a cab to go down to the ship."

"Sparks, for a goddam radio operator, you're all right. Let's do it."

"You get in the back with the two of them; you know, get acquainted." Sparks climbed in the front with the driver. The young mate got in the back and sat between the girls. The cabbie took off, for where the mate did not know, and in a few minutes did not care. Both girls looked fantastic, smelled terrific, and were classy and friendly. They were a lot more polite than the bar girls he had seen in Brazil and other places. They made conversation in English, and, even though it was obvious what was afoot, did not mention anything about it. Even for them, such talk probably wasn't proper.

They pulled up to a hotel. They went into the lobby and an older woman dressed in a kimono came forward to greet them. The hotel was nice looking. There was good furniture, and Japanese music playing softly from hidden speakers. There were bows all around, and they took their shoes off and left them with a row of others off to the side. Sparks said they would like some saki in the lounge area. Mama-san went to get it, and the group went to an area of sofas and chairs. The girls sat down, and Sparks waited for the youngster to take a seat next to the one he liked. He chose one, and sat next to her. The girls had more smiles.

The tray with the saki appeared, and they all started sipping the warm, rice wine. Sparks was saying things about girls from Tokyo coming down on the train to Yokohama on weekends to earn extra money, and how a lot of them had day jobs in Tokyo. The mate heard little of the conversation. The girl next to him was so different than the girls back home. His generation did not have the World War II-era hatred of the Japanese, at least not right then. Just like him, the pretty girl next to him was too young to have any memory of it. He understood better why some guys went nuts in the Orient.

Soon, Sparks said he was going upstairs, and left with his girl. The mate's girl then asked him if he too, was ready to go to a room. Indeed he was. They took an old elevator up a few floors, went down the quiet hallway, and she opened the door. The room was small, but very nice. It had three parts. There was a small living room area, with a low table, cushions to sit on, and a small refrigerator, with sandwiches and beer in it. If you consumed anything, mama-san would charge it to your room. Next to that was the bed area. The bed was low, almost to the ground, and surrounded by mirrors with a stereo built into the headboard. She put on a local radio station, and more soft Japanese music filled the little space. The last area was off to the side, and was the bathroom. It had the usual things, but the tub was deep and large, more like a hot tub, and there was one of those folding screens next to it.

The girl turned on the water in the tub, and took the mate by the hand and led him back to the living area. They sat on pillows, and she got a beer out of the fridge for him. She kept going into the bath area to check on the water level. When it was full, she motioned him to come into the bath, and take off his clothes. As he did so, she went behind the screen. This confirmed another rumor. He had heard that Japanese don't mind being naked, but it considered it rude to disrobe in front of someone. Sure enough, she emerged from behind the screen totally nude. Another story was confirmed when he noticed that she had no curly hair. She was smiling and laughing, and pushed him over to the bath. He got in first, and she followed, sitting on top of him, with her back to him. Japanese girls will always take a bath with you first, he had heard. They're freaks for cleanliness, and don't sleep with anyone who doesn't take a bath first. As her petite, slim body rubbed against him, he thought that this was a good rule.

There was a little fooling around in the sunken tub, but the mate understood that the bath was for cleaning, and preliminaries. Still, he could not keep his hands off the 90-pound girl who seemed so sensual. She got out first, helped him out, dried them both off, and led him to the bed. Next she got oils, and began a massage. Another story came true when she did actually walk on his back. He hardly felt the weight, but wondered if this was something that was for tourists, or whether it was a regular part of a full massage. Throughout the massage, however, she carefully avoided the one part of his body that was the most interested in her. It became clear that the bath, the massage, the music playing, the scented oils and perfumes, all of it was there to heighten the senses before the act. He decided that it beat the hell out of the back seat of a car at the drive-in. Eventually, of course, it was time for the serious stuff. He could wait no longer. She understood this, rolled him over, and got on top. He would remember the next day how light she was, and how she bounced up and down seemingly without effort. He would vaguely recall waking up in the middle of the night, finding himself caressing her little round curves, and rolling her over for more.

In the morning, he awoke to find another bath ready. After that, he found his clothes neatly arranged on the bed. She was already dressed in traditional garb, and served tea for them both. It was time to go. He broached the subject of payment. She wrote down a bill, in yen, so he could determine the charge for the hotel and the food and drinks. He kept trying to get her to write down how much her tip should be, but she would not. You gave what you thought was appropriate. It had been one of the best nights of his life. He gave what he thought was generous, in dollars, for everything. She smiled and gave a bow. They soon went downstairs, found his shoes, and headed for the door of the hotel. The mama-san was there, too. She and the girl followed him to the front door. More bows all around. He knew that his tip had been acceptable, since another habit of these people, was that the farther they followed you, and the more bows they gave, were indications of respect and appreciation, for your payment, or how you treated the girl. They kept talking about a taxi, but he insisted on walking. He had no idea where he was, but he wanted to walk around a while, and take in the sights and sounds of the streets, before looking for a cab back to the docks. It would be difficult to return to work on the rusty old ship; he understood better why sailors throughout history jumped ship in places like this, or Tahiti, or wherever seemed like Paradise to them.

The ship left that night and continued on to Nagoya, another Japanese port. His only new experience was going to a nightclub where young people danced, practiced their English on him, and used a unisex bathroom. From there, they steamed across to Korea, and made Pusan and Inchon for cargo work. He got ashore a couple of times, but did nothing more than drink a little beer. He met a couple of the sailors in hotel bars, and they introduced their girlfriends. Some of these relationships had been going on for years. He did not ask if the girls were in it for money, or whether they really hoped to marry one of the sailors and go to the states. The new mate's overall impression of Korea was a lot different from Japan. The place was a lot rougher. As soon as you hit the docks, there were shore pilots hounding you unmercifully. These young men wanted to take you all over the place for a fee. They would show you where to change money, where to get girls, souvenirs, or anything else you wanted. They were aggressive and a goddam pain. He avoided them all. Cabbies drove around at night with another guy in the front seat with them, for protection. Most of these friends carried guns. Sailors were often cheated or robbed. There were special streets, like Texas Street, for the American soldiers stationed there, where they could get drunk or chase women. Everyone seemed uptight and on guard. The young mate decided to hang out in the Seaman's Service Club, where at least no one cheated you, and the police kept the criminals out.

He was glad when they started sailing across the Sea of Japan, headed for the Inland Sea, back to Yokohama to top off with cargo for the long run back to New Orleans. He was on the night watch in between countries when he ran up on a huge fishing fleet. The boats were rather small, and by the time he saw over a hundred lights spread out all in front of him, it was too late to go around the whole bunch. Many of the boats were not even making a radar target, and there were too many to plot. He then saw two large targets, surely ships similar to his, one on each bow, making their way through the fleet. It was similar to the navy fleet experience, except that these little boats, if they were fishing, all had the right-of-way, and the normal rules for the large ships crossing his bow from different directions, were different. He knew he needed to use the unwritten merchant navigator's rule, that of common sense. He would steam right into the middle of the fleet and zig and zag his way out the other side, like Red had taught him, but he would give way to the ship crossing from starboard to port, taking his own ship to the right, just as he would if they were the only two ships on the ocean.

As decision time neared, he went out on the starboard wing, as was his practice now, and took visual bearings of the boats, and the large ship that was a collision problem. As usual, there was no thought of slowing down. He went right rudder to avoid a boat, then left, then got ready to go right to a clear path to go astern of the large ship, whose lights he could now make out, when a fishing boat he was not aware of suddenly turned on some lights. The damn thing was almost dead ahead, but slightly to starboard, and close -- damn close. It was so near that if he changed course to starboard, as intended, he might hit it. He had no choice. He ordered hard left rudder, and as the ship swung, passed the boat to his starboard side. It was too close; so close that he could hear the guys on the fishing boat hollering at him as they passed. He worried that he might catch their lines in his propeller. Then he worried that the large ship to starboard would not understand his actions. He had time to go right again, and pass port-to-port, as planned, but if the other guy got nervous seeing his current change to port, he might change to port, and collision would be a possibility.

As soon as he got by the yelling fishermen, he ordered hard right, and watched the large ship to starboard every second. He took a bearing of the dark area to his right, which gave him the course he should end up steering. As long as the big ship did not change right now, and no other fishermen suddenly appeared out of nowhere, like the last one, things would still work out. As the old ship came right, he watched the traffic with binoculars, and swept the dark area. He saw nothing. He eased the rudder, and the ship's swing slowed down. When the ship was almost steady, he gave the AB the course to steer, right down the middle of the dark path between the fishermen that he had chosen. Then he would have to go over to the port wing, watch the guy who crossed, and run a plot on the other large ship that was southbound, to see if he would pass safely ahead or astern. As he walked through the wheelhouse to get over to the port side, he saw the captain sitting in his chair, in the dark, with a cup of coffee.

"Have a little traffic, mate?" he asked.

"Yessir -- almost clear of it." The roll of the ship must have awakened him. If you put a lot of rudder on a ship going full speed, she would heel over more than normal. Good sailors woke up when they felt different movements of the ship. Good engineers would wake up in the middle of a deep sleep, if the engine didn't sound right. The captain on this ship was a good sailor. He probably looked out his porthole and saw lights all over the place, and came up to see if the mate was in trouble. It was a mark of confidence that he had not interfered.

Soon, the mate could see that the other sea-going vessel would pass astern of him. He was clear of the traffic. The captain came out on the port wing where the mate was.

"I'm going down below, mate. You're getting the hang of this; you don't need my help."

"Okay, Cap'n." Of course he was getting the hang of it. He was almost 22 years old.

By the time they got back to Yokohama, the weather looked bad. They should have been there about two days, but it kept raining and they could not load cargo in the rain. They stayed five days. The mates and engineers went on 8-hour watches again, instead of four. The young mate got the four to midnight shift again. It was eight hours on, and sixteen off; enough time to go ashore and see something, or get into and out of trouble, as you wished.

Far into his first cargo watch, as the longshoremen were alternately working and waiting for the rain to stop, about 2200 hours, the mate was sitting up in the ship's office. He passed the time studying the cargo papers, and trying to decide if he was going to go anywhere at midnight, or wait until morning and do a tourist trip to Tokyo instead. His peaceful solitude ended abruptly. One of the Japanese workers, who had a boss with him, limped into the office. This was highly unusual; the workers never entered the cabin areas. The boss knew a little English, the worker none. It became obvious, though, that the barely dressed hatch worker had some kind of medical problem. He lifted up his bare foot to the mate; a huge gash ran the length of his foot and he was bleeding profusely.

When a merchant ship is in port, anyone who is hurt goes to a hospital. At sea, one of the mates each trip is designated as the medical officer for the trip. This is normally the chief mate, since he is a permanent employee, typically has a lot of experience, and keeps the keys to the medical locker. Until the 1970's, when the mates got EMT training to give them some knowledge of medicine, what kind of help you got if you were hurt or sick on a ship was hit or miss. Many of the older mates were surprisingly good at fixing you up. At other times, aspirin and bandages were the basic remedies. If someone were hurt badly, the radio operator would send messages to medical services ashore, who would advise you on what to do. "Keep the son-of-a-bitch alive" was the motto. In a life and death situation, you would alter course for the nearest port, or try to meet a ship with a doctor, at sea. This would be a naval vessel, or a passenger ship. If an American merchant ship carried more than twelve passengers, the law considered it a passenger vessel, and you had to carry a doctor. That was why the freighters who carried passengers limited it to twelve. That was risky. Most of the passengers were elderly, and had health problems. Guys on the ship had a standard question: "Who's the doctor this trip?" On this trip, it was the chief mate, but he was ashore. The captain was as well. The young mate was alone with the cut-up foot.

He tried to explain that he was not a doctor, and the worker needed to go to a hospital. The boss left. The guy with the foot sat impassively in a chair, saying nothing, waiting for treatment. The mate looked at the guy's foot again. He clearly needed numerous stitches, something he had zero experience with, to go along with limited first aid training. This stranger just sat there, bleeding, probably embarrassed at getting hurt and being unable to work, and waiting for this young American officer to help him.

The mate at least had to stop the bleeding. He went into the medical locker and found some gauze and iodine. *Let's see how badly this guy wants me to operate,* he thought. He went over, turned the foot up and poured iodine all over his foot. No reaction. *Christ, I know that hurts like hell, but this guy isn't going to show it.* The mate wrapped his foot with a roll of gauze and had him press in on it to stop the bleeding. He tried again to indicate he now should see a doctor for stitches. The longshoreman made no movement. *Okay, we'll play it a different way,* the mate thought.

While he was looking for the gauze, he had gone through a file cabinet. The cabinet had some non-prescription medical supplies -- aspirin, band-aids, etc. He had also seen a roll of sail twine and a needle for repairing canvas. Sail twine is very thick, and the needle used for stitching canvas was about three inches long. In order to push the twine through the heavy canvas, you used a sail palm, a leather glove-like device that fits over your palm and thumb, and has a metal thimble built into it. He put on the sail palm, and took out the twine and needle. He made a big show out of cutting off a length of the twine. Out of the corner of his eye, he checked the longshoreman. He was keenly watching. Next, he drew out the sail needle and held it up to the light. As he started to thread the twine into the eye of the needle, the worker started mumbling in Japanese. The mate tied a big knot in the end of the twine, and then got out the wax. The wax was to grease the twine so it would pass through heavy canvas. Again, he made a spectacle out of waxing down the twine. The mumbling got louder.

"Okay, okay, I fix you. Dai jobo, everything dai jobo!" the mate assured him, now moving in with the needle.

"No, no, nay, nay!" the worker shouted, got out of the chair, and limped as fast as he could, down the passageway, with the end of the gauze trailing behind.

The mate never saw the guy again, and assumed he had indeed gone to a real doctor. He settled back into the chair in the ship's office, listened to the sporadic rain beating on the steel deck above, and thought that everything had worked out just fine.

He stayed aboard the ship. In the morning, he went to breakfast. Sparks, the ultimate shore-hound, was there, which was unusual. In their conversation, the mate mentioned that he was going shopping during the day, and hoped to get some souvenirs for his family, and a radio and tape recorder for himself. The little redhead, of course, knew just the place, and invited himself along as a guide.

Aggressive businessmen, realizing that seamen from other countries had money to spend, would send runners down to the docks and distribute leaflets, or business cards. Sometimes they would offer you a free ride uptown, the first stop, of course, being at their employer's store or bar. The store they went to displayed every kind of stereo, radio, and electronic device made in Japan. What set this place apart was that when you went in, a greeter met you, discovered what language you spoke, and then called over a young girl who spoke your language to act as your salesperson. The mate and Sparks were easy, since English was still a required subject in Japanese schools.

The mate settled on a reel-to-reel tape recorder that weighed 30 pounds, and a transistor radio that had short wave bands as well as the normal ones, that weighed nine pounds. Printed circuits were not common yet. These heavy devices were new, state-of-the-art, and, with the dollar still being strong in Japan, much cheaper than he could get back home. He picked out a few tapes to play, some blanks, and batteries for the radio so he could go out on deck with it during the trip home. The girl converted the price from yen to dollars, and he was happy with the negotiations. Sparks, however, was doing his own negotiating. There seemed to be something going on, but the mate did not catch on until they left, and went to a small café nearby for coffee.

The Old Redhead had arranged for the two of them to meet the salesgirl and one of her friends after they got off work from the electronics store. They would have a drink somewhere, and take the girls out to dinner.

"Well, you old son-of-a-bitch, that's great. But first, I have to work the 4 to 12 watch tonight. Secondly, these aren't geisha-type girls like you found before. These girls are straight; you can't be an Ugly American and try to take them to bed."

"That's right, I know that. I thought it would be a good cultural experience for you, that's all. Besides, the old 3rd mate doesn't go ashore. He'll take your watch, or switch with you. All he cares about is making as much overtime as he can so he can retire."

Sparks was right, but still, the mate would have to go back to the ship and arrange it. They went back in a cab. The old third mate was awake and hanging around, and he agreed to take the watch. If the mate "got lucky," he could stay out all night; the 3rd would cover sixteen hours of cargo watch. If he got back before morning, he could relieve him. The young mate secured his purchases in his room, and got ready to go out about 1730 hours.

They had to meet the two girls at a bar a few blocks from the store where they worked. It wouldn't be proper for their bosses to see them going out with customers. The mate told them that they wanted to go out to dinner, but not at a tourist place. The girls hailed a cab, and after a long ride, they were somewhere in the suburbs, at a local restaurant where no one spoke English except the four of them. The service and cooking were all done right at the table. It had a built-in hot plate, or fire, underneath the center of it. Their waitress brought the raw food and cooked it in a wok right there. They let the girls order, only telling them that they wanted a sample of different things, local fare. The mate did not know what he was eating half the time. He did recognize the steak, vegetables and rice, had a good guess at the jellyfish and squid, but no idea on much of the other food. The waitress kept cooking and keeping things warm right on the table; she put more in their plates as they ate. Enough saki went around and around the table to give all four a slight buzz, but no one drank heavily, it didn't seem appropriate.

When the long meal was over, the sailors paid the bill, with interpretation help. It seemed reasonable. There were stories on the ships about places that kept two price lists, one for locals, and one for tourists. If you asked for the price list ahead of time, they would show it to you. The foreigner list was terribly expensive. Most of the time, the foreigners got the hell out, which was just what such a bar or restaurant wanted. The mate was fortunate that in the 60's, this practice was limited, and that Sparks had the sense to get some locals to take them out, so this would not happen in any case. Still, the mate developed a habit of asking prices when he went to a strange place in another country, not just walking in somewhere and ordering, as you might do at home.

So, the four of them were standing outside of this restaurant, somewhere in Yokohama. The mate really liked his girl, but he did not know what to do next. He offered to continue the date, to take her out somewhere, a nightclub, perhaps, but she and the friend said they had to work the next day, and needed to get home. They lived in different directions, so Sparks got two cabs, and they split up to take the girls home. The mate's girl seemed surprised at this that he would want to see her home, even in a cab. The mate tried to explain this as an American custom, but it was also true that he wanted to ride around the area, talk to her, and get a better look at how this girl lived.

They eventually stopped in front of a large apartment building. The mate got out with the girl. She hesitated. Could it be possible that she was considering inviting him in? He would love just to see how she lived, what her apartment looked like, and, if she was inclined to have him stay the night, so much the better. However, he would not be pushy. This was the complaint about Americans the world over. The cabbie sat silently, waiting to see if he would continue the fare or not. The mate got his question answered soon enough.

The girl said that she would like to ask him in, but there was a problem -- her father. She lived here, with her parents, and her father had been in the war. The mate understood. Her father would have a hatred of Americans. It would be unthinkable for her to bring one into the apartment, even for an innocent cup of tea. He explained that he understood this to her. He explained how his father had also fought in the war, and would be shocked to learn that his son was even going to dinner with a Japanese girl. "It's too bad," he said to her; "that our parents' views can affect us like this." She was greatly relieved, but seemed sad, too. They were both post-war baby boomers, from different sides of the ocean, but had grown up hearing similar prejudices.

It became clear to the young mate that he should not even walk her up to the door, as her father might see who her date was. He told her that he would wait in the cab and watch until she got safely into the building. That common courtesy seemed to surprise her. It was possible that he would return to Japan, of course, but they both knew that to build a relationship so far apart was almost impossible. The evening had been simply a cultural exchange for all four of them. As she seemed ready to walk up the sidewalk, he told her about another American custom.

If your first date is a happy one, he told her, it was customary to give your date a kiss when he took you home. She beamed at this. She probably could not believe that this bucko, rough, American sailor would offer such an innocent gesture. She put her arms around him and gave him a "first-date" kiss so sweet any innocent girl would be proud of it. The mate watched her walk up the pathway. She looked back and waved a couple of times. For once in her life, he thought, she would have a positive experience with a foreigner; one that wasn't rude. Still, it was unusual for him to be so polite when going ashore from a ship. He got back into the cab, and gave the driver a card. It had the name and location of his dock printed on it in Japanese. The ship's agent had passed them out.

He got back to the freighter, paid the white-gloved driver, went up the gangway to his room, put on his khakis, and went out on deck to relieve the old 3rd mate. He learned from the old salt that they were going back on sea watches at midnight, as the ship would sail the next day, probably early evening. This was normal, but because he had swapped hours, the mate would now take the deck until midnight, his shore watch, and then take the midnight to 0400, four of the hours he owed the old-timer. Then the 2nd mate would come out for the 0400 to 0800, and the young mate would be back on duty at 0800. It was fine; he would get two or three hours sleep in between.

As he paced the deck with the cargo plan stuffed in his back pocket, he thought about the girl he had left at the apartment, and thought that there really wasn't so much difference between people as some would think. He also realized, as he checked the work at each hatch, that many of the workers knew him from the cleaning gang/shower incident, and were friendly to him. He also noticed that some of them jabbered profusely when he walked by, making motions to their feet, and with imaginary string and needle. They stared at him. He smiled inwardly at both responses. One would earn him a bit of respect in a country that so valued it and the other would help ensure that the cargo work went along with no problems.

The mate was on deck the next morning, looking forward to noon, when his long night and day would be over. He could get a little more sleep, and be ready for undocking and the trip back home. He was standing by #3 hatch, when the chief mate, whom he had not seen in days, came up to him.

"Okay, mate," he said to the youngster, "I've got the deck. You go up to your room and shave off your mustache, then go see the captain."

"What the hell are you talking about?" The mate thought that the older, chief mate had probably lost what was left of his mind.

"Look, you're a good shipmate. I don't care what you do ashore. There are people in the captain's office. They want to talk to you. Just do what I said."

"I still don't know what you are talking about. It's perfectly legal for me to grow a mustache, I'll be damned if I'll shave it off."

"That's not the point. See, there are some Japanese police aboard the ship, up in the Old Man's room. They caught a girl a couple of nights ago with drugs. She says she got the stuff from an American seaman. She described him as being young, medium height and build, sandy hair, blue eyes and a mustache. There were only two American ships in port that night - ours and one other. They are insisting on seeing anyone in the crew who resembles that description. The captain has to be honest with them, or they'll line up the whole bunch of us. Maybe you didn't hear, but our first night here they busted one of our messmen on the dock. He had some dope in a bag taped to the underside of his foot. They must have known he was smuggling. The result is that we're a hot ship now; they think we're loaded with the stuff. These people don't fuck around with drug dealers. The captain likes your work too, and doesn't want to see you in trouble. We're sailing tonight. If you get detained here, there's no telling what the hell can happen."

"Hey, mate, I don't do that shit. I'm not that stupid. I wouldn't risk losing my license to sail for a little dope, not to mention the jail time. Besides, two nights ago, I was here, on cargo watch from four to midnight. I signed the goddam logbook. If they caught her then, I'm in the clear. I'll go talk to them, but I'm not shaving." The 21-year old mate, with the blue eyes, the mustache, 5 foot 10, 165 pounds, and light brown hair that had bleached in the sun on the way across the ocean, went directly up to the captain's cabin. On the way, he realized that the night in question was the one he ran ashore at midnight, in the cab with Sparks and the two girls. He had stayed out all night. *If I need an alibi for after midnight, I might be fucked,* he thought. He would probably never be able to find that girl again, or the hotel.

He knocked on the captain's open door, per custom. There were two Japanese cops in there, in suits and ties. They were staring at him. The Old Man was stuttering, which he always did when he was nervous. The mate began to feel a little worried. *Did everyone assume he was guilty . . . just because of his age, maybe?* The narcs were very polite, and spoke English. Sure enough, they had caught a bar girl with drugs after midnight on the night the mate was ashore. He told them about the hotel, but did not know its name, or exactly where it was. It sounded fishy, even to him. He was beginning to wonder if he should have taken the chief mate's advice. *Nah, if they found out I just shaved, it would make me look even worse.*

After a few minutes, the captain apologized to him, but said the Japanese police wanted him to go downtown with them, and he would have to go. The engine cadet was going too. *Great,* he thought. The engine cadet was young, but short, heavy, and had red hair and a red beard. If they were the only two Americans in the lineup, which would you chose to match the description? He went to his room to change. He put on clean khakis, rather than shore clothes, and put on a pair of shoulder boards, which he hardly ever wore on this ship. He wanted the authorities to know he was an officer on the ship, not crew. It was very rare for an officer to smuggle, especially dope. They had too much to lose.

He and the cadet got in the back of the police car for the ride downtown. The mate began to worry a bit more. He knew that the Japanese were very strict. He had heard that they offered bribes, or lower sentences, for drug users to inform on suppliers. What if this mystery girl felt compelled to say he was the one anyhow? Would they give him a fair chance to find the hotel? With some time, and help, he was sure he could find it, and get someone there to vouch for his whereabouts, probably even give the name of his girl. Would the cops even bother for a stranger? *Yeah, that's the son-of-a-bitch; lock him up right away.* He began to fantasize about a Japanese courtroom. He would probably understand very little of it. Do they even give you a defense attorney? The goddam ship was sailing that night, what about that? Was the company or his union going to stand up for him, bail him out of all this? Maybe the judge had fought in the War, too, and hated all Americans. *Nuts*.

The engine cadet, in spite of his youth, didn't seem too worried. He had heard the description of the American too, and knew that he did not resemble it. If only the night they were concerned about was last night. The mate could find that girl, right in the electronics store where she worked. They would go there, the cops could question her, even go to the restaurant where they had that long meal. Their efficiency would force them to find the cab driver that would tell them about taking him back to the ship. The alibi would be complete. He imagined the local cops, in typical Oriental fashion, apologizing to him. These scenes all disappeared from his mind as they pulled up to the police building in downtown Yokohama.

He knew being an obnoxious American wouldn't get him anywhere. Demanding to call the U. S. Embassy wouldn't impress them. You were in their goddam country, and their laws were the rule. He decided to act a bit put out by it all, however. As they got out of the car and went in the building, the mate told the cops that he hoped this wouldn't take too long. He was 3rd in command of the ship, he told them, an officer with a lot of preparation to do for sailing. He puffed himself up a bit walking in, acting important. He had heard that Japanese respect authority, so he played up his importance to the ship, and how his record as a ship's officer was spotless. He failed to mention that his record as a ship's officer was only two months old.

The four of them went into the building, past the front desk, down a hall, and into a conference room. It was like a police station in the movies, except that he and the cadet were the only Americans there. They were the outsiders; they did not know what all the people there were saying, and had no idea what would happen. The mate imagined waiting for hours, then the cops questioning him repeatedly, and then going into one of those line-up rooms with the glass in front of it. As they went into the conference room, however, none of these things happened. There, in the corner of the room, a young Japanese girl sat quietly. There were two more detectives, in suits, in the room. One cop told the Americans to wait at one end of the room. The narcs from the ship went over to the girl. There was some conversation in Japanese, and then the girl looked at the two of them. No waiting. She was going to answer right then. The mate held his breath and looked back at her. She shook her head left and right. He exhaled. Then the cops asked her again. She looked at them a second time, and shook her head "no" again. *Thank God, she had told the truth.* The mate had heard many times that Japanese were very honest. It was against their cultural upbringing to lie, cheat, or steal. Still, people involved in drug deals in any country would probably do anything to lessen their problems.

Out of the room, back down the hall, out the door, and into the cop car; the same two cops took the two of them right back to the ship. There, they got out, apologized for the inconvenience, and bowed. They were so goddam efficient. The mate shook hands with them and said he understood they were doing their jobs. There were smiles, but still, he wondered what would have happened if the girl had pointed at him. Would he have been able to convince them, to prove his innocence? He hoped that would never happen to him. He had already heard many ugly stories about seamen getting into trouble in different countries.

They got the old freighter undocked a few hours later. Clear the dock, stow the lines below, sail down the bay, drop the Japanese pilot, and head out into the Pacific. It felt good to be back at sea again. The mate had mixed feelings about Japan and Korea, but he was glad he had gone there.

The seas were choppy the first couple of days, but there were no storms reported, and soon the ship settled down to the boring routine of standing watches and other normal chores. Some guys arranged movie nights, the cooks prepared the usual meals, and the 2nd mate calculated the great circle course for Panama. The mate would spend time off watch with his new radio, tuning in short wave stations from around the world, and getting used to having music in his room from his new tape recorder. Even the captain had some tapes to trade, and seemed happy that his young 3rd mate was not in a Japanese jail. Everything slowed down to the pace of the old ship, as it did sixteen knots across the ocean.

Heading back, as was customary, the chief mate directed the bosun and the deck gang to dress her up for arrival in the company's home port. The mate watched from the bridge as the work progressed. The first few days out, the chief mate asked him to steer the ship through any rain showers, if they weren't too far off course. He did this, although the heavier showers made him wince a little, wondering if there was a craft hidden in the rain. The idea was to get a free, fresh-water rinse of the old ship. It washed away salt and dirt. The sailors routinely washed down the ship leaving the last port, but they either used the fire hoses and pumps, which drew salty sea water, not good for steel, or used up tons of the precious drinking water that the engineers made on every watch. Rain was better. As the deck gang began to put fish oil on the deck, to prevent rust, and paint her up with decorative white coatings on the bitts and stanchions, the chief mate reversed himself and asked all the watch mates to avoid rain when the fish oil and paint needed to dry.

It seemed for days that all would be normal all the way home, but then the engineers had a serious problem with one of the two boilers the ship used to create steam for the turbines. They had to shut down the starboard boiler. The ship limped across the ocean to Panama on one boiler, doing about eleven knots. The older guys said it was like doing convoy speed in the war. The younger guys could not believe how slow they were going, since new ships at the time averaged about eighteen knots. The captain was stuttering again, since his schedule was way off, and, even though the chief engineer was the one to explain it, he was responsible. If they hit a bad storm, it would be more dangerous. If they lost the second boiler for some reason, they would be helpless in bad weather. However, the boiler and the weather held up. It just took 23 days to reach Panama.

Chapter 9: Guns in the Streets

Lykes Brothers Steamship Company, the owners of the ship, had arranged for some repairs in Panama. It wasn't that the ship couldn't make it for three more days to New Orleans, but the chief engineer had radioed in that he needed to work on the boiler as soon as possible. Besides, things were cheaper in Panama, including labor to help with the hot work in the engine room. The ship would stay at a dock on the Pacific side of the canal for two or three days. Before they got there, however, the guys on the ship who listened to their radios heard some news from Panama.

It seemed that a certain General Torrijos, of the Panama National Guard, had decided that he alone knew what was best for the country, and had seized power. In Panama, the National Guard was also the army, the state troopers, and the police. There were rumors of possible sabotage in the locks of the canal, but there were always such rumors. The U.S. controlled the Canal Zone, and there were American bases there to protect it. The canal was open for business. The change in the power structure of Panama caused a lot of debate on the ship, but the company decided to go ahead with repairs anyhow.

The American pilot came aboard and took the ship to a dock in Panama City. More than the typical number of officials boarded the ship, and it took a heavier bribe than usual to clear the ship's papers. There were armed guards on the docks. Many of them were young kids, eighteen or nineteen maybe, with rifles or automatic weapons. The sailors thought no one would allow them to go ashore. The troops might even shake the ship down, in a search for weapons that might be smuggled to anti-government rebels.

However, the Old Man passed the word that shore passes were available. Visions of bands of armed citizens roaming the streets, shooting at General Torrijos' troops, vanished. The word came down to be damn careful. They should stay off the streets at night, but the hotels and the whorehouses were all open as usual.

The crew split 50/50 on places to go. The young mate went with two of the other officers to the Hilton Hotel. They thought it would be safe. Riding in a cab, they came to an intersection where a young Panamanian soldier was stopping traffic. He had some kind of automatic rifle. He waved the cab over, and hollered for all to get out. He checked through the cab and then told the driver to open the trunk. The mate had not thought about it much, but, at this point, he wondered what would happen if this cabbie was part of some resistance movement, and had pistols in the trunk. The soldier was by himself, and about nineteen years old. If he got nervous, he could kill them all. The mate was glad none of the other sailors with him were drunk enough to make any stupid jokes to this kid with the gun. The cab was clean, and they went on their way. The streets seemed deserted.

Inside the Hilton, everything looked normal. The trio of ship's officers, the mate, Sparks, and the 2nd engineer, went to a bar and had drinks. The mate had a couple more drinks, and decided that he would play blackjack. Sparks tried to talk him out of it, but went along for the show when the mate wouldn't listen. He tried to tell him that you don't gamble when you're drinking, but the mate wouldn't listen. They went in, and the gambling rookie chose a table. He changed $20 and started betting $2 and $4 at a time. He got great hands. It seemed like he won all the time. Hand after hand, he took a profit, until eventually he lost a couple of times. Then he walked away. They went back into the bar. He paid for a round a drinks and felt proud of himself for walking away while he was ahead. Sparks, the old red-haired son-of-a-bitch, burst his bubble.

"You did real good in there, mate," Red said.

"Yeah, I'm about $35 ahead, and I walked out. I told you I wasn't drunk or stupid."

"Maybe not, but do you realize what you did?"

"Yeah, I won."

"You made thirteen straight passes at blackjack. You won thirteen hands in a row! Do you realize how much you could have won if you let your bets ride a little?"

"What the fuck do you mean thirteen in a row; were you counting?"

"Damn right I was; I was standing right behind you. You should have been keeping track too. You had beginner's luck. You didn't even know enough to double down on ten or eleven, and you still won. You could have won a lot more."

Now the mate felt badly. It showed.

"Look," Sparks said, "I didn't mean to criticize you. If you got too far ahead, they would have cheated you anyhow. Nobody leaves their bets alone for thirteen passes. It's just that you won't have luck like that all the time. Learn what the hell you're doing, that's all."

"Yeah, well, Sparky, old boy, let me tell you that you're a real no-good cocksucker, but you're a good shipmate, too, which is lucky for you, otherwise I'd have to kick your ass right here for ruining my good time."

"No problem, that's what I'm here for; to keep your young, stupid ass in line."

Another drink and they forgot the casino. At this point, the engineer was determined to go up the hill, to one of the clubs that was open. They decided that they could not let him go alone. The fact that Panama was a dangerous place even in good times, and there was a revolution going on didn't faze him a bit. The three of them got in a goddam cab. The engineer told the driver he wanted to see some girls, and off they went, to the suburbs, and up some lonely road.

The driver dumped them off in front of a large, two-story, old house. There was a large bar on the ground floor.

They went in, sat down at a table, and checked it out. It was even more degenerate than the Moulin Rouge in Brazil. The clientele consisted of drunken seamen, a few locals, and an array of girls who offered various sexual services for as little as five dollars. There were rooms on the same floor, right off the bar, where they would take you. The girls wore very little, and would flash the customers, or sit with you and let you check out the goods right at the table. Some of the crew was in there, plastered. The music was loud, and the place was dirty. It didn't do anything for the mate or Sparks, but the engineer liked some of the girls. The mate told him that he and Sparks were not staying long, and if he wanted to ride back with them, to make his mind up about what he was going to do. He grabbed a girl and disappeared into an adjoining room. He wasn't gone long, but the mate and the radio operator had to fend off the more aggressive girls. The mate gave out some cigarettes to keep the peace, but the rude ones called them "queer," in Spanish. The mate would tell them that they already had a girl somewhere else, and they just wanted to drink. He was glad when their shipmate returned, and they talked him into leaving. Christ, that guy was married, and they would be in New Orleans in about four days. Couldn't he wait? *These aren't the kind of beauties you made an exception for,* he thought. *Hell, to each their own.*

On the ride back to the dock, the engineer tried to talk them into going to one of the bars downtown. *Didn't this guy have enough?* The engineer talked about the Zamba Club, how they put on bizarre shows, even with animals sometimes. "Hell, you want to go see that, you keep the cab after we get out," the mate told him. *And what about the goddam revolution? Did he think he wouldn't have any trouble with that?* On the way back, a soldier searched their cab, as before, at an intersection in the downtown area of Panama City. They were moderately drunk, and he hoped nobody would say or do anything stupid. He felt lucky when they pulled up to the entrance to the docks. There was only a mild argument over the fare, and the mate settled it with a little gutter Spanish. The mate and Sparky headed to the ship, but the other sailor hesitated. The mate told him to forget it, and come back to the ship with them, but he headed back out to get the cab before it left. The unwritten rule was that you didn't leave your shipmate in a jam, even if he was being a jerk. He was sober enough. He made a conscious decision to go out to more bars. Whatever might happen to him now was his own problem.

The next morning, the mate got the report that repairs to the boiler were going along okay, and the ship would sail the next day. The only visit ashore he made that day was to the little duty free shack right on the dock. He bought a case of beer for the ride home, and a bottle of whiskey to take off the ship. The prices were good; a fifth of Johnny Walker Red label was about $1.30.

They got underway the next day, and made it through the ditch in about nine hours, about normal. The canal itself was an engineering marvel. Panama wasn't a place the mate ever wanted to live in, but the canal was worth seeing. The equipment used to pull the ship through the locks, up to the level of Gatun Lake, through that, then down to sea level on the other side, was already over 50-years old, and it all still worked.

When they dropped the pilot in Cristobal harbor, on the Atlantic side, went through the breakwater, and out to sea again, the mate was glad. Panama was full of poverty and revolution, and seemed like a dangerous place. There was talk, as there always was, from time to time, of giving the canal back to the Panamanians. To a man, the sailors were against it. It wasn't that the U.S. had such rights to it, but because they did not believe that such a corrupt, poor country could maintain and run it. Moreover, who would pilot the ships through? The mate thought that if the U.S. wanted to give it back, they should give it back to Colombia. *There was no country of Panama until we created it,* he thought. The land where the canal was had belonged to Colombia. We created the Panamanian government, supported it with military force, and broke it apart from that country. Still, if we hadn't, would there ever have been such a thing built?

The ship made it back to New Orleans without problems, and with all hands. It was the payoff port, and the entire crew signed off articles. Those sailing right out again signed on for the next voyage, along with the replacements for the crew getting off. The mate had a permanent assignment on the ship, and could have kept the job. Instead, he had given the captain notice to call the hall, and have the union replace him. The captain hated to lose him. Shipping won't always be like this, he said, the mate should stick with one company. Still, the mate was young, and wanted to go to different places. The Old Man understood, and they parted on good terms. The mate partied one night in New Orleans then caught a flight home to Jacksonville. He registered for work at the union hall there, and expected to use up his vacation time before he shipped out again. A couple of days later, however, the union hall dispatcher called him at home and told him that there was a ship docked in Cape Canaveral that was short a mate. He borrowed his Dad's car, drove down to the union hall, and took the job. *What the hell,* he thought, *it's a different ship.*

Chapter 10: Captain Charlie

It was late afternoon when he got home from the hall, on a Friday. He wasn't due to join until the next day. His Dad drove him down to the cape to join the *S. S. Seamar*. Two of his younger brothers, aged twelve and thirteen, went along. No one in his family had ever seen one of his ships. Most ships did not allow any visitors, out of lawyer-induced fear over injuries and lawsuits. At least they could probably drive down close to it, and the kid brothers could see how big it was; there was value in that. He was surprised when they drove right to the gangway, and walked aboard without a challenge. The new mate found his room, stowed his gear, and then saw the chief mate, to introduce himself, and give him his assignment papers. The guy was friendly to his family, and said they could all look around, if they didn't go out on deck. The mate was amazed -- this guy had a little class.

The Bethlehem Steel Company, in Baltimore, owned Calmar Steamship Corporation. They had five ships, and ran only from the east coast to the west coast in the states. They handled heavy pieces of steel, and the booms could lift heavier weights than most cargo ships could. They shipped out of Baltimore as a home port, went around some eastern ports, then through Panama to the west coast. Out there, they back loaded lumber for the eastern ports, and then took a full load of steel right at the company dock in Baltimore, at the Bethlehem Steel dock. It was back and forth, and no foreign ports; they went through the canal, but did not work any cargo there, and normally did not stop.

The family left and the mate took a tour of the ship. It had a hatch on the raised part of the foredeck, or "fo'c'sle," which was different from his other ships. It was fully loaded with lumber, and they would discharge it all up the east coast, and then go to Baltimore for a load of steel. The steel would be all types; pipes, plates, fittings, you name it. The crew seemed friendlier than most, typical for ships that sailed coastwise all the time. It was, in effect, like being on a tanker, without as much risk, and docking at piers closer to cities. The mate would learn that most of the guys on the ship were homesteaders, guys who worked only that ship. The young mate could see that if you wanted a steadier life, a job like this could be good. Still, he hadn't been to many places, in his opinion, and still liked the idea of sailing foreign.

The captain was making his last trip before retirement. Behind his back, everyone called him Captain Charlie. He had started sailing on square-riggers, as a boy, and still knew a lot about them. He was writing a book about that; he said he feared that no one would remember the old ways. He was like a kindly, old grandfather. The chief mate was a large, middle-aged guy who lived in the company's home port. He was a real family-type guy, and knew his business. The second mate was quiet, and the young, relief 3rd mate hardly saw him. The other 3rd mate was only three years older than he was, and had gone to the same maritime academy as the mate. They sailed the steam turbine, specially built cargo ship to New York, where most of the lumber was going to be unloaded. They spent one night in port, during which the two third mates went to a nearby, waterfront bar, and shot pool and drank too much beer. Even though Mark was older, the mate had to practically drag him back to the ship to get some sleep. He seemed as if he could drink all night, and enjoy it.

The next day on deck, watching the cargo operations, the mate was a little hung over. The unloading was almost finished in the afternoon, and, as he was the mate on deck, he went ashore to read the draft of the ship. The mate went down the gangway, and walked away from the ship, outboard of the two groups of longshoremen on the dock, who were still unloading the last few slingloads of lumber. He then went forward, fished his notepad and pencil out of his pocket, and walked towards the edge of the pier, to see the draft marks on the bow. As he slowed down to focus on the marks, a strange thing happened.

The sky suddenly went dark. It seemed like a giant cloud had just covered the sun. The mate heard yelling. He looked up. There, a couple of feet right above his head, a slingload of lumber swayed gently. It was about ten feet long, and four feet wide and deep. It must have weighed a ton. The lumber just hung there, swinging slightly. The mate was frozen with shock for a moment, and then got the hell out from under it. The longshoremen on the dock were yelling at him. He was abeam of number one hatch, the one up on the forecastle. The signalman on the deck of the ship was at the railing, looking down at him on the dock. He had two rolled-up pieces of newspaper, one in each hand. With these, he would signal to the winch driver, who could not see the dock, whether to go up or down with one winch, or in or out with the other. The signalman had seen the dummy walk right under the load of lumber, and given the signal to stop both winches. If he had not, the load would have crushed him to death right there. He would have been nothing more than a grease spot on the dock.

Shaken, the mate waved up at him, managed to still read the draft fore and aft, and went back up the gangway. He went up the foredeck to the guy at number one hatch who had saved his worthless hide, and shook his hand. He tried to offer him something, a drink, if nothing else, but the gruff-looking, dirty-clothed old guy just smiled. He just told him to be more careful if he wanted to keep going to sea. The mate went about his business, but felt stupid. He thought he knew his way around ships, but here was another goddam lesson; every ship is different in many ways. The biggest danger of going to sea was not storms; that happened, but many more guys were killed or injured in industrial-type accidents.

They sailed south to Baltimore, and docked at the company dock right next to the steel plant on the bay. They took on a full load of steel for the west coast. The mate was not familiar with the types of booms and rigging they carried. Most of the booms had ratings of ten tons, and some fifteen, which was more than usual. The steel pieces were heavy, and the ship had been built for it. They paid particular attention to securing the cargo down in the holds. If the ship got into bad weather, loose, heavy pieces of steel pipe could punch a hole in the side of the ship. His experience on the dock had made him more cautious. He was careful walking around the deck. He even wore the company-issued hard hat, although it wouldn't do much good if he got whacked with a steel beam.

From there, it was on to Panama. Sailing through the islands in the Caribbean was pleasant, although you had to be careful during hurricane season. They made the Windward Passage, off Cuba, and changed course for the tropical paradise of Panama. On the bridge, Captain Charlie treated the mates well. It was a nice change from some of the maniac, drunken skippers the mate had seen. Charlie would come up for a cup of coffee, check the navigation work, then sit in his chair and tell stories about the old days. He seemed to have confidence in his two young 3rd mates, and left them alone to handle traffic problems and course changes. It was all quiet and normal until they approached the Atlantic side of the canal.

Calmar Lines, because of their frequent trips through the canal, had a special arrangement with the authorities there. Their ships did not sit out at anchor, awaiting clearance and a pilot to go through. They sailed right in through the breakwater, picked up a pilot inside the harbor, while moving, and proceeded directly to the first set of locks at Gatun.

On this trip, they approached at night, on the mate's watch. Captain Charlie came up to the bridge about two hours out. It was his ship to take into the harbor. The mate had positions obtained from visual bearings of lights, with bearing and distance off points of land by radar. Charlie had done this so many times over the years, he knew all the points and lights by memory, and did not look at the charts. The entrance to the harbor was on a bearing of 180 degrees, due south. The canal did not run east and west, but rather north and south. The approach was to steer more to the southwest, and when you were lined up with the entrance, due south, you swung the ship over to about 185 degrees, to allow for the set of the current. Then, you adjusted speed and course to make the opening in the rock-piled breakwater. As soon as you were inside the harbor, you immediately slowed down some more, to allow the pilot boat to pull alongside. A canal pilot would climb up the ladder, go to the bridge, and take the ship the short distance to the first set of locks. Charlie had done it hundreds of times. The mate had only been through a few times, so he was still taking positions for the chart right up until they neared the harbor. Charlie was out on the port bridge wing, watching the lights and other ships moving around, or at anchor. He had the conn, and the mate's job was to check his handling of the ship, and inform him if anything was wrong, or if there was a problem with the ship, or traffic that required attention. They were still on sea speed, about eighteen knots, and rapidly approaching Panama, still steering to the southwest of the entrance, when the mate began to realize that something was indeed wrong -- very wrong.

If you drew a north-south line on the chart from Gatun locks, it would go right through the breakwater and outside the harbor. This was the true course for the harbor entrance. The mate had taken a fix with visual bearings on two lighthouses ashore, and drawn the bearings on the chart. Where they crossed was his location. If your gyrocompass was accurate, it was the best position you could get. The mate's position showed that the ship was already to the west of the line, and steaming at full sea speed for the rocks to the right of the entrance. If they did not change course soon, Calmar would own a wreck instead of a ship. *My position must be wrong,* he thought. *Captain Charlie would never have waited too long to make the turn.* He took the bearings again, and he took a position from the radar, with the distance off the breakwater. Hell, you could see the goddam space the entrance made on the radar screen, and they were definitely to the right of it. Every sweep of the radar showed the rocks closer and closer. The mate began to sweat. He had to convince Charlie, and he had to stay calm. He went out to the port wing.

"Captain, we're off course to the west. We missed the turn. I've got to swing the ship around right now."

"No, mate, that can't be. I'm watching the range lights on the locks. They haven't lined up yet. When they do line up, I'll come left to about 186. That'll allow for the current, and we'll slip right in."

The young mate ran into the wheelhouse and grabbed the binoculars. He searched through the maze of lights on shore to find the range lights Charlie was watching. Range lights are a pair of lights on land, with the one farthest away higher than the nearer one. When the two lights lined up, you were exactly on the range, or bearing, of the lights. The range of the first Gatun lock was due south, 180 degrees. When you got on the range, and steered a course made good of 180, you would then steam right into the harbor. Charlie had done it over a hundred times. He didn't need to look at the chart or the radar. The mate frantically searched for the range lights. The lower one was to the left of the upper one. This confirmed his positions. They were already past the due south line. The quartermaster was steering along, on the same southwesterly course the captain had given him. As the 22-year old mate literally ran from wing to wheelhouse to chartroom, the helmsman could see that there was something panicky going on. The mate checked the radar again, hurriedly. They had less than two minutes to turn. All his training and experience to this point beat one thought in his brain. *Act, and do it now, no matter what. Take the conn away from Charlie, fight the AB for the wheel if you have to, never mind who's legally in charge, argue about it later, do it now, now, now!* He grabbed the telephone and rang the engine room. The engineer on watch answered.

"This is the bridge. Bring her down to maneuvering speed now, as quick as you can; be ready to answer bells, and don't call me back; I've got a problem here!" He knew that if you told an engineer that you had a problem, the son-of-a-bitch would bust a gut changing the speed of the ship. He would know that he didn't have the normal time to get everything ready. The rocks were now less than a mile ahead, not much room for a large ship; hell, it would take almost half a mile to turn the goddam ship. He had no more time. The mate ran out to the port wing again.

"Captain, I don't have time to explain this. The lights are never going to line up, we're past the range. I need you to give me the conn right now!"

"Are you sure?"

"I'm goddam sure, Cap! I need to turn right now, there's no time left to check it again!"

"Okay, okay, do what you have to do."

He ran into the wheelhouse.

"Put your rudder hard right!"

"Hard right, mate?"

"Put the rudder hard right, and don't question my orders! I've got the ship!" Christ, that was all he needed, the quartermaster hesitating. Hell, it wasn't his fault, the captain had given him orders, now the mate was; he was confused as to who was in charge, and he knew there was something serious going on. Who would most people believe the experienced, wise old skipper, or the young mate who had just joined the ship?

"Hard right, mate, okay, hard right, she's going right." Any hesitation from him and the mate would have had to physically knock him off the wheel and spin it himself. As the rudder angle indicator swung to the right, the mate checked the distance to the rocks. If they couldn't make the turn, he would have to ring full astern and hope the engineer had enough time to change the speed of the ship. He knew that he had to open and close valves. He had to redirect steam from the ahead turbine to the astern turbine. They might not be ready. *Don't panic, stay with this,* he thought over and over. If this didn't work, he would ring the general alarm and wake up the whole goddam ship. He wasn't going to crash full speed into the rocks while sailors were asleep. *Wake 'em all up, and give them a fighting chance.* They might not just pile into the breakwater and stick there; the hull could easily burst open. The ship could slide off the rocks and sink right there, in shark-infested waters. He wasn't going to have sailors drown in their rooms. Stories of nautical disasters passed through his mind in seconds.

Captain Charlie came into the wheelhouse, but said nothing. The ship started to move faster, gaining momentum in the turn. They would clear the danger by a couple of hundred yards; it was way too close for a ship that was over two hundred yards long. The mate eased the rudder as they got abeam of the rocks. Charlie just stared out the window. Now the mate had to deal with the next part of the problem. They weren't alone in the waters off the harbor. There were several ships at the outside anchorage and a small one underway astern of him, also headed for the entrance. He ran out to the starboard wing to find a path between them. He would get clear of the anchored ships, make a large circular turn to the north, and then line up again for the harbor when he was clear of everybody else. He found a big enough gap between two of the ships to their right, took a visual bearing on it to get the course he needed to steer between them, and went back into the wheelhouse. He stood in the exact center of the ship, gave the quartermaster the course to steady up on. He would watch the steering like a hawk. Charlie was silent, apparently now convinced that the mate was right. He was letting him finish the turn, getting the hell out of all the trouble.

As they passed right between the two ships the mate had chosen, he could see clear water ahead and to the north. He gave rudder commands to slowly swing the ship to the north, then more to the east. He now had the ship turned around the opposite way from the normal approach to Cristobal Harbor. He checked the radar, and put a position on the chart. The mate figured out the distances and courses for a nice, wide path back to the original course line on the chart, to the north of the entrance and the anchorage. He also checked for ships coming out of the locks; that's all he needed at this point. Nothing was moving out of the harbor. He calmed down a bit; it was almost over.

Right then, the signal station on the hill in Panama began to flash at them with a blinker light. This was routine. Even though the ship had sent messages by radio, there was still an old signal station, and you had to answer them, and give them the name of the ship by Morse code. The mate checked the chart again, and saw that he had time to answer. He gave the quartermaster a new course, and went one deck up on the flying bridge to signal back. It would only take a couple of minutes, as his blinker skills were still good. He uncovered the signal light, turned on the switch, and opened the shutters. He trained his light at the signal station and gave the "answer" signal. The shore station blinked "What ship?" as expected. As the mate started to blink back the name of his ship, he felt the ship heel over to port. The lights on shore started to move rapidly to the left. He finished signaling, having to retrain his light on the shore station all the time. He looked astern. The ship was making a large, curved wake. They were turning sharply to starboard!

Did I miscalculate? Are we already at the point to turn and line up again for the due south path to the harbor? How the hell could that be? He looked at the lights on the shore and saw that they were not. They were still to the west of the range!

He ran to the ladder and down the steps as fast as he could, his mind now racing again with the goddam possibilities. If something had gone wrong with the steering engine or the rudder, they were screwed. The only hope then would be to stop the ship with the engines before they hit anything. Even if he did that, the current could drift them onto shore before they could get tugboats out of the harbor, put lines out to them, and have them haul them to safety. No, goddam it, that would take too long. He would call the chief mate on the phone, and get him to run up on the bow and drop the anchor, hell, drop both anchors. A mechanical problem was his immediate thought, but it also flashed through his mind that the goddam quartermaster was changing course on his own. He had seemed upset about the disagreement between the captain and the mate. Goddam it, if that was the case, he would have to take the wheel away from him, and when this was over, have him logged and fired. Hell, for something like that he would ask to have his goddam seaman's papers taken away. In the ten seconds it took him to get from the flying bridge down into the wheelhouse, the thoughts of steering gear failure or the AB going crazy were the two answers for the change in course that came to mind. But, when he got into the wheelhouse, he got the real reason. Captain Charlie was pacing back and forth in front of the quartermaster, giving him orders. He looked irritated.

"Captain, what's going on? Why did we change course?"

"Goddam it, third, I've been running down here for more years than you've been alive. The signal station always opens up on you from your port bow. The signal light was on the starboard bow; I turned the damn ship around to put it on the port bow, where it belongs. Now I'm going to line up the goddam range lights like they should be!"

With that, the Old Man went out to the port bridge wing again, to look for his precious range lights. The mate was stunned. He had thought they were out of it. A few more minutes, and he would have had the ship all lined up properly. Slow down, rig the pilot ladder and they could forget about everything. He hadn't convinced Charlie. What he said about the signal station was true, but not if you got yourself turned around, which was what had happened. Goddam it, if the light operator hadn't started blinking until he finished the circle, it would have been on his port bow, Charlie would've understood it, and the crisis would have been over. Now, it was worse than ever. The captain was convinced in his own mind that the young mate had fucked up, and put his ship at risk. The conn, the legal command of the ship had now passed from the mate to the captain, back to the mate, and now to the captain again. The poor bastard steering was in a state. He stared at the 22-year old in khakis as if he were completely crazy.

What now? Could he ever convince the captain a second time? If he had more time, the next move would be to get the chief mate up there, explain the situation, and let him talk to Charlie. The chief mate was second in command, and had sailed with Charlie for a long time. The problems with this were obvious. The chief mate did not stand a watch on the bridge. He hadn't for years. So, he might not be any more familiar with the lights than the mate was. *The lights, the goddam lights -- why didn't the captain take bearings or check the radar?* Secondly, there was no point in getting someone up there that would need ten minutes or more to study the charts, determine his own position, and then, if he agreed with the 3rd mate, not the captain, try to take the conn away from him. Hell, the chief mate might just talk to the Old Man and then assume he was right. What a scene that would be. Three of the four guys in charge of the ship would be on the bridge, standing right there, while they cracked it up on the rocks, destroyed it, and probably got some guys killed. What an inquiry that would make!

By now, the mate could tell where the ship was by just looking at the radar or the goddam lights on shore. However, true to his training, he again took bearings on known, charted lighthouses, and a position with bearing and distance off by radar. He hustled, sweating, into the chartroom, just aft of the wheelhouse, and plotted both fixes. Sure enough, they were right back where it had all started, to the west of the range line, headed for disaster. The only difference was that they were now on full ahead maneuvering speed, which was about sixteen knots, instead of the eighteen or nineteen they had been doing before. Big deal, that gave him a few seconds more before he had to turn again. And, as before, they were too far to the right to make a safe turn to port. There wasn't room. They had to make another wide turn to starboard, and run between the anchored ships again.

The good news was that the engineers were obviously ready to answer bells, to change the speed of the ship, ahead or astern, quickly. If nothing else, the mate could ring the telegraph. Neither the captain nor the helmsman would be able to counteract that quickly. He also decided that he would indeed ring the goddam general alarm before impact. He owed his shipmates that, no matter who on the bridge thought he was wrong. The bad news was that the captain was more confused than the mate had thought. It had seemed that, nearing 70-years old, his eyesight wasn't what it used to be, and he depended too much on seeing the range lights line up. Now it had gone way beyond that. He was very confused. At this point, he did not understand the lights, the turn, why the signal station appeared to be on the wrong side of the ship, nothing. The 3rd mate decided to give it one more try with Captain Charlie before grabbing the engine order telegraph, the general alarm, or the phone to the chief mate's office. He looked at the radar one more time. The ship was almost back to the original danger point, only they were farther to the west than the first time. Hell, that was because Charlie never let him finish the turn. Again, he had about two minutes to do something. He gave the helmsman a stern look, and went back out to the port wing of the bridge, where Captain Charlie was standing, watching his infernal range lights on the first lock at Gatun, which would never line up.

"Captain, I don't know how to tell you this, but you have made a serious mistake. This is your last assignment before you retire. If you don't give me command of the ship again, right now, you are going to wreck this ship on the rocks to the west of the entrance to Cristobal Harbor, and finish your long career with one of the worst disasters in maritime history. No one is going to remember you for your 50 years at sea. All they will remember about you is that you crashed a healthy ship, in clear weather, at full speed, in a place you have been to a hundred times. Guys below decks are going to get killed." The young mate had puffed himself up, and looked the skipper right in the eye, in the most serious way he could.

Charlie just looked him back. Precious seconds passed while the old skipper thought about it. The mate's mind raced again. There was no doubt what he would do if Charlie refused him. He would take the helmsman by surprise, and forcibly take the wheel away from him. The AB was a lot bigger than the mate was, but he was also a lot older. He could knock him down if necessary; spin the helm over, then go over the few feet between the wheel and the engine telegraph. He would ring up half ahead, and then see if they would clear the rocks, or if it was too late. If it was too late, he would keep the wheel hard right, ring up full astern, and sound the general alarm. He glanced away from Captain Charlie and looked across the bow. They were close to the rocks again. He started counting to ten in his head; if he got to ten and Charlie hadn't responded, he would carry out the plan. If they cracked up the ship, it would be in all the books. The legalities would include who was legally in charge of the ship and when. The mate had read *The Caine Mutiny,* and although it was fiction, it raised an interesting point. At what point is a junior officer justified in taking command away from the captain? He looked back directly at the Old Man as his count got to five. There were tears in Charlie's eyes.

"All right, mister mate. You've got the ship."

"Thanks, Cap'n. Now, I need you to tell the AB at the wheel to do what I say. He isn't going to believe me otherwise." The Old Man and the mate went back into the wheelhouse.

"Do what the mate says; he's got the ship." The poor AB was more confused than ever, but answered.

"Yessir, Captain."

"Put your rudder hard right!" The young mate used his "authority voice."

"Hard right rudder, okay, mate, yessir, she's goin' over. She's coming, mate, she's coming right." The mate realized he needed to calm him down. If he made a mistake with the helm now, all this would be for nothing. *What was this guy's name? John, his name was John.*

"Look, John, we'll be okay in a couple of minutes. We just have a little problem, that's all; it's nothing to worry about. Just do what I tell you."

"Ok, mate, no problem. She's coming over. Passing 230. . . 240. . . 250."

"Ease to 20!"

"Ease to 20, aye, ease the wheel to 20 right."

The mate stood in the center of the wheelhouse, watched the rocks pass to port again, and looked over to starboard, where he would have to pick his way through the anchored ships again. He ordered the wheel eased to ten degrees, then midships, putting the rudder straight astern. He took a bearing on the anchored ships, and decided to go between the same two as before. There wasn't room enough to pass between the rocks and the first anchored ship. As the ship's swing to starboard slowed down, he made it easy for John.

"Check her."

"Check her, aye, mate." John put some left rudder on to "check" the vessel's swing.

"Steady, now."

"Steady." Now John would use whatever rudder, left or right, necessary to keep the ship on its present course. They were aimed right between the anchored ships, but a little closer to the one on the port side than they were during the first circle. Captain Charlie had pulled up his chair to the window on the starboard side. He sat there and said nothing. The mate could not be concerned about him now. As the ship steadied, the mate looked over the port quarter, astern, and saw the wake of the ship wash up on the rocks. He began to breathe easier. Hell, a close call was one thing, but they just had two of them in a row, in the same place.

As the Calmar ship passed between the helpless, anchored ships, the mate went out on the port wing, since they were closer to that one. Guys on that ship had come out on deck, and some of them were yelling at him. It was a foreign language, maybe Italian, and he could imagine what they were yelling. Sailors sitting on an anchored ship know that they are a sitting target for an out-of-control ship. They must have thought he was crazy. He did not care. They got between the two ships again. Their wake rocked the anchored ships, but that was just too damn bad. In other times, the mate would have been embarrassed about that, but not this time. They had no idea what he was going through.

After passing the anchorage area, he again began a slow, wide turn to starboard. This time, if the goddam signal station opened up on him, he would not answer. He was staying right in the goddam wheelhouse, and not leaving it, not even to go to the chartroom. He felt he knew the area well enough. The only change on this second circle was that now there was a ship coming out of the harbor. The mate swung around to pass it port-to-port, and rang up half ahead. Charlie was still sitting there, confused. He would not be taking the conn back. The young mate realized that he now also had to bring the ship into the harbor, and pick up the pilot by himself. His confidence was up, but he could not relax. He had to handle the ship inside the breakwater, something 3rd mates almost never do. *No problem,* he thought. He picked up the telephone and called down to the AB on standby in the crew's messroom.

"This is the bridge. Rig a pilot ladder on the starboard side, two feet above the water. Then standby the ladder, and send the Ordinary to call out the deck gang for handling lines in the locks." It sounded good, but he had no idea if two feet was right for the pilot boat that would come alongside or if he was supposed to call out everybody or not. If they went directly to the first lock, that would be fine, if not, he had just awakened a bunch of guys for no reason. Well, at least they would be on overtime, and get extra pay. He had to think of everything, not just the navigation of the ship. He steadied the ship on a course of 185, allowing for some current, and headed for the opening in the breakwater. He passed the outbound ship with no problem, and then realized he had better check with the Panama Canal pilots. He picked up the VHF radio microphone from its cradle on the bulkhead.

He made contact with the pilots, who said that they were waiting for him just inside the breakwater, and wanted a ladder on the starboard side. *Lucky me,* the mate thought, *that's where my guys are rigging it right now.* He then noticed a couple small boats moving around near the harbor entrance. Hopefully, they had enough sense not to cross his bow just as he went through. In that case, there wouldn't be much he could do about them. *Guys in small boats had no idea what it took to stop a big ship,* he reasoned.

As the ship with all the steel cargo slid into the harbor, with the rocky breakwater on both sides, the mate went to dead slow ahead. That would take their speed down to about four knots, enough to steer the ship and allow the small pilot boat to get alongside them. The phone on the bridge rang, and the mate grabbed it, keeping his eye on the boat with the display of white light above red light, the signal for the pilot boat.

It was the Ordinary Seaman on his watch. "Mate, the ladder's rigged and the AB is standing by it. I just called out the deck gang for handling lines."

"Very well, Jose, good job." Thank God, things were going smoothly, finally. Captain Charlie still sat in his chair, silently watching. As the pilot boat approached from their starboard quarter, the mate went out to the wing to watch the pilot board. Normally, the captain would do this, but the mate had to keep going, to do everything that the captain would do, plus his own work.

As the boat pulled up to the lit up ladder hanging down from the main deck of the ship, the mate rang up stop on the telegraph that was out on the wing. This was in case the goddam pilot fell in the water; it was bad form to foul your propeller with the body of the pilot. All went well. Two pilots came up the ladder. *One is probably an apprentice,* the mate thought. When they were on the deck, he rang up dead slow ahead, to give steerageway to the ship. He went back into the wheelhouse, and adjusted course to head right for the famous range lights on the first set of locks at Gatun. As soon as the pilot made it to the bridge, he would be legally in charge of the ship, a peculiarity of the Panama Canal, and the mate would just be a mate again. His worries would be over, and, in half an hour, his watch would be over. Then he would grab a cup of hot coffee from the fresh pot in the crew's mess and go aft, to direct the part of the deck gang that worked there, handling the lines from the mechanical mules on the locks. It wasn't long before the two pilots appeared on the bridge. There was an older one, and a young one. The older one found the captain in the corner, and went over to him. The younger one, obviously an apprentice, started talking into his hand-held radio to the control tower at Gatun Locks. The pilot introduced himself to the Old Man, and they shook hands, as protocol required.

"Yeah, Cap, we were watching you come in. Saw you take a couple of round turns out there. Is everything all right?" He would, rightly, be concerned that the ship might have problems with the steering gear, or the engines.

"The ship is fine. I made a mistake. The 3rd mate there, he brought the ship in. If you need anything, talk to him. I'm going to my room." With that, Captain Charlie, one of the most experienced masters afloat, left the bridge. The mate avoided looking at him. No one except the two of them needed to know anything about it. When the captain was below, the pilot went over to the mate, who was now standing by the engine telegraph, and making entries in a workbook, to put in the official ship's logbook when he got relieved. There would be no mention of the extra miles they had just cruised.

"Hey, mate, what the fuck happened out there?"

"Well, pilot, we like Panama so much we decided to take a little extra tour of it."

The pilot read the mate's look. He understood.

"Yeah, okay, I understand. Good job, nice entrance into the harbor. How's the coffee?" It was a tradition to have fresh coffee available for pilots. It would be a long night for them and the deck gang on the ship.

"Well, there is no coffee; I've been busy. But if you have the ship, I'll put on a pot."

"Good, thank you, I've got her. We'll be going right into the locks."

The mate went over to the coffee pot they had on the bridge, and began to fix some. It would take eight to ten hours, if all went smoothly, to get through the 50 miles of Panama and out the other side. He would work overtime through the locks on the Atlantic side, then get some sleep, and then be on watch or on deck through the locks on the Pacific side. There was a lot to do with all that, but the mate thought that it would be easy compared to the last hour or two. For the first time, he had time to try to put it all in perspective. Hell, he only did his job, what he was trained to do. When he got relieved, he wrote up the log, with no mention of the "round turns," took a cup of coffee with him, and went aft. He passed the captain's room on the way and paused. His light was on, which was a good sign. The young mate wondered if old Charlie was depressed, embarrassed, mad at him, suicidal or what.

The next day, things on the ship seemed normal. They exited the canal and headed for the ports on the west coast. No one mentioned anything about the round turns. Off the coast of the Gulf of Tehuantepec, in Mexico, they watched the weather carefully. If there was a storm inland, and the winds blew across the narrow part of Mexico from the east side, the waves would build up in a hurry. Captain Charlie had been by this place many times, and knew that there was no sense beating the hell out of a ship in bad weather.

There was one change for the mate, however, on the northbound leg. The chief mate had started to give him some easy jobs to do when he was off watch. To "call him out" off watch meant a minimum of two hours of overtime pay. These little jobs included things like taking an inventory of the medical locker, checking lifeboats, doing some easy typing, and things like that. The chief mate also told him that the captain had decided that from now on, every time the ship docked, the third mate should go around and take soundings at the dock.

The mate knew the real reason for all this extra work. Captain Charlie had obviously told the chief mate to find some way of getting extra pay to the 3rd mate who had saved his butt and his ship in Panama. No one discussed it this way; they just understood it. As a result, he did not go ashore much, but stayed aboard most of the time in port, doing extra chores.

The trip south to Panama and up to the east coast went without incident. The chief mate continued to feed the young 3rd some easy overtime. Captain Charlie even asked him to look at the book he was writing, and to edit it. The mate thought that the book was too technical for most people, but hoped he got it published. There was valuable information in it, even though very few people would ever need to know how to rig sails on a square-rigger. Before they got back to the company's home port, in Baltimore, however, Charlie approached him with another idea.

Captain Charlie wanted the mate to visit the company's home office in Baltimore. He was to go see one of the executives there, and have kind of an interview with him. Calmar had an executive training program that was unique. They assigned their promising ship's officers to the office, to learn the shoreside aspects of running a steamship company. They also sailed part of the year on Calmar ships. The concept was to end up with company managers who knew the operations of their ships first hand. Eventually, if you succeeded, you ended up working ashore for the company. *So, this is Charlie's big payback.* He could see that this was a big deal to the captain, so he agreed. Charlie was happy, and told him to stop by and see the chief mate on his way below.

The chief mate had more news for him. He explained how he lived in Baltimore, and he wanted the 3rd to come to dinner at his house the night after his interview in the company office. He would get a good, home-cooked meal, he promised. The young mate could not refuse. It was a high compliment. The captain and the chief mate, two, permanent Calmar men, had talked it over and were trying to fix him up for a life with the company.

Back in his room, he dug through his sea bag, and luckily, found a coat and tie he had stuffed there. He had one good white shirt. He took the wrinkled clothes to the officer's laundry, fired up the iron, and pressed everything as best a sailor could. Then he went down to the crew's area and found the 2nd cook. Every ship seemed to have one guy who cut hair at sea, and Cookie was the guy. He agreed to give him a little trim that afternoon out on deck. Hell, he was going to have to shave, too.

The next afternoon the mate got dressed up and went up to the company office in Baltimore. It was a blur of meeting people, seeing the operations, and hearing all the good things about Calmar. Charlie must have really pumped him up to the bosses there. They explained the executive training program, and when it was all over, they told him that he was accepted. Just send a letter when you're was ready to begin, they said. There was no guarantee he would get through it, of course, but Captain Charlie had given him a running start. The mate knew that this was probably his once-in-a-lifetime chance. He also knew that seeing all those guys sitting at their desks, all dressed the same, with their suits and ties, answering the phone, and filling out paperwork, made him uncomfortable.

Back on the ship, he gave a summary of it all to Charlie and the mate. They were all smiles. They had paid him back for saving Charlie's ship and reputation. It was the best anybody could do, and they had high hopes for him. It was almost 1700, and the mate had a car on the dock. He would be ready to drive the mate to his house in 20 minutes. The 3rd went to his room to wait. He would keep the coat and tie on. He looked in the mirror and saw an office type guy staring back. He didn't look like a sailor at all. The tie around his neck began to feel tight, like a goddam noose.

The chief mate lived in the suburbs. On the drive out there, he talked about what a good company Calmar was, and how working steady for one line gave you all kinds of stability in life. They pulled into the driveway at the chief mate's house. It was what the mate expected, a nice four-bedroom brick house in the suburbs. The wife met them at the front door. She was very pleasant. The house had nice furniture, and was spotless. A huge meal was being prepared in the kitchen, and the dining room table was already set.

Then the chief mate's daughter came down to dinner. She was the same age as the mate. Now he really got worried. Showing him the advantages of a steady job for a company was one thing, but now the mate thought he was being set up with a young girl who understood the life of a sailor, and would make a good wife. *Were they planning his whole life out for him?*

After a couple of uncomfortable hours, the mate begged off, saying he had to get back. No problem, daughter will drive you, Dad said. There was no spark between them on the ride, and the mate politely rejected her offers to go to a club. He made up a lie about meeting up with a shipmate downtown, and had her drop him off in front of the Belvedere Hotel. Since he was dressed up, he went to the fancy cocktail lounge on the top floor, and settled in at the bar. He ordered scotch. *Hell, I don't drink scotch. What's happening to me,* he wondered.

He took a cocktail napkin and drew a vertical line down in. He wrote the positives of the Calmar program on one side, and the negatives on the other. The positives included things about steady income, promotions, security, pensions, respect, being home more, and opportunities in business. Negatives were no more foreign travel, and little adventure, the Cristobal harbor incident notwithstanding. It was no contest if you wanted to get ahead in life. He put the list in his pocket, had another scotch, which tasted terrible, and got a cab back to the docks.

The next day the mate went out on deck, as was normal, at 0800. He thanked the chief mate for the dinner as soon as he saw him, and everything seemed all right with him. He spent the morning hustling from hatch to hatch, checking the cargo loading, as usual. In the afternoon, he saw a bunch of people come aboard for Charlie's going away party. All the officers were invited, but he and the other mates had the deck, and would just stop by the captain's cabin for a few minutes. The mate went up there after a while, had one drink, mixed a little with the people from ashore, then asked Captain Charlie to step out on the deck outside his room for a minute.

"Captain, that executive training program is a wonderful opportunity. I know you did a lot to recommend me for it, and I really appreciate it. But, I can't do it. The thought of sitting around an office with a tie on drives me crazy. I wasn't cut out for that." He thought Charlie would be mad. The old skipper just smiled.

"The sea is in your blood, son, that's what it is. I thought that might be the case, but I wanted to do something for you. Once I retire, people will forget about me, and I won't be able to help you."

"Thanks, Cap. I was hoping you'd understand." *Hell, Charlie had run away from home when he was a teenager, to sail wooden-hulled ships. Of course he understood.*

"I need to go back inside. Smooth sailing to you, son."

"You enjoy your retirement, Cap'n, and don't forget to finish your book."

That was how they left it. The grandfather skipper and the kid mate never saw each other again.

Chapter 11: Any Other "-ism?"

The mate shipped out of New Orleans for several years. His life, of course, changed while he was ashore, and, like all seamen, different things happened at sea. There were good ships and bad. One of the only constants in his life was that he stayed a union sailor, in spite of a brief flirtation with the idea of going non-union.

Union hall shipping was different from most methods of obtaining work. New members paid a thousand dollars to join, and all active members paid quarterly dues as well. You didn't go for interviews with a goddam resume in your sweaty palms, you showed up for job calls. There were job calls twice a day, at ten in the morning, and two in the afternoon, or 1000 and 1400 hours. You had to be there in person to bid on a job, if one was available. If you didn't ship out, you could try for a night mate job at a separate call. Night mates worked only union, American ships while they were in a U. S. port. You worked an eight-hour shift, from 1600 to midnight, or midnight to 0800. On weekends, night mates covered the ship for all 24 hours, and had three shifts. The idea was to give the mates who sailed the ship a night off in port. It paid well per hour, but you couldn't snag a shift very often, maybe once a week if you were lucky. At times, however, it was the only money you could make for months at a time, and it helped keep you going.

The guys in the union hall fell into different groups. Some didn't want to ship out at all, and they played the night mate game as much as possible. Some guys derisively called them "professional night mates." It was never enough to live on, but sometimes you could get lucky, and get several nights in a row. When you got the 1600 to mid on a ship in port, you worked it those hours each night until the ship sailed. Many of those guys had wives with jobs, or they ran a small business ashore.

A second group was the guys who were laying for a specific ship to arrive that they knew would have an opening. They had to let their shipping cards mature. Your shipping card was dated and numbered, consecutively and chronologically. The oldest card got preference with jobs, since that guy had technically been out of work the longest. How old of a card it would take to get an assignment also depended on whether there were plenty of jobs, or next to none. How many new members the union took in every year, and how many old-timers retired was also a factor. Another group was the retired guys who still came to the hall and hung around; they seemed the saddest lot to the mate. He wondered why they didn't have anything better to do.

Another group was made up of guys who were ready to ship, but weren't broke yet. If a guy had an old card, he would not waste it on a short assignment, but would wait until he could get at least four months or so. Permanent assignments came up rarely, since guys who had these kept them for years. The last group would be the most desperate -- officers who would take any sea going job at all. Maybe they needed the money very badly, or were young guys without seniority.

Not all mates in the hall were equal. Rookies were class C; after they had a month of union sea time, they were B, after another year, group A. Group A sailors bid first on jobs, then group B, then C. When times were tough, nothing got through to B or C. Young guys would sometimes take night jobs ashore, in bars, or almost anywhere, kind of like out of work actors. They would take any ship, even a seven-day coastwise only job, just to try to advance to Group A.

Most hated of all were the guys who, exercising their rights, came in from out-of-town to ship. You had a right to go to any union hall in the country, but, naturally, local guys who lived in that port resented anyone flying in with an old card and taking a job away from them. Any stranger in the union hall was regarded with suspicion until someone got him talking, and found out how old his card was, and what his game was. The oldest card in the hall was called the "killer card." Everybody hated the guy with the killer card, and was glad when the son-of-a-bitch shipped out, or gave up and went somewhere else.

As the mate became more accustomed to all these written and unwritten rules about the hall, he began to notice other peculiarities. He had been going to the hall for months, unsuccessfully, looking for an assignment. It was the first time he had really hung around the old union hall in downtown New Orleans. Although he tended to associate with the other young mates, he kept an eye on the old timers. He noticed something strange. It seemed that there were some older mates who sat around the hall every day reading the racing form. They never bid on jobs, and some of them were retired. What they did, however, was disappear into the office of one of the union officials just before the 1:00 p.m. post time at the Fairgrounds, the local racetrack. They came out shortly afterwards, and when the races began, liked to go over in the corner and listen to the radio station that broadcast the races.

Even to someone who knew nothing about horse racing, it was obvious to the mate that the union official was making book right in his office in the union hall. Quietly, he asked some of the old timers about it. It was not only true, they said they liked it. It saved them a trip to the track, and, they said, he always paid off promptly if you won. The concept of paying dues to support this activity did not seem to bother them. The mate let it go as just another aspect of the profession, and hoped that if he lived to retirement age he would have something better to do than hang around the goddam, beat-up union hall placing bets with that guy.

Eventually, the mate happened to be in the hall when there was a union meeting. He had never sat through an entire one before, and decided to stick around after job call for it. The union officials kept implying that you should go to the meetings, if you weren't on a ship. He wondered if anyone kept track of attendance, or if anything bad could happen to you if you didn't attend once in a while. *Screw it, stick around for one, anyway, sign the list, it can't be too bad; maybe I can even voice an opinion or two,* he thought. He believed in unions, in general, and participation should be a part of it. He had walked out on other meetings in the past, as they seemed to always turn into gripe sessions, and contained some long, drawn out argument between a 'brother' and a union official. The disagreement was usually about some obscure union rule, or pension issue that he did not understand.

This particular meeting featured, in addition to the usual platitudes and bitching, the official swearing-in ceremony of newly elected union officials. Most of the elected were already in office; being an incumbent seemed to be an advantage here too, not just in Congress. He noticed that the bookie had been re-elected also; probably got a lot of votes from the horse racing fans. All of these proceedings seemed uninspiring to the mate until the officials, in unison, swore, out loud, to uphold the "Constitution of the United States, the Constitution of the Union, and to oppose Communism, Nazi-ism, Socialism, or any other 'ism.'" The mate could not let this go, and went up to the chief union honcho after the meeting. He politely asked this representative of his organization whether the oath the guys just took meant that they were officially opposed to patriotism, Catholicism and realism, things like that. After the blank stare and the expected "What are you, some fuckin' wise guy?" question, he was invited into the back office. There, he got a long lecture about the head-busting days on the waterfronts in the 1930's, when the union started. After the guy ran out of steam, the mate left, saying he appreciated what the old guys did in those days, but that he still thought they ought to get rid of the "ism" crap in the oath of office.

He sometimes went up to New York to ship. That union hall was larger, and older. It was located in the southern end of Manhattan, within walking distance to South Ferry. Right at South Ferry, the southern tip of the island, was the Seamen's Church Institute, where a seaman could get a small, clean room cheaply; it helped keep you afloat, but it wasn't a party. You could have no visitors in the room, the place closed early, and at night, there wasn't much around there to do. McAnn's Bar was the only joint around, and it was for drinking, not much else.

The main room of the New York hall was full of old, mismatched furniture, and ashtrays. There were offices upstairs, and a small room that had one pool table and some lockers you could rent to stow things in. There was a window between the main room and the dispatcher's office. There, dispatcher Lenny would call out the jobs twice a day, offshore work first, if any. He started the bidding on the assignments with the call, "Hear your numbers, please!" Each shipping card had a number on it. They were consecutive, so that the older your card, the lower your number. Lenny would holler something like: "Third mate, 180 days, on the American Archer, hear your numbers, please," and the bidding, just like an auction, would begin. You shouted out your number, and Lenny repeated it, then other guys would yell lower numbers, and he would repeat those too, until there were no lower numbers; then, like an auctioneer, he did the: "Going once, going twice, gone!" routine.

The problem with this method was trying to figure out what to do if there was more than one job, on top of the usual problems wondering if you should bid, say, on a two-month job, when you really needed four months. Would something better be on the board tomorrow? When there was more than one job, you might have the lowest number that would be bid on the first job called, but pass it up because the second was a better one -- longer job, more pay, or going somewhere you wanted to go. If you passed on the first one, however, then got beat by a guy who was waiting for the second job, you went home, or to the Seaman's Institute, empty-handed. It was no work, no pay, and another day of expenses in New York. You would call home again from Seaman's Church and try to tell your family that things would be better tomorrow, all the while sick to your stomach, worried about bills and kids, knowing that you could have been on the payroll that day if you had played it the other way around.

When shipping was bad, more guys would be crowding around the bulletin board where the job listings were, next to Lenny's window. When Lenny tacked up a job sheet, 25 or 30 guys would crowd around it. With two or three minutes until the official call, the tension would mount. *Who's that cocksucker? Does he have me beat?* Shipping cards in those days were good for two years. If you didn't ship out in two years, the card expired, and you had to get a new one, putting you at the bottom for bidding. There you'd be, with, say a nine-month old card. You hadn't shipped in all that time, and could reasonably expect to get at least a four-month assignment. But, you never knew who had a card that was nearing its expiration, and the son-of-a-bitch would throw in on a short job because he had to use it or lose it. It was all a gamble. The mate saw guys beat out for a job by a guy who had registered for work on the same day, but minutes before, thereby getting a lower number. Even tough sailors sometimes looked sick when that happened.

As the years went by, the mate got to know most of the regulars in the halls. Eventually, little groups formed, and sat together. The guys who lived in the port stuck together, and acted as if they owned the union. Younger, academy graduates tended to hang out together, and would go out at night drinking, or hang around the Institute shooting pool. Hard-nosed seamen who had come up the hawsepipe, working their way from crewman to officer, were another group. The alcoholics tended to find large chairs in the corner and sleep most of the day. There were also the loners. These were the guys most likely to beat you out, if they had come in from another port. "Check his dues!" was a typical cry when some stranger snagged a good job, in the faint hopes that the bastard wasn't up to date on his union dues, and could not only be denied the job, but have to reregister to ship, and go to the bottom of the list.

The mate also learned about the various job advisors who always seemed to be present at job calls. These guys would appear at your elbow a minute or two before Lenny did his act, and ask you if you were going to bid on a particular job. If it seemed you were, comments would follow from your new friend, the advisor:

"The captain on that one is a real mother-fucker. Tries to get every new guy fired."

"That thing is a goddam rust bucket. Goin' to the bottom anytime."

"The food on that ship sucks, and there's no overtime. You can't make anything."

Advice like that was frequent and free. At times, it would be amazing to see, a few minutes later, the same helper biding on the ship he had just tried to talk you out of.

It did make sense, however, to try to handicap the process. If you hung around with the young guys' group, you would learn from each other who had what card, and what they would throw in on. Guys would share information that they had about other sailors in the hall; for example, if a guy bid on a job and missed, you would then know what his number was. From then on, if that guy looked ready to bid, you would know ahead of time if he had you beat. After you had sailed with a guy, he became your old shipmate. Guys didn't fuck around with an old shipmate much, and you generally got truthful answers or advice from them. Some of the old timers were actually very helpful to younger guys they had sailed with, and respected. They would tell you what they knew about the ship, the company, the captain, and who else in the hall might be bidding on the job.

After the last job call of the day, most sailors went on their way. Those that had shoreside incomes, from a business, or from a wife who had a good job, were always in a better mood than the poor bastards who desperately needed to ship out and couldn't. Some guys hung around the beat-up hall until it closed at 1700. Some of them simply had nowhere else to go. Others sat in quiet agony over their state of affairs, hoping for a pierhead jump. These were supposed to be "emergency only" replacements for a ship that was sailing that day. Sometimes it appeared that these rare jobs were not just unusual, good luck, but perhaps something else. The ship would still be in port the next day, and the guy who took the job ten minutes before the hall closed, when there was no one else around to bid on it, was an inside guy who knew everybody, especially the officials. Nobody ever seemed to see anyone offering up a bribe, or anyone taking one, but everybody suspected it happened here and there. It was, after all, a waterfront union.

As the years went by, the union changed the method of bidding on work. Cards were good for only one year, long enough to be without a ship if you needed one. And, instead of calling out numbers one job at a time, there was a different system. Before job call, anyone who was interested in shipping put his card in a box on the dispatcher's counter. Lenny put them in chronological order, oldest first. Instead of calling out jobs, he called out your name. You could pass and take your card back, or you could take whichever of the jobs posted were still open. It was a much better, fairer system, but it lacked the color of the old hustle method. When shipping was plentiful, the mate did not worry much. If you missed a job one week, you could tell by the numbers that were getting out, that you would go soon. There would be enough money to send home sooner or later. Guys were friendlier in the hall, not so cutthroat. Guys would have a beer with you after job call, and you didn't need to spot anyone; everyone had cash.

The union was wonderful. But, these times went in cycles. The good days were good, and the bad days were hell.

During the mate's twenty years in the hall, he would see the number of jobs available decline for a variety of reasons. The 250 ships reactivated in the late 1960's for the Vietnam sealift were laid up again, or scrapped, by 1972. Another 200+ ships from WWII that had stayed in commercial service got so old they were also cut up into razor blades, as the old sailor's expression went, by 1973. When the oil companies learned (from the closure of the Suez Canal) that they could sail a huge tanker with a smaller crew than before, increasing profits, the break bulk carriers took notice. The era of the containership, and its increase in size, meant that you could replace three old ships with one new one; fewer jobs again. Many of the WWII era mates retired, but most all the new Vietnam era ones were still bidding on jobs. Then companies like Delta and Keystone went non-union, and were not replaced by new outfits. United States Lines, once perhaps the proudest American company, with its sleek passenger ships, went bankrupt in 1986.

Further, some American companies sold out to foreign ones. All American merchant seamen, officer and crew, suffered then, even the non-union seamen, as well as those who belonged to that curiosity, "company unions." When Easy Money became a mate, Sea Land had 21 U. S. flagged ships. Sea Land sold out to foreign-owned Maersk Lines, and then there were none. The U. S. government operates some ships for MSC (Military Sealift Command), but these jobs are non union, as well as being few in number. Some foreign countries would let an American sail their merchant ships or would issue you a license of their own. This was not a realistic option as you would risk losing your union pension for that. Plus, they paid less and had less vacation time.

The other good thing about having plenty of work in the union hall was on the other end of the employment picture, when you wanted to leave a ship. You had the right to quit, with 24 hours notice, in any U.S. port. If times were good, you wouldn't have to sail on a rotten ship, or work for Captain Attila. You would know you could ship out again soon. "Call the hall, I'm getting off this mother-fucker!" was the normal method of informing senior management of your decision to seek employment elsewhere.

On board a union ship, more than one organization supplied crewmen. The deck officers had their union, the engineers theirs, the radio operator belonged to his, and the whole crew was from yet a different union. Captains on union ships technically belonged to the deck officer's union, but in reality were company men. They, and the chief mates, were permanently assigned to a ship by the company. The watch officers, the 2nds and 3rds, came out of the hall, and were either permanent or relief. It was curious to the mate to hear some captain complain about labor costs, or union rules, when, in fact, he had risen through the ranks in that company from the union, and owed his high wages to union negotiations.

Every once in a while, the mate thought about shipping non-union. If union officials caught him sailing non-union, he would lose his union rights forever. When you first sailed, you usually made a decision to go union or company. If you went company, you applied for a job just as you would ashore. You went for an interview, and if hired, they told you when and where to report for your ship. You usually worked the same ship off and on for years, changing with a promotion to a higher grade, perhaps to a different ship. Some of the oil companies had company unions, which seemed to the mate to be some kind of anachronism, and, being another "ism," it was something any good union man would oppose. Maybe it was just a way for the sailors to have a meeting once in awhile, and feel like they had some say in things, when they really had none. If you wanted to see the world, the union offered more choices. As a young man, the mate didn't think too much about the future; you never knew if you would live until retirement anyway. What did he care, in his early years, about stability? Besides, it was exciting to be standing around the job board, just after Lenny posted an assignment, with your palms sweating, pulse racing, eyes shifting around to the bastards who would cut your throat to beat you on a good job. You stood there, wondering if you were going to get 'out' or not, and how would the ship be, and what would happen to you in the places it was going.

Chapter 12: We Are Not In Galveston!

One of the ships he caught out of New Orleans was an old steamship called the *Jesse Lykes*. It was one of the older Lykes Brothers Steamship Company's ships, named per tradition after a member of the owning family. It was known as a C-2, had five hatches, and was 459 feet in overall length. It made 28-day round trips to the Caribbean at fifteen knots on a good day. It had been built in 1945 and showed its age. It would go to Puerto Rico, Santo Domingo and Venezuela, the last two places ones he had not been to before, and that interested him. As long as you didn't get a hurricane, the Caribbean was good sailing.

He found out quickly that this captain, the old man, the skipper, the master, whatever you called him, was a washed up, drunken, no good, son-of-a-bitch. He should have retired or quit, or the company should have fired him years before. He reminded the mate of Captain One Lung in appearance and demeanor, but unlike One Lung, he did not take care of the ship, as he was never sober long enough to have the slightest idea what the hell was going on. People ashore might wonder how a ship can get around with such leadership, but it was simple. The watch mates, the 2nd mate and the two 3rd mates, took care of the ship. A couple of good engineers and mates was all you really needed to get a ship from point A to point B, provided that damn thing floated with the stack up and the screw kept turning. On the *Jesse Lykes*, that was all that worked correctly.

Their first port out of New Orleans, on the coastwise, was Galveston, as they were loading cargo for the islands. Captains always come up to the bridge about an hour or so before picking up the pilot, to maneuver the ship, and make sure they find the sea buoy without going aground or hitting anything. On the *Jesse Lykes*, the mate had the 8 to 12 watch, and was navigating on the night watch, through some oilrigs that were not on their chart. When they were about an hour out, he called the captain on the old sound-powered phone, but he hung up on him. He checked the night orders, and there was a scribbled note from the captain to make sure he called him for the pilot pick-up. The mate called him again. The captain swore at him this time, and hung up again.

The 2nd mate, a middle-aged, experienced seaman, happened to come up to the bridge for coffee, knowing that the AB would call him out for docking soon anyway, and not wanting to bother going to sleep. The mate had him take the watch for a minute, and went down personally to the captain's cabin. He was mad. *You want me to "make sure," you bastard, I'll make sure,* he thought. He banged loudly on the door, then opened it and went in. The captain was lying in his bunk. The mate went over and shook him by the shoulder.

"Captain, we're making arrival in Galveston in less than an hour."

"We are not in Galveston! Get the hell out of here!" was the reply. Then, the drunk rolled over and went back to sleep. The mate had never seen such behavior before, not even from One Lung.

Back on the bridge, the mate told the 2nd about it, and took command of the ship again. It was standard practice to have two officers in the wheelhouse approaching port, so he figured he had better call the next in command, the chief mate, and get him up on the bridge. He called him on the phone. The chief mate said that his job did not include navigation, just cargo work, and he did not want to come to the bridge. The mate couldn't believe his ears. Chief mates will always cover for the captain. He figured he could handle the ship, but he had never taken a ship to Galveston by himself. It created an unnecessary risk, letting a young third mate handle the ship. *Screw it, it's good practice for me,* he figured, and asked the 2nd mate to officially turn to and call out his watch to rig a pilot ladder. The 2nd mate, being next in line, offered to stay on the bridge and help maneuver the ship, but the 3rd declined the offer. He wanted to handle the ship alone.

He notified the engine room to be ready to maneuver in half an hour; when the engineer reminded him that they were supposed to get an hour's notice, he told them that he had problems and hung up the phone. Just like on the Calmar ship, he knew any engineer would do anything to get the damn engine ready, not knowing if you were going to have a collision, run aground, or what. On this ship, the engineers knew that the captain was no good. He turned his attention back to the rigs that weren't on the goddam chart because the permanent 2nd mate had not kept it up-to-date. It was easy to avoid them, but there were also buoys around, with flashing lights, and he had no idea what they indicated. He swung around all of them, not taking any chances. He called the Galveston pilots on the VHF and gave them an approximate time for arrival at the sea buoy. Then he had to find the damn sea buoy in the maze of lights spread out before him on the horizon. The low land around there didn't make good radar targets, so he backed up his radar work with visual bearings from a couple of lights on land that he could identify. The ship wiggled and waggled a bit, but he picked his way through the lights, the buoys, the fishing boats, and God knew what else, slowed her down, and pulled up near the buoy. He found the lights of the pilot boat, and turned the ship to provide a lee for it, per seamanship traditions. When the pilot got up to the navigation bridge, he looked around for the traditional greeting he should give to the captain. Only the young mate was there.

"Is the Old Man around, mate?" He asked.

"Nope. He is, ah . . . indisposed."

"Okay, I got you. You bring the ship in?" He could see that the mate was young.

"Yeah."

"Good job. We were watching your approach; a little crooked here and there, but not bad at all."

"Well, I've only done it once before. I could probably use more practice, and on this goddam ship, I'll probably get it."

Things didn't get any better when they left the states for the short run to Puerto Rico. The food on the ship was terrible, and the chief steward didn't care; a haze of purple smoke emanated from his room at night. The radio operator was an old bastard who drank with the captain, and didn't take care of his work. He would disappear for days at a time, with the doors to his room and the radio shack locked all the time. The chief mate was incompetent, the captain stayed drunk, and the old ship seemed to be falling apart. The ship was not air-conditioned, which was no big deal to a sailor, but the porthole scoops everyone had for getting air to flow into their rooms had no screens. Every time they got into port, the ship seemed to fill up with flies. It was a hot, sweaty, muggy, dirty ship. No one seemed to make any effort to fix anything. As long as the damn thing moved from port to port, nothing else mattered.

When they arrived off the entrance to San Juan, they had to wait for a pilot; the pilot office said they did not know the ship was coming. It was late afternoon, and the 2nd mate had the watch. The 3rd mate was up on the flying bridge, one deck above the bridge, getting some sun. The 2nd came out on the wing of the bridge and told the mate that the captain had made a rare appearance on the bridge, and was mad that they had no pilot. He had ordered the chief mate and bosun up to the bow to prepare to anchor the ship. He wasn't going to steam around slowly waiting. Then the 2nd came back on the wing and told the young, 3rd mate that the captain was ordering him to tell the chief mate to drop the anchor. This would have been fine, except that the water gets deep quickly off the island of Puerto Rico, and they were in a thousand fathoms of water. The 2nd and the captain were arguing. The mate understood the problem immediately. If you dropped anchor in deep water, the weight of the hook and its chain would cause it to keep going until there was no more chain. Then the bitter end of the chain would be ripped off the bulkhead in the chain locker, and the end would come tearing up the pipe, over the anchor windlass, whip around the bow, and anchor and chain would go to the bottom. The brake would never hold against all that weight; it would burn up. The 2nd was at wit's end with the captain.

"Screw it, 2nd; tell the stupid chief mate to drop it and run. I'll be your witness that the captain ordered it. When we get back to New Orleans with no port anchor, let the bastard try to explain that!"

"That's what I'm thinking, but somebody could get killed. I can't let that happen."

The 2nd called the bow and told the mate not to use the anchors no matter what the captain might say. The captain got mad and left. He went back to his room, and no one saw him for two days.

The young mate and the older 2nd went ashore together in San Juan. They got up to one of the fancy hotels on the beach, and went into the bar for a drink. The mate had gambling on his mind. He had more cash than usual on him, and, based on his initial gambling experience in Panama, felt that he couldn't lose. The 2nd tried to interest him in tourist girls in the bar instead. There were two girls, he said, sitting right behind them that looked like a couple of secretaries from New York who were down for a weekend party on the beach. The 2nd knew his way around the islands, having been a mate and captain with Windjammer Cruises. The young mate would not listen. He figured to win a couple of hundred upstairs first, and then they could chase all the tourist girls they could find. They went to the tables.

The result was predictable. His winning in Panama had indeed been beginner's luck. He started losing. The 2nd tried to pull him away, but he would not leave. He did not know all the odds and bets available, and could not count the cards. The free drinks made it worse. He lost $150. They went back to the hotel bar. There were no tourist girls in the bar, or in any of the other clubs they went to. Then the older sailor took him down to Old San Juan. That section was the real downtown area of the city, the part originally settled centuries before. It was between the fort that guarded the entrance to the harbor, and the cruise ship docks. The bars they went to were more like the run-down waterfront ones he had seen before. There were no tourists in them, and the only girls they saw were plying the old trade. The mate felt stupid for wasting his hard-earned money, but at least he was still single and had not blown the rent money. The older sailor seemed to understand it, and treated his young friend like a kid brother.

They talked over sailor stories at bar after bar in the old city. The 2nd told him about his years working sailing vessels for Windjammer. The best story was about a couple that sailed with him to the islands, and the wife had started sneaking into his cabin at night. She wanted the 2nd, who was captain on that ship, to push her husband over the side and kill him. There would be a lot of money involved. It was the easiest way to murder somebody, he said. As long as no one saw you do it, it was clean -- no body, no evidence. All you had to do was wait until the ship was rolling. It would be determined that the stupid passenger must have gone up on deck and fallen overboard. Guys fell over in bad weather all the time. However, the 2nd had refused her, finding just enough conscience and sense to resist her. He said his main concern for the rest of the cruise was that she would manage it without him, and then blame him anyway. He had to take extra care with the husband to make sure he was all right all the time. He laughed about it.

They ended up in a real dive down near the old docks. It was on the second floor, in a large room with a circular bar. In the middle of the space behind the bar there was a round platform, on which was a steel drum band that played like crazy, while the whole thing slowly rotated in a full circle. Around the outside of the bar, young girls made their own circuit, asking for cigarettes, and brushing body parts up against the patrons. For ten to twenty bucks, they would take you next door to a fleabag hotel. The whole place was about as opposite as you could get from the fancy hotel where they had started. The mate kept eyeing one girl in particular, who had long legs and a very short skirt. The 2nd knew his friend was broke, and offered to spot him a twenty.

"Here, take this, and go next door with that girl and have a good time. Forget about the casino, the ship, the captain, and everything else."

"No thanks. If I do that, I'll feel even worse tomorrow. I don't really want her anyway. I just liked her outfit, that's all." They went outside and got a beat-up cab for the ride back to the rust bucket.

They went to Santo Domingo. It was hot, and more flies joined the ship. The people seemed very poor, and it was a hassle to go anywhere without beggars following you around. The mate was glad when they left, and went on towards Caracas. The next morning, at sea, the mate got violently sick on the bridge, during the morning watch. He threw up several times. The second happened to come up for coffee and saw how bad he looked. He insisted the mate go below, and took over the rest of his watch. The mate had never missed work at sea, not even for one watch. He felt as if he was going to pass out, and he went to his room and slept all day.

He dragged himself out of bed for supper at 1700. He went in and tried to hold down a bowl of soup. The captain was there, glaring at the young mate the whole time.

"Is something the matter, captain? You're staring at me."

"You stand your goddam watch tonight, mister! I don't want to hear any crap about being sick!" He glared some more.

The miserable bastard really hates me, the mate figured. He couldn't believe it. He and the 2nd mate had been doing his job, preventing him from grounding the ship or worse, and here the cocksucker is, yelling? The mate stood up and faced him.

"Listen, you worthless bastard. I'm sick as a dog. I've got food poisoning from eating on this ship, and have received no medical attention. I'll stand my goddam watch if I can stand up. You can just go back to your room and stay drunk. I'll let you know when we reach Galveston."

The captain had no response. He wasn't used to anyone talking back to him. The mate left, but within minutes, the chief mate, the official medical officer on that ship, showed up at his door with a thermometer. The captain told him to check on him, he said. The mate took the thing and took his temperature. He read it himself before handing it back to the chief mate. It showed 103 degrees. The boss mate squinted at it, and shook it down.

"You okay. Everything normal."

"It's 103, you dumb bastard. Get the fuck out of my room!" The mate began to count the days left until they hit the U.S. He wasn't going to wait for the official end of the voyage; he would quit in the first U.S. port, as allowed by union rules.

The mate and the 2nd began to communicate more with the crew. All kinds of violations of rules were occurring on the ship, but the ones that affected the crew would carry the most weight. One officer complaining about another one, to the same union that represented both, did no good. But, the crew was NMU, or National Maritime Union, and their union was strong in those days. Each department, deck, engine and steward, had elected a representative for the trip, as they always did. They had been keeping a log of all the problems.

The mate found out that one of their complaints was that the chief mate had taken a bag of rice out of the cargo hold, and given it to the chief steward with orders to use it for food, to save the company money. The mate fed them other stories, all true, including how the captain and chief mate had refused to come to the bridge, and risked getting the bosun killed with the anchor chain.

He got uptown in Caracas, but didn't feel well enough to see much of Venezuela. It was too bad; he had liked the looks of the place. He did buy a couple bottles of the 150-proof rum he had heard about, and a case of cola for the trip back. He had a few limes he had picked up in Santo Domingo, and he, the 2nd, and the engineers would party a little on the way home. The mate felt lucky that the ship was not on a Far East run, and would be gone for months.

On the way back, the company routed the ship to Houston. The company said they would take off all the cargo there and lay up the ship. "Lay up" meant that they had no immediate plans for the ship. They would lay off the whole crew. Relief guys would reregister for work in their respective union halls, and ship out on something else. Permanent jobholders could retain their rights to rejoin the *Jesse*, if she ever sailed again. Scuttlebutt was that the ship was in such bad shape that Lykes Brothers might scrap it. The mate and the 2nd broke the seal on some rum and celebrated.

The ship would dock in Houston on Christmas Eve. Many guys on the ship had family close enough to Houston to come get them. They made up telegrams to send, and slipped them under the locked door to the radio shack. The mate sent one to his new girlfriend in Corpus Christi, Texas. He had met her in New Orleans, when she took a vacation there at Mardi Gras time. He thought about her long, black hair, and how it looked laying down her bare back all the way to her waist. That image could make him forget the ship. She could drive up, and he would spend Christmas with her, maybe even go meet her family in Corpus. The mood on the whole ship picked up. Being out of a job didn't seem to matter. Everyone hated the ship, the captain, the mate, the steward, and the food, so who cared? After the 2000 to midnight watch, the mate went below, and decided to celebrate with another drink. He opened the drawer where he had put the recently opened bottle of rum. It was gone.

In port, you always lock the door to your room. Not at sea. You don't steal from a shipmate -- that was the tradition. The officers also left their rooms unlocked during the day so the BR, the bedroom steward, could clean it, or change the linen. But, the mate looked everywhere, and the bottle was gone. He opened his locker, which he had secured with a padlock, and took out his other bottle. He sipped a drink, trying to ignore the stifling heat and humidity, and wondered what could have happened.

He casually mentioned it the next morning to the 2nd, and of course, he hadn't been in the mate's room. He learned, however, that the radio operator had not been seen by anybody in a couple of days, and the AB on his watch told him that Sparks was on a hell of a bender. Rumor was that the guy wandered around the ship at night, sneaked into rooms of guys who were on watch, and stole their booze. The mate stepped back behind the chartroom, and pounded on the door to the radio shack, hollering for Sparks to open up, but got no response. The other AB on the 8 to 12 watch told the mate that this had happened to other guys in the crew, and that everyone below decks was locking his door. A drunken thief is still a thief, and no one liked it.

They got back to the pilot station off Galveston Bay at night. You picked up the pilot for Houston in the same place as Galveston, since you passed Galveston to steam up the Houston Ship Channel. It was the shortest foreign trip he had made, and the worst. The pilot who came aboard said his office had no radio notice that the *Jesse* was due.

When they got up to the dock, near the end of the channel, close to the turning basin, their dock was dark. There were no line handlers ordered, and the tugboats that worked the ship had not received any notice either. Somebody finally got up from a tug to the dock, and put the eyes of their lines over the bitts on the dock. This place was close to Interstate 10, yet, there were no cars on the dock; no families waiting to take Daddy home for Christmas. Sparks, on his drunken bender for the last week, had sent none of the messages; none that the company needed to arrange things, and none of the crew's personal messages.

As the mate finished his logbook entries and headed down to the gangway to join the crowd of guys looking for a pay phone, he passed the radio operator's room. Crewmen were pounding on the door and cursing loudly. They stopped as he walked down the passageway. The mate stared at the AB who seemed to be the ringleader.

"The bastard didn't send any of our messages, mate. We all have families around the Gulf, and could have been home on Christmas Eve. Do you have a problem with this?"

"Just don't kill him." The mate went out on the dock. His girlfriend would drive up the next morning, she said, and they would spend Christmas together. He told her to go to the Rice Hotel, and then he called the hotel and made a reservation. The ship's business would finish the day after Christmas, when the whole crew would be "paid off and laid off," as the saying went. The crew's union already had a rep coming down who would insist that Lykes Lines blackball the captain. The *Jesse* and its captain were both finished. It was fitting.

He went back up the gangway to his room. The 2nd mate came in and they mixed up what rum and coke they had left, and shared sea stories. A few other officers came and went, and with enough drinking, they would all handle the night aboard. At least the mate had somewhere to go on Christmas, and although it was a hotel in Houston, he would not be alone.

Chapter 13: I Thought You Were In Paris?

The mate got the urge to go to North Europe. He got a relief job on the *S.S. Andrew Jackson.* It was owned by Waterman Steamship Company, had an SIU union crew out of Mobile, and was another, older C-2 class cargo ship. It was late fall, and there could be some bad weather in the North Sea, but he didn't care. At least it wasn't January or February, when the goddam North Atlantic and North Sea could become your worst nightmares. He knew that the SIU, or Seaman's International Union, was a little different from the other major crew's union, the NMU, or National Maritime Union. A Waterman ship, out of Mobile, meant that most of the crew would be southern rednecks. Part of his growing up was in the Deep South, and he knew how they were. They wouldn't like his hair, since it was longer now, or the fact that he didn't shave much, and now rode a motorcycle.

He drove his bike down to the dock to join the ship. He was wearing a khaki shirt, and had his sea bag and sextant case lashed to the sissy bar. There was no mistaking the fact that he was a new mate on the ship. He parked the bike right next to the gangway, threw the bag over his shoulder, and started up the gangway. A huge, beefy, white guy with a beer belly that hung over the railing was staring down at him. The guy had a white T-shirt and a crew cut. As he got to the top of the gangway, and stepped onto the platform, Beerbelly was standing in his way.

"What are you, one of them fuckin' Beatles?"

The mate put his bag and case down on the platform. A couple of the other crewmembers stopped work to watch. He could smell the beer on his breath. It was obvious the redneck was one of the upstanding members of the deck gang.

"That's right, asshole. And what are you, one of them fuckin' red-necks?" The mate eyeballed him good. He had been to sea long enough to know that you had to stand up for yourself right away, at the first sign of trouble. Never back down. Fight if you have to. Beerbelly mumbled something incoherent, and backed off. The mate had him.

"I'm the goddam new 3rd mate on this ship. Don't get on my watch, or I'll run your ass off of here when we get to the next port!" The fat guy was an AB, but he did not get on his watch, and the mate had no trouble from him during the two-month voyage. Still, he never turned his back on him.

The old *Andrew Jackson* made it out of the Gulf and around the Florida Keys and got in the middle of the Gulf Stream. The stream gave you extra knots for free, just like planes that ride the jet stream. The current added as much as four knots in the strongest part, but for most of it, you could get maybe an extra knot. Still, if you could find and stay with it for a few days, it helped you a lot. Mates on watch would pay attention to the temperature of the sea water that the engineers reported, knowing that when it was warmer than normal, they were in the stream. The effects of the Gulf Stream lasted all the way across the Atlantic Ocean, even changing the climate of Europe.

As they got into the North Atlantic, the mate watched the weather reports more carefully. Winter was nigh, and everyone aboard knew what that meant. The North Atlantic had a really bad reputation for weather. Even in summer, you got fog, and windy, chilly weather that went right to your bones. There were stories about rogue waves that reached a hundred feet or more in height, and could smash holes in the superstructure of a steel ship. Many a ship sailed across with the house of the ship sealed off for the entire passage, with no one allowed out of deck.

The more he sailed, the more the mate liked a gentle roll. When the ship rolled slowly, with a normal sixteen-second roll, he slept better. The motion of the ship rocked you to sleep, as if you were in the cradle, or perhaps the womb. When the ship pitched, bow and stern riding up and down, it was uncomfortable. The mate thought that maybe it had something to do with the blood in your head sloshing around 90 degrees off the normal rolling. Sometimes he thought he didn't have enough to think about to think such things.

As they approached Bishop Rock, the first lighthouse you see in the English Channel, the weather got worse. The seas built up, and the crew lashed things down all over the ship. The mate thought about the Hollywood movies that made you think that there was a terrible storm on every crossing. Hell, it wasn't that bad, or no one would be so insane as to go to sea for a living. True sailors don't like bad weather -- they want smooth seas. What nut wants to bounce off the damn bulkheads all the time?

They got a distance off the rocks near Land's End, and adjusted course to head to the Straits of Dover, and into the North Sea. From there, they would continue on to Bremerhaven, Germany. The English Channel is not very narrow, except when you dash through the Dover Straits. There are shallow spots, wrecked ships, and a lot of course changes, however. What really makes it dangerous is the number of ships, fishing boats, ferries and pleasure craft that go through there; usually over 500 vessels a day and most of them converge on the Dover Straits. It was a pinball game, with ships of all types going north, south, and crossing. In fog, it was especially dangerous.

The mate was on watch when they made the approach to Dover. He expected the captain to be on the bridge the whole time. Most captains would be, and many would put the engines on maneuvering speed, in case some idiot shot across the bow, and they had to go astern. The captain of the *Andrew Jackson*, a guy they called the Rooster, did no such thing. Going through the Straits made him nervous, so he stayed in his cabin, drinking, while the mate did the navigation, course changes, and plotted collision courses. He wasn't a bad guy, nor incompetent, like some the mate had seen, just too nervous.

Their North Europe ports-of-call began in Germany. All the way across, the chief mate, a 40-ish Ecuadorian guy, had been telling the mate to get off the ship as much as possible, and forget sleep. "You can sleep at sea," he said. "You must open your eyes to new cultures." The other two watch-standing mates were old guys, near retirement, and they offered to take his cargo watches in port if he wanted to give up his overtime pay to go ashore. The chief mate ran things in port, and he approved of this with a smile. Hell, he said that he would cover for the mate himself if either of the old guys got tired.

At their first stop in Bremerhaven, they learned that the ship would be in port all weekend. They would not sail until at least Monday. The shipping company was required to post an official notice to all the officers and crew by 1700 on Friday if the ship was leaving before 0800 Monday. They would not. The mate left the ship after 1700 and caught a local train to Hamburg, then changed trains for one to Copenhagen, Denmark. The train service was terrific. The damn cars were even loaded on a sea-going ferry for the crossing to Copenhagen. You didn't even have to leave your seat. Danish customs checked your papers while the German engineers disconnected their engine; then, they pushed the passenger cars onto tracks right on the ferry and the Danish engine later hooked up on the other side of the water. Upon arrival in the city, as usual for Europe, there was a booth right in the station that booked your hotel reservations, found you a youth hostel, or gave information for tourists. The city was crowded, and the mate felt lucky to get a room in a small hotel many miles from town. He went to a platform where the commuter train ran to this suburb.

He went up to the track, but there were no turnstiles or ticket takers. He had heard how socialized Denmark was, but free public transit was a wonderful idea! He spent the weekend traveling back and forth to the city. He went to Tivoli Gardens, walked the city, ate in different restaurants, took pictures, fell in with a bunch of students he went drinking with, and, although he didn't find a blonde to fall in love with, saw several good candidates, and had a great time. The night before he had to go back to Germany, he was surprised to be sitting on the train and see a conductor coming through the car. He stopped here and there, and people showed him tickets. He asked some local kids on the train what was going on, and got the story. They explained that the commuter trains were on the honor system. You bought tickets at machines in the station, and the conductors spot-checked, mostly trusting their sense of honesty. No one asked the mate for a ticket, but he sweated it out. He had no idea what would happen to him if someone caught him; maybe he would have to pay some kind of fine, but it would be embarrassing if nothing else. He got a ticket for his ride to the station the next morning. He made his connections back to Hamburg, back to Bremerhaven, and got aboard Monday morning just fine. He felt like he was more of a world traveler than a sailor. The chief mate was proud of him.

They finished the cargo work the next day. There weren't too many problems with the loading. The German longshoremen, although just as rough as anywhere else, prided themselves on a reputation for efficiency. This was good for their work, but if the ship had anything that was broken or unsafe, they would bitch about it. They expected your operation to run like a damn cuckoo clock.

The last night in Bremerhaven, the mate went into town. It was a small place, but had a downtown you could walk around easily. He started in the USS club, or United Seaman's Service, which was a club like a USO, only for merchant sailors from around the world. It had the convenience of a post office, a place to make telephone calls to the states, a small souvenir shop, a bar that also served food, and a casino that was really only a room full of slot machines.

From there he hit some of the sailor-type bars, but found these unattractive, as there always seemed to be American enlisted men in them, too drunk, and out of line. The downtown had many small shops, and he bought some sausage, cheese, wine, and bread to stock the small fridge in his room on the ship. He found a tourist shop and bought some beer mugs and a cuckoo clock, why he did not know, but it seemed the thing to do. He went back to the ship earlier than necessary. He was into a tourist mode, not a sailor mode. Drinking and chasing women could wait until he got back to New Orleans, or made another trip somewhere else.

From there, they steamed southerly, down through the Dover Straits, and went to Southampton, on the south coast of England. There was a lot of wind, and even though the ship did not pound into the seas too badly, it was bitterly cold on deck or out on the wing of the bridge. There was dampness to the air that would go right through you. He did not really have warm enough work clothes for it, but by layering sweaters and windbreakers, he would survive. He realized that if he were to sail here regularly, he would have to invest in better jackets and boots, but for the couple of weeks they would spend in North Europe he could get by.

In Southampton, he got lucky again. The ship would stay in port over the weekend. The older mates were happy to work his overtime again. The chief mate smiled as the mate went to his office on Friday afternoon and told him that he was taking the express train to London that night. He didn't worry about hotels. He knew that there would be help for travelers in the station in Southampton and in London, and he would find something. He didn't care what or where; he was going to see goddam London instead of the inside of sailor bars along the Southampton waterfront.

He got a room in an older hotel across the park from Buckingham Palace. It was typical for an older, European hotel. The bathroom was down the hall, and the hotel served a continental breakfast in the parlor, off the lobby. As he went out for a while, he tried to remember some of the differences between his culture and language and the English. He knew not to ask for a "napkin" in a restaurant, but a "serviette." He also knew that if a girl invited you to "knock her up" sometime, it was not an invitation to get her pregnant, only to visit her. The local money was still in pounds and shillings, and that took some math to figure out what you were paying, in dollars. He was used to converting currency and doing some math to figure out costs. He found a nightclub nearby and danced with several girls, including a real beauty from Jamaica. No one fell instantly in love, and he got back to the hotel in time to get some sleep. This wasn't the time to stay out all night drinking. He wanted his wits and some of his money for sightseeing.

The next morning he went across the park to see the changing of the guards at the palace. He wasn't a fan of royalty; in fact, he did not believe in it at all, but it was a real show. He was taking pictures of the Royal Guards with their large, fuzzy hats, when he heard a female voice from behind him in the crowd, apparently directed at him.

"Excuse me; do you have a light meter in your camera?"

The voice had an American accent, and he turned around to see a dark-haired woman, about 25 years old. She was holding a camera and fiddling with the lens aperture.

"Yeah, sure." He gave her the reading for the correct exposure. They both took some pictures, and when the marching show was over, and the crowd began to disperse, he turned around again. *If she's still there,* he thought, *she's interested.* She was. Some small talk about London followed, and they agreed to go to see Parliament and Westminster Abbey together. For once in his life, he wouldn't push it with a girl, just be friends.

He found out that she was a secretary from Chicago who had been traveling Europe by herself for three weeks. She was going home the next day. The fact that she was still alone, and on the last night of her dream vacation, registered in his mind as a possible opportunity for romance, but he dismissed it. They fell in with a tour group and went through Parliament. The guide was local, of course, but he seemed to speak much more slowly than other English people do. They heard the stories about Churchill's famous speech in this spot, and Lloyd George's in that spot, and on and on. When the mate gave the guy a few bucks, he asked them if they were from the U.S., and apologized for speaking so slowly, but said that they had tacked themselves onto a special tour of people from non-English speaking countries. The mate laughed it off, and he never did hear an Englishman speak so slowly and clearly again.

From there, it was the Abbey, then lunch, then a ride around town on a double-decker bus. They watched the cars go round Trafalgar Square. They walked around Piccadilly Circus, where, of course, there was no circus. The mate went in a men's shop and bought a Harris Tweed sport coat off the rack, 42 regular.

The two Americans had a fun day of it, the only negatives being a couple of times when they started to step off a curb, looking to the left for traffic, and almost got run over by cars zooming along the curb from the right. The mate asked Miss Chicago if she wanted to go out to dinner on her last night in Europe. She beamed at the offer, and said she would go back to her hotel to get ready. They arranged a time to meet at his hotel, and he thought he could get a recommendation for a restaurant from the desk clerk. Miss Chicago hugged him and kissed him before getting in the cab.

He had one good dress shirt with him and one tie he always stuck in his sea bag. He put them on, with his new tweed coat, and it didn't look too bad. The more he thought about her behavior, the more he thought he might prepare for more than dinner. He went out of the hotel and down the street to a bottle shop, where he purchased a bottle of French wine and a cheap corkscrew. Back in the hotel lobby, he swiped an extra glass from the breakfast set-up counter nearby. He began to wonder if having a female guest in his room, should he be so favored with Chicago's charms, would be bad form. You never knew, in another country, what was acceptable and what wasn't. Hell, if this were France, the desk clerk would be proud of him for having a girl over, and congratulate him for not being a puritanical American. The English seemed more uptight and reserved.

As he waited for her, he remembered her saying that her plane did not leave until the next afternoon, so she would not have to get up early. *Bingo, you dope! How much clearer could she have made it?* It was like a girl on a date asking you what you wanted for breakfast. Had he been so engrossed with London he had missed that signal? Thankfully, he was now prepared to invite her up to the room for a glass of wine.

The old, rotary phone in his room rang. The desk clerk said he had a visitor in the lobby. As they went down the street for the short walk to the restaurant the desk clerk had recommended, he thought about things from her perspective, as best he could imagine it. He also thought about looking to the right for traffic. Tomorrow she was going back on the long flight to Chicago. In a day or two, she would be back at work, in a large office building, as one of dozens of secretaries. All her friends would want to know all about Europe. The girlfriends would have misguided ideas about it, and, naturally, would joke about the foreign guys. They would want to know if she had any romance on such a fantastic vacation. From her conversation, he got the impression she had not. Now it was her last chance to add this to her itinerary. The fact that he was another American wouldn't matter much. She could change the story if she wanted to, make him a Brit, Frenchman, whatever, or tell the girls in the office that he was a dashing, handsome officer who had wined and dined her, some truth to that. She wouldn't have to mention that she had approached him, and was the one drawing him in like a spider with a fly, now including a low-cut blouse and a cleavage show. She had told him that she had traveled on the cheap, staying in some hostels to save money, and that the guys who had tried to pick her up were mostly rude. The French, she said, were bad enough, but the Italians were so obnoxious she had left there early. He had heard that single women should not travel alone in Italy. As they settled at a table at the restaurant, he knew he had to be as charming as possible. He would travel around the world more, but this might be the only time in her life she did.

The service was good, but neither of them cared much for traditional English food. *Yorkshire pudding,* the mate thought, *was best left in Yorkshire.* They had wine with dinner, and skipped desert. He tried to pay the bill himself, but she insisted on paying half; it was such a pleasant surprise he didn't argue with her. On the walk back towards his hotel, he told her that he knew a nightclub nearby, but she suggested they go right back to his hotel.

As they entered the lobby, he mumbled something about coming up to his room for a glass of wine. She said that would be great. Up in the room, he poured two glasses and toasted her vacation. She said something about him being a really nice guy, put her glass down, and pressed in close to kiss him. In the embrace, he ran his hands up from her waist and across the front of her breasts. She didn't try to stop him. He had his hands spread out and could still not cover all of her. She ran her hands down the front of his shirt, unbuttoning it as she went; when she got to his belt buckle, she undid that too. It seemed like only seconds before they were naked on the little bed, in the little room, in the old-fashioned hotel in the middle of London, thousands of miles from home for each of them. Being far from home could make you lose your inhibitions, but she didn't seem to have many to lose. She was hungry for love or hungry for sex, he couldn't tell, and it didn't matter much.

In the middle of the night, she woke him up again. The only hassle during the night was putting on clothes to go down the hall to the bathroom. In the morning, they went down to the hotel parlor for coffee and Danish. He wondered if any of the hotel people would notice her as the girl from the night before, and see that she had the same clothes on, but no one said anything. Maybe the British weren't as uptight as people said they were.

Eventually they went outside and got a cab for her. There were no statements about being in love. They had exchanged addresses, but he knew they would probably not write. She would return to her world in the high-rise district in Chicago, and he would sail back to New Orleans and look for another ship. He wasn't in love with her, but he sure liked the way she ended her vacations.

He got back to Southampton Sunday night and slept aboard the ship. He went down to breakfast and turned to, on deck, at 0800. The chief mate was proud of him, again, for seeing some more of the world. From there, the ship sailed to Le Havre, France. It was across the English Channel from Southampton, but not through the Straits, and the visibility held up. Fog or rain can make it a real bitch, with all the traffic and fishermen around. They docked on Wednesday, and by Thursday, it looked like the ship would be in port for the weekend yet again. The mate went ashore, and in between looking for a restaurant for lunch and finding a perfume shop for souvenirs, he found a travel agent. He booked a ticket on the Friday night express train to Paris. The chief mate said that he was learning, and kept saying that he must see Paris, and not to worry about anything.

Friday afternoon, however, the ship's plans changed, and they posted the sailing board at the gangway to warn the sailors that the ship would sail late Friday night. They were going back to Germany to pick up military cargo to return to the states. The mate went back to the travel office that afternoon and cashed in his ticket. He was disappointed, but still happy over the traveling he had done. He knew how unusual it was for a sailor to get around as he already had.

The ship undocked late that night, and he had duty up on the bridge, with the captain and the French pilot. After the pilot left in his boat, and the ship cleared the harbor, the captain went down below, and the mate was alone to plot their way back north towards Dover again. He was surprised when he heard someone come into the darkened wheelhouse.

"Okay, I've got her." It was the chief mate's voice. The mate was confused. The chief mate undocked up on the bow, and would normally go to bed afterwards, having been awake most of the day and night. He did not stand a watch on the bridge, and rarely came up there. The mate moved closer in the dark, and saw that it was indeed his culture-conscious friend.

"What do you mean? I've got the watch."

"What the hell are you doing here? I thought you were in Paris?"

"Well, yeah, I was going, but the the ship sailed. I have to be here."

"Haven't I taught you anything?" The chief mate seemed mad. "I told you that we had you covered. You could have met the ship in Germany!"

"But hell, I didn't know you'd go that far. No one else has ever done anything like that for me. And what about the captain, wouldn't he be mad?"

"Stupid. You know the Rooster well enough. You know we run the ship for him. He let you take her through the straits by yourself, didn't he? He would not say a word. He couldn't fire you until we get back anyway, and you're only here for one trip."

He had never sailed with a second in command who, tired from working all day, would take his watch so he could miss a goddam sailing. He had never expected such a favor. He was speechless. You never miss a sailing. If the damn ship moves, you'd better be on it.

"Ah, forget it," the Ecuadorian said, "You are a good officer. You did what was right. You will get another chance for Paris some other time." With that, he went below. The mate resumed his watch, plotting traffic and checking the course changes. He felt better, but he did not know then that he would put twenty years in at sea, and never get to Paris.

The ship got back to Bremerhaven without incident, although it turned much colder in the North Sea than it had been before. The worst of winter was coming on, and the mate hoped they could finish their work and get out of the North Sea and the North Atlantic before any bad storms hit them. Sailing back to New Orleans instead of New York meant that their track would take them a lot farther south, once they were a few days out from the English Channel.

There would be no trips outside the port this time. It would only take two days to load the cargo that the company's agent had booked for them. They had no other ports on the schedule. That night in port, then, was to be the last before the long trip home. As usual with the last chance to go ashore, the behavior of the officers and crew of the *Andrew Jackson* was a little different. Guys who usually stayed aboard the ship went ashore, some looking for last minute souvenirs to bring to family, others to get drunk.

The mate went uptown with the engineer from his watch. The engineer was older, but seemed like a decent guy. They started, like most did, in the USS club, where they changed some money, mailed post cards, and got a German beer for a fair price. There were guys from the ship in there; some making phone calls home, others making a nuisance of themselves drinking. Things got noisy, and the two of them decided to hit a couple of bars in town. It must have been some kind of sailor magnetism, as every bar they found seemed to be one for sailors and GI's. There were a few girls here and there, if you looked hard enough, but mostly it was servicemen and seamen getting drunk, and playing the American tunes on the jukebox. The other thing the mate noticed was that every bar had one real beauty, known throughout the world as a "B-girl." The German B-girls they saw were gorgeous. They had the looks you wanted to fall in love with, write home about, and marry. Guys would offer them fantastic prices to spend one hour with them, but they never left the bar. As elsewhere, their job was to entice you to come into the place and order drinks.

As things got louder and rowdier in the bars, they decided to get away from that part of town. The mate had on his new tweed coat, and the engineer had decent clothes. They didn't look like a couple of American bums, as sailors sometimes did, so they agreed not to stop in anywhere where there were sailors, servicemen, or even tourists. They would walk around the town until they found a local place, where only Germans went. Hell, they looked like locals, with blue eyes and sandy hair, and if they kept their mouths shut, no one would know they were off a ship. They passed several other bars, walked through the center of Bremerhaven, past all the closed shops, and kept going. Right here, left there, they had no idea where they were. Then they saw some cars parked in front of a bar. Looking in the window, they saw tables, a long bar, a small stage, and a dance floor. It was definitely a local place, one with a band, no less. They went in, and strode up to the bar.

The bartender came over, speaking German. The mate simply held up two fingers and said "Beck's, bitte." He figured he had ordered two bottles of Beck's beer, please. And lo, the guy brought them over. He paid with marks, not dollars. No one paid them any mind, and it was working. No one knew that they were sailors. Instead of getting drunk with Americans, they would get drunk with locals! A four-piece band was playing, and one of the guys was playing an accordion. Several women in the place were accepting offers to dance. The two merchant officers were having a good time, and kept ordering beers. The prices were fair, unlike the bars where the B-girls worked.

They knew that there was, as usual in all countries, almost no chance that a local girl would want anything to do with sailors, but you never knew for sure, and hell, the German girls never seemed to turn down an invitation to dance, so why not?

He got the bartender's attention again.

"How do you ask a girl to dance, in German?"

"Say, 'Dansk, bitte?'" The bartender smiled. That bastard knew all along that we were tourists, the mate figured. *What the hell.* He walked over to a table they had been eyeing and approached a redhead. She got up right away.

He went around and around with the redhead. She seemed to be having a great time. However, she didn't speak a damn word of English. *Well, you dope, this is what you wanted. Now you can navigate your way around the place with about four words of German.* He took her back to her table, but in a few minutes asked her to dance again. The engineer danced with another girl from the same table, and soon they were sitting with them. There were about a dozen Germans, roughly their age, men and women, around the table. A couple of the guys spoke a little English, and there was some general conversation. They didn't seem to mind the two intruders. The mate knew that in many countries, being an officer on a merchant ship, hell, even being in the crew, was considered a worthy occupation, and got you some respect. It only seemed to be in America that people thought there was something wrong with you if you did that for your job. In their present situation, the massive consumption of beer and schnapps probably helped the feelings of international goodwill.

As the evening wore on, the mate began to think about going back to the ship. The night before you sailed, you generally stayed out late, but he would need a couple of hours of sleep to function. His days of staying out all night, just to prove he could do it, were over. The funny thing was that the redhead seemed attracted to him. She was acting strangely. All she seemed to do was smile, laugh, dance, and stay real close to him. He began to wonder if he really could make out with a local girl on his last night in Germany. Then he went to the men's room, and heard "her story."

While he was in there, one of the young German guys from the table came in and stood next to him. In his limited English, the guy explained that the redhead was crazy. She was the town loony, so to speak. He even called her "cuckoo," apparently understanding the meaning of the word in English. That did it for the mate. He didn't know how nuts she was, but he was now ready to go back to the ship. He had a little talk with the engineer, a married man who was not chasing women, and they agreed it was time to get back to the docks, in spite of the fact they had consumed only six or seven beers each. They thanked all the people at the table, and wound their way back towards the front door. They asked the bartender if he could call a cab. Of course he could; only a few minutes, he said. They went outside to wait. Then the redhead appeared at the mate's side out on the sidewalk. She was still smiling and laughing, and she put her arm in his and hung on to him.

She would not let go. He tried to tell her to go back inside, that he had to get back to his ship. She understood none of it, and clung on. The cab drove up. *Now what,* he wondered. *Just leave her here on the sidewalk? Physically force her back inside?* The three of them piled into the cab instead. The mate began to consider the possibility of sleeping with her. He had sometimes wondered about the sanity of some of the girls he had dated, but he had never shacked up with a certifiable nut, to his knowledge. She might be absolutely wild. The cab driver spoke enough English for basic communication, and the mate told him to drive to the girl's house. She gave the driver an address. The engineer, trying to be a good shipmate, said that if the two of them got out at her place, he would take the mate's packages back with him. "Just don't miss the ship," he reminded him.

The car stopped in front of a large apartment building. The crazy redhead started chattering in German. Questions flashed through his mind. *Was she inviting me in? Do I want to go in? What would happen? Would she be terrific in bed? How crazy was she? Would she attack me with a butcher knife while I slept? Could I stay awake, or wake up in time to get back to the ship before it sailed?* This was their last foreign port. Miss the ship now, and he could find his own way home, and not earn any more money. He figured he could go up with her for an hour, stay awake, and get back, even if he had to walk. It might be worth it, but, then again, it wasn't the right thing to do. *Are you so desperate you have to take advantage of the town wacko?* He could not. He had to have a little honor. His reasoning was easier since the weekend in London. He gently forced her out of the cab, and said goodnight as best he could. Her expression never changed. He never would know her real story, but she walked away, still smiling, and they drove off. The mate gave the driver the name of their dock. The driver pointed a finger at his head, and made circular motions.

"Yeah, I know," the mate said. "Crazy. Nuts. Cuckoo."

"Ya, ya! Cuckoo!" The driver smiled.

The engineer seemed glad that the mate had not pursued the girl any further. The mate figured that occasionally, maybe once a year, you had to do the right thing, even if you didn't want to.

They got out of Germany and began the long haul home. Their track went west across the North Sea, south through the Straits of Dover, westerly down the English Channel, abeam of Land's End and then a Great Circle course for the Florida Straits. From there, they would run the keys as close to the reefs as possible to stay out of the Gulf Stream, round Dry Tortugas, then set a straight course for South Pass, the main entrance to the Mississippi River. It would take about ten days. Some of the guys the mate saw on deck in port, or in a bar ashore, he would not see again until the ship docked. They worked different hours in different sections of the ship. The officers and crew would eat in separate rooms, and a crewman you bought beer for in Germany would not socialize with you on the ship. The mate would stand his four-hour watches twice a day, as usual, and do almost nothing except navigation and collision avoidance. A trip like this gave the mates practice in all three types of navigation: piloting, electronic, and celestial. An accurate compass was essential to all navigation. The ship had an electrically run gyrocompass that gave true north, and, of course, a backup magnetic compass that read magnetic north. A small error in the gyro was not a problem, provided you knew what the error was, and applied it to all your bearings and courses. Every watch you stood, you were supposed to determine the compass error.

The first type of navigating you learn is piloting. This is mostly taking visual bearings from known objects that appear on a chart. You would go out on the wing of the bridge, and use the compass repeater. An azimuth circle, or bearing circle with sight vanes, sat on top of it. You found a lighthouse, for example, and sighted it through the vanes. If you saw that one lighthouse was bearing north, or 000 degrees, and another one was bearing east, or 090 degrees, you would simply drawn lines for those degrees on your chart, away from the lighthouses. Where the two lines cross is your position. Another important aspect of piloting is dead reckoning, which is a good name for it if yours is not any good. This means that when you lay off your course on a nautical chart, you estimate your speed, and estimate your position along your track. A good "DR" at least indicates where you should be, and when you can expect to see land, and so forth. There have been many times when a ship crossed an ocean in cloudy weather, before satellites, and could not get any positions at all. In cases like this, it is crucial that the mates use good estimates of course, speed, and drift. It is embarrassing to see your first light ashore show up on the wrong side of the bow, when making landfall. It is also dangerous, yet in the days before radar, many ships crossed oceans this way.

Electronic navigation, simply, involves the use of an electronic device. When the mate began sailing, radar was the main aid. You can take a bearing of a point of land, and get your distance off it with the radar, giving you a good position, provided you can tell what point of land is showing up. This is not always obvious, as low land makes a poor radar target. In the 1960's, both Decca and Loran were developed. Decca was a European system that gave you readings on dials from stations ashore. Once your receiver locked on to a chain of transmitters, you got continuous readouts that corresponded to lines overlaid on your chart. The U. S. Coast Guard developed Loran with similar functions. The receiver measures the difference in time delay in reception, and from this, you get readouts that are converted to lines. In time, the designers developed converters that translated the readouts to latitude and longitude. As the years went by, both systems got better; they had more coverage, and more accuracy. Many mates, however, have made the mistake of assuming the readouts must be right. Failure to understand this could cause a mate an upset stomach, when, for example, his ship went aground instead of sailing happily into harbor.

Other electronic aids to navigation used routinely would be the fathometer, or depth finder, and the radio direction finder, or RDF. Good mates always turned on the fathometer when approaching land; it didn't give you lines of position, usually, but knowing how deep the water is beneath your ship is always helpful. If it is not what you expect, by looking at your position on the chart, you'd better find out why not, in a goddam hurry. An RDF lets you tune in to a transmitter ashore, and get an electronic bearing from it, even when you can't see it. Although used extensively in the 1940's, mates were aware that the bearings could easily be off several degrees to either the right or left of what they tuned into, and used them with caution. Eventually, the military got some satellites for navigation, and still later, the services allowed private parties, like steamship companies, to use them. In the beginning, there were only four satellites in orbit for this purpose. When the satellite passed overhead, a receiver on the ship measured the Doppler effect of its passing, and, if the elevation was within certain limits, gave you a latitude and longitude. You could go for several hours without a good fix, and in the early years, there were areas on the earth where the coverage wasn't good. When there were more satellites, the positions came more frequently. The mate never imagined a GPS device.

The third type of navigation was celestial observation. In the mate's time, this meant using a sextant to measure the angle from the horizon to a celestial body, such as the sun, moon, planets, or stars. When he had started, every mate brought his own sextant on the ship with him. The knowledge of how to use the damn thing was one of the main things that set mates apart from other mere mortals. Learning to use it took a long time. It wasn't just learning how to look through the telescope and find things in the heavens; it was the damn calculations that followed. If you "shot" the sun, for example, you wrote down the exact time you observed it, in GMT, or Greenwich Mean Time. Then, you looked all kinds of things up in the Nautical Almanac, and other books. There was a list of adding and subtracting all kinds of variables, on and on, almost a full column down a page of notebook paper, until you got the answers that would allow you to draw a line on your chart. The mate on the *Andrew Jackson* still enjoyed doing this. It seemed to connect him to sailors from hundreds of years ago, who struggled with the sun and stars, constantly trying to figure out better methods of getting positions.

In the mate's years at sea, one of the best improvements in navigation was the development of hand-held calculators. He had gone through college physics and calculus with a slide rule, and computed his sights at sea with the help of logarithms and trig functions. He could not believe his good fortune when he bought his first calculator that did algebraic formulas. Mates began to go to sea with calculators stuck inside their sextant cases. Columbus would have been impressed and amazed.

In the years after his trip on the *Andrew Jackson,* the mate would sail long enough to replace his Texas Instruments calculator with a Tamaya NC-77. When it was new, this calculator, more of a computer really, cost about $350, and was worth every penny to a navigator. What it did for a mate was revolutionary. It had the entire Nautical Almanac for the next twenty years in its memory, and took values in latitude, longitude, or degrees and minutes. It did almost all the calculations for you, if you put in the right figures. It didn't replace a good horizon, or improve poor eyesight, but if you knew what you were doing, it cut your time tremendously. Solving a star fix the old way could easily take an hour or more. With the advanced machine in your hand, you could do the same job in about fifteen minutes, and it didn't make errors looking numbers up in books, or simple math errors.

A good mate checked things constantly. As the *Andrew Jackson* sailed through the English Channel and out to the deep ocean, the mates used all three types of navigation, and often combined them. What this meant for a good mate was that if you got a position from visual bearings on lighthouses, you put that on the chart, and then went to the radar. If your position showed you should be 14.3 miles off the nearest land to starboard, then, by God, the radar better show the land that far off, if it was high enough for a good bounced signal. If that were so, then you would look at the chart again, and see what the depth of the water should be. Knowing that, you walked past the fathometer and checked the soundings. After that, you might look at the chart again, and see that there should be a buoy with a flashing light 2.5 miles off your bow. You would casually grab the binoculars, stride out to the wing of the bridge, and look for the damn buoy, and it better look like it was two and a half miles off. You did all this while watching all the other traffic visually and on the radar, and figuring out the time of your next course change, while estimating the current and tide changes, to allow for set and drift. The mate loved steaming along a coast for this reason, that there was a lot to do.

It was the night before they expected to see Hillsborough Inlet lighthouse, and begin the run south between Florida and the Bahamas. The mate was on watch, out on the starboard bridge wing, enjoying the warm weather. He sipped coffee, watched the horizon for traffic, and checked the course. Everything was routine. Then the mate began to notice moving objects in the glow of the masthead light up forward. At first, they looked like large raindrops, but they were swirling, and it wasn't raining on him. First a few, then hundreds of objects were caught in the glare of the white light, all over the place, moving rapidly in all directions. He called the quartermaster to come out on the wing for a look. The two men soon saw that the objects were small birds. Thousands of birds, perhaps blown off course in their migration, were attracted to the ship's lights, and were frantically circling the masts. They couldn't see the wires in the ship's rigging and ran into them. It was bird madness. They hit wires, masts, even the bulkheads of the masthouses. This weird behavior was still going on when the watch was relieved.

In the morning, the mate went up to the bridge for watch and saw that there were thousands of birds perched safely all over the ship, on the masts, booms, wires, radar antenna, everywhere. However, others had not been so lucky in the dark. The bosun and a couple of ABs were sweeping up the dead ones and dumping them over the side by the bucketful.

The weather was humid and warm, and the bridge of the ship was not air-conditioned. As the watch went on, the mate propped himself up against a window, forward in the wheelhouse, and mentally drifted. He pondered the behavior of the birds. *The ship was now a damn aviary of sorts, but why?* What had gone wrong with the birds' natural navigation abilities, usually amazingly accurate? If the ship headed in the same direction as the flock's intended migration, how long would they stay aboard? Did they have some kind of leader who would decide when it was time to head off again? He thought of their own leader, the captain, who was somewhat bird-like. Maybe the birds had one little guy, green and yellow like the rest, but with four gold stripes on his little wings. He would be going around now, from mast to shroud, telling all his troops what the plans were. He would puff up his little chest and show off his captain's stripes, so they could see that he meant business. "All right, you lazy, little, bird bastards," he would shout in bird talk, "two more hours rest, then we fly off to the south, and no bitching this time!" The mate contemplated this scene, and then thought he should give up drinking.

The day-dreaming was suddenly interrupted by an object that came hurtling in the open door of the wheelhouse on the starboard side, went past the mate like a small missile, whacked into a window on the port side, and fell to the deck. It was one of those curious little birds, confused by the glass windows, which had zoomed in there, and not found his way out. He flopped around the deck, hurt. The salty mate and the scurvy-looking AB on watch went over for a look. The crew had just dumped hundreds, maybe thousands of his buddies over the side. Here was one more. However, for some reason, neither the mate nor his quartermaster could just pick him up and toss him to Davy Jones' Locker.

The mate knew that there was a side to sailors that most people never see. A sense of machismo or bravado kept them acting like tough guys. You cannot sail a ship and show any softness. Be a son-of-a-bitch all the time, that's the ticket. Yet, the mate had learned that most sailors were honest, even warm-hearted, although their actions belied this. He picked up the bird and examined it. Before long, the unshaven AB and mate had placed it in a shoebox, with pieces of cloth for blankets, a cut up Styrofoam cup with water, and crushed crackers. They put it on a windowsill, and when their four hours were up, told the next watch that it was the new ship's pet. As the mate expected, when the watch on the bridge changed every four hours, all the tough guys in the deck department checked on the little lost bird, brought things to try to feed it, and advanced numerous opinions on his injuries, and the best method of treatment.

Soon, the flock left, off to who-knew where, and the little injured guy was alone on the ship. He did not seem to eat. The mate took the eyedropper out of the medicine chest, and force-fed it water right down its beak. It took that. Then everyone mixed up various concoctions with the water, to give it strength. Only God knew what different things were in the water. Sailors added sugar, salt, crushed leftovers from the galley, and whatever else they could think of. Then there was the matter of medical treatment. The mate would leave his watch, come back up eight hours later, and find that the guys on the other two watches had totally changed the treatment program. Some thought his wing was broken, others his leg. One morning he would find him with his wing neatly wrapped in bandages. By nightfall, it would be his leg. Then it was the other leg, and back to a wing. Sailors left the little bird all kinds of crap to eat or to play with. *Hell, why not leave him a book to read?* It was amusing to the mate; all these tough-talking, hard-working deck hands and mates doing this. He also thought that the bird, having survived the flock's disaster, and the crash into the window, would surely die from the treatment. However, the feathery, little, son-of-a-bitch hung on to life.

In a couple of days, the ship had run the Florida Keys, as close to shore as possible to stay out of the Gulf Stream, which was against them steaming south. It was a busy time for mates, as there is a lot of traffic through the slot, north and south, and numerous pleasure craft around the keys and making runs to Nassau. The mate always liked doing this. It was called "running the pink." At night, the lights on the little islands that showed a white light when you were in the safe part of their range, and red if you got too close to danger, looked pinkish when you were right on the edge, as close to the reefs as you dared go, and maximum distance out of the opposing current. You had to change course a lot, and avoid the pleasure boats that didn't always give way. Soon, they took Dry Tortugas abeam to starboard, and set a straight course for South Pass. The mate's assignment would end in two days, in New Orleans, and he decided more had to be done with the bird. He introduced an exercise regimen into his rehabilitation program. This consisted of the mate and his AB standing a few feet apart, in the wheelhouse, and tossing the bird back and forth. The little feathery one would flap his wings like mad, fly a little, and the other guy would catch him, offer encouragement, and toss him back. Eventually, they moved farther and farther apart, and his little Wright Brother-style flights got longer. Opinion was evenly divided whether this treatment was helping him, or whether he was so anxious to get away from his lunatic bird doctors he would try anything to fly again.

By the time the ship got up the Mississippi to the wharf in New Orleans, the winged one could go fifteen feet on his own. The mate had to get off the ship, and could not leave the bird in his box on the bridge, as no one stood watch up there in port. He gave the pet to the most caring of the crewmen, a big, ugly guy, who, by the looks of him, you would think would rather eat the damn thing than care for it. The plan was for the AB to keep the bird for the eight-day coastwise run the ship would make around the Gulf, unloading the cargo they had brought back, and loading new things to go foreign. When they topped off the hatches in New Orleans again in about a week, the sailor would release the bird. The concern was that if he took off on his own out at sea, he would perish, either because he was too far from land, or because he might be lost. The mate left the *Andrew Jackson* not knowing the fate of the bird, but feeling good about it. It wasn't just for the bird's sake, but because it had brought out some repressed goodness in the sailors.

Chapter 14: The Banana Girls

One of the ships that the mate caught over the next couple of years was the S. *S. Gulf Merchant,* for a six-week voyage. It was a G.S.A., or Gulf and South American Steamship Company, freighter, going from New Orleans down the west coast of South America. The good part was that the weather was usually very good, except for some long, rolling swells that came in from the Pacific. You could also have a good time ashore without spending a lot of money. You could buy llama sweaters, gold jewelry, Panama hats, and homemade birdcages to bring home as treasures. The bad side was that some of the ports in Colombia and Ecuador were very dangerous. Young soldiers with automatic weapons guarded post offices, banks, and government buildings. It made you feel as if they expected a robbery or a revolution at any moment.

He shipped as a 3rd mate, and the other 3rd mate also came out of the hall for one trip. The other guy who shipped with him was an older, Louisiana-bred guy who smoked a pipe and talked a lot. He seemed like a good mate, and knew everybody in Louisiana, it seemed. He was a real old-time, good ol' boy-type swamp rat, Crafty Cajun. The Cajun took the 12 to 4 watch, and the mate got the 8 to 12. The ship's permanent 2nd mate covered the 4 to 8.

On the voyage southbound, they stopped in Buenaventura, Colombia. The mate had been working the 1600 to midnight cargo watch when, while standing up by #3 hatch, he heard a couple of shots. He did not know where they had come from. He ran back towards the midship house. As he passed #4 hatch, he saw a local citizen standing on top of the hatch cover with a pistol in his hand. The mate froze for an instant, not knowing which way to go and feeling betrayed that he could not have a gun. He continued aft and got to the gangway. The local watchman there explained that the guy he had seen, who was dressed in ragged civilian clothing, was one of the armed guards the company had hired to fend off looters, and he had been the one who had fired.

The mate went back to #4, and saw that a container on top of the hatch cover had been broken into. The thieves were gone. The cargo they had pilfered was cologne. Small bottles of it were everywhere around the hatch. "I'm risking my life for this crap?" he wondered aloud. A small crowd gathered as he filled out a report. Then he picked up a broken case, and passed bottles around to all. The locals were all happy with this end to the crime, and some of them smelled a lot better, too.

The mate went ashore in Buenaventura with the engineer from his watch, but they didn't stay out long. Even in the places the locals said were nicer than others, the two officers thought they were in some kind of hell. There were beggars everywhere. Young men stared at them from every street corner, and they never felt safe. In one club, a guy came up to their table to beg. He was dressed in rags, and was pulling himself around on a square piece of wood with four wheels nailed to it. He had no legs. They gave him a couple of bucks and went back to the ship.

It didn't take long for the mate to realize that the captain was going to be a problem. He was in his sixties, overweight, had white hair and a white mustache, and had been running down to the same ports for many years. He growled and bitched at the two new mates constantly. He went out of his way to make their watches miserable. He told them to turn the radar off when they thought it should be on. He called them on the phone constantly. He bitched for twenty minutes if the pencils by the chart table were not lined up the way he liked it. He had a habit of shouting at the pilots, calling them "stupid foreigners." He gave orders to the bow and stern over loudspeakers, shouting all the time.

Worse, yet, he considered himself an expert on everything. Everybody was an idiot compared to him. The mate had seen this act before. Once a ship left port, some captains thought their title was God, not captain, and acted like it. Nothing they could do would ameliorate his behavior.

The ship also carried twelve passengers. The dining arrangement was unusual. There were two large oval tables set for each meal. All the passengers sat around one table and all the officers at another. The captain, of course, sat at the head of the officers' table. He would charge into the room, sit down, and start bellowing and bragging about himself at every meal. He was a complete asshole. *Fuck him.* The mate stopped shaving, which pissed off the old blusterer even more. There would be no more attempts to get along.

As they began to make ports along the west coast of South America, things continued to worsen with the captain. During one docking, the mate, in charge on the stern, had a large manila line to the dock, and the captain, as was his habit, had taken command of the docking away from the local pilot. He mishandled the ship and a heavy line broke aft, where the mate was directing his men. All kinds of abuse came from the loudspeaker, but eventually, the mate got another line ashore, and they heaved alongside. After docking, the captain hollered for the mate to come up to the bridge. The usual shouting followed. Captain Jerk refused to admit his mistake, as always. He told the mate that he would take the cost of the line out of his pay. Knowing that this was illegal, the mate invited him to do so, and informed him that he was lucky no one had gotten hurt. An eight-inch line snapping under heavy pressure can kill someone.

The mate then told Old Gruffy that he would not obey any further orders that would injure anyone. The captain got all red in the face, and left, cursing. The mate was learning how to get under his skin. When he went below to his room, the mate began a secret journal, setting down all the facts relating to the captain's behavior and orders.

The other thing he did was to have nightly chats with the Crafty Cajun. He was getting the same treatment. It seemed the two of them were outcasts amongst the officers, and they had to stick together, he said. He also was keeping some records of things aboard that were not normal. The Cajun smoked his pipe, put his feet up on his desk, and told the younger mate about the secret room on their deck. The room, he said, was full of contraband, all kinds of stuff from the states, like blue jeans, cigarettes, radios, candy, and so forth. None of it was declared anywhere as cargo, he said. The story was that the captain, purser, and chief steward were in on a smuggling operation, and had been for years. The mate began to like ol' Crafty even more. Crafty had pictures of it.

The mate began to make logbook entries such as: "radar off per captain's orders." This infuriated the Old Man. The mate calmly explained that if his use of normal navigation equipment were to be restricted, he would make an entry of it. If the captain was a decent guy and let him use his judgment, which was good, that would be okay, but he did not want to cover for Captain Asshole. If they had a problem, let him explain why the mates couldn't use the radar, or other devices.

Old Blusterer claimed to have the sharpest eyesight on the ship. He bragged at dinner, mostly for the benefit of the passengers, that his eyesight, even at his age, was much better than that of "those damn young guys," meaning, of course, guys like the mate. He knew the coast well, having sailed up and down it for years. He had a habit of showing up on the bridge just before a lighthouse should be abeam, going out on the wing, taking one look, and declaring that he had seen it. He would then order the mate to put the line on the chart, even though the mate, with 20/20 eyesight and binoculars, could not see the thing. The mate and the Crafty Cajun began to refer to him as Captain Eagle Eye for this extraordinary ability. One night he demonstrated this skill to the mate once again, even though the mate could not find the proper light along the shore. After he left the bridge, the mate looked up the lighthouse in an official publication. The light had burned out two years ago.

Sure enough, at breakfast the next morning, the captain was holding court at the round table, and brought up the subject of the light, and how he was the only one on the bridge who could see it. The permanent officers all let him ramble on, but the mate could listen no more.

"That's right," he said in a raised voice that all could hear. "The captain saw that light when no one else could. I couldn't see it, the AB at the wheel couldn't see it, and the lookout didn't report it." The captain was astounded. He smiled as if to say that he now knew he had gotten the better of his younger officer.

"In fact, I was so astounded by this display of skill that I looked that lighthouse up in the book, and discovered that the light burned out two years ago! And still, our captain could see it!" It took a minute for this to sink in before the captain realized that the young mate was insulting him. He got red, and flustered, and could not speak. The mate got up from the table. He walked around behind the captain on his way out, and gave a wry smile to the other officers.

"Are you all right, sir? You don't look well."

By the evening watch, the mate learned what the next shot across his bow would be. An order came from the captain that, due to the coffee spills on the ladder that led to the wheelhouse, he forbade the helmsmen coming to the bridge to bring the mates any coffee. Old Eagle Eye gloated over this apparent success in pissing off all three of his mates. The mate and Crafty discussed it after dinner, in their usual planning session. It was childish and ridiculous, but they had to do something. They could not let the old bastard terminate one of the finest traditions of the sea, and one of the perks mates the world over had. Even the seamen on their watches didn't like it, as they were expected to "take care" of their mates, and, even if a guy called you a mother-fucker down below, he understood the value of keeping the mate on watch awake. Crafty, true to his nature, had a plan.

He calculated that the mates relieved each other on the bridge eight times a day. Now, he figured, if we visit the bridge more often, say, to get a look at the next chart, or just to socialize, we could add at least four more visits to this. The mate began to smile as he realized where this was going. Suppose, Crafty went on, that every time the three of us come to the bridge, we bring our own cup of coffee? Nothing anyone can do about that, we have a right to do it. And, suppose something were to happen to each cup? If, for example, you went out on the wing of the bridge and set it on the railing, it could easily fall overboard, even with a gentle roll of the ship. Hell, the steward could be missing a lot of cups. Crafty puffed his pipe and put his work boots on his desk, the sign that he was done calculating, and that, unless his younger union friend had a better idea, it was settled. The Coffee Cup War began.

On his next trip to the bridge, the mate first went to the crew's mess, and poured himself a cup of coffee. The crewmen coming off watch always made a fresh pot for the next watch, another tradition. One of the mate's sailors was there, and apologized about not being able to bring the mate his coffee. After relieving the watch in the wheelhouse, the mate went out on the wing. He finished the coffee and paused. *This is childish and stupid,* he thought. He threw the cup over the side.

This continued every watch, and in between, when Crafty and the mate used any excuse to visit the bridge. The visitor would bring two cups of coffee; the mugs never made it back down to the galley. Within a few days, the crew was bitching to the steward that they could not find enough cups. The last thing a steward wants is a whole crew at his throat. In port, he went ashore and bought three large thermos bottles. He labeled them for each watch. The first guy up to the wheel for the watch would bring a full thermos for the mate. There were no spills on the ladders. The helmsmen were again upholding the tradition, and there was no need for all the cups to end up in the ocean. The mates agreed to abide by this compromise solution, and ended their immature battle.

The twelve passengers they carried had been, up to this point, of little notice. You saw them at meals, had brief conversations with them, but no officer was allowed on their deck, or at the nightly cocktail parties they had at sea. The mate had noticed that sometimes, if he left his laundry in the laundry room too long, he found it all neatly folded and stacked up on the ironing board. The passengers shared the officer's laundry, and one of them was performing this chore for them. It was a nice touch, like having a mysterious Mom on board. Then one of the women passengers, a brunette about 40, who was not only a Mom, but was traveling with her husband and two children, did something very un-mom like.

The mate was in the last hour of his eight to midnight watch. The bridge was quiet and dark, and he was in the chartroom checking the distance off land, calculating the ship's speed, and estimating the time for the next course change. The chartroom was on the port side, just aft of the wheelhouse. He looked up suddenly from the chart, and the woman was standing in the doorway. She said she wanted to see where the ship was. The mate was surprised at this, since passengers always asked permission to come on the bridge. They also used the inside ladder, and came in the back door for this purpose, and always during daylight hours.

He composed himself enough to say that he did "have a minute," and she could take a quick look at the chart. She had the top buttons of her blouse undone. In the little chartroom, with no open portholes, the mate could smell alcohol and perfume -- too much of both. She had a drink glass in her hand. He expected her to stand next to him, but she moved behind him to get around to the other side of him.

As she did so, she "accidentally" rubbed her breasts across his back.

He pretended to ignore the contact, and moved away from her. She stood next to him, close enough to press her side against his. *Christ.* He gave her a quick explanation of the ship's position, course and speed, and then told her that he had work to do, in other words, the game was over, and he wasn't playing. She responded by asking him what time he got off watch, and wondering what the officer's rooms looked like. The mate knew it from her angle. A voyage at sea was romantic to most women. A fling with a younger ship's officer could fulfill some fantasy, perhaps gained from reading too many romance novels. He had to get out of the situation, but didn't want to offend her. He made it clear that he thought she was very attractive. On another ship, another time, yes, he would be very interested, but not now. She finally gave in, and left, this time down the inside ladder to the passenger's deck below. The mate went into the darkened wheelhouse and told the AB that if anyone came into the wheelhouse like that, to say something, and loudly. He didn't like such surprises.

There was one woman, traveling alone, who had caught the eye of most of the officers. She was 53, blonde, cute, and had a petite figure. She would lie out on her deck, sunbathing, and you could not help but notice her. The mate thought that he was getting old to even notice a 53-year old woman. She also had a habit of showing up in the saloon at coffee time, and making conversation with the officers. The mate did not know if any of the officers had made a play for her, but he was soon to find out.

The day after they left Antofagasta, Chile, the mate was on watch when the ship's deck cadet came up for some navigation work. The cadet was on his first trip, and he was a good kid. He worked hard and showed respect for the mates. He was unusually quiet for a cadet, and kept to himself during most of his off-duty hours. He looked nervous and upset. The mate liked the Youngblood, and took him aside.

"What's up with you?" he asked.

"Nothing, nothing."

"Don't bullshit me. Something's up you don't want to talk about. You got money problems?" All cadets had money problems.

"No."

"Need to see the purser for a shot of penicillin, and are afraid to ask?" The mate smiled at this one.

"No, no, nothing like that, but you know, I . . . well, something happened I don't know what to do about, if anything. If I tell you, you have to keep it to yourself." Then the kid spilled it. The previous night, in port, he had stayed on the ship. Antofagasta was a decent sailor's town, and almost the whole crew was ashore. He had gone down to the saloon to get a cup of coffee, and the blonde passenger was there. After some talk, she invited him to her room for a drink.

"So, you nailed a fifty-year old woman, and you feel bad about it?"

"No. God no, we were just talking, you know. She asked me about my family and how it was at the school, and all that. I wouldn't touch her; she's older than my mother." The mate wondered if this was true. Was this kid so naive he didn't think a fifty-year old blonde would try it with a nineteen-year old cadet?

"So, I was in her room, just talking, and then someone started banging on her door, wanting to come in. It was the captain." The mate was beginning to like the little story.

"What next?"

"I told the woman that I shouldn't be in her room, and if the captain found me in there, well, he could get me in trouble with the school. She told me to get in the locker, you know, the clothes closet. I went in there, shut the door, and hid. She opened the door and the captain came in. I could hear everything."

"Continue, young man. It's good for your soul."

"He was all over her. She hollered at him, that he was drunk, and was telling him 'no' and all that. I thought I would have to come out and help her, you know, if he was raping her or something. Before I could decide what to do, she got rid of him and locked the door. I stayed there for a while, to make sure the Old Man was gone. She checked the passageway for me before I left. She also made me promise not to tell anyone, so you can't. Right?"

"Right, right, no problem. You did right to tell me, though. As a cadet, you don't have any authority. You can't even make a logbook entry. Two things, though. If the captain gives you any shit, let me know; and, don't go into any more passenger's rooms, but stay on good terms with the blonde. If she wants to make something out of this, let me know. I'll take care of it, and leave you out, okay?"

"Okay, great. I just want to get this trip over with, you know?"

"Yeah, I know, but this is all part of going to sea, Youngblood; you've got to learn how to handle weird situations and people like Eagle Eye." The kid went below, and the mate finished the watch with a light heart. Of course, he would share this with Crafty, in spite of what he told the kid. As soon as he got off watch, he made some notes about it and talked to his Louisiana shipmate. If the woman didn't want to press charges, Eagle Eye would escape, but it might prove useful ammunition anyway. *Knowledge is power,* he thought.

Their turnaround port was next. Valparaiso, Chile, was the seaport for Santiago. From there, they would head north, with only a couple of stops before the Panama Canal. The mate could imagine the end of the voyage. Except for Captain Eagle Eye, it hadn't been too bad. They arrived in the morning, and he took the rest of the 0800 to 1200 watch on deck, watching the cargo operations.

Within minutes of docking, the decks were swarming with longshoremen, and cargo was going off with booms, winches, slings, pallets and nets. He made his rounds about the main deck, from hatch to hatch, counting the hours until Crafty relieved him on deck. He drifted to the gangway at ten minutes to noon. Crafty was waiting for him.

"There are a couple of guys up by our rooms that want to see us," the Cajun said. "Come on, it'll be okay."

"What guys?"

"Local customs officials."

Sure enough, up on the officers' deck, next to the mate's room, were two guys with badges. The head guy said he had to check the mate's room. This never happened. Officers almost never risked their licenses to sail by smuggling drugs or anything else, and especially not in their rooms. The other factor was that it was an insult, especially in South or Central America, to treat a ship's officer this way. However, they had a right to do it. The mate told them that he had a right to have another officer there as a witness, and unlocked the door. Crafty went in with them. The mate spent the whole time standing, chest puffed up, stripes on his shoulders, acting indignant. The lead guy went through the drawers and lockers, but, of course, found nothing. The mate knew the captain was behind this, and he and Crafty kept an eye on the two locals, to see that they did not plant anything in the room. That was the biggest risk. *Would the son-of-a-bitch captain go that far?* After the mate's room, they wanted to see Crafty's room, and the whole group went in there, with the same results. When it was over, the local guys were apologetic. There was no doubt someone had put them up the search. After this, the customs guys did not search any other officer's room. Crafty asked them if they had searched the spare room on their deck. The leader just smiled. That settled the matter for Crafty. He told the mate that the next day, at sea, he should come up to the bridge on Crafty's watch, just after lunchtime, and they would settle things with Captain Eagle Eye.

The next day they began to sail north, for home, with a few planned stops along the way. The mate went up to the bridge on Crafty's watch, after lunch, as arranged. Crafty was really pissed off about the customs search. He picked up the phone, called the captain and told him he needed him to come to the bridge immediately, and hung up. Then he sent the AB on watch outside, on the wing, and closed the door to the outside. When the captain got up there, Crafty did all the talking. He told him how he knew about the spare room, and had pictures of it, loaded with contraband. He told the old guy that there had better be no more customs problems, or any other problems, for the two relief officers. He told the astounded captain that he knew about his improper advance on one of the women passengers. Further, he informed the red-faced old bastard that there was a secret witness to the whole business. Crafty didn't swear or yell, you can't do that to a captain, but he was giving him hell. The Cajun was over 60, had been to sea for over 30 years, had seen it all, and had no fear of retribution. The captain burned with embarrassment and anger, but said nothing, and went below. The two union mates would continue to watch their backs, but figured they had settled matters.

Allende was still in power in Chile, but he was in serious trouble. By the time the ship docked in Antofagasta, on the way north, there were more moneychangers aboard than normal. The official bank rate of exchange was 43 escudos for a dollar. On the ship, the 'cambio' guys were offering more than a hundred. Some of the dock workers told the mate that they expected the government to fall any day. The mate knew that whatever they were offering on the ship, he could get more uptown. The government was trying to hold the line on inflation, somehow, and held the exchange rate at the official level. They were also forbidding businesses from raising their prices. A foreigner with dollars, marks, pounds, or yen could profit from all this, if he took the risk of exchanging money illegally.

Antofagasta had an abundance of bars with cheap booze and young girls. You could buy good Chilean wines cheaply and even have cases of it delivered to the ship. Sweaters and rugs were popular take home items. The mate changed just enough money on the ship for walking-around money, and went ashore after dinner. He got 140 to the dollar right on deck. He went up to the nearest hotel, where there was a nice bar. He ordered a local beer, and after he paid for it with Escudos, he figured that at the exchange rate he got, the beer cost less than ten cents. It wasn't rotgut beer, either. The mate used his gutter Spanish to ask the bartender if he knew anyone who wanted to "cambio dinero."

"Si, Pedro." The bartender went down to the other end of the bar, and had a few words with a fat guy, presumably Pedro. Pedro came over to the mate and motioned him towards the men's room. At this point, the mate's survival senses went on alert. Would the guy try to rob him in there? Hell, it was a nice hotel, and the men's room was nearby, not far away. There were many other people around.

The mate got in the men's room first, and checked to see if anyone else was in there. Two against one was no fun if you were the one. It was empty, and Pedro came in alone. Pedro lifted up his shirt to expose a money belt that went all around his large waist. The mate did not see a weapon.

"What you got, dollars, pounds, marks, what?" Pedro asked.

"How much you give for dollars?"

"200."

"Okay. Here's 60 bucks, then, for 12,000 escudos." Pedro took out a huge roll of thousand Escudo notes, and peeled off twelve of them.

"That's all you got?"

"Si." Pedro seemed disappointed. "Posseeblay mas, manana, in la noche, senor." The mate used his few words to tell him he might have more tomorrow night.

"Bueno." He left, and the mate went back to his barstool. It had been illegal, but he had exchanged money in a dozen other countries in similar fashion. You would never find out who Pedro worked for -- you didn't ask.

He ordered another beer, and calculated that he now could get drunk on less than a dollar. He could never spend 16,000 in that place. As the night went on, he ordered food, bought drinks for some shipmates, and tipped the bartender a lot. Several guys from the ship showed up. They split into two general categories. Some left for the sailor bars. The mate and some others stayed put at the hotel. It was a festive atmosphere. He had never seen a sailor's money go so far. A few local peddlers came through. One had guitars for sale. The mate picked one out, having no idea how to play it. He paid six dollars for it. Blankets, rugs, pottery, and the guitar eventually littered the bar.

He started to feel out of control, and decided to go back to get a few hours sleep before going on cargo watch. He had spent less than twenty dollars. The engineer on the same watch went with him. The street of sailor bars was on the way, and they decided to go in and have one last drink in one of them, and see what was going on. The place was typical. Tables full of sailors from all over, young girls in short skirts, with too much perfume on, circulated around the tables. It was dark and smoky, and there was the usual loud music, a combination of local tunes, and old American ones. As his eyes adjusted, the mate saw the deck cadet making his way over to their table. He had a girl in tow.

The kid sat down, and the mate bought him and his girl a drink. *So, the kid isn't such a goody two-shoes after all,* he thought. He was, however, acting nervous again.

"What's up, kid?"

"Well, nothing, I just . . . well, I like this girl here, Maria, you know, but she doesn't speak any English, and I don't speak any Spanish, you see?"

"Yeah, I see. What are you trying to tell me?"

"Well, I don't know, I just want to figure things out with her."

"Listen, Youngblood, I know you didn't meet this girl in church, so what exactly are you trying to figure out? I know a few words of Spanish; enough to get you in trouble, if that's what you want, but it's your lookout, right?"

"Right. That's it exactly. I mean, I know I have to pay her, and probably a hotel, too, but I don't know how much is right, or how to ask. Can you help me?"

"No problem, that's what shipmates are for." The engineer and the mate then used their gutter Spanish to arrange things for the deckie. The two youngsters got up to leave.

"Hey kid, you okay for money?"

"Yeah, mate. Even I can make out in this place."

"You didn't change your money at the bank, did you?"

"No. I'm a rookie, but I'm not that stupid."

"Good. Can you find your way back to the ship, in the dark, even if you're drunk?" The mate knew the kid was planning on staying in the hotel all night, and walking back to the dock in the morning. He also knew that after an hour in a dingy hotel with a girl who wouldn't seem so impressive after you laid there a while and thought about it all, the kid might decide to leave before then.

"Yeah, don't worry. I'll be there for work in the morning."

The mate slipped the kid 5,000 escudos and made him take it. The youngsters left and the two officers finished their drinks, passed out a few more smokes to the girls cruising around the tables, and began the walk down to the darkened dock. Their walk was a little wobbly, and the mate had his guitar slung over his shoulder, the engineer some rugs over his. The mate figured the negative part of this money-changing business was that many of the locals seemed desperate. If the government, banks and their economy fell apart, they would be hurting even worse. The mate was glad they would get out of Chile before any shooting started in the streets. A few months later, he would read in the papers about the fall of Allende, and wonder how Pedro, Maria, the hotel bartender, and all the dockworkers were doing.

Crafty's talk with Eagle Eye had worked. There was no more bullshit. The trip was winding down, but they had another stop before Panama. They were going to Guayaquil, Ecuador, chiefly to load bananas. The mate thought that it was a close contest between Buenaventura and Guayaquil as to which place was the armpit of the west coast of South America. If he had a vote, he would have said that Buenaventura was worse. In Guayaquil, there were some decent places if you took a cab ride. That, plus the drug trade being stronger in Colombia tipped the scales, but not by much. Just getting to a dock in Ecuador was a hassle.

The port was upriver, and the piloting was difficult. There were strong currents, which made steering a bitch, especially when passing another ship. The pilots just told the helmsman to "steady." The pilot would take you upriver, and then tell you to anchor for a day or two to await dock space. At night, pirates would come around in small boats. They would climb up on deck any way they could, even climb up the anchor chain, or use ropes and grappling hooks. Then they would run all over the ship, stealing whatever they could, and throw it down into the boats, or, if the item would float, like your damn mooring lines, right into the river, to retrieve them later. The crooks running all over the deck would eventually just jump into the river, and swim to their boats.

The local authorities seemed to do little to prevent this. Over time, the bandits got bolder, and would break into containers and crates with crowbars. They sometimes carried guns. Companies who traded there fought back by hiring armed guards. However, these were local guys, and it was hard to tell who was on what side. The deckhands and mates patrolled the deck. They put bright lights over the gunwale, shining down in the water. They rigged fire hoses fore and aft, and upon sighting a small boat sneaking alongside, the deck hands would spray water to keep them away. It seemed a poor defense. Sometimes sailors got hurt, sometimes killed. The mate had told captains in dangerous places that if they really wanted him to patrol the decks like that, he needed to carry a sidearm, and preferably have a crewman with a shotgun with him. In the American Merchant Marine, no company allowed this, although the mate had been on a ship or two that illegally carried weapons in the chief mate's locker. Is the ship safer if everyone knows they have no guns, or do the sailors have a right to defend themselves against attack?

They got upriver to Guayaquil okay, but had to anchor for several hours. It wasn't too bad. A few boats came around, but they chased them away. The ship had nothing out on deck, not even the heavy mooring lines. The watertight doors leading outside to the main deck were chained shut from the inside, with crewmen on watch there with keys, for an emergency.

They got to the dock early in the morning, after the usual shouting and arguing between the captain and the local pilot, and the hassles of getting eight-inch lines to the dock so they could haul the ship alongside. Tugboats in South America did not like to push a ship towards the dock. They towed you with your line near the dock, but the rest was up to you. The tugs that worked the waterfronts in the U.S. were much better.

There was some general cargo to unload and backload -- crates, pallets and drums, the usual variety, but the main event would come that night. All day, the tween deck spaces in some hatches that had refrigeration ducts were prepared for loading bananas. The United Fruit Company was best known for carrying bananas and citrus from Central and South America. Their ships were painted white, to keep the ship cooler, and had entire hatches fitted with cooling ducts. They had non-union crews, however, and the union guys used the expression, "If you have to go fruit, go United," every time they saw one of them.

As evening approached, the tween deck spaces were ready. Shore crews had emptied the spaces, swept them clean, and laid dunnage, wood boards, on top of the steel deck. The dunnage was to make sure that any moisture that collected on the deck drained aft, to the bilge box, and did not damage the cartons. It also created a layer of air under the first tier of bananas. Deck hands dogged down the hatch covers, and the engineers ran the giant coolers, bringing the temperature down. You got into the spaces only through a manhole on the main deck and climbing down a steel ladder straight down into the hatch. There were sideports in the hull for loading. These hinged, steel doors were about seven feet high, and you dogged them down from the inside of the hatch, to make the hull watertight at sea.

The dockworkers would place wooden ramps to each sideport from the dock. As the ship rose or fell with the tide, the angle would change, and they would adjust them. At times, you would have to duck your head going in. It was hot work. They would wear shorts and sandals. Some would go barefoot. A few would step on nails or trash on the dock and cut their feet. Timing was important. Plantation workers picked the bananas at just the right time to be loaded into trucks and immediately driven to Guayaquil, directly to the docks. They wouldn't be stored into the warehouse, as happened with a lot of cargo; the trucks would drive right onto the dock, and the loading would begin. The trucks would come from small towns and villages, usually driven by their owners, who contracted for the work. It was a big deal all around Ecuador.

Everything was ready by dark. Everyone rested. Suddenly, the first wave of trucks pulled onto the apron of the dock, honking their horns. The trucks were gaily decorated with designs painted on them, and had tassels and little lights around the windshields. Several people were crammed into each cab. Lights on the trucks flashed, the foremen began shouting, and the quiet dock area turned into organized chaos. The bearers began to line up behind the trucks. The drivers got down and dropped the tailgates. People shouted to the men inside the ship to open up the sideports.

The tallymen positioned themselves at each ramp, with their paper form and pencils ready. They would count the boxes from each truck that went into each hatch. The workers inside the hatches got up from their naps and got ready. Runners went to fetch coffee for the bosses. It would be along night. Inside #3 hatch, the mate made a last check that all was in order. The temperature in the hatch was acceptable, although the temperature would rise with the sideport open. He didn't have to concern himself with the tallymen. The ship's agent would settle with them later, agreeing eventually on the number of cartons that actually went into the ship. He did have to check the temperature of the bananas, however, and carried a thermometer with a probe in his pocket. It was a sign of importance, along with his khaki uniform and shoulder boards with stripes. An officer on a merchant ship got more respect in Ecuador than he did in the United States, and it helped to look and act like one.

Soon there was activity everywhere, in several hatches at once, and with trucks all over the dock. Sweaty men ran up the ramps with cartons on their shoulders. The ones who had done it before had a folded cloth on their shoulder to place the box on. It would be a long haul, and they could not afford to get a sore shoulder quickly. One of the most important workers in the hatch was the stickman. He had little sticks, like square dowels, in bundles. As the layers of cartons were stacked in the spaces, it was his job to run around and place the sticks just so. The idea was to leave a little air space between tiers of cartons, so the cool air the engineers would pump into the hatch would circulate. As the bananas got stacked higher and higher throughout the night, workers put dunnage against the sides of the cartons, to leave a vertical shaft of open space for the air to move.

The mate spent most of his watch climbing into and out of each hatch, checking on all this, and taking temperatures. He made his customary appearance out on the dock also, acting as if he was checking the work habits of all. Standing silently, watching, acting important, was an art form appreciated in Ecuador. The truck drivers would stand around, nervously watching, like expectant fathers, over their cargo. Their responsibility was over when their trucks were empty, and others pulled up to take their space.

Two other things came with the bananas. The first was tarantulas. They hid in the bananas, and liked the leaves. Some of them were huge. The locals got a good laugh when the mate jumped back after surprising a particularly large one.

The other was "banana girls." These enterprising young ladies rode the trucks from small villages and plantations, and hung around the dock until they could get a chance to board the ship. Once on board, they would roam the passageways, offering to participate in various gymnastic exercises with whatever sailor they met up with, in his room. The going price for a room visit was only a few dollars. Five or ten would get you special treatment. They especially liked being able to take a shower in the sailors' rooms. It seemed many of them did not have that luxury in their homes. The sailors, for their part, were grateful that they got the service right on board; no need to chase around bars uptown, or on the dangerous waterfront. It saved them time and money. Tips for the girls included cigarettes, gum, and candy bought from the slop chest, and soap and laundry detergent, which cost the sailors nothing.

Captain Eagle Eye, however, gave orders that the girls were not to board the vessel. The main worry was stowaways, although it could be an ugly business if the passengers ran across half-naked girls running around the decks. In reality, the girls knew better than to go above the crew's deck without an invitation. An officer would sometimes take one up to his deck, but it had to be more discreet than the party going on down in the crew's quarters. The order forbidding this activity would go to the watch mates, and to the local gangway watchmen. The watchmen would tell the girls who started up the gangway to forget it. This would make both the girls and the sailors who wanted to participate, unhappy. One sailor was insistent to the extent that he went down the gangway, approached a girl by the truck she had ridden on, made his bargain, and took her behind a shed right on the dock. The mate was in the middle, listening to the pleadings and complaints of both parties. He just blamed the captain, but it was a legal order, and he did his best, without a weapon, to enforce it. You would always get the bosun and check the rooms before sailing, mostly to make sure no one had forgotten the sailing time, and was asleep. A life at sea can be difficult, and the banana girls provided some relief from it, for those that were interested. The sailors got what they paid for, the girls were happy, and what the hell. But, orders were orders.

The main problem with enforcing the order was the tide. Guayaquil had a large rise and fall of the water level. The mate knew that at one point, the ship would be so low in the water the main deck would be even with the dock. This happened towards the end of his watch. Now the game was at hand. You could now easily board the ship from almost anywhere along its length, not just by the guarded gangway. Soon, out of the corner of his eye, he saw the first shadowy female form, up near #2 hatch, step the few feet between the dock and the ship's railing. She grabbed the railing and easily hopped over it.

The mate had to make at least the appearance of stopping her, and walked forward on the main deck. Of course, by the time he got up to #2, the girl was gone. *She's done this before,* the mate thought. He turned quickly and looked aft. In the dark, he could make out two or three more forms, back near the stern of the ship, boarding the same way. Everyone knew where he was. By this time, some crewmembers were out on deck, and the mate knew that they were helping the girls. He could not stop it, and did not care to get in a fight over it either. Soon, there were girls all over the crew's deck, and a couple on the officer's deck, but there were none near the passengers or captain. The mate walked back by the gangway and gave the watchmen a stern look. He ended his watch by telling the watchmen that every damn girl had better be off the ship an hour before it sailed. He told the chief mate that he had better get a few reliable sailors to sweep the quarters well before sailing. The boss mate nodded sadly, knowing that he could not stop it now either.

By noon the next day, the ship was ready to go to Panama and New Orleans. As planned, a large group of officers and crew made a thorough sweep of the ship. The mate went along with a passkey and knocked on, then opened, every door. The sailors understood the importance of this. If they screwed it up this time, Eagle Eye would have a dozen guards the next time, and there would be no on-board parties. The ship was clean when it sailed. It was uncertain if the crew would be clean on the trip back, or if some of them would go to the purser for penicillin, but that was the chance they took. The banana girls didn't seem to worry about anything.

It was only about five days to New Orleans, but it went without incident. Thanks to the Cajun's lecture, Eagle Eye left the mates alone. They docked, signed off the official ship's articles, and got their pay. The mate called a friend to come get him, said his goodbyes to the mates, engineers, and crew he liked, and took his gear down by the gangway. It had been a short trip for a sailor, only six weeks, but had seemed longer, thanks to Captain Jerk. It would be good to get off and look for another ship. However, Eagle Eye appeared on the main deck, by the gangway, somewhere you rarely see a captain. He approached the mate.

"You turn your goddam keys in, mate?" he growled.

"Yeah, Cap', I turned them in."

"Well, goddam it, I don't want to see you on my ship again!"

The mate gave him a cold stare. "Cap', I didn't know you owned this ship, I thought the company did; and if a goddam job comes up on it, I'm going to bid on it. I like it here!"

Eagle Eye stormed off, red-faced, and cursing, as usual. The mate's ride showed up, and he hauled his stuff down the gangway, happy that he was leaving the crusty old bastard in his normal emotional state.

Chapter 15: Brazilian Rerun

The mate eventually got tired of New Orleans, although he had friends there, could get dates regularly, and managed to even save some money. The new style of dating, with those hippy-looking girls who were not impressed with a three-piece suit, didn't require expensive ritual dates like the traditional southern girls did. In spite of these good times down in the French Quarter, or uptown along Charles Street, the mate yearned for a different culture and geography. Perhaps under the influence of several other mates and engineers who were from New England, he moved to Boston. He had been born in Connecticut, and thought it was a return home, in a way.

He rented an apartment in the city and explored the area. He enjoyed being able to visit the "House of the Seven Gables," and stand at Concord Bridge. The Salem witch trials came alive. The fishing harbors around Boston had character, too, but the mate had no desire to go commercial fishing. You could stand on an old, damn old, widow's walk on top of a sea captain's house from the 1800's and imagine the whaling or clipper ship days. He loved the history of Boston, as well as autumn, a season he had almost forgotten about, living down south.

He took some college courses and began to imagine there could be a life after the sea, if he ever got tired of it. There wasn't much shipping out of Beantown, but he had a brother in New York who would put him up, and the mate usually went there to ship. He sailed to North Europe more, sometimes on the newer style "container ships." It was the way of the future, everyone said; ships with no cargo gear, just packed with trailer truck bodies stuffed with cargo you never saw. The old cargo work with booms and hooks, pallets, drums and crates lashed all over the place was disappearing. Some docks now had giant cranes that lifted an entire truck body from the dock to your ship, where longshoremen secured it with metal stacking pins and heavy wire lashings on deck. Ships had more automation, especially in the engine room, and the new invention, the computer, began to go to sea. There was talk about getting navigational positions from satellites, something the mate could not imagine. He had been happy to get a calculator that could handle algebraic formulas.

A cute girl he knew from New Orleans came to Boston for a visit, and stayed. A fun weekend led to a longer stay. They got married and had a son. He was a family man now, something else he had not thought likely. He tried to work ashore, but nothing paid very much. The wife stayed home with the baby, and for the first time, he felt pressure to earn a steady living. He liked teaching school, but even around Boston, it only paid about $8,000 a year. He wasn't quite 30, but felt older. He kept shipping out.

Down to New York he went, again and again. One trip he caught out of the old union hall was a relief trip as 2nd mate on a Moore-McCormack freighter. The ship wasn't a containership, or "box ship;" it was a freighter, or a "boom ship." It was 550 feet long, had six hatches, could make 24 knots, and had some early automated functions. He would sail to Brazil, a country he had not been to in many years. The weather would be a big improvement from the North Atlantic, and that was a bonus.

When you shipped out of New York, the union sent you a few blocks away, near Wall Street, to a clinic. The pre-employment exam was routine, but the 300-pound nurse who filled out your fit for duty slip was special. When you were all done, she called you into a little office. She would have the paper right in front of her, but before she would sign it, she gave everybody a VD lecture. If you were going to the Far East, she would say that there was a new strain of disease in

Hong Kong that penicillin couldn't touch. If you were going to South America, she would say the same thing about a new Brazilian disease.

The ship was in Brooklyn, at old pier #4. The elevated subway ran right by it, and there was a real tough waterfront bar on the corner, the first place you saw going out, and the last place going back. The warehouse was filled with all kinds of cargo; bags of fresh coffee, ingots of metal, frozen shrimp and fish, crates of household goods, and a special locker with more expensive items locked up. The mate liked walking through it on the way to the ship. With the smells of all the cargo, the buzzing of forklifts that almost ran you over, and the shouting of the longshoremen, he thought the place had character. On a containership dock, all you saw were huge rows of parked trucks, and you had no idea what was in them until you got a list. The containers were already loaded before they got to the piers. Those docks were cold and sterile.

There seemed to be an unusual amount of activity on board the ship. When he got to his room, it looked like someone had given it a going over. The mattress was off the bunk, and all the lockers and drawers were open. The BR, or bedroom steward, the guy who took care of the officers' quarters appeared suddenly, with fresh linen in his arms. He apologized for not having the room ready, and explained that a group of drug agents had been searching the ship all day. The mate found the chief mate out on deck, and introduced himself. He would go right to work, as soon as he got into the room and changed. The chief mate told how the drug agents, apparently acting on a tip, had met the ship in force when it had docked the previous day. They found a bundle on the ship that contained 23 pounds of high quality cocaine. The ship was hot now, and could expect similar treatment everywhere. The agents were mad, he said, because the coke was in a public space, an area that was accessible to everyone on the ship. They had no fingerprints, and so far, had arrested no one. Someone had secured the bundle in a passageway that led out onto the main deck, up above some pipes, lashed so that you could not see it even if you walked right underneath it. Between the tip, and with the help of a dope dog, they had found it. They had tossed all the crew's rooms, and, not finding anything, went after the officers, a highly unusual thing for them to do. They even had gone into empty passenger rooms, and the galley. Three agents had rooms on the ship, and stayed aboard all night. They were working the cargo hatches now, huge spaces to search. The ship, and the company, had been nice as hell to them, hoping they would not delay the sailing of the ship, and not caring if they caught the dumb bastard who had gotten the ship in trouble.

They made Philly, Baltimore and Norfolk on the coastwise, loading all the time. They were hassled by drug agents in every port. In Philadelphia, one even came aboard with a dog that sniffed every room on the ship. A few days later, the coastwise was over, and they sailed past Cape Henry, headed south for Brazil. It had been many years since the mate had been there. He was happier sailing through the Caribbean than the north Atlantic. The officers and crew seemed like a decent bunch. The captain was competent and sober most of the time. The engineers seemed okay, and a couple of them were in their 20's or 30's. Even the radio operator didn't seem as batty as most of them were, and, on this trip, the purser and chief steward were not in a smuggling racket with anybody. The chief mate didn't say much, spending all his time with day work with the crew, and working on his stability and cargo plans. The mate was sailing 2nd, which he liked, and standing the 4 to 8 watch, which he always thought was the best watch. The 12 to 4 third mate was about 30, still young for the merchant marine. He was a hawsepipe mate, having worked his way up from the crew ranks over the years. He and the mate got along well, at work and off. The only potential problem was the other third mate, who had the 8 to 12 watch. His name was Jack, and it was his first trip as an officer.

Jack was just 22-years old, fresh out of one of the state maritime academies. Five states had four-year programs to become an officer in the merchant marine. A lot of good mates and engineers came out of them. The drawback was they did not get their sailing experience on regular merchant ships in service, but on training ships. Jack had said that on his training cruises, ten students would crowd around a small chart table to learn something from the navigation officer, and if you were standing in the back, you didn't see anything or learn anything. Jack must have been standing in the back a lot. He had enough basic book knowledge, but couldn't apply it. He also didn't catch on right away to the way things were. The mate and the other 3rd mate figured he could learn what was what, or fail. They had made their first attempt to teach him in New York.

Late in the afternoon back in New York, before they sailed, a technician had come down to the ship to install a new type of Loran receiver, an electronic navigation device. It was just about quitting time for all the mates, but the 2nd and 3rd mates were going up to the bridge to have the technician show them how to use it. They stopped by Jack's room.

"Hey, Jack?"

"Yeah?"

"There's a guy up on the bridge putting in a new Loran. He's going to teach us how to use it. If you want, come on up with us."

"Well, we're officially off duty, right?"

"Yeah, that's right."

"Well, I'm going ashore then. I'm meeting a guy I went to school with, for beer."

"Okay, Jack."

The other two mates went up for the lesson, on their own time. It took an hour or so, but they not only learned how to use it, they learned to tell when the readings were not reliable. The device was an advance in technology. It not only received the radio signals, it converted the results into latitude and longitude readouts. It then gave continuous positions, but these were assumptions. You couldn't just read it and rely on the position.

Their last port in the states was Norfolk, and they left for sea early in the evening. Jack came up to relieve the mate at ten minutes to eight, the traditional time for officers to take over the watch. He spent a few minutes looking around, and then passed the course, officially taking over. As the mate was leaving, however, Jack asked him to step into the chartroom. He did so.

"Second, you know this new thing here, the Loran?"

"Yeah."

"Well, I've never seen one like it before. Could you show me how to tune it in and all?"

"I could, but I won't. The manual is right beside it. You read that." He left. Jack looked forlorn that the mate wasn't ready to give him a lesson; he didn't quite get it.

The cycle of watches repeated throughout the night, and the next morning, Jack again came up right on time. This time the mate asked Jack to step into the chartroom. As navigation officer, he had a habit of checking all the navigation work on the chart, not just his own. He had seen some positions from Jack's watch the night before that he did not understand. Jack had the marks on the chart showing the ship close to the course the mate had drawn, then suddenly veering off five miles to the east, and then going parallel to the intended course. He pointed these out to Jack.

"What happened last night; traffic? The navy play war games, you went around all of them, something like that?"

"Oh no, nothing like that. I turned this thing here on, you know, the thing that shows you how deep the water is, and I was getting readings. I figured we were in shallow water, so I hauled her out to sea more, you know, to deeper water."

"That's nice. It's called a fathometer. How deep was the water?"

"Oh, I don't know, about 30."

"Thirty what?"

"Fathoms, I think."

"Is that below the keel or with the draft of the ship added?"

"Well, that's what the fathometer said."

"Jack, look at the goddam chart. How deep should the water have been along the track where you did this?"

"Well, there's a number 35 right near there."

"Right. If you look in the corner of the chart, it says the soundings are in fathoms. We're drawing about five fathoms more. A reading of 30 or so is perfectly normal along there. You took us five miles off course for no reason." The mate took stock of Jack's blank expression and left.

Over the next couple of days, the mate and the other 3rd mate talked it over. The 3rd mate had worse problems, since he relieved Jack's watch, just before noon and again at midnight. If Jack got the ship into trouble with his poor navigation, or collision avoidance, he had to fix it up. Jack was happy-go-lucky, and didn't seem to notice any problems. When he fucked up, he would always say, "I didn't learn that in school," and that seemed, in Jack's opinion, to be the end of it. The mate and the 3rd decided to have a talk with Jack. The 3rd mate got up for breakfast, and came up to the bridge at 0800, when Jack and the mate were relieving the watch. They took Jack into the chartroom, and shut the door. It was just the three watch mates, all of whom were young for the merchant marine.

"We've got to talk to you, Jack," the mate said.

"Okay, guys, what about?"

"You," the 3rd said. "You're dangerous, and you don't have a fucking clue what is going on. I'm tired of relieving you with things fucked up. Your radar plots aren't right. The other night you told me there were two fishing boats out there, when both of them were clearly showing the lights of ships, underway."

"And," the mate added, "this crap about teaching you. Why the fuck should we teach you anything? This isn't the goddam schoolship. This is real. You take the same pay we do, but you can't do the job. You belong to the same union. You are our competition in the union hall for work. Why should we help you? You think this is a vacation? Do you know that if you have a collision or grounding, you can go to jail if someone gets hurt? Do you realize that you can lose your license to sail? No more career, no job, no money?"

Jack was silent. He looked like a little schoolboy who the teacher caught throwing spitballs in class.

"I'm sorry, guys. I mean, I want to sail, I've always wanted to. I'm just not sure what to do out here with everything."

"Look, Jack," the mate said, "you seem like a nice kid. You work hard when you work. But no one cares what happened to you in school. You can cut it or get off. The captain's on to you, too, isn't he? He started standing most of your watches with you, and gave you strict orders to call him, day or night, whenever another ship is within eight miles, right?"

"Yeah, he did."

"Well, that doesn't cut it out here. The next captain you sail with may not be so kind. The next guy won't want to hear your goddam whining about why you don't know this or that. This guy is willing to help you, and so are we, but you have to make more of an effort."

"What do you want me to do?" Jack was beaten. At least he knew he needed help. He finally recognized the difference between a student cruise and being a responsible mate.

"Don't come up here right on time, and then ask me all kinds of questions," the mate said. "I don't get paid for being your goddam teacher. You want to learn from me, you come up here an hour early. Then, you watch what I do. If I'm not busy, you can ask questions, and I'll help you."

"And, when I relieve you," the 3rd said, "you don't leave until I say so. If you have a poor position, or radar plot, we'll work on it right then. Also, when you leave the bridge each watch, you take something with you, down to your room, to study. Let me know what you take. Start with the Loran manual, or the radar instructions, for example. You need to make up for some things you didn't learn in school. Got it?"

"Yeah, I got it. Look, I appreciate this. You guys are right. I've got a lot to learn. It's just that, well, I was so happy to get out of school and get out here, you know? It's the first time I ever made good money, and my parents are real proud of me, and all that. I was so happy to be an officer; I guess I didn't realize how serious this could be. I'll work real hard."

That was how they left it. Jack had his chance. He could work at it, in which case the other two mates would help him, or he could be lazy, or have an attitude, in which case they would not. They would not let the ship get in danger, if they could help it, but they would not protect Jack anymore.

The mate had half expected Jack to tell them to mind their own business, or, the sailor's equivalent, "fuck off." But he hadn't. His behavior changed rapidly. He came up to watch early, to work with the 2nd mate, and stayed late to learn from the older and wiser 3rd mate. He studied the manuals, as they told him to, and began to catch on. There was hope for him, and it made the mate happy they had spoken to him. The captain, however, continued to stand watch with him. He just didn't trust him with collision avoidance. The mate thought that if Jack survived his first year at sea, he would probably become a terrific mate, and someday a captain. Some of the least likely guys in the mate's school had gone far, mostly on dogged determination, rather than brains.

They began to hit ports in Brazil. Belem was the first one southbound. It was about 100 miles up the Amazon

River, but the water was deep enough for ships like theirs to get to. They anchored in the river overnight, and went to a dock in the morning. The only remarkable things the mate experienced there had nothing to do with the Amazon River. He went along with a couple of others in a small boat, from the anchorage to a wooden pier. There was idle chatter amongst the crew whether the Amazon had crocodiles or alligators, but they saw neither. On the pier, they found an old beat up car that served as a taxi. There was no meter, and the passengers negotiated a price to take the group to Belem. The road went through the jungle for several miles. It was dark, and the mate noticed that the cabbie did not have his lights on. Then they saw a shape in the dark coming towards them, and the driver flashed his headlights at it. The shape was a car coming the other way, and that driver flashed his lights on, then off, too. They passed each other, and the mate knew that rural drivers in Brazil were still saving their headlights. He hoped the driver had good night vision.

The city of Belem was one of the poorest the mate had ever seen. There didn't seem to be a nice section of the city anywhere. There were apartments at street level that had no glass windows, only wooden shutters. On some of the streets they walked, young girls hung out of these windows and hollered at them to do a little business. The sidewalks and streets were full of trash. Everyone seemed poor. There were beggars and hustlers all over the damn place. The group tried to find a quiet bar to get a beer, but they were unsuccessful. They settled on a place anyway. There were girls hustling their wares, and the beer was local, tasted terrible, and wasn't very cold. Loud Brazilian music played from an old jukebox, and they heard the usual requests for American cigarettes. It was a familiar scene to the mate. There probably was a better section of the city, but none of them knew Belem very well, and the cabbie had been no help.

After the second beer, the mate was thinking of giving up for the night, not being interested in cheap, rowdy bars.

Then a couple of girls began doing table dances. One of the guys at the mate's table gave one of them a buck or two for a dance. She happily jumped up on the table and began gyrating to the local beat. It wasn't exactly a striptease, but she did make a show of lifting her dress now and again. The mate could sense the evening degenerating even further, and left with one of the engineers. The two eventually found a little bar with no music, just a few local guys drinking quietly. They got a couple of looks, but no hassles. This time they saw a bottle of rum behind the bar that they recognized, and had that, with some coca-cola. They even got slices of lime, and knew they were in a higher class of bar. They left soon after, tipping the bartender for finding them a cab, of sorts, to drive them back. The mate had his usual piece of paper with directions written in Portuguese, and they got a similar, no-headlight ride back. The mate pulled out a couple packs of Marlboros he had hidden in his socks for the bribe to get a small boat to take them out into the river, to their anchored ship. As he went to bed, he wondered what the smaller towns and villages up the Amazon were like.

Salvador, known popularly as Bahia, was the next stop. The mate had been there before, and, after working his cargo shift, rode the tram uphill from the dock area to the main part of the city. He wandered around until after dark, and found himself near a church the sailors called the Church of Gold. There was a service going on, and he went in, even though he was not Catholic. It was located in a poor section of the city. The outside of the church looked just like the hundreds of others in this city that claimed to have a different Catholic church for every day of the year. It was standing room only inside and the mate edged his way to the side of the pews, at the back. There was gold everywhere. From crucifix to goblet, it was all gold. Gold frames on the windows, gold thread in fabric, gold was everywhere, it seemed, except the stained glass windowpanes themselves. It all glittered and shone brightly. The service went on, in Latin, and the people sang, prayed and crossed themselves. The mate left quietly. He was glad he had seen this place, but outside, the contrast with the poor neighborhood hit him as it must have hit all non-Catholics. Why did they need all that gold in a church meant to serve this poor part of town? It was a question he could not answer.

Rio was the next stop, and the mate's favorite place in Brazil. One might assume it would be the favorite place of all sailors, but this was not true. Not everybody made it out to the beaches or the other world-famous tourist spots. The ports that had more honky-tonk bars with cheap booze and women were still popular with many guys. They docked just before midnight. The mate was on the bow, the salty 3rd on the stern, and Jack on the bridge, their normal docking stations. The three watch mates met at the gangway after docking, to watch the rigging of it, and see who came aboard -- port officials, company agent, or workers. The mate looked at his watch and realized that it was midnight. The ship would be there two days. He and the salty 3rd told Jack that they were breaking sea watches, going on 8-hour cargo watches, instead of 4-hour watches. Jack thought this was a great idea until they then told him that he had the midnight to 0800, was now on watch, and would stay awake all night until relieved by the mate after breakfast. To his credit, young Jack did not complain. He had begun to learn that you often had to work fourteen-hour days with no sleep, in order to get a few hours uptown. Then, right there at the gangway, still dressed in officers' khakis, with their walkie-talkies still slung over their shoulders, the two older mates decided to go ashore for a quick beer or two. The mate had cash in his pocket, and they walked down the gangway, waving goodbye to a quiet, young Jack as they went.

They walked a few blocks along the waterfront, which they both knew, and past the Florida Bar, to the Subway Bar. It was still open, no surprise with the time, as Rio is a party place, but they knew that occasionally the police shut the place down.

The two mates sat at a booth, letting their eyes adjust to the dim lights. Soon, the scene the mate had seen years before unfolded. A waiter took drink orders, and the girls began to circle the club. They were, as he had noticed years before, some of the prettiest girls in Rio, and were dressed up. They did not dance on tables, or offer to perform services right at the table, or under it, like in some places in Panama or Colombia. If business were slow, they would get up on the little dance floor in the middle of the club, with all the lights, and dance with each other. It was not cool for a customer to get up and dance there; the polished wooden floor was for the girls to showcase themselves. The mate passed out a few American cigarettes, but declined offers to buy drinks, or allow a girl to sit at the table. The other patrons late that night were locals in business suits, and some Japanese from another merchant ship. The two mates noticed that, in typical fashion, the Japanese were dressed in suits, spent a lot of money, and were having a great time. The mate had seen this behavior all over the world. He figured that such places in Japan would be much more expensive, and Japanese officers liked to act like big shots anyway. They would buy girls drinks and throw cash around as if it was nothing; Japanese, Brazilian, or American money, whatever you preferred.

The mate liked the Subway mostly for the fact that it was a sinful place where you could just drink and watch everybody else. If the girls who worked the club were poor and uneducated, they didn't act like it. Somebody had selected them carefully, and trained them how to act. Maybe that's what the Japanese or local businessmen liked. They had more class than the usual Brazilian working girls. The two mates had a couple of drinks and walked back to the ship. It was another sign the mate was getting older. He had ignored some of the prettiest girls in Rio, and had put sleep ahead of drinking and chasing girls.

He got up at 0715, had breakfast, and found Jack by the gangway, the traditional place to relieve the cargo watch, at 0750. As young as Jack was, he looked exhausted. The mate saw that his khakis were filthy. The best sign that he had been working properly was a mark across his back. It had the unmistakable tread mark of a greased lashing wire.

"Okay, Jack, I've got her. Looks like you've been down in the hatches, eh?"

"Yeah," he replied weakly. "Had to check a bunch of stuff. Here's the cargo plan. I crossed off the cargo that's gone."

"Good job, Youngblood. Have a good breakfast."

"Breakfast, hell, I'm going straight to bed." He left, dragging himself up the ladder, and the mate thought, *There is hope for him yet.* It wasn't a party all the time; you were going to have some rough days and long nights. The mate left to cruise the deck, and check on the discharge of cargo in every hatch they were working. The backloading of cargo for other ports would begin by afternoon, and then, he would get a new stowage plan from the chief mate to start checking that also. Jack would be okay by supper, and, if things went normally, would then find enough energy to go ashore. He would still be back by midnight to do another eight hours of climbing up and down the steel ladders in and out of the dirty hatches, interspersed with trips to the bow and stern to check and handle lines, if necessary, deal with longshore bosses and company agents, and so forth. It was a great job if you liked all that.

In Rio, the mate repaid a favor in a traditional way. He arranged with the captain and the chief mate to give the cadets on the ship the day off, and he browbeat some money out of all the officers to send them off to Copacabana Beach, Mount Corcovado, and wherever else they wanted to go. Others had done this favor for him, years before. It made the mate feel older that he did not want to go with them, and they, once they got the going-ashore money, did not invite him.

Santos was the next stop. Most of the crew felt this was the best place. Monkey Wrench Corner was still in business, full of bars, girls, cheap beer, and souvenir shops. He intended to bypass the sin pit and go out to the beach area, but agreed to stop there for a look with the engineer from his watch. They left after their shift, and went into one of the bigger clubs. He had not been to this area since he was a cadet, years ago. It looked the same. The mate thought it would never change, as the people who controlled the waterfront bars, hotels, restaurants and shops, and the crime that was associated with them could make a lot of money. Local guys looking for trouble went there, too. Down on the corner, no one cared who you were, only how much money you had.

As the two officers sipped their drinks and got their eyes adjusted to the darkened bar, the mate instinctively noticed the patrons at the table next to theirs. It looked like a couple of Scandinavian merchant sailors and a local blonde girl. There were many empty drink glasses on the table. All that was normal, but then the thin blonde started staring at him. He turned his attention away from her, but in another minute, she came over, stood right in front of him, and pointed her finger right at him.

"I know you."

"Well, I don't know you, and I'm sorry, but all I want is a drink."

He thought that would be the end of it, but it wasn't. She repeated the assertion, then amazed the mate by telling him about the time they had met, years ago. She told him that he had been a cadet, what ship he had been on, and how they went to the beach and the movies. Then she told him things only that pretty, little, hippy-looking girl could have known. The mate was shocked. He was years older, twenty pounds heavier, had longer hair and a mustache, and there, in the dark, she knew him. She didn't look as pretty as she had back then. She looked tough and mean, the kind of girl who might have needle tracks on her arms. He was saddened to discover that this girl was now working the bars. The knowledge destroyed his memory of the happy time with her. She hadn't made it out of the poor section of the city, and had become part of the worst of it.

He did not deny her claim, as she clearly remembered him, after all that time. Then she said she wanted him to go with her. Now he had a little problem. He did not want her, and there were still two big sailors at the next table who had been buying her drinks. If they thought he was trying to steal this girl from them, he might have to fight his way out of the damn place. The engineer also sensed it was time to go, but he did not want to ride out to the beach area with the mate. The mate told him to go ahead. Turning his attention back to the tough blonde, he politely declined her offer to leave with her, and got up to leave by himself.

She got angry and started yelling at him. She demanded money. He had seen this before. A drug-crazed Brazilian bar girl who felt insulted in any way would often yell, using all the profane words she knew, in Portuguese and English. He walked towards the door, keeping an eye on her and the Scandinavian guys. The guys stayed put, but she followed him out onto the sidewalk. He walked quicker, away from her, but watched her all the while. She ran up to him, and he turned all the way around.

"I cut you!" It was in perfect English, and no bluff. She reached into her blouse and, from an apparent hiding place in her bra, pulled out a razor blade. Tape covered one side of the blade, but the other edge sparkled brightly. She raised her arm to slice him across the face. He punched her, hard, and she went down. He had never hit a woman before. He saw that she was not seriously hurt, but she was not getting up right away, and he turned around. All he wanted to see now was a taxi, but what he saw instead was a Brazilian cop, in uniform, with his nightstick out, running up the sidewalk towards him. *Christ.* Memories of the brawl in the Moulin Rouge, in Recife, years ago, flashed in his mind -- cops whacking everybody over the head with sticks, not bothering to ask for explanations. *Run or stay? Does the cop have a gun? Will he shoot me in the back if I run?* The one thing he could not do was fight the cop. He faced the wall, assumed the position, and braced himself for a possible beating.

Maybe the cop spoke some English, and he could explain, or buy him off with a bribe. If he only saw him hit the girl, and not the razor attack, it could be bad for him. Just how do you say "crazy bitch," or "razor" in Portuguese? The cop grabbed his shoulder and spun him around. The mate turned, raising his arms to protect his face. The cop wasn't swinging the stick. Instead, he pointed it at the dirty blonde on the sidewalk.

"This one bad. No good. You go. Go!"

"Obrigado!" At least he knew the word for "thank you," and took off, walking quickly down the street. He took the first corner and the second, to get away from the scene, and found a cab. He told him, "La Playa," or "beach" in Spanish, and, if not the same in Portuguese, the driver understood. In twenty minutes, he was sitting at a sidewalk cafe, ordering shrimp and beer, feeling the ocean breeze. The mate vowed to leave the Santos waterfront to those who appreciated its colorful qualities more than he did.

They finished cargo work the next day. There weren't many problems, except for a little arguing over some refrigerated cargo. A large part of #5 hatch was fitted with wooden planking on the decks and bulkheads. In a section accessible from the manhole ladder, there was machinery for producing cold air. The air circulated around the tween deck through ductwork, and under the planking. It wasn't too much trouble for chilled cargo, but this trip they were bringing back frozen fish and shrimp. The mate deemed the temperature acceptable for loading, but the bosses on the dock wanted it colder. Eventually, it was understood that while the damn hatch cover was open, the space could not be kept below freezing, but as soon as the boxes were stacked and secured, they could close the hatch, and bring it quickly below 32 Fahrenheit. The loading commenced.

The ship began its northbound leg, up the coast of Brazil, around the hump of the continent, and back to the U.S. The mate got the charts in the proper order for all this, with the usual layout of general area and weather charts on one side of the chart table, and the local charts for the legs near land, and the little ports they would make. Recife, Natal and Fortaleza were all small, compared to Rio and Santos. They would not stay long in any of them, unless there was rain that delayed the loading of the burlap coffee bags. As he put the charts in their order of use, he drew penciled courses up the coast. He also got the correct pilot chart for that month out. This was more of a weather map, and it showed average wind conditions and ocean currents on it.

Looking at the general charts, he wondered what kind of charts existed centuries ago, when the Portuguese got the area now know as Brazil. His memory of the history was vague, but it seemed that the Spanish and Portuguese both claimed the same parts of the New World, without, of course, consulting the local inhabitants. To settle the matter, the Pope had taken a chart of South America, and drawn a north-south line down it, declaring everything to the east to be Portuguese territory, and to the west, Spanish. Most of Brazil was in the hump that stuck out into the Atlantic. At least it explained why Brazilians spoke Portuguese while the rest of the inhabitants of the continent spoke Spanish.

He stayed away from the worst of the sailor bars in the little ports, preferring instead to go into the center of the little towns, find the public square that always seemed to be there, and then sit quietly at a sidewalk cafe. From this vantage point, especially if it was Sunday evening, or just after dinner, he could watch how the locals acted. The way the young boys walked together and eyed the girls they liked was much the same as in Spain and Italy. The girls would have an older female relative with them, or they cruised the town square in groups. There was little evidence of dating rituals, which may explain the existence of places of sin, which every town also seemed to have. The one exception he made was to return to the scene of the brawl in the Moulin Rouge, in Recife, for a quick beer with a couple of guys. It hadn't changed either, but at least there were no fights in his brief, historical visit.

Fortaleza was the last stop before sailing up through the Caribbean Islands. It was a pretty, little place, and the mate liked it. The people seemed friendly, and frequently came down to the docks to see big ships. While he was standing by the gangway during daytime duty there, he noticed a young boy on the dock, looking the ship over. The kid was about ten, and was dressed poorly, in sandals, shorts, and a tee shirt that needed a washing. In his arms, he was cradling an animal. It looked like an armadillo, and must have weighed 25 pounds. It was ugly. Then he saw that the boy had a piece of dirty rope lashed around its neck. *It's the kid's pet, for chrissake.* Then, the mate thought of a way to brighten an otherwise boring day, and maybe give the kid a bit of fun.

The ship had a purser, an officer who did all the ship's paperwork. The guy on his ship who did this work was a fat, red-faced older guy who was extremely nervous -- nervous about everything, and afraid of everything. How he had sailed this long, no one knew. However, he was friendly, and liked to play jokes on people. Probably that was how he dealt with his nervous state. The mate figured he had one coming, and motioned to the boy. With sign language, the mate got him to understand he wanted him to come up the gangway, on the big ship, so he could see his pet. The boy lugged the ugly thing up to the main deck with a smile on his face. Some of the local longshoremen also gathered around, to see what possible interest the ship's officer could have with the urchin and the animal. The mate smiled at the boy, and reluctantly petted the creature. The boy and the other locals thought this was great, that he was being kind to the poor kid. However, the mate wasn't done.

He motioned the boy to stay put for a moment, and walked into the main house of the ship. He sneaked down the passageway to the ship's office, where the purser worked. He had a small office on the port side, forward. The mate peeked inside the open door, and could not believe his luck. Fatman was in the head, or bathroom, that adjoined his office. It was perfect. He ran up to his own room, put a few things in his pocket, then ran quickly back to the gangway, and led the boy and his pet into the interior of the ship, motioning him to be quiet. They got to the door of the purser's office, and the mate pointed at the armadillo, and to the room. They could hear the purser around the corner, in the john. The kid was bright, and understood.

The boy lowered the animal down on the deck. It immediately began moving around the room, sniffing, and exploring. The mate quietly reached behind the door, took off the hook that held it open, and closed it. The boy's smile got bigger. The mate took him back about ten paces to wait. The mate motioned to stay quiet, and keep their eyes on the purser's door. It was like a delayed action fuse, and it would go off any second.

Ten more seconds of silence, then it happened. There was a horrible scream from the room, followed by heavy bumping noises, and more screaming. The door flew open, and the red-faced purser stumbled out of his room. Down the passageway he came, yelling about something. He had his huge boxer shorts mostly pulled up, but his pants were still at knee level. He ran past them, pulling at his pants, sweating, and yelling. He got a hold of his belt, and went up the nearest ladder, probably to report to the captain that the ship was awash with giant rats.

The mate took the boy back to the office, and the kid went in and retrieved the pet. Back out on deck, by the gangway, the mate fished things out of his pockets for the kid. Gum, candy and a few dollars went happily into the pockets of his raggedy shorts. He was too young for Marlboros. He took the armadillo back down to the dock, and walked along it. The mate could see him talking excitedly to other locals, and pointing up at the ship. Soon, he was gone. The mate went for a tour of the main deck, hoping that he had given the little kid some excitement for the day. On the rest of his cargo watch that day, the mate thought about other experiences with animals and ships.

You could not have a pet aboard an American ship. This was not true on some foreign ships, and the mate had seen many where there was a ship's dog or cat aboard. He had also seen the films from WWII where soldiers or sailors had sneaked a kitten or small dog onto a troop transport. In the mate's time, he had seen guys buy birds in handmade cages right on docks in South America. On one trip, so many crewmen bought the damn things that the captain had to order all the cages hung on pipes back on the stern, as they were making too much noise. When you got back to the states with an animal, you couldn't just take it home. You had to have it quarantined first, to check for disease. It could take 30 days or more, and you paid for it. Then, if the customs had a problem with the animal, they kept it and killed it.

Ships sailing to West Africa frequently came back with a pet monkey or two. Locals would capture them in the jungle, and bring them right down to the dock, for sale. The mate could never understand the attraction, but some guys must have thought they were cute, or interesting. The quarantine was restrictive, however, and more than one guy had a story about being bitten by these wild creatures. Rabies shots are no fun, it seems. Like most merchant sailors, the mate had been on numerous ships that carried animals as cargo. Mostly it was cattle or horses, sold to someone in places like Italy or Puerto Rico, for breeding. It was funny to watch the owner of a horse stare, as a guy running a crane hoisted the wooden stall 50 feet in the air, and then swing the prized animal onto the deck of the ship. They went on deck, not in a hold. Stevedores lashed the stalls to the deck, in a part of the ship protected from the seas. There always seemed to be at least one crewman who had been a farmer, and that guy would be happy to take care of the stock at sea. The mate had heard stories of ships that carried more exotic animals for zoos, or the entire animal population of a circus.

The most common animals associated with sailing were not pets or cargo. Wharf dogs and wharf rats lived on many waterfronts. Late at night, along the dock, you could see the mangiest, skinniest, scummiest dogs you have ever seen prowling the waterfront. They would hang around the side of the ship, hoping for a handout. If a crewman threw them some lunchmeat or bread, the damn things would hang around day and night until the ship sailed. Rats were common in some places. Grain docks were the worst. The mate recalled his first time at a grain dock, in New Orleans. When he left the ship at night, he carried a large stick to tap on the ground to scatter the rats. They would temporarily create a clear path, but you had to move your ass. Grain-fed rats are large, and they get familiar with people quickly. They show little fear. More than one mate carried a pistol to use on these waterfront animals, as well as protection against the two-legged variety of rat.

From his travels, and talks with other mates from different countries around the world, the consensus about the worst type of animal to transport was sheep. There is a trade route from Western Australia to the Middle East, where specially built ships carry nothing but live sheep. They are food in Arabic countries, but only Islamic butchers can slaughter them; you can't just ship frozen meat. The mate had heard that a ship of this type could carry more than 50,000 sheep at a time. If you had to overtake and pass one of these ships, the advice was to do so to windward. The claim was that the smell could reach you several miles downwind.

No one ever told the purser who had played the joke, or that it was a joke at all. They all said they had seen no rats on the ship, and he must have imagined it. The mate suggested he quit drinking, if he was seeing things like that. They all noticed, however, that all the way back to New York, he kept the door to his office closed.

Not much of interest happened on the return leg. The salty 3rd mate came up to the bridge on the mate's 4 to 8 watch in the evening to take stars. He had a new 2nd mate's license, and wanted to practice. The mate liked the company. Sunset was usually towards the end of the watch, and the two mates followed the unwritten rule. As ship's navigator, the 2nd mate would work out his sights and plot them first, adjusting course as necessary. Then the visitor on the bridge would take the Almanac and tables, and work out his. Being new at it, it took him much longer. The mate frequently left at 2000 hours while the salty 3rd mate was still working his observations out. Upon his return to watch at 0400 the next morning, the 2nd mate would check the positions obtained during the night, and enjoy seeing how closely the 3rd's star fix came to his own. It was all normal until the day of the coffee spill.

The mate came up for the 0400 watch one morning, and, as usual, checked the position and course to make good before relieving the watch. They were using a chart that showed the coastline of Brazil, their track parallel to it, and some ocean to the east. To the east of their track, someone had spilled coffee on the chart. This was not normal, as it was a habit of mates never to place a coffee cup on a chart table. It could leave a ring on it, or, if the ship rolled, spill all over it. Mates liked their charts to stay clean looking. It was no big deal; they could order another chart for a couple of bucks. What made it more noticeable, however, was that the culprit had not stopped with the coffee stain. He had then used the marks as the basis for a drawing of a woman. Something in the shape of the stain had reminded the guilty one of somebody he knew very well. It was a large drawing, in ink, and the woman was nude. The drawing was very complete, and showed talent, of a sort. It also showed that somebody needed to get home in a hurry.

He went into the wheelhouse to relieve Salty. Salty confessed and apologized for the coffee stain, and said he had already put the chart number on the requisition for New York, and told the purser that he would pay for it. He had struggled with his position the night before, and been careless with a coffee cup. The mate made a joke about the woman in the drawing, and forgot it. The mate got a laugh out of it all, and didn't think anymore about it, until the evening watch, when the captain called him on the phone, and asked him to stop by his room after watch.

The captain was more than competent, but a guy some would describe as a moralist. He didn't drink, smoke, or go ashore. He told the second mate that he had seen the drawing, and that it offended him. Then he astounded the mate by informing him that, since he knew none of his licensed officers would do draw such a thing, let alone spill coffee on a chart, he knew the deck cadet had done it. He was telling the mate about it because he was responsible for the charts, and had gone to the same school. Before the second could respond, the captain informed him that he had written a letter to the academy about it. A vision of *The Caine Mutiny* and stolen strawberries crossed the mate's mind. It took the mate twenty minutes to convince him that he was wrong, and not to mail the letter. He told Captain Morals that although the deck cadet wasn't the best he had ever seen, he wouldn't dare do anything like that. "It was an accident, Cap. I'll have the guilty party in your office in the morning," he told him. The salty third mate had to go see the Old Man the next day, and confess.

The trip ended in New York. They docked in the afternoon, and would pay off the crew for the voyage the next morning, and start a new one. The relief assignments and the cadets' assignments were over. By the time customs officials cleared the ship, several guys were waiting at the gangway to go ashore. The mate came down, dressed in jeans, to find a pay phone on the dock. Both cadets were there, dressed in full khaki uniforms, with brass buttons, striped shoulder boards, and their high-pressure hats. They were going into Manhattan to the academy office, to get their next assignment.

When the ship cleared customs, the mate, cadets and six others went down the gangway and walked up the dock. About halfway up the pier, a guy who was dressed like a longshoreman came out from the shadows and flashed a badge. He asked the mate to step aside, and let the others continue. It had happened before. Pick out the guy with longer hair and jeans; he must be the one smuggling something. The cop patted the mate down, had him empty his pockets, and asked him some questions. By the time the mate got up to the end of the dock, the rest of the guys were gone.

The next morning, guys were lining up in the officers' saloon to sign off, be paid, and some of them to sign on for the next voyage. The kids went through the line, and then stopped by the mate's room to say goodbye. They seemed to be smirking a little, so he asked them what was up. They started joking about how funny it was to see the mate pulled aside by the narc, while they all walked ashore.

"What's so funny about that?"

"Well, we were the ones he should have stopped."

"What do you mean, *should have*?" The mate smelled a rat.

"You remember down in Santos, you saw us in a bar, sitting in the corner, talking to some local guy?"

"Yeah?" There was definitely a rat here.

"Well, we made a little purchase there. A hundred joints of Brazil's best, already rolled."

"You dumb bastards."

"Yeah, we knew you'd say that, so we didn't tell you."

"How did you get them ashore?"

"We put 50 joints each inside our hats, around the edge, at the top."

"You dumb bastards."

"Yeah, mate, well, you got searched, and we didn't. We figured with our short hair and uniforms on, we'd go ashore with a group of scurvy-looking seamen like you. Who would you search?"

"Yeah, well, you're more lucky than smart. If you had a license to lose, you wouldn't try such a thing. I'll give you credit for having some balls, but you're both still a couple of dumb bastards. Now get the hell out of here, and I hope I never sail with you again."

There were smiles and handshakes, and the kids left, still grinning. The mate never did see either of them again, but he later learned that the deck cadet had dropped out of the academy after his sea year, and gone home to try a civilian college.

Chapter 16: Hafvilla

Fog is a mate's worst enemy. Even with radar, there is always a danger. A fog bank could show up, faintly, on the radar screen, but usually, it didn't. The visibility would just get worse and worse, until you saw nothing. Ships would save their radar in good visibility, by turning it off, or leaving it on standby. Good mates learned to smell the fog. During the day, you could easily see the horizon appear closer and closer, but at night, it wasn't obvious. Standing out on the wing of the bridge at night, you could smell the moisture in the air. If there were stars visible, you could see that they were getting fuzzy, and then disappearing. If you were watching the lights of another ship, you could tell how far away the fog was when their lights disappeared. Heavy fog messed with your senses, and the damp air went right through you. A Scandinavian officer the mate knew would joke about being in a state of "hafvilla," an old Viking word for "lost in fog." If you had the knack to be a mate, you quickly developed a sixth sense about fog. Instinctively, you would turn on the radar twenty minutes before the ship hit the fog bank.

Small boats, like yachts, were the toughest to detect. The older ones, with wooden hulls, did not give much of a return even from a good radar set. You had to be close, and you had to watch the radar like a hawk. Over time, sailboats began to hoist radar reflectors aloft, on the tops of their masts. At first, small boat guys hoisted pots and pans up the mast. Later, nautical suppliers sold commercial ones.

The mate or captain watching the radar had to know how to interpret the blips on the screen. The standard method for years was to mark the range (distance) and bearing (compass direction) of a blip, at intervals usually of six minutes, since that was a tenth of an hour. You made a mark on a plotting sheet, and drew lines for the target's relative course. The mate always disliked the word "target," as in the merchant marine instructors trained you not to hit anything. You figured out the true course and speed of the other vessel, and its CPA, or Closest Point of Approach. If this was less than two miles, you then determined who had the right of way, and if it was the other ship, how much to change course, in what direction, to increase the CPA. The idea was to keep your ship in a position where the other guy couldn't hit you. All this went out the porthole if you had numerous targets that were close, like when you went through a fishing fleet. A good mate could just look at the blips all over the screen, and pick his way through, without taking his eyes off the radar to plot anything.

In the mate's early years, many of the older ships still had radar sets from WWII. Newer radars had joysticks, like the ones on video games. You moved the stick to acquire the target, and the radar would then track and plot it for you, showing the target's course with a glowing green line. After that, the new sets started to automatically acquire and track targets. All this was fine, as long as you understood the limitations of your set. Every time a mate joined a different ship, he checked out the radar, and learned how to use it. It was dangerous to assume the new sets would find all the targets. Signals bounced off waves could look like those from a small boat. It was the same for rainsqualls; you still had to adjust things, and interpret things, and, when in doubt, avoid a blip that might or might not be a vessel. Take no chances, and don't wait until the last minute, that was the way.

Some places in the world had, of course, more fog than others did. Warm, moist air over cold water could produce a terrific advection fog that hugged the water. A temperature inversion over low-lying land would produce radiation fog. The Grand Banks off Newfoundland, the Northern California coast and the English Channel were notorious foggy areas.

The southeast U.S. frequently had morning fog that burned off by noon. Ships sailed these areas for centuries without radar. In modern times, ships almost never slowed down for fog, in spite of the rule about reduced speed in reduced visibility. You would simply never keep a schedule or make a profit for the company if you slowed down every time the visibility got bad. The captain had the final word, but a captain who was late all the time didn't stay captain for long.

The frequency of fog also affected the operation of a port. Local pilots and tugs had to work in the fog at least some of the time. Savannah was one place the mate had been to where they would take a ship in or out in fog. The first time this had happened, the ship was at the dock, but before they finished their work, the fog had crept up the river all the way to the city. They were prepared to leave at night, and the visibility was getting worse all the time. The pilot came aboard and checked out both of the ship's radars. They were working fine; you could see blips from the buoys in the river. He said there were no inbound ships, and he would take her out if the captain wanted him to.

The mate walked up to the bow with a huge flashlight. The bosun stood by the anchor, ready to drop it. As they sailed downriver, the mate would spot each buoy with his light. He got the number of each one, and reported it to the bridge, with a distance off the bow. The first time you stand on the bow like that, it is a spooky experience. If you're going to hit anything, you wouldn't see it until it was right in front of you. Many guys died on the bow of a ship when they hit a dock, a bridge, or another ship. With no other large ship moving in or out, the most likely accident would be going aground, or hitting a small boat. The mate had been glad when they got out of the river.

One of the mate's trips was as second mate from New York to North Europe, on a Farrell Lines containership called the *Defiance.* The master of the vessel was a tough sailor the crew called Captain Hardass. The weather going over was typical for the North Atlantic. It was rough as hell for a couple of days, but then got calm and damp, perfect conditions for fog.

They made Land's End, in England, abeam to port, and set course for Le Havre, France, making about 21 knots. Fog set in during the night. No one got much sleep, with the ship's steam whistle sounding the fog signal every two minutes. When he went up to the bridge for the 0400 to 0800 watch, the mate arrived early. He checked the ship's position carefully. He made sure the Decca receiver was set up properly, and getting signals from the chain of stations for their area. He memorized the currents and tides for his watch, and double-checked the courses he had laid out on the charts all the way to port. If the fog stuck around, he wouldn't have much time to spend in the chartroom. Visibility was less than a half-mile, and, naturally, they were steaming at full speed. The captain was at the long-range radar on the port side of the wheelhouse. He had been up there all night. The AB had the ship in hand steering, and the engines were on standby. The 3rd mate on watch was at the short-range radar on the starboard side. The 3rd showed him the plots he was running on the targets on the scope. When the mate understood all of them, he repeated the course, and said, "I've got her," assuming the watch. It was typical for the English Channel in fog, and no big deal.

Within an hour, it became a big deal. They couldn't see the bow. Small targets began to appear on both scopes, along with the larger ones. The captain said he would take care of the large ships; the mate was to concentrate on small targets. The mate knew what all the small targets were. On the way over, he had read about a sailboat race in a "Notice to Mariners" warning. The racers had left England, were racing around an island off the coast of France, then were going north to Ireland, and back to England. The mate thought that the guys who did that were tough as nails, and completely insane. They should have cleared the channel before the

Defiance got there, but lack of wind had delayed them. It became clear that they were steaming right through the lot.

Targets on the scopes for the big ships in the Channel were easy to see. They would show up at fifteen or twenty miles, and you had plenty of time to run a plot on them and change course if necessary. You also knew that big ships would get on a course and stay with it until they reached a certain point. They didn't tack back and forth like sailboats did, and they didn't turn on a dime, either. They also all had radar, and, if they were using it correctly, knew where you were and what your course was.

A guy in a sailboat would hear a ship's signal, but sound bounces around in fog. Without radar, he might panic and make a sudden change in course, not knowing if the ship was clearing him or not. The racing boats were making only a knot or two, with the current, and a tiny bit of wind. It would have been better for the ship if they were completely motionless. In that case, you would know that any course change you made would miss the boat, since that bastard was sitting there, helpless, praying that you could pick him up on radar, and that you were competent enough to interpret his blip.

The men on the bridge tensed up. There were targets to starboard and port, and dead ahead. There were too many to go around the bunch. The captain and the mate dodged right and left, and were doing fine, until the mate saw a tiny blip on his scope just off the starboard bow. It was so small he could not even be sure it was another sailboat. Before he could run a plot, even a quick, three-minute calculation, the blip disappeared into the small area of sea return at the center of his scope. It seemed to have a steady bearing, which meant that the racer was making a little headway, across their bow, from right to left. Their whistle went off again, and the mate wondered if the sailboat guy could tell where they were, and would he tack?

"Cap', I've got one close, just off the starboard bow. Lost him."

"I didn't see anything; you sure?"

"No, but if it is a boat, and we don't change, we're going to kill the son-of-a-bitch."

"Do it."

"Hard right!"

"Hard right rudder, mate."

The mate left his radar and went to the center of the wheelhouse. As the ship heeled to starboard, he watched the rudder angle indicator swing right -- no time for any mistakes. Then he stood by the gyrocompass repeater in the center of the bridge, and watched the course change. She started swinging pretty good; just then the lookout on the bow began ringing the bell rapidly. It meant he saw something dead ahead, and with the visibility the way it was, it must be right under the bow. The mate prayed the sailor had not tacked to port. If he had, it would be too late.

"Midships the wheel!"

"Midships."

"Left 20, now!"

"Left 20."

The idea then was to check the swing, and straighten the ship out. The bow would either clear or not, but if he had gotten the guy off his port bow, as intended, but swung her too much, there was a chance he would clip the guy with the stern of the ship, which was swinging left.

The mate and the captain saw the light at the same time. A white light appeared suddenly off the port bow. It looked like it was hanging right over #2 hatch. They both ran out to the port wing of the bridge. They got to the skin of the ship, leaned over the side, and looked forward. A yacht was right below them, not more than 40 feet from the side of the ship. He was still on a westerly course, away from them. The yacht was so close that they could have spit on it. The mate could see the radar reflector hanging below the mast light.

Within seconds, the hull of their ship slid right past the boat, maintaining the same distance off. The stern cleared the guy. They had seen no one on its deck, and heard nothing from the sailboat. They were probably asleep.

"Midships!" The mate hollered back into the wheelhouse.

"Midships!"

The mate went back into the wheelhouse and gave the quartermaster the course to steer, and told the AB that he had done a good job. He went back to the little radar. The captain appeared at his elbow.

"I can watch them both for a few minutes, mate. Why don't you make some fresh coffee?"

"Okay, Cap'." Captain Hardass didn't give many compliments, but he gave the mate "The Look." The Look was meant to mean that maybe he didn't believe the mate had a real target there, because he hadn't seen one, but he was damn glad the mate had done something about it, 'cause, *yeah, we almost killed those guys.*

The mate got fresh coffee for the captain and himself, rechecked the ship's position, adjusted the course a little, and went back to the little radar. The AB at the wheel got relieved and the watch was half over. It looked like they were clear of the rest of the sailboat racers. All they had to do now was avoid hitting the other cargo ships, supertankers, tugs with tows and fishing boats that were all over the Channel, and navigate electronically into Le Havre -- no problem. He wondered if the sailors on the yacht had really slept through all that, and he decided it was better if they had.

His most memorable experience with fog happened a few years later. He shipped out as relief 2nd mate on a Sea Land Service container ship called the *San Juan*. It was an older ship that had two mobile container cranes on tracks on its deck. She sailed from the Sea Land docks in Port Elizabeth, New Jersey, across the Atlantic Ocean to the Mediterranean, with a stop in Cadiz, on the Atlantic side of Spain, first. The mate liked Med trips a lot better than North Europe ones. There was better weather, interesting places to go, and good food to eat -- this, of course, if you had time to go ashore. The container ships did not stay long in port.

The weather on the crossing was good, and everyone settled into a boring, but pleasant routine. Sailors appreciated quiet days at sea. On one clear day, steaming near the Azores, with only moderate winds, and a small sea running, the captain came up to the bridge on the mate's watch. He was a competent, experienced master. While they were standing around, talking about nothing in particular, the mate spotted a small dot in the water, dead ahead. He routinely picked up the binoculars, and zoomed in on it.

"Watcha got there, mate?" The captain now saw it too.

"I dunno. Looks like maybe an oil drum, or some other trash somebody threw over, but we're going to be real close to it. Want me to change for it?"

"No, the wake from the bow will push it aside." He looked through the other set of glasses. "It's just a piece of junk."

They got real close to it. It would pass down the port side of the ship. With nothing better to do, the captain and the mate went out on the port wing, and looked down at the object. They had the binoculars with them, and stared down at it. It was right underneath them, not 30 feet from the side of the ship. What they saw left them silent. It was a floating mine, complete with spikes sticking out all over it. It had barnacles growing on it, and was greenish in color. It was likely a leftover from WWII. It could have been floating around for years, or more recently had broken its mooring from the bottom somewhere, and begun traveling around in the ocean currents.

The mine washed astern, without going off. The two officers breathed again. You wouldn't expect a mine that old to still be active, but it did happen. In London, they were still finding bombs imbedded in the basements of buildings.

"I'll, uh, I'll fill out a warning for the 'Notice To Mariners,' Cap'."

"Yeah, good idea." He said nothing else, but his face showed a little concern. He was the one who had said not to bother changing course for it. The mate wrote down the ship's position, and filled out a form to warn other ships. Then, he got the stack of previous warnings out of a locker, and flipped through them. Sure enough, a few months earlier, another merchant ship had reported the same thing, not far from their present position. The mate thought that it paid to read the notices.

They reached Cadiz without incident. Cargo went off, and on, and the mate got a few precious hours ashore. He had something to eat, a couple of beers, and wrote postcards. He liked Spain, and was glad their next port was Barcelona, inside the Mediterranean Sea. It was a pretty, large city, and a good shore port. You could sit and watch life go by, or go to the bars that catered to sailors from around the world. He mostly liked walking the narrow streets, and sitting in the cafes.

They undocked in the afternoon, cleared the harbor, and shaped up their course south, for the Strait of Gibraltar, and its famous rock. They would head south, cross the outbound ship traffic lane, then enter the eastbound, or inbound lane, along the African coast, at a sharp angle; then they would change course to the east, get in the middle of the lane, and steam right through the strait. The traffic lanes, a recent innovation, were about two miles wide each, with a separation zone in the middle. It was plenty of room, if everybody played by the rules, which not everyone did. They would watch carefully for crossing traffic, like ships and ferries going to and from Morocco and Spain. The captain and the mate had done it before. It could be a hectic time, but nothing unusual -- nothing unusual until this time.

They were beginning to dodge the outbound ships, but hadn't shaped up for the strait yet, when the fog set in. Then the radar crapped out. The captain was on the bridge when it happened. The plots the mate had been running on other ships now became guesses. They got the radio operator up there immediately, put the engines on standby, kept the ship in hand steering, and began to sound the fog signal. Sparky looked things over, and said there was no way he could fix the radar. It probably needed a part he didn't have. It was time to settle matters.

"Do you have the conn, captain?"

"Yes." He was competent and sober. With all kinds of possibilities, and crucial decisions to make, the mate had to know who was going to make the choices. The mate knew what they should do. Either turn around and head back towards Cadiz, to get a technician to repair the radar, or retrace their steps back to where the visibility was good, and wait until the fog cleared. The captain chose "none of the above."

"See what kind of position you can get, mate. We'll proceed on towards the strait." The mate thought that was completely insane. He spoke up loudly, for effect, and for the quartermaster to hear.

"Captain, I recommend that you turn this ship around immediately." The captain gave him a look that meant, "I know you don't approve, but this is my decision, and this is what we are doing."

"I understand your concern. Hold your course, and give me an ETA for the course change to Gibraltar." The mate started to walk back to the chartroom, but gave it one more shot.

"Captain, if you leave this bridge, even for a second, I will turn this ship around and head back as far as I need to go for the visibility to clear up."

"I understand, mate. Just get me a position." *Shit. He won't give it up.* He wanted to make their docking time in Barcelona, to save the company money. Delays cost money. There would be labor already ordered to work the ship there;

the company would have to pay them something, even if they didn't show. But, to head into a highly used traffic area like this, in an area of restricted movement, totally blind, was nuts. The mate went into the chartroom, knowing that he didn't have a good means of getting a position, but failing to think of a legal reason to wrest command of the ship away from him.

The mate checked the chart they were using. He put down a DR, or dead reckoning, position, and labeled it. It was an estimate. Then he tried to find a way of obtaining a fix, or position. In those days before satellite navigation, and without a working radar, there wasn't much. There were no Decca stations to use. The only Loran coverage was for airplanes. He got out the air chart for Loran coverage, tuned the receiver into the station, and got a reading. It was just one line of position that indicated to him that he was near the Strait of Gibraltar. Hell, he knew that. He turned on the RDF, or Radio Direction Finder, and checked the tables for local stations. He found one in Morocco, and tuned in the frequency. He heard its distinctive Morse signal in the headphones. He twisted the dial until he got a bearing. Then, he drew the bearing on the chart back from the charted position of the transmitter. All he knew was that, theoretically, his ship was somewhere along the line. It was a poor line of position. The bearing could easily be off a few degrees to the right or the left. The farther away you were from the transmitter, the more miles you could be off, and they didn't have many miles to play with.

He took another bearing on the same RDF station twelve minutes later. He drew the second line, and then advanced the first line with an estimate of the ship's course and speed. The result was what mates called a running fix. If each of the two bearings could be off just a couple of degrees, and the estimated speed used was off a knot, the resulting position was really a guess. Instead of an exact point where the two lines crossed, what you really had was a diamond shaped box, a few miles on each side, and you knew that you were somewhere inside it; maybe. Nobody in their right mind would change course, in fog, without radar, into a strait full of other ships, based on a position like that. He told the captain what he had, and the Old Man went into the chartroom and studied it. *Now he'll turn around,* the mate thought; *he's got to.* The captain drew a course from the running fix into the strait's eastbound traffic lane, on the African coast, and ordered the course change. He was going in anyway.

The fog did not lift as they swung to the east. The mate could tell that the quartermaster was getting nervous. The lookout started reporting what he heard, since he could not see anything. The mate began to sweat. Hell, it may not matter if the fix on the chart was any good or not; running aground and tearing the bottom out on a rock wasn't going to happen. They would surely have a head-on collision with a ship first. He wondered if the guys down below would like to be awake in their final moments. If they knew what was going on, they would want to be, but they did not awaken the crew. Only the people on the bridge knew the extent of the danger.

The mate's watch was only the usual four hours, but it seemed to last forever. Soon, the lookout began reporting by phone that he was hearing ships' fog signals to starboard. The mate and the captain heard them, too, and went out on the starboard wing of the bridge, where they could hear them better. The blasts from whistles were on that side; they got louder, and more to the right all the time. They came from forward of the beam of their ship, and then passed astern. It was clear what that meant. They were on the wrong goddam side of the strait! The westbound, or outbound, traffic lane was on the Spanish side of the strait. If they had been in the correct lane, on the African side, all these ships would be passing down their port side. But, how far over were they? They did not know. If they were far enough to the north, they would run aground on the rocky Spanish coast. It wasn't a sandy bottom, where they might slide to a stop and get stuck, oh, no. Hitting the rocks now, at full speed, would tear the bottom out. The ship could go down, and the sailors with it.

If they still had enough water beneath them to port to avoid land, their problem was the westbound traffic. Their very survival now would depend on every other ship in the area having a working radar set, a mate who understood how to use it and plot their course, and a captain or mate who would make the correct decision to avoid these idiots who were in the wrong lane. They would surely be cussing them profoundly all the while. It was too much to hope. Even if all the big ships did this, there could be ferries crossing, or fishing boats that didn't run a plot on them. The mate confirmed that the captain understood their predicament.

"Cap', do you want to try to cut over to the right some, to get closer to the inbound lane?"

"No. We might cut right in front of another ship."

"Okay. I'm just concerned that we might be so far over towards Spain that, well, you know."

"I know. Hold course for now." The more the captain told him to hold course, the more nervous the mate got that all this was based on his running RDF fix. *Christ.*

Sparky flitted in and out of the wheelhouse the whole time, putting on a show trying to fix the radar. He brought in parts, opened up the circuit boxes, and all that. He couldn't fix the damn thing, and the mate thought he was just getting in the way. He figured if the radio operator really wanted to be useful, he should go into his shack and establish contact with a station ashore, ready to send out the SOS when they bought the farm. It might save a life or two. *Christ.* When the AB at the wheel went below, what would he tell the other guys who were awake? Old stories of mutinies and fights on the bridge came to mind, but he knew none of that would happen. The crew had faith in the two of them -- the two in charge, who were now engaged in risking all their lives.

The horrible thought of colliding head on with another ship would not leave his mind. Maybe it would be better to hit a supertanker, and die quickly. There would be no damn hearings to go to then, to try to explain all this. Surely, they would ask him why he didn't try to take command of the ship away from the captain. He had no legal reason to, of course, but he pictured the courtroom full of widows and orphaned, small children, crying, and their lawyers tearing him apart. Could he justify taking the ship over at some point? Would the helmsman obey his orders or the captain's? If he ordered the engineer to reduce speed, and the captain called down and said not to, who would win that? What if he knocked the captain over the head to prevent this? The lawyers would love that, and what if he hurt him badly, or killed him? These crazy thoughts flashed through his mind and were gone. They held course and speed, but did not say much. They continued to listen to the blasts of whistles on the starboard side, trying to judge how far away they were. Disaster could come at any second, but they were too far in now to turn around, even if they wanted to. That would be just as risky. What about any small boats that might be around? They did not all have radar. They could easily run over a fishing boat, kill a few guys, make the headlines in the Spanish papers, and end up in jail in Barcelona; another pleasant thought.

With all these distracting thoughts, the mate at first did not realize what it meant when a bright white light flashed through the wheelhouse, and was gone. He ran out to the starboard wing, and soon, it flashed again. He got a bearing on it. The light was high up, and breaking through the fog. *My God,* he thought, *there's another ship so close to hitting us that they're searching for the idiots with their searchlight!* Then it flashed a third time. The bearing of the light had changed a bit to the right. It wasn't on a steady bearing, which meant that it wasn't on a collision course. Then he got it, and began counting seconds. Sure enough, the light was flashing at regular intervals. It was a lighthouse on the African coast. The fog was closer to the water, and lights above it were beginning to show through! The wheelhouse was about 60 feet above the water, and they could see something else that was high up.

He ran back into the chartroom and looked at the characteristics of lighthouses along the coast. He found the one that matched the period of flashes, and laid down the bearing. Then he took another bearing on the RDF station he had before. Now, he had one good line of position, the visual one from the light, and a second, not as good, from the radio signal. He crossed the two lines and circled the intersection. He labeled it with the time. The captain was at his elbow, also having realized the significance of the light. The position showed them right in the middle of the wrong lane, but with enough water to their portside that they would not go aground. They still had serious worries, but at least had a good idea of where they were, and how far to the right they needed to go to get into the correct traffic lane. The two went back out onto the starboard wing. Soon, they saw the white masthead and range lights of another ship, off to starboard. The ship passed them starboard to starboard, about two miles off. The fog was still thick close to the water, but the two could see ship lights, being high up on the masts.

The captain said that now that they could see another large ship, at least a mile or so, it was time to come right and get in the correct lane. The mate ran in and got a course and time to run, and ordered the ship right. He would take her about three miles to the south. Then, when they were in the middle of the eastbound lane, go east again. The captain watched for traffic. The mate prayed silently that there were no small ships hidden in the fog, and that other large ships that were plotting them on radar would not panic and change. It took about ten minutes to go far enough south. They had to dance between two ships before they could swing east again, but luck, fortune, or God, was with them. They hit nothing, and, in another 30 minutes, the fog cleared almost completely. Now the mate could see lights on both shores, and get all the reliable positions he wanted to. They made their docking time in Barcelona, right on schedule. Sparky made extra money watching the repairman fix the radar.

Author on the bridge wing, taking a sunline with a nautical sextant. Photo: K. Zahn

Author on bow (R) of the S. S. Mormactide, in Capetown, South Africa

The Austral Pioneer in Sydney, Australia

Author at the automated bridge control, M. V. Sea Land Express. Photo: K. Zahn

Part Three

The Old Salt

Chapter 17: Aussies, Kiwis, Limeys and Yanks

Years passed. The mate was now in his mid-thirties. His hair was shorter than it had been in years. He shaved his mustache off during a voyage, but started growing it back again the next day. He no longer identified with the young guys he occasionally saw on the ships. He had taken up smoking cigarettes, and had gained weight. He drank too much. He felt he could still handle himself in a fight, but he was not in as good a shape as he used to be, and he didn't care.

His wife hated the winters in Boston, and wanted to move back down south. The mate compromised, and they moved to Baltimore, partly for the climate, and partly so he could still be near a seaport to look for work. There weren't many offshore jobs in the Baltimore hall, so he often went back to New York.

When he couldn't get a ship, they argued about money. He thought a wife should take a job, or grow vegetables, anything to help the family. She was a southern belle type, however, and thought the husband should provide everything. Most sailors had wives who begged them to give up the sea. "I don't care if you sell shoes, I want you home," was a typical argument. The mate's wife would pack his sea bag for him. They got divorced, and it wasn't friendly. The mate stayed in Baltimore to be near his son, who suffered the most. Her lawyers made much of the good years, when he could make $40,000, and ignored the bad years, when he struggled to make half that.

He tried working ashore. He sold advertising and taught junior high school. There was no time to go back to college and learn to be a businessman, or more about the new age of computers. He could not avoid the fact that he could make more money in three months at sea, than he could all year with jobs like that, and back to the union hall he went, looking for another ship.

Shipping wasn't good. Companies like Keystone Tankers and Delta Lines were going non-union, others were declaring bankruptcy. Foreign shipping lines, many of them subsidized by their governments, were getting more and more of the cargo business. The end of the Viet Nam war meant that many older ships were laid up or scrapped. No one cried about the rust buckets, but the mates who sailed them were now in the union hall, competing for jobs. What jobs he did get took the mate to few new places. He went to Puerto Rico. He sailed to South Africa, and rounded the cape to Mozambique. He went to Greece, Israel and Hong Kong and stops in between, but there was no time to explore anywhere. It wasn't an adventure, it was a job.

He was keeping an eye open for a chance to go permanent with a company -- chief mate, and then captain. He had taken a couple of months to study for his chief mate's license, and had passed it. He was at the age where one had to make serious decisions about all that. You could stay a relief mate for your whole career, hoping that shipping was good enough to get you jobs, or you could become ambitious and make permanent chief mate with one company, then bust ass for four stripes. There didn't seem to be much opportunity for that, however, and he kept finding himself in the union hall, listening to the goddam numbers.

Large containerships and supertankers continued to replace smaller ships. It was a simple concept -- carry more cargo with a smaller crew. Automation and computers enabled the companies to do this. The newer tankers carried ten times, then twenty times the amount of liquid a World War Two ship could. An old freighter that might spend three days in a port, at an old dock right downtown, was replaced by a larger, faster containership that could unload four times the tonnage, in 24 hours, and docked at a new container terminal, twenty miles from downtown. You went "near," not "to," interesting places, and saw nothing. The cargo work went on 24 hours a day, in almost any weather. With the more efficient cargo handling, you got very little time ashore. No one built more nuclear merchant ships; the *Savannah* was retired, and became more of a white elephant than ever.

Companies also figured out that it was more efficient to do major maintenance on ships in shipyards, rather than pay overtime for the crew to keep up with it. Automation took over engine rooms to the point that no one stood watch in them at night. The engineers simply locked them down at night, with alarms to go off in an engineer's cabin if anything major went wrong. Companies decided that the chief mate could stand a watch at sea, in addition to all his other responsibilities. He could be physically exhausted while in command of the ship, after working a sixteen-hour day in port, but what the hell, you could eliminate one of the 3rd mate's jobs.

The unions caved in to company demands again and again. They allowed the shipping companies to reduce the number of men, and reduce their overtime. A 500-foot ship with 45 officers and crew became an 800-foot one with 23. The members bitched that the union officials were just trying to save their own, easy, office jobs. The non-union guys continued to take whatever their companies were offering.

The supertankers were too large for most traditional docks, so they built offshore platforms, with pipes running under the sea to the oil terminals. The ships docked alongside them, essentially still at sea, and pumped their oil there, never even getting to a port.

All these changes affected the way of life for merchant seamen. With smaller crews, the ships looked ghostly at sea. Guys were either working or sleeping. There weren't enough guys off duty at one time to get up a card game. There was no more movie night; there was a case of videos in the recreation room. Guys drank alone -- a bad sign. Even the crew's deck became quiet. Most cargo liners stopped carrying passengers; nobody wanted to carry extra crew to take care of them. Guys worked, ate and went to their rooms, and you didn't see them for days at a time.

In the early 1980's, he snagged a six-month job as 2nd mate on a new Farrell Lines containership, the *Austral Pioneer*; it was only on its fourth voyage. It sailed to New Zealand and Australia, places he had always wanted to visit. The ship was over 800 feet long, and displaced 27,000 tons. The schedule was 84 days, round trip.

The trips to the South Pacific, however, were different from the typical runs he had made to North Europe, South America, or the Med. They weren't just longer; most of the time was in the South Pacific, one of the calmest parts of the oceans. The down side, if there was one, was that you didn't see much. There are no large ports anywhere; just hundreds of small islands, and you almost never passed any of them close enough to see anything. You could get bored, but the mate loved it. It was a chance to relax, read, see a different part of the world, and make money doing it. The divorce lawyers couldn't bother him out on the ocean.

The captain was a spit and polish guy who liked to wear dress blues and gold stripes. The chief mate was a drinker, but an old hand. One of the third mates was British by birth, American by choice. The other was a young guy who had gone to the same academy as the mate. They had several young engineers aboard, a real oddity for the American Merchant Marine, and two cadets, one deck and one engine, who would both turn 21 during the voyage. Farrell Lines was one of the last American steamship companies to carry passengers, and they had the usual allotment of twelve.

Norfolk, Virginia was their last American port before going foreign. As soon as they let the lines go and the tugs pulled the ship away from the dock, she heeled over to port about three degrees and stayed there. The vessel wasn't loaded right, and they needed to increase their stability. It was nineteen days at sea to Brisbane, and even though you would expect good weather, you didn't want to sail with such a condition. The captain got on the phone to the chief mate, bitched at him, and ordered him to start ballasting whatever empty tanks he had to correct it.

When they got to Panama there was another problem. Before they got in line to transit the canal, the emergency generator in the engine room burned up. The twelve-foot shaft bent with the heat, and was useless. The insurance underwriters would not approve of their passage across the Pacific without repairs. The problem was that there were no deep-water ports, or repair docks, along their track, and no ocean going tugs to come get you if the main plant failed. They stayed at anchor in Cristobal harbor to fix things.

The delay in Panama was not a hardship. The ship was still new enough that the shipyard that built it had to pay for the repairs, so the company didn't suffer financially. The passengers, mostly retired, arranged for tours of the canal and jungle excursions. The mates stood their watches in eight-hour shifts instead of four, and rode the launches to shore. The mate hung out at the Yacht Club or the Washington Hotel, two of the safer spots. The watch mates caught up on paperwork, like making the tedious corrections to charts and navigational lists of lights. The deck gang worked their hours outside, and it was hot. The engine crew helped with the repairs, and the work was a bitch.

A private company with small boats provided transportation to and from the dock from their anchorage. The last one left the dock at 2300 hours, and if you missed that one, you were stuck ashore until the first one at 0500 the next morning. The mate did not care to cat around in Panama, and considered it a dangerous place. One night, however, he and an engineer missed the last launch back, by minutes, and looked stuck for the night. Then the mate got an inspiration, and strolled into the launch company's office on the pier.

Within minutes, a special launch appeared at the dock, and the two officers got a private boat ride out into the harbor. The engineer was impressed, and asked him how he had done it, or what the bribe had been.

"No bribe. I told them I was the captain, and the company would pay for an extra trip. I signed for it. The Old Man never leaves the ship, and it'll be weeks before the bill hits somebody's desk back in New York. They'll never know the difference."

The mate was more punctual the next night he went ashore. The only excitement of the evening happened in a casino. By this time, the mate had learned the basic strategy of blackjack; he knew some rules about splitting hands, doubling down, and insurance. He had $320 in front of him and only two drinks in him when he decided to quit while ahead. The dealer told him that he needed to change all his $1 and $5 chips for larger ones before he went to the cashier's window. When the guy gave him his chips back, there was only $275 there. He had stacked his chips neatly, and knew the count was short. He got no help from any of the other players, and called the pit boss over. The pit boss was a big, ugly guy. He stared at him, told him he was mistaken, and observed that he had been drinking.

"Okay, I understand how it is." He left to get a cab outside, watching his back all the while.

Farrell Lines shipped two three-ton generators to Panama. The deck gang lashed them to the after deck. The engine crew ran all kinds of electrical cables from there down to the engine room, and got them working. It turned out that the chief engineer was a whiz at electrical problems, and he got high marks for directing things. The insurance underwriters tested the "jury rig" repair, and certified them to cross the South Pacific.

Panama to Auckland, New Zealand, their first stop, was about 7,500 miles. It was another 1,400 to Brisbane, Australia, their next port. From there they would make

Melbourne and Sydney, followed by a run through the Cook Straits between the north and south islands of New Zealand to Littleton, the port for Christchurch, N.Z., then Wellington, then back to Panama. After The Ditch, the schedule called for stops in New Orleans, Charleston and Philadelphia before the voyage would officially end back in New York. Even at twenty knots, it would take fifteen days to cross the open sea. If the mate had not gained an appreciation for the vastness of the oceans before, this would surely do it. The North Atlantic run, for all its misery and trouble, was less than half the distance.

Everyone settled down to his own routine; the watchstanders and the day workers, the cooks and the passengers, all had different schedules. The younger guys got bored the quickest, while the older sailors enjoyed the relative peace and serenity of the South Pacific. The mate thought about the guys in the past, on the sailing ships, who had wandered around this part of the world for a year or more at a time, exploring or exploiting, as the case may be. Ships were sent out to find the "missing" southern continent that experts figured had to be there to balance the weight of the land masses in the Northern Hemisphere. They found Australia, but many still believed there had to be more. Mapmakers were still redrawing the area well into the 20th century, with so many islands scattered over such a vast area. He thought of how Magellan never finished the trip he got credit for, and how Cook was killed in the Hawaiian Islands, but his navigator and cartographer, Bligh, sailed on into history for other reasons. It seemed there was nothing out there -- nothing but ocean day after day.

There was almost no traffic to deal with. If another ship did pass, even many miles away, the mate on watch would call it on the VHF radio and have a conversation. Passengers would come out with binoculars to see it. The mate thought none of them would have survived in Cook's time. Even on a large ship, there was nowhere to go, and guys began to form partnerships; some played cards, some drank together, and some sat around the lounge, sipping coffee day and night, talking incessantly about nothing of importance.

The British 3rd mate came calling one night after supper, and the two became friends. The Limey was a good mate, and well traveled. He had survived World War II in the Polish Merchant Marine, and sailed English and American merchant ships ever since. Like most Englishmen, he had a good sense of humor. He also had been buying gold coins ever since the 1940's, and stashing them away.

He did, however, like to criticize all the other English-speaking peoples. The Yanks, the Kiwis from New Zealand, and especially the Aussies; all had inferior cultures to that of Dear Old England. The mate would let him ramble on and on about what was wrong with the American government, or how there was little to see in 'Kiwiland' except sheep, and how the Aussies were the descendants of prisoners. He made English tea for them both, and the mate had to admit it was far superior to the Lipton crap on the ship. He also learned the best way to shut him up. He had become an American citizen, so he paid less tax, and lived better than he could have in England. All the mate had to do was say something like, "If England is so much better, 3rd, why the hell don't you go back there, tend your teeny little garden somewhere, and kiss the hem of the Queen's gown, or whatever it is the British do?"

The captain kept up his image, even at sea, with stripes and blues at dinner. He forbade the other officers from socializing with the passengers, but went to their lounge every night before dinner for their daily cocktail party. The Chief Steward himself would open the passengers' liquor cabinet, and mix drinks for everyone. After many days of this, one of the passengers remarked to the mate at supper that she did not understand why the other officers were so unfriendly to them. The mate informed her that the captain did not allow them to come up on their deck at all. The information had the desired effect, as that passenger told the other eleven, and, within two days, there was a party for all the officers to attend. After that, the Old Man allowed them to visit during certain hours, with the stern warning that any officer who got drunk in the presence of the passengers, or, God forbid, had a personal affair with one, would be fired. The mate took to playing chess with a couple of the older guys. One was a retired surgeon, and became valuable for medical advice. Another had brought his own sextant, and came up to the bridge to take stars with the mates. It made the passage more civilized. The real slobs never socialized with the passengers anyway; they didn't want to clean up, put on shoulder boards, or behave themselves.

There was a lot of drinking, one way or another. Their delay in Panama had given everyone plenty of time to go ashore to the duty free shops and stock up for the trip. The young guys had come back, night after night, with cases of beer under their arms. The older guys would bribe a launch driver to bring it out to the ship for them, thereby, in the mate's opinion, proving their superiority of intellect to the younger crowd. The young third mate brought so much back that he set up a bar in his room, complete with cocktail shakers, tequila mix, liqueurs, beer, ice buckets, and so on. The captain probably should have clamped down a bit, but he had a competent bunch and he did not seem anxious to piss off all his officers. The mate could not believe what a tame kitten he was, compared to some of the real bastards and nuts he had sailed with. That was worth a lot; so, in spite of a few eccentricities on his part, the mate would back him up in any situation.

Their run of ports finally began. In spite of being a modern containership, capable of discharging and loading massive amounts of cargo in 24 hours or less, it did sometimes stay in port overnight, almost unheard of with the new ships. Part of the reason was that in New Zealand, the dockworkers did not work after 7:00 p.m., unless your ship was sailing in an hour or two. They did not understand the dock work in

America, where different shifts of longshoremen worked 24 hours a day. Everyone needed to be home at night, they would say. What kind of life is that, to be at work in the middle of the night? It was, they said, an American or European attitude, to work all the time, just to make more money. Their docks were quiet at night, and the ship's crew could go ashore, or have a quiet ship to sleep on. It was great.

The mate saw a bit of the countryside in New Zealand, and thought it was beautiful. He didn't care how many sheep they had. He also learned that there was a difference in cuts of lamb in restaurants. The Kiwis prided themselves on it, and said the junk that passed for lamb in America, England, and Australia, was, of course, inferior. The mate had to agree. In the pubs, the people were friendly. Their biggest cities were small, compared to the U.S., but he liked that. You could walk around them. It felt safe. The New Zealanders were also fond of sailing, and you would see their yachts out, even in rough weather. Almost everyone he talked to had traveled a great deal. Maybe it was because their homeland was small, he did not know, but he had met Kiwis all over the world. One problem they had was that many of their brightest young people moved to other countries as soon as they could arrange it. He met a doctor who told him how difficult it was to keep a medical student in New Zealand when he finished school, and began a practice.

"Why would they stay," the doctor mused, "when they can make so much more money doing plastic surgery in Chicago or London?"

"But you're here."

"Money doesn't mean so much to me, as it does to the young ones."

They had to anchor in the mouth of the river near Brisbane for three days awaiting dock space. There was launch service day and night to the city. Almost everyone went ashore. The first Aussies the mate saw belonged to an engine room repair crew who arrived on the first launch from town. The first thing they unloaded was not their tools, but several cases of cold beer. The mate got friendly with the launch driver. He told him that he had heard Australians made good beer. On the next trip out, the launch driver brought him three cases of his own favorite, a brand called XXXX, or Fourex. The mate happily paid him, and carted the prize up to his room. In further conversations, the driver told the mate how he had always wanted to show his family what a large ship was like. The mate got permission from the captain, and told him that when they docked, he could bring them for a tour. Sailors and dockworkers spent years working the big ships, but their families never knew what they were like. Most companies did not allow any visitors, for fear of injury or lawsuits.

The mate thought the guy would never show, but when they pulled alongside their dock, the launch driver was standing on the wharf with a woman and two small boys. They were the first ones up the gangway. The mate met his new friend, John, at the head of the gangway. The launch driver introduced his wife as "me cook," and his two boys as "me half-pints." They had never been aboard a large ship, and were impressed with its size. He took them up to the bridge, answered questions about navigation, then out on the wing, where they could look down at the foredeck. From there, they could see the giant cranes lifting the 40-foot containers off the ship. Like most visitors, they were surprised how high the bridge was, more than 80 feet above the water. The little boys held onto their parents' hands tighter.

The tour ended in the mate's room. He got soda for the boys and beer for the adults. They asked about America. Like most Aussies, they planned to visit there someday. They said they would rather go there than to Europe, which the mate found interesting. The "cook" was impressed that an officer would treat them so nicely. Class distinctions didn't mean much in Australia, she explained, unlike England. He began to understand why Aussies liked Americans; they had a lot in common. When the mate had to get to work, they went back to the gangway. John insisted that he take the mate out for steak and beer that night. The mate tried to back out, then realized it was a good chance to get to know some locals, rather than end up in a strictly touristy place, or, worse yet, a sailor's bar with the same guys from his ship. John would pick him up that evening.

The mate met up with John and a buddy of his, and they drove to The Rose Garden Restaurant for steak. It was better than any American steak. He did not tell John that he thought the beef in Argentina, raised by grazing on the Pampas, was as good, or better. The mate did not try to keep up with John's ability to consume beer. *Only a Dane could drink more*, the mate thought. Asked why his wife didn't come along, John explained that Aussie men don't do that much; they preferred to go out with their "mates." Perhaps that was why Australian women, whom he thought were mostly very pretty, had historically liked American men. From the Big War on, Americans who spent time there came back with great stories about the girls, and frequently the girls themselves. An Australian girl was impressed if you held a door open for her. Aussie blokes thought something like that was a sign of weakness that would only lead to their women demanding better treatment. Better to leave 'em home with the half pints.

The mate got back to the ship early for a sailor. The younger guys went bananas chasing the pretty, local girls around the clubs and discos. Stories went around at breakfast about it all, who had made out, and who hadn't. It reminded the mate of his younger days.

From Brisbane they went to Melbourne, then Sydney. The ship carried a supercargo on the runs from port-to-port, something the mate had not seen in years. He was British, and had lived in Australia many years. He made all the arrangements for the ship and its cargo -- labor, docking, clearances, etc. A supercargo in the olden times would ride the whole voyage, not so in modern times. A good supercargo made the job of the chief mate, in particular, and all the mates, easier. He knew how far you could push the longshoremen, for example, helpful in Australia where the waterfront labor unions were still powerful. The interesting part was that, because he was British, he and the Limey 3rd mate became instant friends. The mate noticed a change in attitude from his shipmate as they began to make the Aussie ports. It seemed that the old antagonisms between the British and the Australians had not disappeared. People on both sides made jokes, but with elements of resentment still there, from centuries before. Some Aussies even called the Brits "Pommies," a derisive term that implied they drank too much gin.

The mate wondered why the Australians and the British didn't get along better. Some Aussies told him that it was because of several wars, when the Aussies had sent troops to be part of the Allied cause. They felt that the whenever the commanders were British, the Aussie troops were used as cannon fodder. The Battle of Gallipoli, in World War I, was a prime example. A British general ordered a Light Infantry of Aussies to charge entrenched positions of Turks. Mistakes with British artillery barrages doomed them. In typical fashion, the Aussies followed the orders of their own leaders, and charged machine gun nests over open ground, wearing their traditional felt hats. Many died. The mate wondered why the English-speaking peoples did not get along better. It would seem that if they couldn't get along with other cultures, they could at least get along with each other.

In Melbourne, the mate got a few hours to visit an American friend who had moved there. He had done the reverse of what many Americans had done. He met and married an Australian girl, but he moved there. He was a former merchant officer who had given up the sea, and he and his wife ran an antique shop. It seemed he had been learning and gathering things from all over the world for years, in his travels. He had a natural eye for the value of odds and ends, and learned the rest. They seemed happy.

He also got to a couple of souvenir shops. He bought a boomerang, guaranteed to return, a piece of coral, certified to be from the Great Barrier Reef, and a "Digger Hat," the same as the Australian Armed Forces used, guaranteed to attract attention. He thought that anyone who went into battle with a hat like that, instead of a helmet, was foolish, but that was the way of the Aussies.

Sydney was last, and the mate loved it. During the first day, he took a ferry across the beautiful harbor to the zoo. It was the only place he was going to see kangaroos and wallabies; they didn't run wild in the streets. From there, he crossed back, and lined up for a tour of the famous Opera House. It was indeed amazing, but he found it strange that the guide kept talking about the labor problems and the tremendous cost overruns. She implied that the most interesting part of the facility was that it ever got finished.

They stayed two days, a rarity for a containership. At night, he went up with a few officers to an area of Sydney called "The Rocks." This was one of the original areas built in the harbor, in the settlement years. It was close to downtown, and had pubs, restaurants, and shops. Many groups of locals went there for drinking, eating, dancing, and to meet. He thought the typical Australian guy there was loud, and drank too much, but this in itself was not offensive to a sailor. The girls were dressed up more than you would expect. They would talk to you, or dance with you, if you asked. He ran into most of the young guys from the ship that night. Most of them were drinking and chasing the pretty, Aussie girls. He also learned that there were other bars around that the Aussies called "chaps bars." You didn't go there looking for women. You went there to meet other "chaps."

It was back to New Zealand the next day. The ship had a huge capacity for carrying reefer boxes, and the mate got a kick out of discovering that the largest contract the ship had for reefer cargo was frozen beef from Australia; the majority of it would be unloaded in Philadelphia, and the receiver was the McDonald's restaurant chain. The usual jokes about kangaroo meat went around. He knew Australia had great beef, but wondered how it could possibly be cheaper to ship it half way around the world, rather than buy it in the states. Overall, the crew survived the time in Australia without much trouble, and the mate was glad he had gotten to see it.

They sailed through the beautiful Cook Straits. The mountains of the two islands of New Zealand loomed large to starboard and port. The mate was glad to have the watch sailing through there. Theirs was clearly the largest vessel around, and he enjoyed making the course changes and avoiding the other vessels going through. Cook himself would have been shocked to see how large ships had become.

They went to Lyttleton, the port for Christchurch, first. They didn't stay long, and the mates kept sea watches, which meant that the mate, being 2nd, would be off from 0800 to 1600. He got a ride to Christchurch, and in a shop, he bought a couple of handmade woolen sweaters. They were thick, heavy ones, and cost about $50 each. They made great ski sweaters, and the craftwork was beautiful. Sweaters like that could last many years.

Wellington was the last stop. It was a short passage from Lyttleton, on the South Island, to Wellington, on the North Island. They stayed overnight, mostly due to the civilized approach of the longshoremen. The mate didn't do much in the small city. He got a haircut, had a meal, walked around the downtown shops, drank a couple of local brews in "stubbies," or little glass bottles, and went back. They left New Zealand the next day, and were shortly back at sea, with nothing but ocean surrounding them. The mate calculated the great circle courses for Panama, and everybody sobered up and settled back down for the passage. Even though you might like the ports you went to, you always knew you'd be at sea soon, and it was kind of a strange relief to cast off the damn lines and get out there again.

The trip east was typical for the South Pacific -- good weather, boring routine. There were two exceptions. The first happened when the mate was casually looking through the Nautical Almanac during a lazy watch. The mate noticed that there would be an eclipse of the sun during their passage, visible in the Southern Hemisphere. He figured out when and where the ship would be, and the chart in the Almanac indicated they would be in the area of total eclipse. He posted notices for the passengers and crew, but didn't expect much of a response. He was wrong.

On the afternoon of the event, a crowd gathered up on the bridge, including passengers, officers, and crew. Many brought all kinds of devices to watch the eclipse safely, but there were also some macho types who scoffed at the idea of burning their retinas, and just used sunglasses, no matter what anyone said. The mate used binoculars, turning them backwards and focusing the sun's image onto the white bulkhead. Passengers had crude cardboard boxes with the little hole punched in them. The favorite device was a welder's faceplate that an engineer brought. His theory was that if the glass could protect you against the glare of welding, it must be good enough for the sun. In the absence of scientific evidence, the group split evenly on the theory. Overall, it was a fun time, and, if nothing else, gave the passengers a story to tell, since their friends back home could not see the eclipse.

The second event of interest had to do with their route. With a minor course adjustment early on, they changed their great circle track so that they would pass close to Pitcairn Island. The surviving mutineers from the *Bounty* had sailed there. Their descendants still lived there. The island itself was only a couple of miles across, and was, as the islanders had told Christian, far to the east of all the other islands in the chain. It was not marked on any chart in Bligh's time. The mate had always considered the mutiny the greatest true sea story ever told, and thought it was a rare opportunity to see where the adventure had ended.

As they got closer, the mate figured out what time they would pass it. The time of arrival off Pitcairn was crucial, and mostly a matter of luck. There was no thought of stopping. First, there was no port there. Bounty Bay wasn't much of a harbor, just an inlet, big enough for only a small boat, and there was no dock. The locals went out in small boats, more like the longboats used in Christian's time than anything else. Secondly, the company would not be happy if they hove to, even for a couple of hours. Time is money in the shipping business, and the company didn't pay the seamen for sightseeing. The last reason was the islanders' behavior. Their reputation was that they loved visitors. If you stopped, they would row out to the big ship, and climb aboard. They would trade handmade goods for food, magazines, and building items they could not manufacture. It was hell to get them back off your ship. There were smaller cargo ships that did call there as part of their schedule, but not Farrell Lines. They would have to be content just to see it. They would not adjust speed for it. The ship had luck. They would approach Pitcairn at sunrise, on the mate's watch.

A couple of days before passing, the mate posted notices again for all. He told them about their passing of the famous island, and invited all up to the bridge for the event. It would be a Sunday morning, with sunrise about 0600, ship's time. On the appointed day, the captain came up to bridge about 0430, in his dress blues. The mate, in his usual clean khakis, plotted the course and picked up the island on radar. It was still dark when the first crew and passengers came up. The mate was surprised and happy to see some of the scruffiest engineers and crewmen, guys who would normally be sleeping, come up, rubbing their eyes, looking for the island and a cup of coffee. *Who says sailors aren't interested in history?*

The sky to the east was getting lighter as the target on the scope got more definite. They headed right for it. Bounty Bay, the place where the mutineers scuttled their ship, was on the north side of the little, mountainous island.

"Cap', how close can I go to it?"

"The water's deep there. Stay one mile to the north of Bounty Bay."

"Yessir, that'll be good. Give everyone a good look."

A mile was close for a big ship. With binoculars, they would be able to see it very well, and the mate was happy. As they got closer, the sun rose up, as if on cue, right behind the island. He had the ship in hand steering, took positions off the island itself, and began to maneuver the ship closer. The visitors on the bridge were all out on the starboard bridge wing, sipping coffee. The Chief Steward sent up pastry, and the captain left the navigation to the mate. It was a good feeling, that your captain totally trusted you, and the mate loved maneuvering a ship.

The mate took visual bearings outside on the wing, and distance off by radar, inside, and plotted them. To the delight of the visitors on the bridge, the mate changed course again, this time to starboard, to get closer for the final run abeam of the island.

The *Austral Pioneer* sped past Pitcairn at 21 knots. They could clearly see the shore at Bounty Bay, and those who knew the history of it no doubt thought about the mutineers and their Tahitian women and men, all standing on the little beach, right there, watching their ship burn, knowing that they were stuck there probably forever. They could see houses the islanders had on the sharp slope up from the little bay. The radio operator worked his key, and "talked" to a descendant of Fletcher Christian, in Morse code. The mate wondered how someone could be happy living on such a small island, away from everything; then again, there were problems modern society had that they could avoid, too. A couple of the younger officers came up at the last minute. They had an old, large paint bucket, with a stick attached to it. They had been going around the ship the last couple of days asking for donations for the Pitcairn Islanders. The mate had contributed some cigarettes and magazines, along with a postcard asking for someone on the island to send him a card. They brought it into the wheelhouse, and the mate gave them a signal flag, the "Y" flag, to attach to the stick. The "Y," or "Yankee" flag, had a meaning of, "I am carrying mail." It was an old-time signal. The young officers stapled the flag to the stick. The mate checked the prevailing wind and current, and told them when the time was right. They heaved it over the side, in the hopes that it would drift right into the bay, or at least somewhere, where the inhabitants could get it.

It didn't take long before the bay and the houses were out of sight, and the steep hills of the island were astern of them. Soon, everyone left the bridge. The mate adjusted the course one more time, putting the ship on a slightly altered course for Panama. He had her back on the Iron Mike, and the AB at the wheel went around and collected the coffee cups from the little party, and cleaned them up. The mate would end his seafaring career without ever getting a card from Pitcairn.

His friend, the British 3rd mate, had other opinions on the story of the mutineers, and, true to his nature as an ex-patriot Brit, thought the original inhabitants were all criminals, and should have been brought to trial in England, and hanged. The mate's nightly, polite, cocktail hour with his Limey friend continued, but when they neared Panama, a new story came out. The 3rd had come up to the bridge on the mate's watch, unexpectedly. He seemed lost in thought as he gazed out at the shoreline to the north, in the Gulf of Panama. When questioned, he simply told the mate to stop by his room after watch, for a drink and a story.

The story he got was true and enlightening. Some years ago, the English 3rd had sailed on a different American merchant ship, also as a 3rd mate. Upon the approach to the Pacific side of Panama, while on watch at night, the Limey had gone out on the port wing of the bridge, and thought he heard a voice in the water. He had listened more intently, and heard a voice cry, "Help," in English. He saw nothing but dark water, and the distant shapes of the land. He immediately called the lookout to tell him to listen carefully, called the engine room to tell them to stand by for possible maneuvering, and called the captain to come to the bridge. He was sure he heard the cry of a drowning man in the water, although there was no emergency message about any sinking, and nothing on the radar.

The Old Man was a company guy more than anything, and did not want to slow the ship, or alter course. He kept telling the mate on watch that he "must have been hearing things." The 3rd had insisted that he clearly had heard a cry for help, from the water, now astern of them. Furthermore, if the captain did not turn around and conduct a search, that he would enter all the particulars of his observations in the logbook, especially his refusal to give aid to those stranded at sea. The captain had fussed and fumed, then given in. The Brit called extra men on lookout, woke up the first assistant engineer to handle the throttles, and turned the ship around. Before long, the bosun, out on the wing as an extra lookout, heard the same plea for help. They turned on some searchlights, stopped the ship, and readied a lifeboat. Eventually, they spotted two men swimming in the water. The ship's crew rescued them. It turned out that they had been in the crew of a sea-going tug that had been towing a large barge, and had capsized in a storm. Now the captain pitched in, getting the radio operator to send distress messages. Being near the canal, of course, meant that there were numerous ships in the area, and several vessels spent the night searching for the missing crew of the tug. The tug guys had been swimming all night without lifejackets, in water frequently inhabited by sharks. Their survival was a miracle, and it was another miracle that the 3rd mate had heard them, and insisted on a search. The Limey had a copy of the logbook entry, to prove all that had happened. He said he felt funny every time he passed the same area of the world.

The mate had more respect for his fellow officer, whom, in spite of his anti-American statements, was a damn good sailor, and shipmate. However, part of the telling seemed to imply that he thought it exemplified the difference between British and American, the American captain having no class, to do things the way he did. The mate went back to his room, and returned with two drink glasses.

"What's that, then?" the 3rd inquired.

"It's Irish whiskey, damn your eyes."

"Irish?'

"Yeah, Irish. You ever heard of good English whiskey? Shut the hell up, and take the glass." The older mate did.

"Okay, you no good, son-of-the-queen -- here's to my Limey friend, third mate Clarke, the hero of the Panama tugboat rescue!"

"No, no, that's not why I told you the story. I think you're different, you know, there's hope for you, in spite of being a bloody Yank and all."

"Too bad. This is all the recognition you're going to get. Drink up!" With that, the toast, and unofficial award ceremony, was complete, and they both went to bed.

The big ship squeezed through the canal without a lot of room on either side in the locks. The widest ships that could go through were 108 feet in the beam; their ship was 100. They went up 85 feet to the level of Gatun Lake, and later down the same amount to sea level. No matter how many times the mate had been through it, the canal was still an engineering marvel. Panama, however, had hot, humid weather, and mosquitoes. He was always glad to clear the harbor on the other side, and head out to sea. They set course for New Orleans, about 1600 nautical miles, and three days steaming away.

The rest of the trip, from New Orleans, to Charleston, Philadelphia, and New York, where the voyage ended, went without much excitement. The young guys overdid it some in The Big Easy. They started their night there by going directly to Pat O'Brien's, in the French Quarter, and drinking Hurricanes. When the mate was done visiting old friends and having some shrimp, he went back to the dock. Walking into the cargo complex, he found the young 3rd mate passed out on the pavement. He helped him up, back to the ship, and put him to bed. Before the end of the voyage, the chief mate showed him the personnel reports the captain filled out on everybody. For his record, it stated that the mate drank "casually." For the young 3rd mate, the same section said, "abstains." *Well, captains don't know everything,* the mate thought.

The scene in the officer's saloon in New York was typical. Everybody lined up to sign off the official articles of the voyage. The mate stepped right to the next table and signed on again. He watched the usual scene of guys carrying their bags down the gangway, happy, and others toting bags up, apprehensive. It was the beginning of another 84-day trip, and at the end of that one, he would go right back again. It would be the longest he sailed in a 12-month period since his first year as an officer.

At payoff, before he left, the Englishman told the mate that the tugboat story had an epilogue. His former ship was up for an award for the rescue, one of those "Ship of the Year" things. The captain went to the award dinner. No one notified the 3rd mate or invited him to the ceremony. The captain accepted the award, and gave a talk about following the moral law of the sea to always aid a fellow seaman in distress.

Chapter 18: The Party

The mate could never understand how anyone could refer to an event as a party if there were no women there. However, that is what seamen called the casual, on some ships, habitual, sessions of drinking and storytelling. At least this was true until the supertankers and containerships took over, and there weren't enough guys around at night to have such a gathering.

It would usually begin right before supper, which was 1700-1800. The day workers, the guys who did not stand a watch, like the chief mate and first engineer, would clean up beforehand, and congregate in some officer's room for a drink or two before dinner. That's how it would start. "Just a quick one before dinner," they would tell themselves. The most important part of the cocktail party was to remember to get in the messroom early enough. If you went in right before 1800 hours, the cooks and messmen would be pissed off, and your food and service would suffer.

After dinner, the guys not on watch on the bridge or engine room might go out on deck and look at the sea for a while, then drift into the house, where the quarters were. The guy who had started the party that night would have his door open. If you wanted to sleep, or didn't want to be bothered, you shut your door. An open door was an open invitation.

"Hey, mate, how ya doin'?" would come the call from an open door, as you walked past.

"C'mon on in, and have a fuckin' drink!" went the formal invitation.

Soon there would be five or six guys crowded into the small room. The host would pull out whatever beer or booze he had, and glasses, sometimes clean ones. Others would go back to their own rooms and grab something to contribute. It

, kind of a crude BYO party. On some ships, even the captain would host these drink-a-thons. Being the captain meant you always had a supply of booze, much of it paid for by the company, for entertaining port officials and the like.

The mate remembered in the older, colorful years of shipping, when drinking was normal. Sailors would say no one would go to sea if he couldn't have a drink after work, but some of the new containerships tried to enforce a ban on alcohol. The enforcer was typically a captain who was a reformed drinker himself. The only time there was not a party going was the first night at sea after leaving a port. Everyone was too tired from their work in port, lack of sleep, and their going uptown.

The crew, living on their own deck below the officers' deck, had their own parties at sea. Usually the bosun or dayman would host for the deck department, since they made the most money, worked the hardest, and usually drank the most. In the steward's department, it could be anyone, but usually it was the chief cook. On some ships, the crew kept to themselves, drank quietly alone in their rooms, or holed up in pairs here and there. These were not happy ships. They were ships where many in the crew had bitches against one another, even fights, and there was little socializing. On happy ships, there would be nightly card games at sea, and numerous open doors. Loneliness, sulking, and drinking alone were bad signs. Often it was a bad weather run that caused this, and at other times, how the ship was managed by the officers, and rarely, just a bunch of damn guys that could not get along.

The next stage always seemed to begin the same way. Guys would say they didn't want to talk about the ship, but the conversation always turned that way. After a half hour or more of bitching about the conditions in the engine room, or what an asshole the captain was, everyone would tire of this line, and it would turn into a sea story contest. The stories always began the same way:

"Well, I was on this ship one time and ________" someone always began it unexpectedly, with no prompting, other than the drink in his hand. The mate remembered one such party.

One of the mates had begun. It seemed he had been on a ship one time, sailing with old Harry Such and Such. Old Harry was an engineer who went ashore in Haifa, Israel, for a drink. He was 2nd engineer on the old ship So and So, with Whatzizname as chief, and, well, anyway, he went ashore and didn't come back until morning. Guys were lined up by the gangway right before turning to, with their coffee mugs, when ol' Harry came stumbling down the dock, with only his boxer shorts on. The wharf rats rolled the poor bastard, and the cocksuckers had stolen his damn clothes and shoes -- everything except his shorts. With no money for a cab, he had to walk all the way back to the ship like that. At this point, everyone had a good laugh at Harry's expense, and reflected on some of their experiences.

In response to the boxer short story, other officers told of times in places like India or Africa where guys got rolled and stripped completely naked. The first story had been one-upped, and that set off the inevitable race to come up with more interesting stories.

The officers' parties would usually be an equal combination of mates and engineers, with an occasional radio operator thrown in. If you were on a ship where the mates only drank with the mates, and the engineers did the same, it was not a good ship. Since the first story was about an engineer, the good-natured competitiveness forced an engineer to tell a mate story. He had been "on a ship one time" where the 3rd mate on watch was so drunk that he passed out right on the deck of the wheelhouse. The ship was approaching port, and the AB at the wheel was steering. As the story went, the guy just held course until he thought the lights on shore were getting too close, and called the captain for help.

Guys who hadn't spoken would kick in with something, and it didn't matter anymore if it related to the previous story. The higher the alcohol consumption, the more this rule applied.

Another mate had been on a ship where they had a guy in the crew everyone called The Phantom. It was an old ship, and had the standard, sound-powered telephones. You turned a dial to a number for the place you were calling, and turned a crank to make it ring. They were all over the ship -- the bow, the stern, engine room, bridge, messroom, etc. They had to stay on, for safety reasons. The phone would ring in the wheelhouse or engine room, at all hours, day or night, at different times, and the mate or engineer on watch would answer. The message was always the same:

"This is the Phantom. Fuck you." For the whole voyage, everyone tried to figure out who was doing it, but no one caught anyone.

For some reason, some bitching started about the Coast Guard, and how they didn't know what the hell they were doing when they came aboard merchant ships to enforce regulations. The mate contributed a story about a radio call he had overheard on VHF channel 16, while steaming off the Florida Keys. A small boat had radioed in to the Coast Guard that another boat was sinking, and gave some details. The response from the radio dispatcher was classic:

"Vessel calling, this is U.S. Coast Guard. Is the vessel sinking in any danger?"

Guys then bitched about the lack of respect the merchant marine got, partly because of the damn Hollywood movies, partly because many more guys served in the navy. One bitch was about the story told at Navy OCS to all new naval officer candidates. According to the story, a navy ship had passed a cargo ship at sea, fairly close. The officers on the navy ship looked into the wheelhouse of the merchant ship, with binoculars, and saw only a dog. The dog began to bark, and a merchant officer came running into the bridge, and changed the course. There was no proof of the story, and no one ever said what nationality the ship was; the damn navy instructors just lumped all merchant ships together in one category, and implied they were all no good. The mate observed that he would love to have a dog like that. Someone else opined that it was like saying that the Turkish Navy and the American Navy were just the same.

The stories about the other sea-going services ended with a confession from one of the engineers. He told how he had first joined the navy when he was a kid, and been assigned to the deck department of his first ship. He didn't know anything about ships. He got the job of a talker on the bridge. All he had to do was stand next to the captain, with headphones on, and repeat his orders into the microphone, which would send the orders all over the ship. It was simple. Everything was fine, although he did not have any notion what the orders he repeated meant. After a few days, the ship was docking, and he was again next to the captain. While approaching the pier, the captain said, "Tell 'em fore and aft we are going 'portside to.'" This meant simply that the portside of the ship would be "to" the dock. Deckhands needed to know this to arrange the mooring lines in the proper places. The guy had repeated the order into his headset, and then broke protocol by speaking to the captain:

"Captain, if that's Portside Two, where is Portside One?"

The captain stared at him, speechless. The next day, they assigned the guy to the engine room, and told him never to come to the bridge again. That's how he started learning about boilers and pumps. He spent his navy career in the engine room, and then got a license as a marine engineer. He laughed at himself, a good sign, and said it was the rookie question that had given him his career.

The topic turned to women. There was some bitching about wives and girlfriends at home, how they didn't understand the sea life, and so on, and then it turned to girls in foreign ports. All lamented how things had changed in Japan. It was sad, they said. You used to be able to get a pretty, young girl, a nice hotel room with a sunken bath, and food and drink, for the night, for about $30. No more. It was rare to find these things, and it cost too much. The famous street of hookers in Genoa, the Pigalle, was mentioned, although the usual mispronunciation was used, "Pig Alley." Italian stories included the famous washerwoman of Genoa, Anna Banana. Spain and Brazil got high marks. The most disgusting place award went unanimously to Panama, and stories went around about the usual lewd behavior seen there. No one was old enough to remember Havana, but all knew of its reputation.

One of the watch engineers started telling about a captain he had sailed with who was drunk all the time. Engineers liked to tell stories showing how fucked-up captains or mates were, but the mates in the room let it pass. This particular captain would disappear for a week at a time, only to reappear looking like hell. The ship was one that came out of mothballs for Vietnam duty, and the crew was a real piece of work. The chief mate was along for the ride, the 2nd mate was 70 years old, and one of the third mates never came out of his room except for work. The trip dragged on for months, much of it spent at anchor in Nam.

Crewmembers got into fights, guys had injuries that sent them home, and, with the supply of booze bought from the bum boats that came alongside the anchored ship, most everyone was drunk all the time. Many never turned to for work. Finally, with all the tension of such a long, hot voyage on an old ship, the captain had apparently snapped, and decided that he hated the door to his room. One night, while drunk, he, being the only one on the ship allowed to have a firearm, took out the company-issued pistol and emptied it into the door. The third mate on watch heard it, and began looking around the passageways. The engineer telling the story met him, and they went up to the captain's deck to see what had happened. There were six bullet holes in his door, and six spent slugs lying around the deck in the passageway. The captain did not show his face for the next few days, and there was much speculation whether he was alive or dead. No one seemed to care either way.

Then it was Christmas night, and the chief engineer had a party in his room. Most of the officers were there when the captain stuck his head in the doorway, looking like death itself. He wanted a drink. The chief said he would give him a drink if he first told why he had shot up the door.

"Go fuck yourself, chief," was the captain's reply, and he left.

A few minutes later, he reappeared. He must have been out of booze, and wanted a drink badly.

"I'll tell you why I did that. I've been looking at the inside of that goddam door for seven months, and I hate that door, so I shot it up. Now, give me a goddam drink!"

Someone fetched the drink. Apparently, the engineer went on, the captain ran out of booze again, and sobered up enough to tell the chief that he wanted his door fixed. The engineer telling the story, a young guy at the time, went up to the Old Man's room. He patched up the bullet holes with a traditional remedy -- epoxy putty known as red hand. He ended the story by saying how nervous he had been the whole time he was on the other side of the door, hoping that the captain would not decide that he hated the door again.

At this point, the radio operator spoke up for the first time, and pitched in with a story. This was significant because on many ships Sparks stayed to himself, and rarely could match stories with mates or engineers anyway. Many operators went batty after years of listening to dots and dashes. The Sparky on this ship seemed almost normal, and it was a good sign that he drank with the mates and engineers, and now, even participated in the story telling.

His story was about a time he was on a ship in bad weather, and had a message from the company for the captain. It seemed important, so he went right down to the captain's cabin with it. Normally, he left messages on a hook by the door, but the door was open, and he knocked. The captain hollered from his bedroom to come on in with the message. When he got through the outer office and into his bedroom, he saw that the captain was in the shower. The captain opened the stall door and reached out his hand for the telegram. Just then, the ship took a heavy roll, and the captain lost his balance. The stall door slammed shut right on his dick. He screamed in pain, and went down on the deck. Everyone considered this story satisfactory and amusing, and there was hope that they had a regular guy for a Sparky.

The mate then added his own heavy roll story. He had been a cadet on a ship and was drinking with the third mate, in his room. The ship had just left port, and he hadn't stowed all his gear. His sextant was sitting up on the dresser. Next to it was a bottle of scotch he had just opened. The ship took a sudden roll and everything in the room that was loose began to fly across the room. The mate had immediately jumped for the dresser, and caught the bottle of scotch before it hit the deck. His expensive sextant crashed to the deck, but he didn't care.

A spate of weather stories followed. Everyone in the room had been through hurricanes and typhoons, so it wasn't impressive trying to show that you had been in rougher weather than somebody else. They had all seen tough times, and accepted it as part of the life. Mates thought they were primarily responsible for ships safely riding out storms, since they had to handle the course and speed just right, to keep a ship out of the trough of a huge wave. Engineers would remind them that if they did not keep the screw turning and the steering engine working, it wouldn't matter. The mate thought they were correct. You could take your engineers for granted until there was hell to pay. Many ships had foundered in rough seas because they couldn't steer, or make any headway. If you lost the plant in a storm, the ship would broach to the seas, sideways, and take the huge waves and swells broadside; it was a dangerous time, and many a ship and fishing boat had not survived it. He didn't want the party to turn into a pissing match over who had the more important job; they all had to turn to and get their jobs done. He stuck in a weather story about St. Elmo's fire. Some of the guys did not know what that was, although they had all heard of it.

The mate had been out on the wing of a bridge, at night, when chain lightening surrounded his ship. It wasn't raining, but there was a terrific lightening show all around. He apparently had been out there for a long time. He was open to the atmosphere, which was highly charged with electricity. Suddenly he noticed that his hands, which hung over the dodger, the forward bulkhead, had blue electric flames shooting out from his fingers. There was no feeling of pain, just the blue fire. He had called his AB out from the wheelhouse to look at the phenomenon, and the old salt had immediately proclaimed it to be St. Elmo's Fire. He said he had seen it before, but it was rare. It was fascinating, but the mate went back inside the wheelhouse.

Several stories followed about guys who had been hurt in odd ways. Some of these guys had died, and it was not funny. You didn't want to get too serious with your stories at a party. It would change the tone of the evening. Laugh at things, that's the ticket. So the older hands steered things around to lighter fare with stories and memories of the ex-cons, gamblers, drunks, thieves and green first-timers they knew. It saved the party.

The First Assistant Engineer turned the injury topic around with a story from his younger years. The first, as sailors called him, had been sailing on an old C-2 cargo ship, and had severe back pain. The ship went to Vietnam, and he went ashore to the army hospital. They checked his papers, saw that he was a merchant seaman, and told him to get in a certain line. On getting to the doctor, the medical man told the engineer to "take it out" and let him see it. This caused the realization that the army, in its wisdom, had assumed that if he was a seaman, he must have VD, and had put him in that line.

After some arguing, he got to see the other doctor, who prescribed rest and Darvon. This didn't do any good. The ship went to Manila, and his back still hurt like hell. The bunks and mattresses were old and no good and he could hardly sleep at all, let alone get through the workday. He took matters into his own hands, and went ashore to find a doctor. He got to the dock and was immediately approached by a couple of shore pilots, locals who offered to take him to places with the best girls in the Philippines, or the coldest beer, or whatever else you wanted. They would charge a fee for the service, of course. He insisted he wanted none of this, as his back was killing him, and he needed a chiropractor.

"Mister, chiropractor in this town no good, nobody go to them."

"Do you know what a chiropractor is?" The first asked.

"Of course I do, my English very good, but I take you to doctor that the people go to."

He agreed. He had been desperate. The one local got in an old 1950's vintage Japanese car on the driver's side, the right. The other shore pilot removed the back door off its hinges for the engineer to get in the back. He was in such pain that he didn't care about the danger of such a situation. The two guys outnumbered him, and he did not have any idea where they were taking him. The second pilot replaced the back door on its hinges, and off they went. It had been hot and muggy, and there was a terrible stink in the air. He asked why.

"Garbage trucks on strike, one week now," the driver answered.

They drove quite a while and ended up in a shantytown. The engineer didn't care. He would try anything. They pulled up in front of a shack with a thatched roof.

"This guy not real doctor, you know, witch doctor; no speak English, but he will fix you real good."

The first paused to sip his drink and told how, at the time, he was sure he was going to be robbed and beaten, maybe even killed. However, he was in pain, and, in front of the shack, there were a bunch of people waiting. Small, naked children followed the American curiosity around. There was garbage everywhere, and flies all over it. He asked the pilot how much this "doctor" would charge him. The guide said there was no fee – "Just give what you want."

The doctor was a gray, wrinkled, skinny little brown man, who greeted him with a toothless smile. He bowed, smiled, and took the first's wrist in his hand. He said "back sprain" in English, and motioned the patient to lie down on a wicker cot. The first said he figured if he was going to be knocked over the head, it would happen right then. The doc poked him sharply, with acupuncture needles, in three places in his back. That was it. The doc said, "Okay," and was done. When the engineer got up, he reached into his pockets. He only had a $1 bill, and two $20's. He hadn't gotten change. He felt embarrassed, but took out the $1 bill and held it out. The doc took it, smiling.

He got back in the jalopy with the two hustlers, and they rode back to Manilla. He was amazed that no one robbed him. The shore pilots now gave him a serious pitch about going for beer and girls. His back was better, but he wanted to get back to the ship for some sleep before he went on watch again. He lied that he would be back out later that night, and they could take him then. Then they negotiated the price for the pilots' services. They wanted $40, American, a lot in those days. He settled with them for $20. He said that he felt bad; he paid $20 for a couple of hustlers, and only $1 for some village doctor who had really fixed his back.

As everyone drank more and more, guys would start to yak about family or home. This was not good. It did you no damn good at all to discuss your worries about people or things you could not have any effect on until you got home. Just sail the goddam ship, earn your money, and deal with family when you got back.

The bullshit going around the room turned to sea-going stuff that was less personal, things that happened to other people on ships, many of whom they did not know. The case of the union chief mate jailed in Turkey came up. His ship had been unloading containers at a dock when the crane driver had lowered a loaded 40-footer on top of the cab of the truck that was supposed to drive it away. It seemed the truck driver had not stopped his truck in the exact correct spot, and the crane driver was careless. It killed the driver. The Turkish authorities, knowing that the chief mate of a ship is responsible for the unloading of cargo, arrested him for murder, and threw him in one of their infamous jails. The fact that it happened on the dock, and he had zero control over the crane driver, meant nothing. It had taken great efforts by the union and some Congressmen to get him released, and it took months. Even then, although they allowed him to leave Turkey, they could still charge him if he ever came back there. It was a bizarre case, but typical of what can happen to a sailor in a foreign country. You could holler all you wanted to about seeing the American ambassador, but, in many places, people would just laugh at you.

The mate contributed something he had read in a paper about a ship called the *Aegean,* which had been in a collision. The Greek 2nd mate had testified at a hearing that he saw the other ship only moments before impact, and had, "according to the old law of the sea, immediately turned his ship to port," hoping that the other ship, the *Atlantic Empress,* would do the same. The mates in the room got a good laugh out of that, but had to explain to the younger engineers that there was not only no such law, but, when in doubt, if you can't change engine speeds, you would usually turn your ship to starboard. There followed remarks about Greeks selling licenses to people who had no training, and stories about them sinking their own ships for insurance money. That brought on the true story of the tanker that left New York with its compass 180 degrees out of whack and went aground on Long Island. Things were degenerating. Stories didn't necessarily follow one another. People got sloppy. A couple of the guys would be on watch soon, and would need a little sleep or a lot of coffee.

Someone thought about a classic, New Orleans story. A freighter was returning from a foreign trip, and the chief mate, in checking his records of the voyage, realized that he had not test-fired the line-throwing gun. The Coast Guard was due to make an inspection of the safety equipment, so he figured, even though the ship was in the Mississippi River, that he still had time to do this. He got the bosun, and they went up a few decks to rig it. The line throwing apparatus looked like a small canon. You put a powder charge in it, and then loaded it with a metal projectile that had a cylindrical, heavy end, attached to a rod with an eye in it. You attached a small line to the eye. The pre-coiled line would feed out from a bucket. The idea was that you would fire the projectile, with the thin line attached, over the deck of a ship in distress. Then you bent on a larger line to the small one, then a larger one, while the guys on the other ship hauled it in. Eventually, you sent over a mooring line, one big enough to tow the other ship to safety. It was effective if used properly.

By the time they were ready, the ship was in the New Orleans metropolitan area. The river was wide, and there were no other ships near them. Because the ship was getting ready to dock, Mate Laurel thought he would save a little time. He did not attach any line to the projectile. If they bent on a line, they would have to haul it back in, and that would take time. While this made sense, there was one problem. Without the weight of the line holding it back, the projectile would carry much farther than usual. Chief Mate Laurel gave the word to Bosun Hardy, and he lit the fuse. The projectile cleared the river, and flew over into a suburb of New Orleans.

It crashed through the roof of a house, and fetched up in a washing machine. Fortunately, no one was doing laundry at the time. The mate always thought that some kind of comedy award should have been given to the cannoneers, but all he heard was that the shipping company gave the woman of the house money to fix her roof and buy a new washing machine. He was damn sure, however, that the chief mate made the standard logbook entry: "Line-throwing apparatus successfully test fired this date."

This led the mate to repeat a story he had heard from an English North Sea pilot. The pilot told about a British ship that was at a dock in England. The engineers were working on the condenser. Someone opened the wrong valve, and flooded the engine room to a height of eighteen feet. The ship settled to the bottom, still at the dock. The 2nd mate was due to be relieved that day for vacation. He went down the gangway with his gear, and began walking across the pier. On the way, he passed his relief coming the other way.

"Anything new?" the relief mate had asked.

"Yes, she's sunk," went the typically British reply, and the second mate had kept on walking.

This last bit of sea lore offended none present, there being no Englishmen in the room, and seemed a fitting way to end the party. Everyone got up and made his way back to his own room, in different states of drunkenness. There would be another party in somebody else's room the next night, with different stories, and every night at sea until the ship reached the next port.

Chapter 19: You the Man Now?

He picked up a one-trip relief job as 2nd mate on an A3 class United States Lines containership, headed for the Far East from New York. It had spaces below and above decks only for containers. There was no cargo gear at all, except for a small crane to hoist ship's supplies up from the dock. The trip down to Panama, through the ditch and up the west coast towards Long Beach, California, was uneventful. The captain was sober and competent. The Old Man seemed to like the mate, especially when the younger mate learned to work the new computer that was on the bridge. They had programs for stability and navigation solutions. The captain would come up every morning about 0600, on the mate's watch, and the two of them would recalculate the ship's stability for fuel oil burnout, changes in ballast, and anticipated cargo work in the next port. Then they would refigure the ship's courses and speeds. It seemed this would be the routine until the trip was over, but things changed as they approached Long Beach.

The chief mate got very sick. No one knew what was wrong with him. They docked on a weekend, and the captain arranged to send him ashore to a hospital. By afternoon, the word came back that he needed an operation. The captain brought the news to the mate directly.

"I want to promote you to chief mate. The union hall here is closed anyway, so we can't get a relief. The company never hires chief mates out of the hall; they always take somebody off the list of permanent mates and captains. One of the third mates will go second. When we stop in Oakland, we'll pick up a relief 3rd mate for the foreign trip."

The mate was thrilled, and accepted immediately. He had gotten to the age and point in life where he had to get on the permanent chief mate list, sail with only one company, and be in line to become captain, or get the hell out. Shipping relief out of the hall was getting tougher all the time. He would earn almost double the money, considering the rate of pay, and the incredible amount of overtime a chief mate could work. He would stay on board the ship for the whole voyage, and bust his ass. He would make a name for himself. When you were on the list, the company called you with an assignment; all you did in the union hall was clear it, letting them check that you had paid your dues, and you were on the protected list. He would earn a larger pension, and might even make captain before retirement. The captain even gave him a pair of chief mate shoulder boards, with three gold stripes on each of them.

That first day as chief mate, in port, was busy as hell. He had a talk with the bosun about deck maintenance for the voyage. He took over in the mate's office, going through all the cargo papers. The word got around there was a new mate. He checked the lashings on all the cargo, and had both 3rd mates turn to in order to check them again before sailing. They left late at night; he had gotten almost no sleep, and would still stand his 4 to 8 watch for another day, until they made Oakland. Then, he would move into the chief mate's room. It was bad enough to take over for another guy, but he hadn't even had a chance to discuss the ship's business with the ill mate. No matter -- he could do it. They docked in Oakland late at night. He stayed up until 0300 talking with the company rep about cargo, and going over stability and fuel oil burnout calculations. He went to bed exhausted, but felt great. He planned to sleep until 0700, then get breakfast and go back at it. Four hours sleep was enough. The union would send down a relief 3rd mate that afternoon, and he could stop standing watches and concentrate on chief mate's work. It wasn't, however, going to be that simple.

He heard a pounding on his door at 0530. He opened it, bleary-eyed. The chief cook was standing there, in his white apron and hat.

"You the man, now? You the chief mate now, right?"

"Yeah, yeah. What's the matter?"

"That damn guy from the engine room down in my galley, right now; he's threatening everybody! There's going to be trouble, I tell you."

"Okay, I'll be right there. Does he have a weapon?"

"No, no weapon, but you get him outta there, or somebody gonna get hurt, for sure."

"Calm down, I'm coming." *Christ.* He had known immediately something was wrong. A cook wouldn't come to a mate unless there was a discipline problem, or a medical problem. In addition to everything else, the chief mate was the ship's policeman and doctor.

He threw on some khakis, decided against bringing a club or handcuffs, and went down, half-asleep, to the galley. One of the crewmen from the engine department was drunk and running all around the galley and the crew's mess, shouting nonsense. The mate confronted him, eyed him good for a weapon, and watched his hands.

"You listen good! I'm the goddam chief mate now, and I am giving you a direct order to go below to your room! I'm not going to put up with this shit -- I'll run you off the ship!"

He braced for an attack, but none came. The offending oiler went to his room. The mate followed him to see what room he was in and that he did not come right back out again. He would now probably sleep it off. He went back in the galley, calmed the cook down, and took a cup of his coffee. There was no sense trying to sleep for one hour. He was too mad and fired up anyway. He went back to the mate's office, and struggled with more paperwork.

The bosun came by just before breakfast to get the day's assignments for the deck gang. He had already heard about the galley incident, and seemed to be looking at the new chief mate a little differently. *Good,* the mate thought. *Let the word get around to the crew that they can't fuck with me.* At 0720, he went down to the officers' saloon to eat. He now sat with the captain, chief engineer, and the first assistant engineer. It was these four men that managed the ship, and he was now one of them, not just some guy out of the union hall.

Over the meal, he mentioned the galley incident to the captain and the chief engineer. The captain wanted to know if the guy was going to be a problem. The chief engineer said that he was a permanent crewmember, but had pulled stunts like that before.

"Well, what the fuck do you put up with it for?" asked the mate.

"Well, he's got problems at home, you know the routine."

"I don't care. Do you want to make the trip with him, or get rid of him?"

"Hell, I'd love to get rid of him. He's not much of a worker," the engineer answered.

"Okay, what's his work schedule today?"

"We're taking on bunkers this morning. He's supposed to turn to at 0800 and rig the hose on the outboard side, for the fuel oil barge."

"Good. I'll meet you there at 0801." Now the new chief mate was getting looks from the chief engineer and the captain.

The mate left the table, took a cup of coffee with him, his fourth so far that young day, and went down to the main deck. He stood by the valve where the ship would take the hose from the fuel barge and bolt it onto their valve, eventually sending the bunkers down a pipe, through the engine room, sped on its way by their pumps, and into the fuel tanks. The bosun and dayman were already out on deck, blocking up the scuppers, or drains, on the main deck. He saw the mate on watch and had him go up to the bridge to hoist the red Bravo flag, post the "No Smoking" signs around the ship, and make the usual logbook entry about safety precautions. The fuel barge was now coming alongside; the deckhands took their lines and began to make them fast. The second engineer, in charge of fueling, was there to supervise. The chief engineer was there too, but there was no oiler.

"What time you got, chief?"

"It's five after eight, mate."

"Well, let's go. I want you there too."

The mate led the way into the house, down a deck, and through the passageway to the oiler's room. He pounded on the door, but got no answer. He used his passkey to open the door.

The guy was still lying on his bunk. He had made no effort to get up for work, just as the mate figured. There were empty vodka bottles in his trashcan. The mate shook him by the shoulder.

"You're drunk, and late for work. You also threatened people in the galley this morning. You're fired! Be up in the captain's office at 1000, dressed and ready to go." Then he took two of the bottles out of the trashcan for evidence, turned on the lights, and left.

The mate went up to his office, and stowed the bottles. He went up to the captain's office. He was there with a company rep. The captain told the guy to call the crew's union right away and order a replacement. He set the logging for 1000, as the mate had wanted. The chief engineer should be there too, he said, and he told the mate to wear his stripes.

The mate did not really expect the oiler to show up for the logging, but he did. He was showered and dressed, and his bags were packed. The captain conducted the brief ceremony, reading him the entry from the ship's log that the mate had made. He gave the oiler a copy of it. The guy admitted he had done wrong, and would not fight the logging or the firing. He even signed the logbook. The captain then paid him the money he was due, and had him sign off articles. In five minutes, he was down the gangway, and slowly walking across the pier with his bags.

The mate stalked the deck with renewed confidence. The cargo work was going okay, he had solved his first discipline problem, and the captain and he had just about settled on stability figures, what tanks they needed to burn fuel out of, the securing of cargo, and their great circle track to Guam, their next stop on the way to Japan. They would sail the next morning, and he would have plenty of time at sea to really settle into the job. Then his union representative came up the gangway.

The mates' union, like the other seamen's unions, had guys called patrolmen who visited ships, supposedly to settle any union beefs, collect dues, or just show the union flag. This guy went right up to the captain's office. Twenty minutes later, the captain came on deck to find the mate.

"The union rep says I can't promote you and the 3rd mate like this. He says we have to hire a chief mate out of the union hall today, and leave you guys in your assigned positions. I'm sorry; I can't seem to change his mind. He's sticking to a technicality." The mate was depressed and angry.

"Cap', the company isn't going to hire a chief mate out of the hall are they?"

"No, they never do that. They'll delay the ship if they have to, to pick a guy off the permanent chief mate list, and fly somebody out here. They have the right to do that, in an emergency."

"Where's the rep now?"

"He's down in your office. He wants to explain it to you. Keep calm, I don't think there's anything we can do."

The mate went down to the office, closed the door, and sat at his desk. He had never seen the union rep before. The patrolman launched into a long explanation of the rules, and how they could not get a promotion in the field when the ship was in a U.S. port, and could order a replacement from the local union hall. The mate eyeballed him good, but could not get a read on him.

"Look, you may be right, technically, but what the fuck do you think is going to happen? United States Lines is not going to call in a relief chief mate's job in your hall. You're doing this because you want to tell everybody in the hall that you got a job for somebody today, but the company is going to take a guy off their permanent list."

The rep hemmed and hawed, insisting they would call in the job.

"Look, what's better for the guys trying to ship out of San Francisco? No job at all on this ship or a 3rd mate relief job that everyone in the hall has the license to bid on?"

The rep was adamant. The mate changed his tactics.

"Look, let me ask you something else. You or your wife got a favorite charity?"

"Huh? Whaddya mean?"

"You know, you help the Red Cross, or the Boy Scouts or something? Listen, I give to charities all the time. I've got $300 in an envelope right in this desk. It's for your charitable work. Give it to whoever you want, you understand? If that's not enough, I can get more. I've been a union man for over fifteen years, and you don't get chances like this very often."

"I don't want your goddam 'charity,' I'm just enforcing the rules, like I'm supposed to."

"Well, bully for you, but you are not just screwing me and the 3rd mate out of a chance, but you are screwing somebody in your own damn union hall that really needs a job, 'cause you won't get one!" The rep left, and it was a good thing. With little sleep, the oiler problem, and this news, he didn't really give a damn.

Sure enough, the captain made a phone call to the company in New York, and they said they would have a chief mate on a plane that night. The mates' union hall had no job on the board that day. Some son-of-a-bitch who would have been happy to get a six-week assignment went home, or back to a cheap hotel, without work. Late that night, an old, grumpy guy came aboard as chief mate. The next morning, the captain had the mate sign off as chief mate and sign on again as 2nd mate. The mate was pissed about not finishing the trip as second in command, and the new guy was pissed because U.S. Lines had pulled him off vacation early. One felt betrayed by his union, the other by his company.

They crossed to Guam without anything exciting happening, just the way good sailors like it. The mate hit a few bars with a couple of guys in Apra, but didn't care for it much. There were too many navy guys getting drunk and looking for whores; either that or he was getting too old to enjoy such debauched scenes. There was a seamen's club near the dock that had souvenirs to buy, phones to call the states, and beer and sandwiches. It suited him more. When they left the harbor, at night, the third mate on the bridge forgot to turn on the ship's running lights. The ship was dark as it left the harbor and headed for Japan. A Russian trawler chased them for several miles, no doubt trying to figure out why the sneaky Americans were slipping away without lights. Those crazy Russian "fishermen" must have thought they had secret military cargo.

They docked in Yokohama at a new containership dock far from town. Conditions in Japan had changed so much over the years that some guys did not even leave the ship. Things had gotten very expensive. You could spend $40 or more in a cab, one way to the city. The bars, if you went to them, were no longer full of pretty, young girls who pretended to like Americans. He thought about the Japanese girl from the stereo store, years before, and wondered how her life had turned out. The mate only made it as far as the Seamen's Club near the docks, which had, as usual, telephones, a bar, souvenirs and stamps.

Korea and Hong Kong were much the same as in the past. The economy wasn't strong in Korea, and the people still chased sailors. In Hong Kong, the ship had hired a shore gang to do some painting and engine room cleaning. They worked all night, and never seemed to get tired. At one point on his watch, the mate had gone into the void area around the smokestack, which they were painting, and seen several of the workers shooting up. Some longshoremen told him that many of those guys worked for drugs. The mate got ashore to a world-class hotel on the Kowloon side, but no farther. It had fantastic service, including an attendant in the men's room, dressed in white dinner jacket and black tie.

Kaohsiung, in Taiwan, was the port where they topped off cargo for the return. The time ashore in Taiwan was better. The shopkeepers and bars still needed the American dollar. The furniture shops sent vans down to give free rides into the city, stopping first, of course, right at their shops. The mate bought a carved tea table, some ship's wheels to make coffee tables out of, and a brass clock. He especially enjoyed the negotiation. You did the best you could with the clerk who waited on you, and then the owner offered you tea or beer, and sat you down. That's when you worked out the final price for everything. When both parties had agreed on the total price, there were smiles and beer or tea all around. The shopkeeper would deliver all the goods right to the ship, and his men would carry them right up the gangway and store them in your room. You didn't have to lift a finger.

The champ of the souvenir buying was the older of the two third mates. This guy had been here before, and, in the union hall, would lay for a Far East run. When they left Taiwan, his entire room was chocker-blocked with tables, lamps, folding screens, brass clocks, and so on. As long as he declared them all on his customs declaration, he was okay. He spent thousands. Most of the guys on the ship thought he was nuts. You could hardly get into his room. There was only a small pathway to get to the bunk and the head. He had told the mate, however, that a brass clock he paid $35 for would easily bring $80 where he lived. *He's crazy like a fox*, the mate thought.

The ship only stayed in port about 24 hours, but with all the good shopping, almost everyone got off the ship for five to seven hours. It was also the last port, and that always sent guys uptown who might not otherwise have gone.

Kaohsiung also had its share of bars and girls. Some of the girls approached him on the sidewalk outside of the furniture shop. They wanted him to go next door for a drink, but if he wanted to skip that part, there was a convenient hotel nearby. He politely declined, even though a couple of the girls were very pretty. He liked Oriental girls, and felt old that he could refuse their charms. So, those who wanted to buy things did so, whether it was furniture or otherwise.

The captain called the mate up to the bridge before sailing. He was not happy. It seemed the company had loaded more containers than he thought they should take. He had the mate run the computer stability program. It took into account the weight of all the cargo on each deck of the ship. The program showed the same result no matter how many times they ran it. They would have enough stability to sail, but the burn out of the fuel would leave them with a negative stability figure before they reached Oakland. This was extremely dangerous, and no good captain would sail like that. One bad storm and you never knew. The captain had been arguing with the company reps about it, but they insisted he was wrong. They loaded all the cargo. The captain finally gave up, but saved all the computer printouts.

A couple of days out, a fierce storm came up astern, and threatened to overtake them. The ship would roll and yaw a lot more. This was enough for the Old Man, and he changed course more to the south. Storms across the North Pacific follow a similar pattern as the ones in the North Atlantic. They follow the wind and current patterns, and drift farther north. He wasn't taking any chances. Then they had a crack in a double bottom tank.

The double bottom tanks, in the very lowest part of the ship, carried the fuel. The fuel in that particular tank was almost gone, and they transferred the rest to another tank. The captain wanted more weight down low, for stability, so he had the chief engineer and his guys weld the crack. This was not proper procedure, but he didn't care. They did it as safely as possible. Then, he had the chief mate fill the repaired tank with seawater ballast. This was strictly against company instructions, and could get the Old Man in trouble. The mate respected the captain for doing it, and recalled his very first trip, when that captain had ballasted a cargo tank. Most captains would just sail on, hoping the storm would not hit, or that the ship could withstand it anyway. Most times, no one in the crew and only a few officers knew the real risk. You can't tell how stable a ship is by looking at it.

The mate thought the captain deserved some good karma, and he got it. The storm moved off to the north. The trailer truck bodies, which were stacked up five high, creaked and groaned at their wire lashings, with all the rolling. The chief mate was not happy that the company had decided to stack them that high. It was harder to lash them. The watch mates were not happy because the containers blocked their vision from inside the wheelhouse. You had to run around from wing to wing to see anything dead ahead.

They docked again in Oakland, at the same pier as before. The union patrolman came down, a different guy than before. The mates all had a talk with him about the loading, especially the new practice of stacking containers five high right in front of the bridge, with the reduced visibility, and the stability. The rep told them they were lucky to have jobs, and they shouldn't complain. He sounded more like a company go-fer than a union rep. He was on a yearly salary, and didn't have to haunt the hall for a job.

One of the diversions during the trip had been talk of baseball. Several officers on the ship followed the sport, including the mate. Everybody had a favorite team, mostly east coast ones. They had tuned in games on the short-wave radio in the officers lounge, and argued about baseball strategy and all the other baseball trivia. After they sat at the dock a few hours in Oakland, the word was that the ship would not sail until about 0400 the next morning. Night mates and night engineers would come down. The entire crew would be off duty for the evening. It was a rare night in port for a containership, and this one had just finished an ocean crossing. The mate went on the dock and found a newspaper stand. Checking the sports section, he saw that the Oakland A's had a home game that night.

He went back to the ship and informed all the baseball fans of their good fortune in being in a port where there was a home game. They could all get together, go see the A's game, drink a few beers, and feel right at home again, forgetting this life they had at sea for a while. The response he got from the sports nuts was a surprise. Not one of them wanted to go to the game. They all intended to head right for the bars near Jack London Square, right after supper.

He should have expected it. He had been going to sea long enough to know that reason seldom gets in the way of a seaman with a night off in any port. It was too damn bad. Only yesterday, the captain had put out a cash draw. Every son-of-a-bitch on the ship probably had at least $200 in his pocket. Money was not the problem, old habits were. His disappointment turned to hard-headedness, and he decided to go the game anyway.

The mate walked to a pay phone on the dock and called a cab. The guy showed up in ten minutes, to his surprise, and got right up on a freeway to the Coliseum. When they neared the ballpark, however, there were lines of traffic, stopped. The mate wanted to get out right there and walk. "Hang on," the cabbie said, "we'll be there in a minute." He pulled out into a special lane, cops removed the barriers, and he stopped right in front of the ticket window. *That's terrific service,* the mate thought. He gave the driver a good tip, and went in and bought a ticket.

He remembered the game years later for two things; he saw Ricky Henderson steal a base the year he set a record for it, and he bought his son a good A's uniform shirt. He always bought him things on his trips, but thought he would like that more than the Oriental stuff he already had.

When the game was over, he did not know how he would get back to the ship, or anywhere else. There was no need to worry. Right outside the stadium, there were several cabs lined up right outside the gates, and he got one immediately. They went out the special lane, and soon were up on the freeway. The mate told the cabbie to take him to Jack London Square.

Jack London Square was a relatively new area of shops, restaurants, and bars. He figured he would walk around, it being one of the safe areas of Oakland, and get a sandwich and a beer somewhere. On the short ride, he remembered the earliest baseball games he had been to, in the 1950's. His family had lived in Connecticut, and his Dad would take him down to New York on the train once in a while. He had been to Ebbitt's Field, the Polo Grounds, and the original Yankee Stadium. He had liked the Dodgers.

They got to the Square, and the mate got out and walked around. He went in some shops; the most interesting to him being one that sold magic tricks. Then he saw a large bar on a corner, and went in. It looked more like a nightclub inside. He saw almost all the officers and crew from the ship in there. It was not yet 2300, and they were smashed. The baseball fans were there, and seemed amazed that he had gone to the game by himself. He sat with them and listened to their drunken chatter.

The place was a hangout for navy wives, they said. While their husbands were at sea, they would come to this place in groups or pairs. Easy picking, they said. "The ship is sailing in a few hours," the mate told them, "and if you think you're going to score with one of them in that short a time, go for it." In his sober state, he could see that, as usual, the seamen were spending lots of money, and that the women, whoever they were, were happy to let them treat. They would at least dance with you, however, and the mate danced with a couple of them, just to see what it was like to be next to a woman again. He didn't buy their drinks, however, or try to pick one up. Time, if there was no other reason, was running out.

The bar closed at 0200, and they all had to be on board, for sailing, at 0300, one hour before departure. It took several cabs to get all the ship's company loaded up, and it took more than one guy to force a couple of the real drunks in the damn cabs. Still, in true sailor fashion, everyone made it back, changed, and stumbled around to their undocking stations. The mate got his coffee and went up to the bow, his station. He would supervise the undocking there and then get up to the bridge for his normal 0400-0800 watch. He was tired, but not shit-faced, and glad of it. Nights like that could be long, and you never knew when things would happen outside of the harbor that would command your attention.

The ship let go the lines, the tugboats pulled her away from the dock, and soon they were outbound in the channel; from there to go under the Bay Bridge, the Golden Gate, and south for Long Beach, then Panama and the U. S. The captain called the mate on the radio and told him to knock off on the bow, and get up to wheelhouse as soon as possible. Yeah, it was his watch, but he didn't usually tell him to hurry. When he got up to the bridge, he saw the reason. The 3rd mate, the one who talked baseball the most all trip, was unconscious right on the deck, next to the engine order telegraph. The mate had to call down below for a couple of deckhands to come up and haul the guy away to his room. The captain was pissed off, and threatened to log him and fire him. *Fuck Mr. Baseball Fan*, the mate thought.

While in the Santa Barbara Channel, approaching Long Beach, the mate had a close call on the afternoon watch. The seas were kicking up a bit, with good-sized whitecaps. He had both radars on, and there weren't any problems with the traffic. He moved around the wheelhouse, pacing and watching, not standing in one place. It was his habit, and now that there were more obstructions with the cargo stacked right in front of the bridge, it was more important.

He noticed a white cap just off the port bow; it was noticeable because it did not dissipate, as whitecaps do. He picked up the binoculars and looked. As had happened so many times before, when something doesn't look right, it isn't right. It wasn't a whitecap at all. It was a fishing boat. Her hull had fresh blue paint, and the little superstructure was white. It blended in perfectly with the sea and the whitecaps. It had a wooden hull, and was not making a decent target on the radar. He was crossing, and not engaged in fishing. This, by law, made him a power-driven vessel, just like the mate's ship. He was less than a mile, and on a steady bearing, which meant a collision course. According to the rules, the ship had the right of way, and the little boat was supposed to change course to starboard, pass him port-to-port, and go under his stern; the mate had the right to hold course and speed. As had happened countless times, the guy in the wooden boat was doing nothing. The visibility was good, he could surely see him; that meant that he was one of those guys who think that fishing boats always have the right of way, and he was keeping his course.

The mate swung the large ship to the right, watching the little guy all the time. When he was back on his original course, he read the name of the boat off its bow, and went to the VHF radio. He contacted the boat on channel 16, and then switched to channel 6 for a conversation. They exchanged friendly greetings. Then the mate asked him if he had gotten a recent paint job. The fisherman said he had; he seemed proud of it. Then the mate told him how the blue hull with a white top made his boat blend in to the sea. The fisherman became quiet. The mate told him that anything, even orange would be a better color, even though it might not look so good. Then he asked him if he had his lines out. No, he didn't, he was on his way to the fishing grounds. "Well," the mate explained, "that means I had the right of way. You only get the fishing boat rule when you are actually engaged in fishing." There was silence. The mate went on to explain how close he was before he even saw him, and how it took a half a mile to turn the ship. When he was done, the fisherman sounded sick. He began to realize how he had screwed up with the paint job, and the rules, and how the mate could have killed him with the 650-foot ship. The mate signed off, telling the guy that he was just trying to help him out. Maybe his advice would help the guy.

They didn't stay long in Long Beach. The mate only got ashore for a couple of hours. He did notice that the city was attempting to rebuild their downtown area. There were actually some decent restaurants, shops, and hotels near where there used to be tattoo parlors and seedy bars. The captain had so far survived the ass chewing about the ballasting, but had lost the battle over carrying cargo so high. In New York, he would have to answer to the company for the salt-water ballast, but he had his printouts of the stability numbers as evidence.

They left the harbor in the daytime and headed south in the marked, deep-water channel that led the big ships in and out of the port. The mate had the watch leaving. Not far out, he started watching two pleasure sailboats crossing the channel from his port to his starboard. They appeared on course for Catalina Island. They were on a collision course with him, but, of course, he had the right of way in the channel. He kept watching to see how close they would get before they swung around, or hove to, and let him pass ahead. They didn't do either. The mate had to swing the large ship to port, and he was not happy about it. He got the names of the two boats, one following the other, off their sterns, and called them on the VHF. They both answered, and he switched channels to have a talk with them.

The fisherman was different; he made a living on the sea, and the mate knew what hard work that was. He respected that guy; these two were weekend sailors, guys who bought a boat, didn't know squat about the sea, and thought everyone should stay out of their way. After some small talk about Catalina, the mate's tone changed.

"You guys got a copy of the Rules of the Road on board?"

"The what? No, I don't think so. What do I need that for?" one responded.

"Well, you just broke several rules. First, while I am in this channel, I have the right of way."

"Hey, wait a second. This is a sailboat."

"No, it isn't. Do you have your sails up?"

"Well, not right now. We use the engine to get clear of the land, and then we'll put the sails up."

"Right. So, right now you're using an engine, which makes you a power-driven vessel, just like me. Even if we ignore the channel rule, when two power-driven vessels are in a crossing situation, the one who has the other to starboard must give way. If we were on the open sea, you would be required to change course to starboard, and go astern of me. That is the rule, and I had every right to expect you to follow it. It takes a mile to stop this ship, and over a half mile to turn it. Do you read me?" He normally wasn't so tough on the radio, but these guys pissed him off. They would be the first ones to get a lawyer and try to sue the shipping company, if they survived a collision.

"Yeah, yeah, okay. We're sorry. We didn't know about the engine thing, or the channel."

"I'm just telling you for your own good, and the good of the other ocean-going ships that have to steam through bunches of weekend sailors. The last mistake is common sense. No matter what the goddam rules are, don't ever cut right across the bow of a ship like that. If your engine quits right then, or you have sails up and the wind shifts or dies, even if the mate on the ship sees you, he may not be able to do anything except run your ass over. Over."

He made it all the way around to New York without running over any small boats, in spite of several attempts by those guys to force him to do so. He ended the trip on good terms with everyone, except Grumpy Chief Mate, who didn't like anybody, and thought he was the hero of U.S. Lines for finishing the trip as chief mate. The captain said he would probably survive the ballast tank incident. The mate went home, to his little furnished apartment in Baltimore.

The mate, knowing that it would be months before his union shipping card would be old enough to even consider getting an assignment, tried his hand at some shore side jobs. Nothing seemed to work, especially those commission-only types of sales jobs. He figured he just couldn't lie well enough to be a good businessman. He was getting deeply into debt, and as soon as he thought he might get lucky, he went back to New York, to stay with his younger brother in New Jersey, and try to ship out again. His younger brother said he looked like hell. He had gained weight, was smoking and drinking too much, never had enough money, did not have a steady girlfriend, frequently went around in rumpled clothes, did not shave much, and didn't seem to give a damn about any of it.

At one point, the brother had come into Manhattan in the afternoon on business, and gone down near South Ferry, to the union hall, right after the afternoon job call. He thought he would offer the salty brother a ride back to New Jersey. He found the mate in an old, green, beat-up reclining chair, fast asleep in the midst of 30 other guys yakking and arguing. Brother shook him to wake him, and the mate jumped up out of the chair, ready to fight. He thought for a moment that he was on a ship.

Chapter 20: Don't Call Me Ishmael

He grabbed a 28-day assignment out of the hall in New York. It was one trip in the North Atlantic on an old, converted tanker that was now a containership. He normally wouldn't have taken such a short job, but he was desperate. The ship was in poor condition. It was slow, and the navigation equipment and steering gear looked like they would fall apart any time. The Coast Guard had hassled them over the condition of the lifeboats. Worst of all, the bridge was right up on the bow, and the mates lived there too. Forward houses, common on old tankers, were a bad business for cargo ships, which sat higher in the water than a tanker. Heavy seas would lift you up and smash you down into the waves. When a big wave hit the bow, it was only 40 feet away from you, and it sounded like someone was pounding against the bulkhead of your room with a sledgehammer. He hated living up forward. The motion was so different than what he was used to that he had constant headaches.

The first night out the weather wasn't bad, and he tried to relax and make the best of it. The captain was one of those guys who left a night order book on the chart table every night, when he went to bed. You had to read his orders and sign the book. It was a standard routine. The mate thought it was mostly bullshit, meant to cover the captain's ass, or protect the company in an accident, so they could try to blame the mate on watch. The trick was that after you signed off on these orders, the captain would tell you verbally to ignore them, or give you conflicting advice.

He signed the book and relieved the watch. He routinely checked the compasses, the AB at the wheel, and the ship's position. Then he got a cup of coffee and went out on the wing of the bridge. He leaned up against the dodger, and looked up the stars overhead. Years ago, he could have picked out at least 20 or 30 by name, but no more. Four hours to go.

He was bored and felt lonely, but a sailor never admits those things; shipmates would consider that a sign of weakness. When he was younger, he would have used a quiet watch to study charts. Now he could spend five minutes looking at a chart and know enough to take a ship anywhere. He had lost any ambition to learn anything more than the absolute minimum to get his four hours over safely.

Standing there, doing nothing, your mind wandered. People ashore who sat and watched television every night would never understand all these mental wanderings. Night after night, you have little to do but relive the past, and try to plan some type of future. You couldn't tell anybody that the majority of the time you spent on a ship was boring; they only wanted to hear about the adventurous parts. You could become a sea-going vegetable. He knew many guys who had lost their mental sharpness, and he wondered if it was happening to him, too.

You could stare at the horizon and imagine all kinds of things. Your mind would play tricks on you. Was that a light on the horizon, or a low star coming up? Was that rain or fog ahead? Should you turn on the radar? He wondered how the hell he had gotten into this crazy business. He was the only one in his family who had gone to sea. Maybe it was from books and movies.

He wondered how much the stories he had read as a kid had directed his decision to go to sea. One of the first stories he remembered was that of Huck Finn. Although Huck never went to sea, his trip on the raft had seemed like great adventure to the twelve-year old who read it. The deeper meanings of the book were lost on him, but it was clear that some type of waterborne craft could provide travel and excitement.

Pirate stories were more to his liking. It didn't matter who wrote them, and the lack of historical accuracy was not evident to him at the time. It seemed like high adventure to a kid, and a ship could enable one to live such a life. Well-meaning adults who said he should become an accountant or work for the post office just didn't get it. *Treasure Island* was the best of these. He wasn't alone in imagining himself as young Jim Hawkins, dealing with the scoundrel Long John Silver in a fight for treasure, and good versus evil.

Robinson Crusoe did not compare, as it didn't have much to do with the sea, except for when one ship left him on the island, and another rescued him. Still, it seemed that a sailor had good survival instincts, as exemplified by ragged ol' Robinson. Years later, it became more interesting when the mate learned that it was based on a true story.

Characters like Tugboat Annie and Captain Hornblower popped up here and there. Life on a tugboat did not appeal to the youngster; they didn't go far enough out to sea. Hornblower was better, but even as a kid the mate thought it impossible for one person to always have such storms and problems every trip. The history about seafarers like Magellan and Drake suited him more. *Captains Courageous* seemed more realistic, although the future mate liked Kipling's stories about India better.

In his high school and college years, he discovered other writers. Jack London was a favorite, and his books didn't seem to have all the hidden meanings that teachers kept saying others had. It was adventure, pure and simple. Man against man, man against the frozen north, and man against the sea. Other kids loved *Call of the Wild* and wished they had a dog like Buck. The future navigator liked *The Sea Wolf* better, and wondered how he would fare with the hardships of life on a whaler with a miserable captain.

Hemingway appealed to him. His works seemed straightforward; cut out the bullshit and tell it like it was. For a change, he liked stories like *The Sun Also Rises,* and *For*

Whom the Bell_Tolls, stories that happened on land, better than *The Old Man and the Sea.* He thought that Hemingway himself was appealing, being a hard-living, action-loving guy, but his sea experience was as a fisherman, and the mate did not see himself cutting bait and staying close to shore.

Hermann Wouk's *The Caine Mutiny,* although fiction, posed a serious question for the future merchant marine and naval reserve officer. Was an officer ever justified in seizing control of a vessel from the captain? Could it ever happen to you? What would be the circumstances, and what would you do if others did not join you, even though you were sure the ship was in danger? The captain always looked right on land, with his stripes. People had misconceptions that a captain was, by definition, a wise, experienced seaman who all must obey for the common good. Of course, people ashore had never sailed with Captain One Lung.

Long voyages gave the opportunity to read the hefty books that people always said they were going to read, but didn't. *The Rise and Fall of the Third Reich* went along to Japan. Even a shorter, two-month trip to the Med or North Europe was long enough for *War and Peace* if you read some every night. He had not stopped reading sea stories, but he mixed in new interests in history and politics. Still, before taking the second mate's exam, he had completed a project to read the navigator's bible, Bowditch's *The American Practical Navigator,* cover to cover. It was over 1,000 pages of technical stuff, but even though a struggle, he felt he should do it once in his career. Otherwise, he felt he would be like the self-proclaimed religious guy who had never read the Bible all the way through.

The old timers who told stories about how tough sailing was in the 1920's and 30's led him to go back further in time, and read *Two Years Before the Mast.* Dana's masterpiece was of interest not only for a description of how things were in the sailing ship days, but because his efforts started a discussion in Congress about the treatment of merchant sailors. The mate thought that people ashore who didn't understand why there were sailors' unions should start their homework with that book.

The story of the mutiny on the *Bounty* was always a favorite. The mate thought it was the greatest true sea story of all time, but the various movies made about it were misleading. The book *Captain Bligh and Mister Christian* eventually came out, and it seemed to provide some sense of accuracy to the often-told story. Bligh was a great sailor and navigator who, although he made some mistakes in judgment, was far from the ogre most people assumed he was.

Melville was another matter. The mate had studied *Moby Dick* in college, with a professor who taught an entire course about this one book. There was so much hidden meaning, or reading between the lines, you could get lost. It was one of those sea stories that had more than one level, the action level with Ahab and his whale being only the surface one. The story became more meaningful when the mate discovered that a true incident had inspired it. Killer whales had sunk a New England whaler in the Pacific. Surviving crewmen had resorted to cannibalism.

Billy Budd, although it also had its philosophical messages, was easier to handle, partly because it was much shorter, and partly because the mate had sailed with young kids who, in a different time, could have fallen into the dilemma that young Billy had.

The Cruel Sea, by Nicholas Monsarrat, was a more modern classic. Although it centered on a British Navy ship in World War II, and not a merchant ship, it was a great story. The mate's favorite part of that book was when the crew of a torpedoed merchant ship was found floating in the water in their lifejackets. They had tied themselves together with rope; the only problem was that by the time anyone found them, the lifejackets held only floating skeletons.

No matter what he read, the mate had a personal favorite since high school -- Conrad's *Lord Jim.* Even with the direction of a good English teacher, the seventeen-year old could not grasp all its meaning. What he did get, however, was the story of a mate on a steel-hulled, power-driven, merchant ship. The ship in the book was older than the ones he sailed on, but similar to some of them. He could not imagine a ship's officer, even on an old tub like the *Patna*, deserting the ship and its passengers. A rereading of the book after he became a mate provided more understanding. Jim could easily have escaped his fate, but the point was, he had to face it, to end his life with the honor he had lost. It made the older mate wonder whether, if he ever did anything on a ship to disgrace his honor, would he face it, or run from it?

The AB at the wheel had been relieved, and passed by the mate out on the wing, giving him the course. The mate walked back through the wheelhouse, checked the new guy, and the compass, and got more coffee. There was still nothing on the ocean except them. He continued out to the port wing, sipped his coffee, and drifted again. Two hours to go.

The impression most people had of seafaring didn't come from reading; it came from Hollywood movies. The earliest memories he had were of the old swashbuckler films, like those of Errol Flynn. He was dashing and romantic, in addition to being a great sailor and fighter. He became the stereotype of the buccaneer. The lack of historical accuracy meant nothing.

The television series "Victory At Sea," which he saw first in the 1950's, fascinated him. Who were these guys who would risk their lives on aircraft carriers, battleships, and cargo ships? In later years, he would watch the reruns on PBS repeatedly. There were only 26 half-hour episodes, but it seemed like there were more. He never grew tired of watching the same show repeatedly. Others saw the great sea battles, and wondered how they would handle a kamikaze attack on their carrier. The future mate focused on the Murmansk run, and stories of "Torpedo Alley" and wondered how in the hell guys could volunteer to sail unarmed ships in the face of such danger. He would learn that the U.S. Merchant Marine was second in casualty rate in the big war only to the Marine Corps.

The mate liked "China Seas," in which Clark Gable was the captain of a merchant ship fighting modern pirates in the Orient. It was hokey stuff, but there was a scene of the Chinese Boot Torture, where a metal boot is placed over the victim's foot, and screws tightened until he talked. Gable didn't talk. He was tough.

Guys like Gable and Burt Lancaster also made submarine movies, like "Run Silent, Run Deep." The kid who saw these could not imagine himself cooped up underwater like that. He wanted to stand with his feet planted firmly on a shifting deck, scanning the horizon, and watching the compass. You could feel claustrophobic just watching those guys rig for silent running. He had great respect for the guys who could do it, but when he saw sub movies, he identified with the sailors on the surface, whom the subs were hunting.

Humphrey Bogart didn't just sit around his bar in Casablanca, waiting for "her." He went to sea, too. The mate liked "Passage to Marseilles," most of which took place on a cargo ship trying to get back to France during the war. They fought the sea and Nazi planes. "Action in the North Atlantic" was better. Bogart played the chief mate of a freighter. There was even a cadet in the movie. The mate also thought Bogart acted more like a real mate than anyone else in the war movies did. Bogart played the nutty captain in "The Caine Mutiny," too.

Many classic books about the sea also became movies, some of them more than once. It seemed every twenty years someone decided to remake "Mutiny on the Bounty." If you didn't read up on things, the image of Charles Laughton as Bligh would forever be stuck in your mind. His portrayal made for a great movie, but in reality, Bligh was not so evil, and Christian less "Christian." The mate always thought that "The Sea Wolf" and "Two Years Before the Mast" were more accurate depictions of the life at sea. His favorite book, *Lord Jim*, became a film in the 1960's. He thought Peter O' Toole did a great job acting like a mate with a troubled mind, and the early scenes on board the rusty, old ship were great.

His feelings of claustrophobia reached new heights with the making of the German film "Das Boot." He first saw the film in its original form, in German, with subtitles. Although too young to have sailed torpedo alley, he had a merchant sailor's hatred of U-boats. He went, expecting to find a typical movie that glorified that side of the war, but it wasn't like that. It was fascinating, realistic, and did not glorify the war at all. The scene with the sub trapped on the bottom made the mate feel ill. At the end of the movie, it was easy to be glad that those Nazi killers got theirs. It was more difficult to accept some sense of kinship with other sailors from a different country, a different time, and the "wrong" side of the war. The mate felt that it was, perhaps, only fate or the hand of God that put one sailor in a German U-boat, and another on the deck of a merchant ship, looking for periscopes.

His favorite movie of the genre was not a well-known classic. It was a black and white movie made in 1956 called "Abandon Ship." A passenger ship begins to sink rapidly, and 27 surviving officers, crew, and passengers take to the sea. Only the captain's shore boat survives, and they all end up in it or holding on to it. The ship does not get an SOS off. A mate is in command; there are a few crewmen in it, but the rest of the people in it are passengers. The problems they face are two-fold. First, there was no emergency message sent, and there are no other ships around. They might have to row for it. Secondly, there are more people in the boat than it can safely hold, and more in the water, hanging on to the manropes along the side of it. The weather is bad, the boat is taking on water, and the officer realizes that, with all the people in it, the boat could sink, and they all could die. With an approaching storm, the mate makes a fateful decision that some of the people have to be cast adrift, to give the others a chance to survive. Anyone thrown out of the boat, or cut loose from the side, will surely drown. Who then, stays, and who goes? How would you decide? Was it legal to cast anyone adrift?

The movie had great appeal for any mate. Do you assume you would keep all the women and children? Would you cast adrift strong men who can row, and keep women who can't? Do you separate family members, or keep them together? Does an elderly passenger go because of his age? Do you eliminate crewmen who might have experience rigging a sail or catching fish? Maybe you just draw lots for it. What then, if a child draws a short straw? What do you do if some of the losers refuse to go? Is it a mutiny? In the movie, the officer makes such decisions and cuts several passengers and crew loose, to their certain death. One passenger refuses, and the officer kills him. The rest survive, and a passing ship rescues them. Authorities charge the mate in the lifeboat with murder. A court finds him guilty, but he receives a light sentence. A true, similar incident was the basis for the movie.

In four hours alone on the bridge of a quiet ship, it was easy to drift off to all these thoughts and many more. The next night would be the same. You constantly relived the past, and wondered about your future. Some would say it was fate and some that you manifested it yourself. Once you were at sea, all you could do was sail on.

Chapter 21: Ming Line

The next couple of years were not good for the mate, ashore or at sea. He built up a shipping card that was almost a year old, and went to New York. He hoped to snag the maximum allowed four-month assignment on the biggest, best-paying ship he could find. The first night in New York, he went to a health club with his brother, and they played racquetball. At one point during the game, he felt a terrible, sharp pain in the back of his ankle, and he went down, in severe pain. He thought at first that somehow, his brother had swung his racquet and hit him full force just above the heel. He hadn't. They got an ice pack and wrapped it. He couldn't put any weight on it. He hoped it was just a severe ankle sprain. Brother had a girlfriend who was a nurse, and she met them at a local bar. She confirmed his fears. He had torn his Achilles tendon in half.

He had surgery the next day in a local hospital. His leg was in a cast. Brother drove him home to Baltimore, and he was stuck, alone, in his little apartment. His union medical plan paid for the surgery, but when he applied for disability, he found out that the plan only paid $50 a week for a maximum of thirteen weeks. If he had been injured while employed on a ship, it would have been different. He had no one to sue for injuries, no one to help him get around, and the doctor told him it would be six months to a year before he could walk right again. He went deeply in debt.

Work in the industry remained hard to find, whether you were union or not. The American Merchant Marine had fewer and fewer ships. Foreign shipping lines carried more and more of the nation's commerce. There were five or six guys in the union for every job they had, a terrible ratio. When it was two or three to one, you could make out okay.

The mate, like others, worked what jobs he could in between. Without much experience working ashore, it was tough. You could get entry-level things, or commission jobs. Worse, you had to lie and say you wanted to make a career out of the damn job to be hired. Most employers could see through it, figured you wouldn't stay, and did not hire you. He rehabilitated his leg in four months and limped back to the New York union hall.

He made a voyage with Moore McCormack, on an older C-4 class freighter, one with real booms and hooks for cargo gear. The ship went to South Africa and Mozambique, then sailed west across the South Atlantic to Brazil. There, they went from port to port, northbound, loading coffee. It stopped in Jacksonville, and the mate had his Dad visit the ship. Dad loved seeing the rough work, and hearing the guys call him "mate." He did not tell Dad how terrible shipping was.

The trip was interesting for a couple of reasons. He had never been to South Africa, only to North Africa on Med runs -- Tunisia, Libya in the days before Ghadaffi, and a brief visit to Egypt. In the middle of their struggle over apartheid, South Africa was interesting, but a very dangerous place. The black guys in the crew had a terrible time. Some of them never left the ship. Even the white guys, if the locals could tell they were American, had trouble. The Afrikaners did not like the pressure the U.S. was putting on their country. It was none of your damn business, they would tell you, and there were threats and fights. The smaller ports, like Port Elizabeth, were the worst. Even in Durban and Capetown, when the mate went to the best places in town to eat or drink, he and his fellow officers got tables segregated from the locals. The service at these tables was terrible on purpose. They did not care if you walked out; that was what they wanted you to do.

Maputo, formerly Lorenzo-Marques, in Mozambique, on the east African coast, was worse. The Portuguese had left, and local communists had taken over, with help from Russia.

Even their pilot to enter and leave the port was Russian. The downtown looked like it had been bombed. The whole place seemed poor and destitute. There were almost no taxis or cars on the roads, and the sailors were told not to be on the streets after dark. Anti-American slogans were written all along the warehouse walls on the waterfront. The mate was glad when they got the hell out of there.

The other reason the trip was memorable was the presence of a young woman on the ship. She was only 22, and was making the trip to do oceanographic research. Some ships now had women crewmembers, but they stayed on the crew's deck, and did not mix with the officers. This woman lived in a spare room with the officers, and they treated her as if she was one of them. The mate found it curious how the presence of one woman changed everything. Guys did not swear much around her, and they shaved more often. She was a college graduate, single and smart, and she improved the conversations at parties at sea. She also had a firm, young body, and this fact was not lost on anybody. It became apparent that all of the younger officers, and at least one of the older ones, had tried to make out with her; she had rejected them all. The mate made no effort, as he was pushing 40, and considered their age difference too great. He observed her with interest, however.

On the long, 6,000-mile crossing from New York to Capetown, however, she started standing watches with him, as he was sailing 2nd mate, and she wanted to learn about navigation. He sometimes helped her get samples of the water and the ocean bottom. He had never been in the middle of the ocean, in a little chartroom on a ship, and had a pretty, young woman right next to him. The passage to Capetown took two weeks. Day and night, she was right there, and her little curves were there with her, with a hint of perfume. He pretended not to notice, but she must have seen the way he sometimes looked at her.

As they neared the Equator, she wo flying bridge, above the wheelhouse to get invited the mate to join her one day. When th smokestack, she took off her shirt to reveal figure was better than he had thought. After th ould stop by his room after watch, supposedly to get h p with her research problems. She would accept a glass of wine, or a drink, however, and talk about things other than research. She got friendlier. If she was looking for a shipboard romance, and had picked him out, for some strange reason, he would not be able to resist. Still, he felt that she would have to make the first direct move.

One night on watch, she asked the mate if he locked his door at night, and implied that maybe he didn't need to. He wondered about the strange question, but that night, about midnight, he got the answer. He awoke in the darkened room when he heard his door open and close. Then he heard the lock turn, and could make out her shape. She stood quietly, then took off her clothes and climbed into the bunk with him. He made no attempt to resist. She was terrific, and no beginner. Later, she told him that she liked older men, had no intention of spending two months at sea with a ship full of men without getting laid, and had liked him partly because he was one of the few guys who had not immediately gone after her.

It was the only time in his career when he had a girlfriend on a ship, and he loved it. They went ashore together for dinner in Capetown, and dancing in Durban. She had only brought work clothes and jeans with her, so the mate bought her a dress to wear ashore. They tried to keep the affair quiet on the ship, but soon everyone knew. There was nothing illegal about it, but some of the younger guys were jealous. *The hell with them,* the mate thought. *If they didn't act like such jerks around her, they would have made out.*

In Santos, Brazil, the girl had insisted on seeing the seedy side of the waterfront bars, rather than go out to the areas of the beach, as the mate had wanted to. Over his protests, he took her down to Monkey Wrench Corner and she saw it all. The mate had never taken a normal girl into places like that, but she loved it. The research girl was most interested in these girls, how they lived, how their poverty and lack of education had pushed them into such lives. The mate thought about how great it would be if American shipping companies would allow guys to bring wives or girlfriends on trips with them. Many foreign lines did. They wanted their officers to stay employed with them. Hell, if you had a woman with you, you acted better, and liked your job more. Guys would sail longer for less if they had such a privilege, but he knew that the Spartan, Puritanical attitudes in the U.S. maritime industry would never change.

The little romance ended when the trip had, in New York, and there was no pretense that it would continue. Out at sea, age didn't matter much, but now, he would go his way, and she hers. It was a wonderful memory for him, and he hoped it had been for her. The only negative was that in future voyages, the lonely nights at sea would seem even worse.

The trip had given the aging mate new confidence. Having a young woman go after you was a great ego boost. He went home and began to work out. He played tennis, got back to his normal weight, and hoped that shipping would get better. He took some temporary shoreside jobs and tried to pay his bills. He helped coach his son's baseball team, and acquired a couple of new buddies to hang out with. For a few months, he actually felt a renewed strength. He thought that he might find another opportunity to go chief mate and captain. He could finish his career at the top, and make some serious money. The uncertainty of his future was becoming too much to bear.

His newfound optimism lasted almost six months, but things again went downhill. He went up to New York again, and hung out with his brother. He could not get an assignment, and drove home on weekends with less money than before. From Monday to Friday, day after day, he came back to the apartment in New Jersey depressed. No work, no money. Night after night, he stayed up too late, drinking. The two of them would bitch about things to each other. He didn't exercise, didn't eat right, and didn't give a damn. He couldn't decide if he should make a major change in his life or not. Hanging on to the sea as a way of life was getting tougher again. He went back home and tried to work ashore for a while so his shipping card would build up. By the time he got a ship, he had been off the ocean almost a year and the second mate assignment he got was only for a single voyage to the Far East.

The ship belonged to United States Lines. It was a sister ship of the one he had been on the last time he went across the Pacific. The differences were that this captain was a jerk, the officers didn't socialize much, and the trip dragged on. Nothing exciting happened the whole voyage. The mate didn't even go ashore in some of the ports. They had rain and fog in the North Pacific and around Japan. There were narrow escapes with fishing fleets, the food wasn't very good, and the crew gave the officers problems. It wasn't that all these things were that unusual, but the mate was getting tired of the bullshit that could happen at sea. Compared to his last voyage, it was the pits.

As the trip dragged on, he thought more and more that he was wasting away. The ships didn't stay in port, and bills ate up whatever money he did earn. His son was growing up without him, and he didn't have a steady girlfriend. The situation on the ship itself didn't help. On the long trip back, the captain went on a drinking binge, and no one saw him for two weeks. He didn't even come down to the officers' saloon for meals; the steward sent food up. No one knew if he ate any of it, and no one cared. The chief mate, next in line of command, was a moose who only cared about his cargo figures, and was anti-social. No one played cards, or got together at night for bullshit sessions. The way shipping was going, the mate figured it would take him fifteen more years to get enough time at sea to retire. You earned retirement credits only while on a ship or on paid vacation. The mate felt beaten by all kinds of forces beyond his control. It was difficult to concentrate on the ship, which was the one thing he could control.

After what seemed like years, the ship cleared Panama on the return, and came up the Atlantic. They were offshore from the Carolina coast, on their way to New York. The mate thought about little else except what in the hell would he do this time, when his assignment ended. No one had seen the captain since a brief appearance in the Panama Canal. The ship wasn't rolling much as he came up for the 0400-0800 watch, but there was rain all around. The weather matched his mood. The radar was on, and, even though it was old, it still worked. It was like the ship itself, and the mate in charge -- old but still functional. The mate and the AB at the wheel were the only ones on the bridge, as usual, and except for his other two deckhands and the people on watch in the engine room, the only ones awake, as usual.

It began to rain more heavily, and the mate warmed up the secondary radar. He put the ship in hand steering, and the engines on standby, making a logbook entry about it. Even in his confused state of mind, these things were old habits. The visibility got steadily worse with increasing rain. You couldn't see anything. He checked with the lookout up on the bow. He was there, and awake, but he couldn't see anything either. He didn't see any targets on the big radar. The sea return images built up a bit in the center of the scope. The rain was getting heavy, in patches, and he turned up the rain suppressor button to minimize the bounces off it. A small boat in the middle of the rain would be very difficult to see, and he would, as always, walk back and forth between the radars to check both of them.

Soon, the mate thought he detected the image of a target on the port bow, in the middle of a rainsquall, about fourteen miles off. He turned on the plotter screen light, made an "X" on top of its position with a grease pencil, on the plastic overlay that fit over the screen. The pencil marks would glow with the plotter light turned on. He would mark two or three positions of the target, and then draw lines and figure out its course and closest point of approach. It was no big deal. If there was a ship out there, coming close to him, they would be in a crossing situation, and the mate would have the right-of-way.

Six minutes later, he made another mark, and drew a line. Six minutes was a tenth of an hour, and made your mental calculations easier. It had been his habit for twenty years. The line he drew from the target's last position ran right through the center of the scope. It was a collision course, but he did not worry. It had happened hundreds of times before. The other guy would be plotting him, and would change course, passing port-to-port. All he had to do was hold course and speed. He went out on the port wing with the binoculars, but could see nothing. It was raining all over the horizon, and more heavily than before. He was still eleven miles off. The mate made fresh coffee. His mind put the target to rest, and he again dwelled on his problems ashore. Could he possibly straighten out all the difficulties? Was it worth it to keep sailing, trying to pay for things he could no longer afford? Would shipping ever get good again in the old hall? What should he do about this or that? After two months at sea, these things increased in importance. When you got close to the end of a trip, you had to decide all kinds of things. He sipped some of the fresh coffee, lit a cigarette, and thought things over. Then he remembered the target. *How long has it been since I checked it?*

He saw that the visibility was even worse, maybe half a mile or less. He walked quickly over to the large radar and looked down at the scope. The other ship was still on collision course, coming right down the line he had drawn. It was only five miles away, and at the relative speed of the two ships closing on each other, he didn't have much time. *Damn it! Why hadn't the bastard changed? Couldn't he clearly see him on his scope, and realize what he must do by the rules?* The target was a big one, surely a ship as large as his. He reached for the VHF radio, on channel 16, and started calling, saying things over and over like, "This is American Containership calling the vessel bound southeast about four miles on my port bow. Come in."

He got no response. Maybe he didn't have his radio on, or maybe he didn't speak English. The Coast Guard station in Wilmington heard him and responded, saying that a large, Ming Line containership had recently left that port. The mate called again, asking the Ming Line ship on his port bow to come in immediately. Nothing. The mate cursed himself for waiting so long. You never wanted to depend on radio communications. *Why have you gotten yourself in this position, you dumb bastard,* he told himself. *You should have just changed before this, to starboard, and gotten across his bow.* He ran out to the wing again with the glasses. No good. He only got wet for his efforts. He was sweating and getting nervous. He was supposed to hold course and speed until the situation got to . . . what was it, "extremis," the legal term for an emergency, then he could change any damn way he wanted to, wasn't that the rule? No, no, wait, that rule only applied to "vessels in sight of one another," didn't it? They weren't in sight of each other with this rain. Some other rule flashed through his head about "a vessel which detects another vessel forward of the beam may take," what was it, "early and evasive action to avoid a close quarters situation." Some damn thing like that. *They meant radar, but they didn't say radar in the damn rules, but clearly you, if you couldn't see the guy, could change, if you did it early, you bastard, but you didn't, no, not you, not this time. You're not concentrating, you're losing a step, you stupid son-of-a-bitch, and now you're in for it, and you have only a couple of minutes to decide.*

He ran back to the radar, and now the guy was only two miles away, closing fast, still on the line. *Get a hold of yourself, dammit, you must act! All these years, you have avoided collisions with large ships and small boats, and now you let yourself get in this situation!* He had never let himself become confused or indecisive before, but now he was. The standing orders were to call the captain if in doubt, but that would do no good. Even if he wasn't drunk, he could not wake up in time to understand the situation. The mate took pride in never calling the captain for help anyway. The chief mate was next in the legal line of command, but that too, would be useless; it would only alert everyone that he, the mate on watch, and next in line of command, had gotten the ship into trouble. The old chief mate wouldn't know what to do anyhow. He hadn't stood a watch in years, and wasn't very quick to begin with.

Screw it, it's your problem, he told himself, *do something, and do it now!* He checked the radar one last time. The target disappeared into the circle of sea return on the scope, right in the center of it, and was now a mile away. *Think, goddam it!* The AB at the wheel was watching him nervously now.

"How's your heading now?" he asked the AB.

"023, mate, she's steady on 023."

In all these years, in all these situations, he would never have gotten this close, no matter what the other guy did, or didn't do. He would have been across the guy's bow long before this, and would have eased the ship back to its original course, calmly watching the target go astern of him. Now, he didn't know if there was time to go right. He would be crossing right in front of Ming Line, if he hadn't changed course. A lot of guys in Ming's position would turn left at the last minute, away from him; if so, and the mate went right, they would collide. *What the hell was the turning radius of the ship? A half-mile? More? Less?* Captains had trusted him to handle their ships. He had always been right and early with assessments of danger from traffic, shoals, you name it, and he had always done the right thing. *Dammit.*

How long have you been pacing around thinking all this? People didn't understand. He could ring full astern on the engine order telegraph, and it would still take several minutes for the engineer to get ready to change turbines and speed. If he did not change course, but the other ship did, they would miss each other, but be too close. Since Ming had never changed course an inch in all this time, it was clear he had an incompetent on the bridge, or he was sailing with no radar, hoping that any other ship would have theirs working, and avoid him. The mate had been through that drill. It was dangerous, very goddam dangerous. *Is that his game?*

He was shaking, and he lit a fresh cigarette. Ming Line was probably oblivious to him, for one reason or the other. *So,* you *only have two choices -- with no engines to back down, you can go right or left, that's it. You could have done something minutes ago, but no, you dumb bastard, you didn't, and now you are seconds away from colliding two huge ships at full speed. How many people are you going to kill? Will the ships sink? If you survive, do you want to spend the rest of your life like some character in the books, Lord Jim maybe, disgraced?*

"Standby, quartermaster!" He never called that guy "quartermaster."

"Okay, mate, standing by."

The mate went out on the port wing of the bridge, in the drenching rain, wondering if this was how it would all end -- alone. Not a soul in the world would ever know all that had taken place, all that was in his mind. He still could not see the lights of the other ship, although Ming Line had to be right in front of him. The question was, had he changed course?

"Hard left rudder!" he hollered into the wheelhouse.

"Hard left, mate!"

His cigarette was soaked and dangling from his lips. He looked up at the rudder angle indicator. The red lights showed the rudder coming left, as ordered; first 5 degrees, then 10, 20, and fetching up at about 35 degrees, the maximum angle of the ship's rudder. *Come on you bastard, move!* The ship hesitated, and then started to swing to the left. A few more seconds, and the bow was swinging sharply. She heeled over as the turn got faster. Now was the moment of truth. He had made his move. It was too late to go midships then right. If Ming Line had changed course to his right in the last couple of minutes, all was lost. There would be a horrible collision.

He lifted the binoculars again, and stared into the rain. If he saw a red, or port, sidelight, that would mean that the fucker had finally changed course to his right, and they would collide starboard to port. Even if Ming had held course, the mate might still hit him, maybe head on, because he had waited too long to decide what to do. Experts and admiralty lawyers would investigate the collision. Teachers and students in maritime schools the world over, including the one he had gone to, would study it as a prime example of what *not* to do.

If he saw a green light on Ming, that would be the starboard sidelight, and would indicate, as the mate had guessed, that Ming never had changed, and they might miss each other green to green, or starboard to starboard. The mate heard the phone ring inside the wheelhouse, but he did not go answer it. It would be the lookout, reporting a light. That poor bastard would be the first one killed if he hit Ming bow on. The mate lifted the glasses again, but saw neither red nor green, he saw white. It was the masthead light of the Ming line, high up from the water, and it was dead ahead. Until he saw the white range light farther aft and higher than the masthead light, he could not determine the heading of the other ship. The bell on the bow rang three times, loudly, then again, the same signal. The lookout was now using the older method of reporting lights; one ring for a light to starboard, two off to port, and three for dead ahead.

Suddenly, he saw the second white light, above and to the left of the first white light! Then he saw the green sidelight. The fucker had never changed, as he had guessed, and they would pass starboard-to-starboard!

"Ease to 20!" He hollered, and went into the wheelhouse, and out the other door, to the starboard wing.

"Ease to 20, mate."

He now saw that the Ming ship was not swinging; the lights were steady. It had been his last fear that while he was going left, the Ming would go right, but the two white lights stayed in the same relative position. They would make it, but close. He eased the rudder to ten degrees left, then amidships. The swing of his ship slowed down. They were so close he got worried that he might swing his stern into the bow of the other ship, and had to steady up to get on a parallel course.

"Check her," the mate hollered in.

"Check her," the AB answered, putting right rudder on to slow their swing to port.

"Steady now!" the mate hollered a few seconds later.

"Steady, aye," the helmsman answered, checking the heading.

Within seconds, the two ships slid by one another. No one blew his whistle, no one got on the radio. The mate figured later that Ming was about two ship lengths off when they were abeam; it could have been closer -- he was shaking so badly he wasn't sure. He could clearly see the white letters painted on the side of the other ship spelling out "Ming Line," even with the heavy rain. He had never passed another large ship that close at sea.

The mate was soaked, in rain and sweat, and looked like hell. His cigarette had disintegrated, leaving only the filter stuck to his lower lip. He threw it over the side, cursed himself again, and went into the wheelhouse. He composed himself enough to begin a gradual course change to the right, back to his original course. The AB said nothing. He called the lookout and told him that he had heard his signal, but had been busy. Neither the AB steering, nor the Ordinary Seaman on lookout said anything. It was a sign that they had faith in him, that they respected him. Otherwise, a guy in the merchant marine would ask you, "What the fuck happened," to let a ship get that close. They probably assumed that the other ship had done something stupid, and his course change had saved them.

He went into the chartroom and dried off a little. He got a position off the Loran, adjusted the course, and figured the ship's speed again. By the time the four-hour watch was over, the rain had let up, and he presented a calm exterior to the 3rd mate, when he came up to relieve the watch. The 3rd mate repeated the course and took the watch, and the mate went below, as he had done a thousand times before, to his little room. He had vowed to quit drinking this trip, but now he took the bottle of vodka he had stashed in his sea bag, and poured it straight. It was 0800, time for breakfast, but he didn't go. He sat alone, in a room of bare, steel bulkheads, drinking vodka and wondering what in the hell had happened to him over all the years.

When he had been younger, he used to laugh at the older guys who were a wreck. He remembered a story a bosun had told him about being on a ship in the middle of the ocean, in the middle of the day. The bosun had been working around the main deck when the captain had suddenly showed up. The Old Man had a suit and tie on, and was holding a suitcase. He ordered the bosun to lower the gangway. When the bosun had asked him what he was doing, the captain had replied, "I'm going to get the bus and go home." They had to sedate the poor bastard until the next port. Could he possibly end up like that? He sat on the edge of his bunk, and saw the soggy footprints he had left on the deck. *You're losing it, you dummy, and that's what's going on. You stupid bastard, you're losing it.*

Chapter 22: The Deep Six

By the time he went back for the afternoon watch after the Ming Line incident, they were passing Cape Hatteras. The compass course was good, they had frequent positions, the weather had improved, and there were no other ships around. The mate felt a little better. Most of the guys were celebrating the end of the trip, but he still felt a little depressed. The sailors on his watch said nothing. There were no rumors around the ship about the near collision. No one except him knew how close they had come. There wasn't much to do, but he felt tired.

He passed the course, got a cup of coffee, lit a cigarette, and leaned against a window on the forward bulkhead. How was it that he had survived all these years when others hadn't? He even had all his fingers and no tattoos. He knew that he was slipping, after the events of the previous night. He stayed there, lost in thought about the union pension plan, and how long it might take him to finish his accredited 20 years. When he was a bucko mate, he cared nothing about pensions and things like that.

An alarm going off in the wheelhouse suddenly shattered his silent reflections. He saw that it was the radio operator's automatic alarm. He was relieved it wasn't the gyrocompass failure alarm, the engineer's alarm, the steering gear alarm, or any of the other many alarms. All he had to do was make sure that Sparks heard it and went into the radio shack to get the call. He looked in the shack, and sure enough, within 30 seconds, Sparks was there. The mate went into the chartroom and estimated the ship's position. If the emergency was real, he would check how far away the ship was from their position, and whether the ship was anywhere near their intended track. If so, he would call the captain, and he would decide whether to divert or not, assuming the captain was sober enough to make any decision.

The message was typical. There was a ship in the North Atlantic, in bad weather, and heavy waves had washed one of their crewmen over the side. They couldn't find the poor son-of-a-bitch, and were asking any other ship in the vicinity to respond, and keep a sharp lookout. It was hundreds of miles away, and not along their track. There was no need to do anything. The mate knew it wouldn't matter anyway. If they hadn't rescued him right away, he would have died in about 25 minutes from hypothermia, lifejacket or no lifejacket. He shuddered a little inside, as he always did reading these messages. It wouldn't make the local news anywhere. Some bastard had probably gone on deck when he was told not to, and been surprised by a heavy wave that crashed over the deck. It seemed that drowning at sea was a fitting end for a sailor, but the mate thought all sailors dreaded the thought of it.

Sparks went down to post a copy of the notice outside the captain's door, and go back to his room until it was time for him to go on watch again. The mate got relieved to go down to supper, and was back in fifteen minutes. He went back to the coffee pot, then his perch in the window. He thought about the sailor who had drowned that day, far away from any land. He would never even know his name, but he felt a kinship with him. What had that poet said? "Any man's death diminishes me; therefore, ask not for whom the bell tolls, it tolls for thee," or something like that. Thinking about death did not help the state of depression he was in, but he could not stop thinking about it. Every time he was near Cape Hatteras, he thought about death. Part of the reason was all the wrecks that had happened near there, earning it the nickname Graveyard of the Atlantic. Part of the reason was personal. His mind wandered to deaths at sea.

People who have not sailed always seemed to think about death at sea in terms of ship sinkings, collisions, wrecks on reefs, and fires. They knew about the *Titanic,* or the *Lusitania* disaster. They had Hollywood versions in their heads of huge storms cracking ships in half, with the hero and his friends swimming safely to shore. There were, indeed, ships sunk every year, but the more realistic danger for seamen was an individual death, like the one that day.

One of the most common ways to die was poisoning or suffocation in a cargo tank. A sailor would go down into a tank that was empty, but not gas-free, meaning that there were still pockets of cargo giving off fumes that would kill you. In one classic case, a guy did that, and another sailor saw him unconscious in the deep tank. Playing hero, the second guy had immediately climbed down the steel ladder into the tank to rescue the first guy, and the fumes immediately knocked him out, too. The mate could not remember how many bodies piled up before someone got the proper gear, with an oxygen mask, to enter the tank. Out on a ship, you would read the latest safety magazines and warning notices about things to avoid. Don't do this or that, it would read, because so and so on the ship such and such had, and he's dead; this was the gist of the articles.

There were dozens of ways to die on a ship. Simple falls were probably number one. Almost everything on a ship is made of steel, and a fall from ten feet or more can crush your skull. In the heyday of the freighters, mates climbed over the hatch coamings and down into hatches all the time. If you lost your grip, you could fall 30 feet or more onto a solid steel hatch cover, or double bottom tank top. The engineers and crew were similarly exposed in the engine room, or doing routine work or repairs up on deck. He remembered working a ship in port on which a guy had come back from ashore, drunk, and taken a fall down a ladder inside the house, which was really like a staircase. The ship wasn't moving, of course, and there were handrails on both sides. However, the guy had fallen down about fifteen steps, and had hit his head just right to kill him. It didn't seem a fitting end for a sailor.

Guys who worked on the ships while they were at the dock were vulnerable too. Many longshoremen died from falls, or had heavy cargo crush them. Stevedores running the winches and working on deck were in constant peril from swinging loads and wires that broke under tension. The strangest case the mate knew of had happened long ago, in Baltimore. Just before his containership had docked, there had been a terrific windstorm. The new Dundalk Marine Terminal had giant cranes that moved along railroad-type tracks. The wind had gotten such a push on the cranes that some of them began to slide along the track. The crane at the end hit the barriers, and toppled over into the Chesapeake Bay. Witnesses told the mate they had seen the crane operator running madly down the outside ladder while this happened. He didn't make it.

Someone might murder you while you were ashore, and considering the places sailors frequently ended up in, the mate wondered why more weren't lost that way. He had also heard stories about guys who had gone ashore, drinking, and made it back to the ship, only to fall into the harbor and drown, right next to the gangway. There was also the possibility of murder right on your ship. Just get the son-of-a-bitch alone out on deck, at night, and push him over the side. By the time anyone noticed that the victim was missing, even if you turned the ship around and looked for him, it would be too late.

The mate also remembered the story of a particularly gruesome murder on a ship. An old tanker had been out in the Pacific, and one night, apparently after much drinking, some of the crew decided to murder another sailor. They lured him into the room where they had been drinking, and stabbed him to death. Then they got scared about taking the body out on deck to dump it over the side, fearing somebody would see them. They cut up the body and stuffed the pieces out the small porthole, into the ocean. They left blood everywhere; it was all over the room, themselves, and even dripped down the hull outside the porthole. They did not get away with it.

He checked the compass again, got a position off the Loran, and then began pacing thwartships, from wing to wing, as was his habit. All was quiet. It was getting dark, and his mind went right back to darker thoughts. All these guys lost over the years, why should he have survived? Bones of sailors past littered the ocean right underneath him, and they had been piling up for hundreds of years. Who were they all?

He remembered the first dead guy he had seen who wasn't in a funeral parlor. It was when he was eighteen years old, and was shipping out of New Orleans on his sea year from the school. The night before his first shipping assignment he had stayed uptown at the YMCA, which wasn't full of scumbags in those days. He had gone downtown at night. When he came out of a rowdy bar on Canal, headed for Bourbon Street, he had started walking down the street, and there, right on the goddam sidewalk, was a dead guy. It was over twenty years ago, and he could still see his face. He was lying on his back, and his arms and legs were crooked, and in strange positions. There was a big cop standing next to him, and he was talking into his radio. A pool of blood was seeping out slowly from underneath the dead guy. The sight shocked the young man, and the cop must have seen the look in his face.

"He's dead. Somebody stabbed him. It's all over, kid, he's gettin' stiff already. You'd better move along."

He had stumbled down the street, but kept looking over his shoulder, back at the guy. The guy on the sidewalk was in his late 20's, too young, the kid had thought, to end his life like that. Or, did he do something to deserve it? As a green kid, he had wanted to know more, but kept on going, keeping a better lookout behind him all the while.

Then he tried to remember the first time he had seen a dead guy on board a ship. An electrician had not turned to for work one morning at sea. The chief engineer had come to the mate and asked for help, since he could not open the guy's locked door. The sailors knew that the guy was a drinker, and they suspected that was merely unconscious in his room. The mate unlocked the door, and went in. The electrician was lying on his bunk, and the mate went over and shook him by the shoulder. His skin was cold, there was no pulse or breathing; he was long gone. He had clearly been dead many hours, and no one tried CPR.

The captain made the official logbook entry -- things about the latitude and longitude of the ship when they found him, estimated cause of death, next of kin, and money due him. Every time you shipped out, you had to list somebody as next of kin. A message from the company came back, telling them to keep the body until they returned to the states. The Chief Steward came around that night, with all kinds of extra servings of melon, and things like that. He had to make room in his chillbox of stores, for the electrician. The mate hadn't been able to eat any of it.

He made another pass through the wheelhouse, checking things, and went out to the other wing. *Nights like this are easy,* he told himself; *too much time to think, really.* It took a strong mind to keep from going batty; if you did this long enough, it would get to you. At least the electrician he thought about had been 60 or so; unlike the young guy on the sidewalk, he had his run. His time was up, and that was that for him.

The next time he could think of had happened in Korea. He had been on a freighter that was at anchor in the harbor off Inchon. The crew had to take launches to get ashore, while the ship waited for a space at a dock. After a night of moderate drinking, he had gone back to the dock where the company-hired boat service was. He remembered that there were hundreds of small boats tied up to each other, and he had a hell of a time trying to find the right boat. Just like in the movies, there were whole families living on the boats. There wasn't much light, and no signs. He had felt funny about walking over the decks of the other boats, as there were people on them, some sitting there as you walked right across their deck. He had gone down below decks in the little launch, into a cabin in which there were about a dozen other guys, also needing launch service to get back to their ships. There was one other American ship at anchor, and several foreign ones.

There was good-natured joking going around the little cabin in several languages, and the air smelled like whiskey. Then they all heard shouts for help, in English. It had come from topside. The sailors all went up the little ladder to the foredeck of the launch to see what the hell was going on. Up there, they discovered an American guy shouting and waving his arms, all upset. They got it out of him that he and his drinking buddy had been climbing over the decks to the launch, when his friend had stepped off a darkened deck of one of the bumboats and fallen into the water. Right there, in the open space between the boats, he was beneath the water, drowning.

It was too dark to see anything. The young mate knew that there was a terrific tide in Inchon, and the rise and fall of it caused a lot of current. The mate and some other seamen ran from boat to boat, bent down, and stuck their arms in the water, trying to grab hold of an arm or leg. Somebody else was trying to get the hysterical one to calm down enough to tell exactly where the other guy had fallen in. Koreans from the boats nearby came over and stared. The surviving shipmate kept mumbling about how he couldn't swim. *And you went to sea?* the mate thought.

They found nothing, and never even saw anything in the darkened water. The current had taken him underneath, somewhere. The cops came and took statements. There was confusion in many languages. After much delay, the launch driver said they had to go, and the sailors went back into the cabin below. The ride to the various ships at anchor was quiet. The friend who did not, or could not, save his friend, went too. Someone tried to console him by saying that the current was swift, and that there was nothing he could have done; that, if he had jumped in, he might have drowned too. The next day, the news went around the mate's ship that the body of an American merchant mariner had washed up somewhere in the harbor, far from the launch dock.

He paced around the bridge some more, and thought of another death. He had been on a Farrell Lines ship going to North Europe with twelve passengers. One of them was an elderly woman, about 70, who traveled alone. She surely had been someone of importance, because at the dock in Rotterdam, Holland, the captain had taken her ashore for dinner. The mate had been on deck when they returned. The captain was helping the woman up the long gangway, and at first, the mate thought she was drunk. When they got up to the main deck, however, he could see that the woman wasn't well. The captain told him that she had fainted during dinner, and told him to fetch the chief mate, who was the doctor that trip.

The mate went up to the passenger's cabin with the chief mate. Right then, the woman went into cardiac arrest. The chief mate immediately began giving her CPR. The mate, having had this training by then, offered to help, but the chief mate said he could handle it, and sent him down to the dock to call for help. He took the gangway watchman, who was Dutch, with him to help with language problems on the phone. When the ambulance arrived, it parked right at the gangway, and the mate took the two medics up to her room. Soon, the two Dutch medics came out, and said she was gone. There was nothing more they could do.

Within an hour, the mate was helping carry the shrouded stretcher down the gangway and out to the ambulance on the dock. It was incredibly light. The captain was standing by the gangway, and looked shaken. He kept mumbling about how he didn't know she was having a heart attack.

Union hall sailors worked many different ships. When there was news of a disaster, guys would say, "I sailed that ship!" The *Marine Sulphur Queen* disappeared at sea without a trace. There were rumors that it blew up or capsized. The *S.S. Poet* was a union ship that never made port. The majority owner of the ship cried at the testimony. He had also been president of another ship, the *Silver Dove,* which had sunk, and he cried at that hearing, too. The *Poet* was 36 years old, far past a normal retirement age. The owner discounted reports of rust and worn rivets in the hull plating.

The mate had never liked ships that carried bulk cargoes. They generally were older, slower ships that sailed to only one port, and sat there, in Egypt, India, or some other rotten place, to unload it all, then sailed slowly back. It wasn't exciting. He learned over the years, however, that it was also risky. A full load of grain gives off gases which, if not vented properly, can explode. Other bulk cargoes cause fatal conditions when mixed with sea water.

He had been in the union hall more than once when there was a moment of silence "for our brothers, lost at sea," or in the Seaman's Church Institute in New York, when they had a special service for the same reason. There was no body brought back, and no sense of closure. Everyone knew about the *Edmund Fitzgerald,* from the famous song about it, but did not read of all the other disasters.

His mind drifted back more. He had joined a ship one time and, when undocking for the first time, went back aft, to his undocking station. As he supervised the crew handling the lines, he had noticed that he was standing over a red spot on the deck. One of the sailors told him that an AB had been killed right there, in that very spot, the trip before. The ship had a crane on the stern, to load ship's stores. The wire that lifted the boom up had snapped. The crane's boom had come straight down, hitting the poor bastard right on the head. The mate remembered looking up, and seeing the damn boom right above his head.

The mate always felt he had bad joss with tankers. The two he had sailed on as a cadet had their share of trouble. One was involved in a collision in New York harbor with a containership. There was an explosion, and guys died. The other was a more personal loss. The salty chief mate, the one who liked him as a cadet, had died at sea, but it wasn't from natural causes.

His ship had undocked and broke a mooring line on the bow. A piece of it hung up on the anchor, and they put to sea like that, with it trailing in the water. It wasn't a threat to anything, but the salty ol' sea dog of a mate could not stand his ship looking like that, something sailors derisively called an "Irish pennant." The ship went to Jacksonville, Florida, and they certainly could have removed it safely at the dock. But the chief mate could not wait for that, oh no, not him, by God. At sea, he put a rope ladder over the bow, and, not wanting to order anybody else to go over the side while underway, did it himself. He climbed down with a knife to cut off the mooring line. He fell, and went under the water. No one ever saw him again. The damn ship no doubt ran right over him. *It was another preventable death,* the mate thought, *but it was in character.*

Then he remembered the Puerto Rican Marine Ro-Ro ship, the *Bayamon.* The mate had caught a relief job on the "roll-on, roll-off" ship out of Baltimore. It went back and forth to San Juan, Puerto Rico. The cargo was all in trailer trucks, and the huge ship used three giant ramps that extended from huge openings in the side of the ship down to the dock. The drivers drove the damn trucks up the ramps, right into the side of the ship, parked them into place, and then drove down a different ramp to get another one. Cargo went off in a similar fashion. Longshoremen lashed the truck trailers to the deck, wheels and all, with wires and turnbuckles. There were no cargo booms on the ship. The main deck looked like a giant parking lot, and from a distance, the ship looked like an aircraft carrier. It was bigger than some of the WWII carriers.

He recalled the first undocking he did, on the stern. The winches and bitts to make the lines fast were one deck below the main deck. This deck was the same one where the huge ramps fit into the side of the ship. The third ramp was right near the stern undocking area. After the shore gang took the ramps down, to leave them on the dock, the mate and his gang singled up, leaving only one stern line, and the spring line, the one that led forward, to keep the ship from sliding aft. Soon, they got the order to let go aft, and they winched in the last two lines, as he had done many times before. During all this, the mate had noticed something unusual. Near the opening in the hull where ramp #3 went, there was a cross painted on the bulkhead. It didn't look like some accidental slopping of paint. It was neat, and clearly meant to be a religious cross.

After he had been on the ship a couple of days, he asked around about the cross. Just like the ones you might see by a highway, someone put there in memory of a dead person. The deceased, in this case, was a vice-president of the steamship company. The rumor in the company fleet, at the time, was that the company had four ships, and 13 vice-presidents. Many sailors are superstitious. What happened to the VP only added to their beliefs.

This particular VP had little experience with his own ships, they said. He had come aboard, at the dock in San Juan, with his tie and his hard hat, to get a look at what really happened aboard the ship while it worked cargo. What he did was stand next to the #3 ramp, and watch the drivers race up and down with the trucks. The traffic on the ramps was one-way, and, at the time, the #3 was for outbound trucks. There wasn't much room anywhere inside the ship for the drivers; when they made turns all over the ship, there was only a foot or two to play with. Trucks came down ramps inside the ship, got to the deck where the ramps were, and made their turns to shape up for the ramp.

A truck had come down from the main deck, and made the wide, left-hand turn to line up for the ramp. The driver had gone a foot too wide, and the body of the truck, weighing several tons, had slid up against the bulkhead where the VP was standing. The executive had not seen the danger in time; in fact, he never should have been standing where he was. The body of the truck had slammed him up against the steel bulkhead. The force was so great that it had lifted him up off his feet, and crushed him to death. The truck was stuck right there, and the driver could not move it.

Sometime after all this, a sailor had painted the white cross on the spot where the truck crushed him against the bulkhead. From time to time, when the area got dirty, some mysterious crewman washed the bulkhead and repainted the cross. It seemed that every ship had some unknown seaman who was very religious, and kept quiet about it. In the four months the mate spent on that ship, he never, ever, stood near the cross.

The four-hour watch was almost over. The mate checked everything, and put down a dead reckoning position on the chart, for the change of watches. He went into the wheelhouse and put on a fresh pot of coffee for his relief. It had been one of those quiet nights at sea, when your mind wanders, and he wondered why, on this watch, his thoughts had turned to death. Why so macabre? *You know why, you dumb bastard,* he thought. *It's the Hatteras thing again, and you don't want to think about it.* He wondered if he would end up in the ocean, somewhere, somehow. Then he thought of those who ended up on the bottom by choice.

Many a sailor was lost at sea; the reality was the bastard had gone nuts and jumped over. Could that happen, if he continued too long? He had felt depressed recently. The trips were lonelier than ever. You could work yourself into a real mental state on the ocean. His upbringing and philosophy should prevent that. Yet, it was so easy; you stood by the railing, at sea, at night; it would take one second to just slip over the rail, and you would be gone. He wondered how many had done it.

There was another way to end up on the bottom, of course, which was more fitting. You had your ashes scattered over the sea. That seemed more fitting to him, and he did not think the lack of a normal, Christian burial was any offense to God; not for a sailor. Was that a fitting end for him also? He had participated in a couple of such events, and thought the service, although people read the right words, was best left to the navy. On a merchant ship, the captain might be dressed up with some stripes, but the other witnesses would have work gear on. The chief mate would tell the bosun to drop his work and get a couple guys to go back aft. They would stand there, heads bowed, in paint-splattered blue jeans or overalls. The navy could muster up a bunch of guys in sharp uniforms, and play taps and all. The words would be the same, "commit the body to the deep," and so forth, but the lack of military protocol in the merchant marine lessened the effect. Moreover, sometimes the ashes blew all over the deck, if the wind shifted.

He thought about the union newspaper, which carried a column called, "Crossed the Final Bar." It listed the names of members who had died. Most of them were old, retired guys, but every once in a while the mate would see the name of a shipmate of his. Some of them were younger than he was, and not all of them died peacefully.

He was in the darkened wheelhouse, and heard the door to the chartroom, right aft of him, open and shut. His relief was in there, taking a quick look at the chart, and adjusting his eyes to the dark before coming out to take the watch. In a couple of minutes, he would be back in his steel-enclosed room, feeling like he had wasted another day of his life. He used to think, when he went to sea that he had already died and gone to heaven, he liked it so much. It didn't matter how old the ship was, or how rusty, or where it went, or what dangers existed in his path. Now he would go below and have one, maybe two drinks, sit on the edge of his bunk, think about the Hatteras thing, and wonder how in the hell he had gotten this way. It had taken years, he supposed. Still, there were those sailors who had not lived so many years, and had not been to all the places he had been to. The third mate came out, repeated the course and the traffic situation, and took the watch.

He left the bridge, as he had so many times before, and walked quietly down the ladder to his room. His mental wanderings for that night would keep him awake for a while. He could not shake his maudlin state of mind. In years past, he would have found a party going on, and joined it. On the containerships, this rarely happened. He wouldn't have gone to one now in any case. He could not just go to bed, not this night. There was one more remembrance of guys who got the deep six to rehash. He took out the bottle of vodka from his sea bag, and a jar of Tang, and mixed a crude screwdriver. He had no ice in the room. He used plain tap water. It didn't matter. He took a sip of the tepid, strong drink, and went back to the locker. He found what he was looking for. It was an old, beat-up copy of the National Transportation Board's report on the *S. S. Texaco Oklahoma.*

He sat at the metal desk in his room and threw the report in front of him. His thoughts drifted back to when he had started sailing as a mate. In that year, shipping had been good. He had started, like anyone else, as a Group C member in the hall. When a job was up for bid, the dispatcher called for Group A members, then Group B, then Group C. As soon as you made a month at sea on a union ship, you went from Group C to B. Then you had to get twelve more months of union sea time to become Group A. He had shipped right away, got his first trip in, and it didn't seem like it would be much of a problem to get the twelve months in after that. He thought it would take a year and a half, two at the most. In the winter of 1969-70, however, jobs tightened up for some reason. He was stuck in the New Orleans union hall, day after day, week after week, with no work.

It was during this time that he met a mate named John. He was the same age as he was, also still a Group B member of the union, and had graduated from one of the other maritime academies. They became friends, and bummed around together. Neither one of them could grab a ship, so eventually John came up with a new plan. He pitched it to the mate over beer in the Quarter.

His plan was simple. As union mates, their union prohibited them from shipping out on any non-union ships. If the union caught them doing that, they could lose their union membership. John kept saying that they had paid $1,000 each to join the union, plus the quarterly dues, and the union had an obligation to find them work. Both John and the mate needed about four months at sea to become Group A. It didn't seem like that would be possible for a while.

They would both ship non-union, with a tanker company, John continued. They would keep mailing in their dues, and when on vacation from the tanker outfit, they would visit the union hall, see how things were, go to an occasional union meeting, and ship out if an assignment came down to them. Eventually shipping would get better. This way, he said, they could make money in the meantime. They would keep their tanker jobs until union shipping was better, that was all. There was a risk of the union finding out, but it seemed remote.

John's last part of the plan was more direct. He had already called the home office of Texaco, in Port Arthur, Texas. They were hiring 3rd mates, they had said. The personnel guy had also told John that if they had graduated from a maritime academy, and had some sailing experience, there should be no problem hiring them; they could plan to ship out soon. The mate sipped his drink and thought it over.

Money was getting tight. He lived rather cheaply, but still, things were getting worrisome.

He agreed to try it. *The union wasn't the goddam CIA, how would they know?* Maybe he would learn to like tankers. *The food was better, the runs were steady.* He knew that would not happen, but it would be good experience, and the union had some jobs, like the ones with Keystone Tankers, that he could then ship on. John said he would make the call, and arrange things.

The mate went back to the present. He mixed another vodka and Tang, cursed the lack of ice, and sat back down at the desk. He started to tilt the chair back, but the bad weather hook beneath it prevented this. He kneeled on the deck and unhooked it. He sat down, tilted back, and put his feet up on the desk. He thought back to the trip to Port Arthur.

He and John had shaved, put on interview clothes, and driven over to Port Arthur. They got there early, and drove around the place a bit, to get the feel of it. It was a lot different from New Orleans. It was not only much smaller, but it had the feel of a beat up, dusty, old town. The smell of oil was everywhere, and they saw the tanker docks. There were refineries nearby, but only one movie theater. The Texaco building was in the middle of all this. It was definitely a company town.

They filled out forms and interviewed, but it seemed a formality. The company needed mates fast. The pay was less than union scale, but it would do. The guy who had interviewed him extolled the virtues of the company. The young mate had said things about being tired of the union (they wouldn't want any union trouble-makers), wanting to get married and settle down (company guys liked that), and how interesting his time on tankers as a cadet had been (a lie). They offered him a billet as permanent 3rd mate on the *Texaco Oklahoma,* and John a similar position on the *Texaco Illinois.* They both agreed.

Back in New Orleans, the mate began packing his sea gear and sextant. He was to join the *Oklahoma* when she docked in Portland, Maine. Texaco had arranged a flight to Bangor the next morning, and a rental car there for him to drive to Portland. John had to go somewhere else to join his ship. After all the years, he could not remember where John had to go, but he remembered that he did go.

He remembered that the night after returning from Port Arthur had been a sleepless one. He had been worried about the union finding him out. He hated tankers. He wasn't keen on going to Maine in the middle of winter, and he didn't like flying much, either. Working a ship running from Texas to Maine, back and forth, back and forth, snow or ice, didn't sound like much fun to a young man. Before he went to bed, though, he stacked up his packed bags by the front door of his French Quarter apartment.

When he got up the next day, he got dressed, put the airline ticket in his pocket, and drank coffee. Everything bothered him about the *Texaco Oklahoma*. If the union caught and expelled just one guy in the whole goddam union for sailing non-union, it would be him. *Christ.* He was young, and did not know how much of a risk he was taking. He did know, however, that he had just enough time to make the 1000 job call at the union hall, and still make the plane to Bangor. He didn't have much hope, but it was worth one last try.

He got into the union hall about ten minutes before the first job call of the day, and there was commotion. Several offshore jobs were on the job board. He had seen this before -- all the Group A members would bid on them, even a guy who had just registered for work that day, before he would have a chance to call out his number. It had been a long time since he had heard the dispatcher say, "Group B, hear your numbers!" Still you never knew what could happen, that's why you always went to all the job calls, no matter what, if you really wanted to ship.

The first job called was a four-month, second mate relief assignment. It was a small Sea Land ship, called the *M. V. New Yorker*. The rate of pay was lower than the other posted jobs. He knew that it was a diesel ship, and ran from New Orleans to San Juan. He figured he had no chance. He figured wrong. When the rep called the job for Group A, there was silence. His pulse quickened. Could it be? *What the hell was wrong with that ship? The pay isn't that much lower.* Agonizing seconds went by while the dispatcher went through his routine. Then the mate heard: "Group A, last call." Now it would happen. Some wise guy was fucking around. The asshole would wait until the last second, and then call out his number, knowing he was getting the hopes up of the younger guys who were still Group B or C. *If that happens, I ought to wait outside for the cocksucker, and beat the hell out of him,* the mate thought. But, it didn't. "Group B, hear your numbers."

He couldn't believe it. It would solve many of his problems. The mate hollered out his number, and the dispatcher repeated it. The mate tensed as he waited for someone to call out a lower number. No one did. The dispatcher spoke again: "Going once, going twice . . . gone!" He had a legitimate job again, and on a union ship.

Job calls were always tense when there was work on the board, but he felt more excited than usual. Of course, no one there knew he had a non-union, permanent assignment in his pocket, next to an airline ticket. Now he could stay a union mate. He would go to a fair weather port. With the four months, he would get enough sea time to become Group A in the union. He would be home every ten days or so. He was oblivious to the other jobs, and did not even notice who got what, normally a source of great entertainment, and comment by all in the hall.

He was impatient, but he eventually got the assignment slip. The union routinely checked that you had paid your dues on time, and you had a valid license for the job. He also got the medical slip, and headed for the usual clinic. He wondered how many other professions required that you pass a physical every time you went to work. The clinic was the usual pain, but he got the "fit for duty" slip and headed back downtown, a happy man. Then he remembered Texaco.

Damn. It was after noon. The plane he was supposed to be on was long gone. The *Texaco Oklahoma* would dock in Maine later that day, and no 3rd mate would be waiting on the dock. Maybe they could get someone else up there from New York, or Boston, in time. He hated the idea of screwing the company, or leaving the mates on the ship short-handed, but what the hell, they were non-union anyway. They probably sat around at night and bitched about the union. *To hell with them.*

He also realized that he had to call the Texaco guy in Port Arthur who had hired him. He got back to his apartment, opened a beer, and looked up the number for the personnel guy in Port Arthur. He hated lying, but he made up some bullshit excuse about an illness in the family, and how he couldn't ship out right now; he said he was sorry, and that was at least partly true. The guy at Texaco surely knew he was lying, but he didn't accuse him of it, or argue. The young mate had felt badly, but not for long. *It's all part of the business of going to sea,* he thought. *You made choices, you took chances, and sometimes, you did what was right for you. Sometimes, you just got lucky.*

He picked up the report again off his desk. It was getting late. He should be getting some sleep, but he knew he couldn't until he had gone over the whole thing again. It happened whenever he was near Cape Hatteras. *It's a sign you're getting older, you jerk,* he told himself. He had to finish recalling the events.

He had served out his assignment and had a good time. It was a good ship, although small. He became Group A in the union. He never again thought about sailing non-union, but that wasn't the end of the Texaco story.

He looked at the title of the report again. "Marine Casualty Report," it began. "Structural Failure and Sinking of the *Texaco Oklahoma* Off Cape Hatteras on 27 March, 1971, With the Loss of 31 Lives," was the official title. The official date of the report was July 26, 1972. He had written away for a copy soon after publication, and had kept it since. *Why do you look at this, you dumb bastard?* He sipped his drink. He knew why. *You could have gone to the bottom with it, that's why,* he told himself.

The *Texaco Oklahoma* was one of several similar tankers built in the late 1950's. It was a standard, split-house ship, which meant that the deck officers, radio operator, and the bridge were forward, and the crew, engineers, and engine room were aft. It was 632 feet long, average for a coastwise tanker at the time, drew about 35 feet of water when loaded, and carried a little over 200,000 barrels of liquid cargo. On her last voyage, she had been almost full of black oil.

She had left Port Arthur on the 22nd of March, and was bound for Boston. It was routine for a tanker. The *Oklahoma* was one of a handful of ships Texaco owned that flew the American flag, being registered in the U.S., and had an all-American crew. It was another one of those Jones Act ships, like the Keystone tankers. They ran their ads on the goddam TV, telling people how much they cared about America, and then registered most of their ships in Liberia or Panama. The ones that they *had* to crew up in the states, like the *Oklahoma* and John's ship, the *Illinois*, were all non-union. *Christ.*

He was digressing from the main issue, and he knew it. Sailors were sailors, it didn't really matter who they were. He had drunk and joked around with union and non, guys from a dozen different countries, and they all had a common bond. When the *Texaco Oklahoma* left Texas on her last voyage, she had 44 guys on her. Only thirteen came back. The third mate who had replaced him wasn't one of them.

The ship had proceeded normally for three days, around the Florida Keys, into the Gulf Stream, and north off

Hatteras. The captain was a relief guy, taking the place of the permanent skipper for vacation. He had lots of experience, and had skippered seven other Texaco ships. The mate flipped through the report. By the 25th of March, the ship was off the coast of Florida, and was beginning to fight heavy seas and bad weather. Soon, they slowed the ship down, a routine in bad weather. You can't try to go full ahead into heavy seas. The *Oklahoma* had not made that mistake.

By the next day, they had slowed down some more and altered course. They got to 50 rpm's, about half their normal speed. They were then in a full gale, and waves of 30 to 40 feet were hitting the decks. They were very stable, but it also meant that waves hit the deck hard. The wind increased to 60 to 65 knots, almost hurricane force. The ship was only thirteen years old. The company had lengthened her to allow for a deeper draft, and more cargo, but was still within the official limits of her stability figures; within, but right up to the limits. In the middle of that night, at about 0330 on the 27th, there was a tremendous cracking sound. The ship broke in half, just aft of the forward house. The crew in the aft section woke each other up, and began rigging the starboard lifeboat on the stern. The stern section was not only afloat, the propeller was still turning.

The bow section, with no propulsion or steering, then drifted aft. The huge chunk of twisted metal rubbed up against the starboard side of the rest of the ship while it rose up and down with the heavy seas, and drifted farther aft, helplessly, but still afloat. The bow angled upwards, and the anchor smashed into the lifeboat on the stern that the survivors aft were rigging. The engineers ran down into the engine room and backed the propeller. They backed away from the bow section, which they feared could sink them, if it continued to smash against their hull. The last anyone on the stern saw of the bow section, it was taking on water, and sinking. Someone on the bridge was signaling with a flashlight. It was the SOS signal, but there was no help available. It could have been the 3rd mate, who would have been on watch, or it could have been someone else. The signal mattered little; the captain's cabin was already full of water, and neither he, any of the mates, or the radio operator, survived. The crewmembers that were on watch on the bow, or happened to be visiting on that half of the ship, went with them. The mate tried to imagine the horror of such a thing, or how the poor bastard with the flashlight felt, but he could not. He had always felt, over all the years that it should have been him. That was his ship. It was a permanent assignment. A steady job on a ship was highly prized by most sailors. He had passed it up at the last minute. The guy who took his place went down with the ship. He had been the same age as the mate, and had graduated from the same maritime school. The mate had known him, as everyone who attends a small college for four years knows everybody else, but they had lived in different dorms, and had not been friends. The mate held onto the idea that even if he had stayed with Texaco, he might have been on vacation when the ship broke up. As much as he hated tankers, he might have quit or been fired long before, too.

Searchers never found the bow, and assumed it sank soon after the stern reversed away from it. Not all the guys on the stern section would survive, but it seemed many more could have, if not for a series of errors, or fateful circumstances.

In the next day or so, three other vessels came into visual contact with the stern. The engineers and crew on the stern shot off flares, flashed lights, and rigged a red light. The red light, to them, was the signal they used when loading cargo. It meant danger. However, by itself, it was not a proper distress signal. In fact, when they hoisted it up high, it shone above the white deck lights that still burned. What the other vessels saw was a red light "over" a white one. This was the International Signal for a fishing boat; every deck hand knew the saying, "Red over white, fishing at night."

From a distance, the stern section would look about the same size as an ocean-going fishing boat. The ship that came the closest to them read the lights that way.

When they had flashed the lights at the three vessels, they apparently never gave a proper SOS in Morse code. The radio operator, captain, and all the mates would have known it easily; they would have been able to send more information than that, but they were all dead. The ship's powerful signal lamp was on the bow section, sinking to the bottom of the ocean.

The guys on the stern did have the ship's portable emergency radio transmitter. The device needed some rigging to properly put up its antenna. It was hand-cranked for power, and they took turns. They cranked and cranked for 24 hours. They thought they were sending out the automatic SOS signal. It had a range of 100 miles, but no other ship or shore station heard any distress call. It seemed that they had accidentally left the test antenna plugged in the whole time. The test antenna was there so that when Sparks tested the thing every week, he would not transmit a false emergency signal. All you had to do was remove it, but the guy who knew that best was gone.

One of the crew heard distress signals on his AM radio, in his room. They all concluded that the signal was theirs, and kept cranking. They belonged to another ship, however, far away. During this time, one ship, the *Bougainville,* passed within five miles of them, and saw their lights. They read the red over white signal as a fishing boat, but, to the captain's credit, he radioed in to the U.S. Coast Guard, and asked if any ships in the area were in distress. Not having heard anything, the Coast Guard told him no. They also tried to communicate with the *Oklahoma* with flashing light in Morse code, and by radio. They got no response, and went on their way.

Only the radio operator was required to know how to rig the emergency antenna, although most mates could do it. Morse code wasn't required of engineers or crew. As he sipped his drink and shuddered at all this, the mate thought the transmitter was the key. It had a range of 100 miles. If you operated it properly, it would send an SOS call automatically, and you could even use the key on it to send anything you wanted; anything you knew how to key in Morse, that is. It seemed such a shame. It was a miracle that the stern section did not sink quickly. Another miracle was that they had electricity for so long. However, in the heavy seas, the stern would not stay afloat forever. The survivors had to decide.

Like most split-house tankers, there had been two lifeboats on the bow, and two on the stern, one on each side of the ship on each half. The drifting bow wrecked the starboard boat on the stern. At about 2030 hours on the 27th, a Saturday, a heavy wave washed away the last lifeboat, on the portside of the stern. No one could have prevented this. By midnight, the stern began to sink. The angle got to about 50 degrees from level. The report didn't say who took charge on the stern, but all the sailors knew that a pitch of 50 degrees was serious. They secured the engine to prevent an explosion.

There were 31 guys still alive, and they all met aft to abandon ship. They had one inflatable liferaft, designed to hold fifteen men. They successfully got this into the water. A line called a painter held it fast to the stern. Guys went down a rope ladder to get in it. They also put over two rafts they had made out of empty oil drums. Everyone had a life preserver on. Some guys also grabbed life rings, and held these in their arms when they went into the water. Then, fate jumped in and screwed them.

The painter to the inflatable raft broke in the seas. The raft's canopy collapsed. About fifteen guys had gotten in it, but then a cargo tank broke open and a mass of oil washed over the raft. The oily goo washed them all off the raft. They began to choke on the combination of oil and seawater. Eleven sailors managed to get back onto the raft. Four others clung to some boards, and the rest drifted off.

Within half an hour, the stern section went vertical, and then sank. Whoever convinced everyone it was time to abandon the stern was damn right. They would have all died if they had waited any longer. The guys in the raft and the guys in the water drifted around all day. About 1700 hours another ship sighted the raft, and saved the guys left in it. It was a pure accident that this happened. Texaco had not sent any warning out about an overdue ship until after it should have docked in Boston, 28 hours after the ship had split in half. No one in Texaco requested a search for eight hours after that. The company men who first knew about it being overdue said they had limited authority to make inquiries or notify the home office. The rescue ship sent out its own messages, and a massive search began. No one ever found any part of the bow. Another Texaco tanker rescued two of the guys who were floating around without a raft. A couple of bodies were spotted, but not recovered. No one else survived. Of the 44 men on the ship, thirteen had died with the bow section, and eighteen had died after abandoning the stern. There were thirteen survivors.

The report continued on, with all kinds of details about structural strength, and all that engineering talk. The mate didn't reread that part. The mate thought the worst part of it all was how close the *Bougainville* had come to them, and how seriously they had tried to make contact in the storm, and make sure it was not an emergency situation. Most ships would have just sailed by, not hearing or seeing any distress signals. They had tried to call the ship, and did call the Coast Guard. One or two proper distress signals to the *Bougainville* would probably have saved the eighteen souls who had survived their ship being broken in half, only to drown in the water a day later. *What a goddam shame,* he thought.

The mate also knew that if he had done what he said he would do, what he was supposed to do, he might have gone down with the other mates, with the bow section, without a chance. As much as he hated tankers, though, it was just as likely that he would have quit or been fired before then. He walked down the passageway and out on deck, on the leeward side. He looked over the ocean. It was somewhere right out there, where the ship broke and sank. He threw the report into the sea, and deep-sixed his drink glass as well. He tried to come up with an answer for all this, but it was beyond the grasp of a mere, mortal sailor.

Chapter 23: Time for Go

Following the end of the Ming Line trip, the mate stayed on the beach for almost a full year before he went back to New York to try to ship out. The maximum his shipping card was good for was a year, the maximum assignment was four months, and he couldn't get anything. On the last day his card was good, he got a four-month assignment to North Europe, on a Sea Land containership.

He got over to the Sea Land docks in Port Elizabeth, New Jersey, a place he had been to dozens of times. It was still nothing more than a huge storage space for the thousands of truck bodies that would end up on the hundreds of ships that docked there. It was a busy place, and a depressing place.

He had tried working ashore during the long time off, but couldn't seem to get anything worthwhile going. Everyone wanted computer skills he didn't have, or an MBA. He calculated that everything he would earn in the four months in the North Atlantic would just about catch him up with bills. He was 40, and had little to show for his 20 years at sea. He calculated potential sea time yet again, and still figured it would take about fifteen more years of trying to ship to get enough time on board ships to earn a full retirement. It was a depressing thought. He was living as cheaply as he could, but was still struggling. He knew he had wasted some years when he was younger that he could have used to learn other skills. However, when he was younger, he could not imagine a time when he could not ship, or wouldn't want to.

The money and the job problems weren't the worst of it. In the last few years, he had rarely enjoyed being at sea. There was no sense of camaraderie on the containerships. You got little time in port. The guys who drank, drank alone.

The watchstanders never broke sea watches in port, so you could have more time ashore. You kept the same schedule every day, at sea or in port, every day, for four months. The mate had slowly felt his physical abilities slip away; he gained weight, and then lost it. He would quit drinking for weeks, then start right up again, same thing with smoking. He would make an effort to work out, but it never lasted long. He always had done a lot of reading while at sea; now, he seldom took any books with him. In his lucid moments, he thought all this was due to a lack of stability in his life. He had no steady girlfriend or job. He never knew from year to year how much he would make. It seemed impossible to get ahead, no matter where he might go to ship out, or how he lived. He began to understand why some sailors went nuts out at sea. He remembered helping put a guy in a strait jacket on the Calmar ship, so many years ago, and hearing the stories about guys jumping over the side, and seriously wondered if he could possibly ever get so depressed as to end up like that.

The months in the Atlantic didn't help much. When it wasn't cold, rainy or foggy, there were gales that bounced them around the ocean. Their main port in Europe was Rotterdam, but, like most containerships, they docked so far away from the city they weren't even in Rotterdam, they were in a little town named Pernis. At that dock, you could walk a mile or so, and get to a tavern where you could get a beer and a sandwich. That was all he saw of Holland. At times, sitting there in the tavern in Holland, he tried to think more positively, but sooner or later, a few other guys from the ship would come in, sit next to him, and start bitching about the ship, the weather, the life of a merchant seaman, and his mood would turn black again.

He thought he had put the narrow escape with the Ming Line ship behind him, but he had not. He did not feel confident handling the ship in poor visibility. He drank huge amounts of coffee and smoked constantly on watch, hoping the weather would be good. Sailing through the heavy traffic in the English Channel, especially the Dover Strait wasn't the challenge it used to be; now he hated it. When he looked in the mirror, he didn't see the fearless, young bucko mate staring back -- he saw a tired mariner.

When the four months was up, the ship docked in Port Elizabeth in the morning, and the mate went on deck to finish out his eight hours of work. His khakis had grease marks from bumping up against wire lashings, the gloves in his back pocket had holes in them, the soles of his work boots had little tread, and he no longer carried a stowage plan. He rarely roamed the deck, and did not care who the hatch bosses were. He just hung out by the gangway with his foot propped up on the railing. The company guys in the office decided where all the cargo went; the mates had little to do with it. After his eight hours were in, he would pack up and go up to the union hall. The old hall in Manhattan had finally closed, and the New York hall was now in Journal Square, New Jersey.

He saw a young man come up the gangway, and ask several people questions. Before he could get over to the visitor to ask what business he had on the ship, the young man came over to him, and asked for him by name. When the mate said he was that person, the young man handed him an envelope, and left. It was very strange to get a delivery right like that. The mate thought it was some company papers, and someone in the office sent the kid to give it to one of the mates. Still, it was odd that he asked for him by his last name, not by "mate," or "the mate on watch." When he opened the envelope, he saw why.

It was a summons from the local court back home. His ex-wife wanted more money, and a new lawyer, her fifth, had filed the papers. There was also some paper from a Circuit Court Judge about his vacation pay; this one apparently instructed his union not to pay it to him. He was furious. He threw the papers on the deck and ran to the gangway. He shouted and cursed at the kid down on the dock. He started down the gangway, but the young guy took off running. Twenty years ago, he could have caught the little bastard; no more. He went back and picked up the papers. An AB from his watch had seen the whole thing. He came over to the mate.

"Trouble, mister mate?" Nick asked. Nick was in his late 50's. He was Greek, and had been sailing since he was a teenager, all over the world. He was a quiet guy, and one of the best sailors the mate had ever known. He was an excellent quartermaster, had eyes like a hawk, and knew his deck work. He could splice wire and rope, any way you wanted to, and still knew his knots. He was a terrific worker on deck. The whole voyage, he had spent his hours on the bridge with the mate in a quiet, observing way.

"Yeah, Nick, more goddam lawyers and money troubles." The mate launched into a tirade about his problems with them, the union's lack of work, the change in the designs of ships, and how that had ruined sailing. He went on and on, stuff about the goddam weather, and the rotten way of life it had all become. Nick just listened, until the mate, still waving the papers, ran out of steam, and paused for a breath.

"Mate, maybe for you, is time for go." Nick was looking him right in the eyes. He wasn't smiling. Nick was a wise old seaman who had seen it all. He didn't give advice or make judgments quickly. The mate had the wind taken right out of his sails. He froze, and looked at Nick, thinking it over.

"Goddam it, Nick, you're right. You're a smart ol' salt. You're exactly right! This is no good for me anymore! It's just no damn good. But what about you, Nick?"

"Well, mate, for you, is time; but for me, no is yet."

"Dammit it, Nick, you go back to Greece and stay there. Everybody knows you save all your money. Don't wait too long, Nick. Retire and buy a damn island somewhere, get a young wife, and leave all this bullshit behind." Nick smiled, but did not answer.

The mate shook his hand, in itself rare, the two being an officer and a deckhand, and he turned to go up to his room. The mate felt a great relief. It was like the old saying of feeling "like a huge weight had been lifted off your chest." *The hell with it. Why wait until you end up like so many others, washed up and useless, or worse yet, nuts or on the bottom of the sea?* He could learn to do something else, surely. He only felt old out here. Twenty years of this was enough for any man.

As he packed up his sea bag for the last time, he thought of the old sailor's story about retiring from the sea. When you've had enough, the story wen t, you would throw an anchor over your shoulder and start walking inland. Every time someone said, "Hey, mister, why do you have that anchor over your shoulder?" you kept on walking. When you got to a place where someone asked, "Hey mister, what's that thing you have over your shoulder?" you dropped anchor and retired right there.

His packing was a little different from normal, for leaving a ship. Most of his work clothes went in the trash. He took his little short-wave radio and sextant, but doubted he would have much use for them. At least he wouldn't be like some guys he had seen who filled their den with things like that, but had never been past the old three-mile limit. The sextant would probably go into a closet, along with the navigational calculator, the stopwatch and a few books. The memories of all the years, the ships, the characters he had sailed with, the storms, the ports, and all that would go with him, but would have to be pushed back to the closet of his mind. He had met too many old sailors, merchant and navy, who could talk of nothing else. He had no idea what kind of work he would get into, but he knew it had to be something with nothing to do with the sea. Maybe from time to time he could tell a story or two.

He got up to the union hall in New Jersey right after the afternoon job call. It was the usual scene. A couple of old guys were asleep in the back, slouched down in beat-up chairs. A few of the younger guys were standing around the empty job board, bitching about not finding any work, discussing living arrangements in New York, and how long they could hold out around there before they would give up and go home. The usual dissenters gathered near the union patrolman's office, threatening to sue the union over some issue about their pensions.

The mate went over to the paymaster's window, filled out a vacation form, and turned it in, with a copy of the official discharge from the ship, for his vacation money. While he waited to see what the guy was going to do about the judge's legal papers concerning his vacation pay, the mate drifted around the union hall. From the window he could see the Hudson River, and a few ships; a couple at their docks, one underway. They were all foreign ships. The notices on all the bulletin boards were nonsense about this regulation and that one. Copies of the union paper lay all over the place. It had the usual pleas to donate money for Congressmen who supported maritime legislation, and the death notices of members. The ashtrays were dirty, and the rug needed cleaning. He looked around the hall for the last time. He was resolute in giving it up. For the first time in twenty years, he had gone to the union hall after finishing an assignment, but *not* reregistered for work.

The union patrolman called him into his office. The home office of the union had put a hold on releasing his vacation pay. Although by now the mate half expected it, he was still pissed off.

"I've been a member of this union for twenty years! Always paid my dues on time. Never a problem on a ship. Now, goddam it, you give me that check!"

"Look, we can't. The home office got legal papers. You need to go home and straighten this out first," the union rep said.

"Screw that. I am standing in the state of New Jersey, the company I just worked for is based in New Jersey, and a circuit court judge in another state has no goddam jurisdiction over my wages. In fact, federal law protects the wages of a merchant seaman. There is no attachment of wages, and I am not behind in child support. You need to stand by a member of this union, not some scum bag lawyer and his bullshit paper filed in a rinky-dink court somewhere else!" However, the union would not hand him the check he needed so badly. He knew that going home and going through another round in court with the lawyers would mean, one way or the other, most of that money would be lost. He got up to leave, as he felt himself getting mad enough to take a punch at somebody.

"Until you pay me every dime of that money, you're not getting another penny of my goddam money in dues. If this is how my own union treats a twenty-year member, you can stick it."

He went down the elevator with his bags. He was burning his bridges, and he knew what that meant. It was tough to do. If he didn't pay his union dues, he would lose the right to ship out with his union. He knew from the moment Nick had said it, that it was the right thing to do, but how the hell do you just walk away from something you once loved, and a way of life you had known for so long? He got down to the street and stepped out onto the dirty sidewalk. It was cold, and there were a few street people eyeing him and his bag. He threw the sea bag over his shoulder and walked a ways. Around the corner, he found a bar, and went in.

~ ~ ~ ~ ~

The memories vanished from the mate's mind as the cab pulled up in front of the terminal at Newark. The mate paid the driver and got his own bags out. The cabbie came around anyway. The guy was still babbling about the mate's sailing all over, and how great it must be, and all that. The mate still wouldn't tell him the negative side of it. He reached into the bag and pulled out a small box.

"You got a wife?" The mate asked.

"Hell, yeah. I got me one of those, and three kids."

"Take this. It's good perfume. I bought it in France; I dunno why, I don't have anybody to give it to. You take it home and give it to that wife, and just be glad you go home every night." The mate walked away, into the terminal. *What the fuck do I do now?* he wondered.

Epilogue: Watch Your Head

In the early part of the 1800's, a British surgeon, a man well respected in his time, conducted a study of insanity. He found that insanity aboard Royal Navy ships was seven times the national average. His conclusion was that the reason for this was the low heights of the spaces below the main deck, and the sailors bumping their heads.

Suggested Reading - A Short List

Conrad, Joseph. *Lord Jim*. Garden City, N.Y.: Doubleday, 1920.

----------. *Tales of Land and Sea*. New York: Hanover House, 1953.

Dana, Richard H. *Two Years Before the Mast*. Danbury, CT: Grolier, 1980.

Esquemeling, John. *The Bucaniers of America*. Amsterdam: Jan Ten Hoorn, 1678.

Hemingway, Ernest. *The Old Man and the Sea*. New York: Scribner, 1952.

Johnson, Charles (Daniel Defoe). *A General History of the Robberies and Murders of the Most Notorious Pirates*. Originally published in 1724: reprinted by Routledge and Kegan Paul, Ltd., 1926.

Junger, Sebastian. *The Perfect Storm*. New York: HarperCollins, 1997.

Kipling, Rudyard. *Captains Courageous*. Chicago: Children's Press, 1969.

London, Jack. *The Sea Wolf*. Mattituck, N.Y.: Amereon House, 1964.

McPhee, John. *Looking For A Ship*. New York: Farrar Straus Giroux, 1990.

Melville, Herman. *Moby Dick.* New York: Macmillan, 1962.

----------. *Billy Budd.* New York: Penguin Books, 1986.

Monsarrat, Nicholas. *The Cruel Sea.* New York: Knopf, 1951.

Mostert, Noel. *Supership.* New York: Knopf, 1974.

Stevenson, Robert Louis. *Treasure Island.* Jackson Heights, N.Y.: American Reprint Co., 1911.

Wouk, Herman. *The Caine Mutiny.* New York: Doubleday and Co., Inc., 1951.

Acknowledgments

Although this is an individual effort, there are those to whom I owe my gratitude. First, I thank my wife, Kathleen. She understood the need to write that inhabits my soul, and encouraged me to attempt it. She was often alone while I shut myself up in another room, but she never complained. I was a mate when she married me, but she never once asked me to give it up; it was my decision alone, and she carried much of the load during those first few, tough years as I made the transition to shoreside work. I may never be inspired by sailing past the Rock of Gibraltar again, but I don't need to be -- she is my rock.

A special thanks to my daughter-in-law, Angela Poland, for her technical support and proofing, both with this version and the eBook version. Thanks also to my brother Jeff, who put up with me during many years of union hall hell in New York, providing a home away from home, visiting many of my ships, and spending some of my rare nights off in port taking me around. Thanks also to my brother Larry, for providing encouragement, and setting an example of what one can do if he sets goals and works hard to achieve them. Other family members and friends helped in other ways, although most did not know that I was working on a book. I believe it is a writer's privilege not to tell people what he is working on; it prevents others from unwittingly putting even more pressure on you than you already do yourself.

To a good engineer and shipmate, Butch Williams, my thanks for his contribution to "The Party" chapter. There are many other merchant seamen, officers and crew, who I have sailed with, who I owe for their help in teaching a young officer the ropes, both good and bad. I hope they will enjoy reading this as much as I have enjoyed writing it.

To my classmates at the U.S. Merchant Marine Academy, my thanks for being friends during those four rough years. Special thanks to classmate Ron Heimburger for his critique of this work. For teachers, my fondest memories are of Professor Giddings, the only one I knew at the academy who went out of his way to encourage his students to read the classic literature of the sea, while they learned to make a living on the sea.

I tip my hat to my friends at my day job, some for listening to my occasional "sea stories;" little did they know I was practicing telling them to see if I should include them here. Others helped an old sailor make the transition from a typewriter to a computer.

To the majority of the officers and crews of the American merchant vessels that I sailed on, my thanks for being good shipmates. To those who were not good shipmates, I offer appreciation for being who you were -- goddam merchant seamen -- no more, no less.

Finally, to sailors past, both merchant and navy, of all nationalities, my debt is great, and my gratitude insufficient, for all the sacrifices they made, including the ultimate one, that resulted in imbuing my spirit with a desire to go to sea.

Appendix

Author Zahn went to sea on the following ships:

1965* - S. S. Thompson Lykes, M. V. Del Campo, S. S. Key Trader

1966* - N. S. Savannah, S. S. Key Tanker

1968 - S. S. Almeria Lykes, S. S. Gulf Merchant

1969 - S. S. Green Island, S. S. Seamar, S. S. Pine Tree State, S. S. Del Norte, S. S. Sue Lykes, S. S. Jesse Lykes

1970 - M. V. New Yorker, S. S. Andrew Jackson

1971 - M. V. New Yorker, S. S. Cristobal

1972 - S. S. American Accord, S. S. Santa Lucia

1973 - S. S. Arizpa, S. S. Afoundria

1974 - S. S. San Juan (Sea Land)

1975 - S. S. American Legend

1976 - S. S. American Archer

1977 - S. S. Mormaclynx

1978 - S. S. San Juan (Puerto Rican Marine)

1979 - S. S. Defiance

1980 - 1981 - S. S. Austral Pioneer

1982 - S. S. American Lynx, S. S. American Legion, S. S. Mormactide

1983 - S. S. Amco Voyager, S. S. Santa Elena

1984 - S. S. Bayamon, S. S. Export Patriot

1985 - 1986 - M. V. American North Carolina (formerly the M. V. Sea Wolf)

1987 - M. V. Sea Land Express

*Cadet (Midshipman) years

Shipping companies the author sailed for:

American Coastal Lines
American Export-Isbrandtsen Lines
Calmar Steamship Corporation
Central Gulf Steamship Corporation
Delta Steamship Lines
Farrell Lines
Gulf and South American Steamship Company
Keystone Tankship Company
Lykes Brothers Steamship Company
Moore-McCormack Lines
Panama Canal Company
Prudential-Grace Lines
Puerto Rican Marine Management
Sea Land Service
States Marine Lines
United States Lines
Waterman Steamship Company

Countries & locations the author sailed to:

Argentina
Australia
Brazil
Chile
Colombia
Cuba
Curacao
East Coast, U.S.A.
Ecuador
Egypt

England
France
Germany
Greece
Guam
Gulf Coast, U.S.A.
Hawaii
Holland
Hong Kong
Israel
Italy
Jamaica
Japan
Korea
Lebanon
Libya
Mexico
Mozambique
New Zealand
Panama
Peru
Puerto Rico
Santo Domingo
South Africa
Spain
Taiwan
Tunisia
Turkey
Uruguay
Venezuela
Viet Nam
West Coast, U.S.A.
Yugoslavia

End

About the Author

Kevin Zahn is a graduate of the United States Merchant Marine Academy at Kings Point, New York. He also holds a master's degree from Boston College. He sailed all over the world as a mate, or deck officer, for over 20 years (1965-1987), some years full time, some part time. His ships were a variety of steam, diesel and nuclear powered. They carried every kind of cargo imaginable.

He was also a junior high school teacher and coach. His last occupation before retiring was as a Geographic Information Systems Analyst. Kevin likes to play tennis, walk his dog, Sassie, and go for hikes around his home in northern Arizona. He is married, and has three children and two grandchildren. He is working on another manuscript. Please visit http://www.kevinzahn.com for more information and samples.

Made in the USA
Columbia, SC
03 December 2022

72638894R00222